POSTERS, PROPAGANDA, AND PERSUASION IN ELECTION CAMPAIGNS AROUND THE WORLD AND THROUGH HISTORY

PETER LANG
New York • Washington, D.C./Baltimore • Bern
Frankfurt am Main • Berlin • Brussels • Vienna • Oxford

Steven A. Seidman

POSTERS, PROPAGANDA, AND PERSUASION IN ELECTION CAMPAIGNS AROUND THE WORLD AND THROUGH HISTORY

PETER LANG
New York • Washington, D.C./Baltimore • Bern
Frankfurt am Main • Berlin • Brussels • Vienna • Oxford

Library of Congress Cataloging-in-Publication Data

Seidman, Steven A.
Posters, propaganda, and persuasion in election campaigns around the world
and through history / Steven A. Seidman.
p. cm.
Includes bibliographical references and index.
1. Advertising, Political—History. 2. Political campaigns—History.
3. Political posters—History. I. Title. II. Title: Posters, propaganda, and persuasion
in election campaigns around the world and through history.
JF2112.A4S45   324.7'309—dc22   2007015984
ISBN 978-0-8204-8617-8 (hardcover)
ISBN 978-0-8204-8616-1 (paperback)

Bibliographic information published by **Die Deutsche Bibliothek**.
Die Deutsche Bibliothek lists this publication in the "Deutsche
Nationalbibliografie"; detailed bibliographic data is available
on the Internet at http://dnb.ddb.de/.

Cover image "Prosperity at Home, Prestige Abroad"
from the 1896 McKinley presidential campaign
Book interior design and layout by Tamara Seidman
Author photo by JJ Ignotz

The paper in this book meets the guidelines for permanence and durability
of the Committee on Production Guidelines for Book Longevity
of the Council of Library Resources.

© 2008 Steven A. Seidman
Peter Lang Publishing, Inc., New York
29 Broadway, 18th floor, New York, NY 10006
www.peterlang.com

Printed in the United States of America

To my wife, Tamara, and my mom, Sylvia,
with love and gratitude

ଔ୬୭ CONTENTS ଔ୬୭

Illustrations

Chapter One

Chapter Two

Chapter Three

Chapter Four

Chapter Five

Chapter Six

Chapter Eight

*All efforts have been made to contact the copyright owners of these illustrations. If
the source for an illustration has not been cited, the original is in the collection of
the author.*

*   Issuer or copyright holder unknown.
†   Organization disbanded.

Posters—and the broadsides that preceded them—have played a key role in political campaigns since the beginning of democratic elections in the United States over two hundred years ago. My interest in posters and politics began at the age of ten in 1956, when President Dwight D. Eisenhower paraded through my neighborhood in New York City, and I received a poster celebrating his sixty-sixth birthday. This poster was part of a special campaign kit, one of several posters distributed during his reelection campaign that year. My interest in the politics of other countries began when I visited Chile during its 1970 election campaign that culminated in Salvador Allende gaining power. *Posters, Propaganda, and Persuasion in Election Campaigns Around the World and Through History* includes three poster illustrations from Allende's campaign, as well as almost two hundred other election campaign posters, billboards, banners, and broadsides from five continents, the earliest of which is from 1828. It was in that year that Amos Kendall, the first noteworthy "political consultant" (although that was not his official designation), plied his promotional skills to help elect Andrew Jackson the U.S. president. Kendall orchestrated a campaign that featured broadsides, along with news articles, speeches, parades, and other events, all tailored for various groups in an expanding electorate, based on rudimentary polls and demographic analysis. He was the first of many practitioners from the worlds of newspaper publishing, advertising, public relations, and marketing to work worldwide in the service of political parties and their candidates. This book, in part, tells the story of how these practitioners used media, particularly posters, in the political propaganda process—manipulating images and words to try to persuade masses of voters.

Posters, Propaganda, and Persuasion in Election Campaigns presents an extensive discussion of broadsides and their deployment in election campaigns. Other books have neglected this topic, which deserves treatment that is more comprehensive. As technological advances made mass-produced, full-color posters and billboards less expensive, they largely replaced broadsides (although modern, direct mail pieces functioned similarly). This work is interdisciplinary. Artists and graphics persons, who incorporate slogans developed by political and advertising consultants, design election campaign posters. These are then disseminated by communications specialists, used in promotions by public relations personnel, and studied by historians and political scientists, as artifacts of political campaigns. This book examines how and why election campaign posters and broadsides have been designed and used, their effects, and the contexts in which they were created. In other words, the approach taken is to place them in the context of history, advertising, mass communications, art and graphic design, technological change, and election campaign management. Special attention is paid to the changing place and functions of posters and other printed material in political marketing. As radio and, later, television supplanted posters as the primary media in much of the world, what role was left for such printed propaganda? Furthermore, what about countries with less developed mass media, lower literacy, or legislative restrictions on electronic media and/or negative political commercials? *Posters, Propaganda, and Persuasion in Election Campaigns* attempts to answer these questions.

℘ **Chapter One** provides an introduction, and gives the background on trends in technology, social attitudes, education, legislation, marketing, and the art world—all of which were influential in the design of election posters.

℘ **Chapter Two** examines the role of election posters, as well as more primitive broadsides and cloth and paper banners, before radio and television became dominant in the United States. Posters were prominent in American election campaigns in this period and helped shape candidate images and voter perceptions on issues.

℘ **Chapter Three** explores the ways that election posters adapted in the age of mass media in America.

℘ **Chapters Four and Five** examine political developments—and posters, broadsides, and billboards—in France and Great Britain, respectively. The social, economic, political, technological, and artistic trends that influenced the campaigns and their posters in U.S. elections affected those in these long-standing democracies, as well as others around the world. Chapters Four and Five cover these developments in these two countries.

℘ **Chapter Six** discusses posters and broadsides in the rest of the world, concentrating on key campaigns in Africa, Asia, Europe, and Latin America. The examination of their worldwide dissemination reveals the propaganda approaches employed in political campaigns. These reflected nationalism, class divisions, and ethnic and racial intolerance, and used a plethora of symbols and slogans designed to appeal to voters' emotions.

℘ **Chapter Seven** presents research findings in the first full literature review of the effects of political posters, in an attempt to answer this question: How effective are political posters? One purpose of this book is to better understand how this propaganda medium has been used to shape public opinion, and how poster messages are designed for voters. This chapter helps in our understanding of the impact of election posters.

℘ **Chapter Eight** summarizes principles and explores present and future trends. What principles have the designers of these posters applied? What symbols have been used to convey essential meanings? What can be concluded about the use of posters in election campaigns?

℘℘

Posters, Propaganda, and Persuasion in Election Campaigns is an investigation of the roles of election posters in different societies and eras. It explores how political systems, ideology, education, literacy, suffrage, financial conditions, legislation, social change, artistic movements, graphic design trends, advertising, and social and technological change have affected the content, style, and utilization of election posters. My intention is to present a multifaceted political history of the world in the last two centuries, with a focus on political communications, particularly broadsides and posters, during this period.

Steven A. Seidman
Ithaca, New York
May 2008

०३৪০ ACKNOWLEDGMENTS ०३৪০

I am indebted to many people for their help on this book. Foremost is my wife, Tamara Seidman, who with love and devotion spent countless hours reviewing the manuscript, preparing the images for print, and creating the graphic design and layout. Her innumerable suggestions on wording made this work far better.

I would also like to thank my research assistants Margaret Fay, Mariko Pimental, and Caroline Wells for their help in obtaining articles, and, particularly, research assistant Rocio Trujillo Chavez, who worked determinedly to secure permissions for many of the illustrations, and Ms. Fay for contacting and interviewing several political consultants. Additional thanks to Aya-Akkenzhe Alimzhan, Akmaral Alimzhan, Nelson Barnica, Cécile Bugnet, Ursula Granite, Maxime Herbelin, Katalin Lustyik, Wei Ruan, Nathalie Sin, and Ms. Trujillo Chavez, for translating slogans, letters, and articles and/or making telephone calls to gain permissions. I thank everyone who granted permission for posters to be included in this book.

Gratitude also goes to the following people who provided, or arranged to copy, illustrations: Mark Beveridge of the Harry S. Truman Library; Marco Cacciotto of the University of Florence; Joanne O'Dell of the Hudson Library & Historical Society; Stanley Rosen of the East Asian Studies Center, University of Southern California; J. F. Seijlhouwer of the Historical Documentation Center for Dutch Protestantism, VU University Amsterdam; and Sepp Hartinger, Christoph Hofinger, and José Manuel Talero of Hartinger Consulting.

My appreciation goes to Frederick Esterbrook for his copying of slides, as well as original posters in my collection; John H. White for his technical advice about image control; Ari Kissiloff for his suggestions and assistance concerning computer software; Dianne Lynch, dean of the Roy H. Park School of Communications of Ithaca College; and my editors, Mary Savigar and Damon Zucca, and production supervisor, Sophie Appel, of Peter Lang Publishing, for their support.

Additional thanks go to Thomas Mills and Jim Spencer of The Campaign Network, Hank Sheinkopf of Sheinkopf Communications, and Todd Olsen of Olsen & Shuvalov for providing their insights on political communications and consulting; Marcel van de Graaf of Beeldrecht for information about Dutch copyrights; Alan Wright for his insights on British parliamentary history; Legacy Americana for helpful responses to several questions about U.S. election posters; and Diane Gayeski and Patricia Zimmermann for their advice on the process of book publishing.

I am also grateful for several grants that provided funding for many of this book's illustrations, along with its indexing and publishing software: two James B. Pendleton Grants from the Roy H. Park School of Communications of Ithaca College, and funds provided by the Roy H. Park School of Communications Faculty Resource Fund.

Appreciation is extended, as well, to the Center for Faculty Research and Development of Ithaca College for a grant for release time from teaching, and to my college for a sabbatical leave, to work on this book.

Finally, I offer special thanks to Tamara Seidman and my mother, Sylvia Seidman, for their faith and encouragement; and to my son, Joshua Seidman-Zager, for his interest in this project and for helping me obtain materials from the Swiss People's Party.

ᏣᏛᏋᎧ

Parts of this book were previously published in three articles authored solely by me, and the periodicals in which they appeared granted permission to use these in this book. The articles are:

"Studying Election Campaign Posters and Propaganda: What Can We Learn?" *International Journal of Instructional Media*, 35, no. 4 (2008).

"The Poster: A Once and Present Medium of Instruction," *International Journal of Instructional Media*, 34, no. 2 (2007).

"The Design of Nazi Election Posters, and American Advertising and Public Relations," in *Selected Readings* of the International Visual Literacy Association (2007). Paper presented at its annual conference in Curitiba, Brazil, October 2007.

Introduction

Elections are important events in democratic societies. There are few other rituals and events on which people in a nation focus, and which are often remembered for a lifetime as influential occurrences—even turning points. Many memorable election campaigns have helped national parties and their candidates to secure or maintain power. Among them are Andrew Jackson and Abraham Lincoln in the elections of 1828 and 1860 in the United States; Benito Juárez in Mexico, 1867; Woodrow Wilson in the extraordinary three-way U.S. race among Theodore Roosevelt, William Howard Taft, and himself, 1912; Adolf Hitler and the Nazis in Germany, 1932; Salvador Allende in Chile, 1970; Margaret Thatcher's Conservatives in Great Britain, 1979; Lech Wałęsa and Solidarity in Poland, along with the Magyar Democratic Forum's victory in post-Communist Hungary's first free parliamentary election of the same year, 1989; Helmut Kohl and the Christian Democrats in Germany's first election after its reunification, 1990; Nelson Mandela and the African National Congress in South Africa, 1994; Vicente Fox in Mexico, 2000; and Junchiro Koizumi with his image as "Lionheart" and slogan "*Kaikaku*" (Reform) and his Liberal Democratic Party in the first elections of the twenty-first century in Japan. The marketing material used in election campaigns, depending upon the country, its laws, and the political circumstances, has often been notable and significant in its impact on the voters, as well.

Posters, billboards, and even banners have played a large role in election campaigns for the past two centuries. They were the primary media of political communication in the nineteenth century, and they continue in importance in many countries today. This is particularly so in nations such as Poland, South Africa, and Turkey, where legislation restricts the use of other media, and elsewhere such as Russia, where the majority of the political parties cannot afford to purchase expensive television time. Although in many nations television has become the most important means of delivering political propaganda during election campaigns, posters not only can help candidates establish name recognition and a theme, but, as Franklyn Haiman noted, they also communicate "a sense of immediacy and of being surrounded by an event that they [the voters] are not likely to get from watching a television screen."[1] Modern election posters typically feature smiling candidates, posed appealingly, with colorful backgrounds, including flags and other props—all designed to gain the notice of voters who are confronted by rows of competing posters—often on sanctioned notice boards, such as this one in Japan (Fig. 1.1). Furthermore, posters

Figure 1.1

can be used during election campaigns to capture attention for a party or candidate. This is the case not only for the voters passing by them, but also for the mass media audiences who see them in newspapers and on televised newscasts. It is especially true for those election posters that are striking in design and/ or visually outrageous. One such poster, issued by the British Labour Party in 2001, caricatured opposition leader William Hague sporting Lady Thatcher's hairdo; another was distributed by the German Green Party/ Alliance 90 coalition in 1990, with a nude statue and a comic "fig leaf" serving as the focal points (Fig. 1.2). Owing to the expanding influence of political marketing consultants worldwide, such posters have been used in campaigns to spotlight dominant themes or to shape political images.

Art has been employed for thousands of years, as a means by which to inform the public, to promote leaders and ideas, and to propagandize for movements and regimes. As Gary Yanker pointed out, "art has been propagandistic since the pharaohs of ancient Egypt."[2] In Pompeii, two thousand years ago, the city's walls were painted with official notices and proclamations, along with graffiti that communicated political beliefs.[3] These official dipinti (commonly having to do with elections) probably were more effective because of their large, stylish lettering and bright colors.[4] Other authorized announcements were written on plaster-coated wooden boards, which were placed in Pompeii's squares.[5] These were not much different from the standing billboards erected in town and city squares at election time today in France and other countries. Posters and politics have been linked for almost five centuries, and the use of political posters has helped

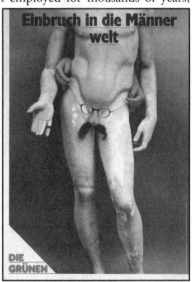

Figure 1.2

people gain or hold on to power, oppose entrenched interests, or advocate for a cause.

In the 1500s, European artists produced social-protest woodcut engravings, such as *Peasant Beating a Rent-Collector* by the Master of Petrarch.[6] By 1539, the French king, Francis I, had his edicts posted on billboards, and was concerned enough about others' posters to mandate an order of control; about a century later, posters in France could not be printed or displayed without the consent of the authorities—death was the potential penalty for failure to obtain it.[7] A number of woodcut prints, however, acclaimed the monarchs of the sixteenth century, often portraying them on magnificently plumed and armored horses. A few centuries later, rulers such as Louis XIV distributed engraved prints that informed their subjects of events at the royal court, which included everything from births to bleedings.[8] The wars of Europe during these centuries also were glorified: heroic soldiers were depicted alongside mythological figures in many engravings, and recruiting broadsides, with simple illustrations, were circulated on both sides of the Atlantic.

Such mythologizing can be seen in nineteenth-century French and American election posters. In France, lithographs of the first Napoleon on a rearing horse or with a crown of laurels were distributed by his nephew Louis Napoleon Bonaparte, a little more than half a century after his uncle rose to power, during electioneering campaigns in the 1860s (as is noted in Chapter Four). In the United States, posters of several presidential candidates in

Figure 1.3

military attire, on horseback in Napoleonic poses and hats, were disseminated (as is discussed in Chapter Two). A good example is the 1840 U.S. election poster for the presidential candidate William Henry Harrison, presenting him in his general's uniform, along with the slogan "The Washington of the West," connecting him to the mythologized first leader of the country (Fig. 1.3). In the latter part of the twentieth century, U.S. candidates' military "exploits" were emphasized more in speeches and pamphlets, rather than in posters.

Propaganda or mass persuasion campaigns seek to influence public opinion. The first posters designed to accomplish this goal were printed in the first half of the sixteenth century, during the Protestant Reformation in Germany. The word *propaganda* is derived, in fact, from the Latin *propaganda fide*, which means, "propagating the faith"; today, there is a propaganda department of cardinals in the Roman Catholic Church called "the Sacred Congregation of Propaganda," which supervises missionary work.[9] The artist, Lucas Cranach the Elder (a friend of Martin Luther), produced quickly drawn "posters" that were displayed throughout Worms when Luther was tried there in 1521.[10] In 1534, Counter-Reformation posters were put up in Paris, forcing John Calvin to leave that city for Basel (a result of what was called the "Poster Affair").[11]

Key Definitions

CR **Broadsides, Banners, and Posters.** The prints Cranach created were rather crude, with limited print runs, and were designed to be tacked up and handed out immediately. Such prints were known as *broadsides*, and were circulated extensively in most parts of the world well into the early twentieth century. They were employed by businesses, big and small, to advertise their products and services; by political parties and protest groups to promote candidates and movements; and by governments to issue proclamations and notices. The American Declaration of Independence was a broadside, printed on the evening of July 4, 1776, and distributed the next day.[12] Seventeenth-century European broadsides reported other news of the day, often in a sensationalistic manner (murders and rapes were favored subjects), with rhymed text that could be sung in public gatherings.[13] When both sides of a sheet of paper were printed, the product was referred to as a *broadsheet*, although many persons have used the terms synonymously.[14]

Figure 1.4

Most broadsides were simple, with large type, and usually printed in black ink on poor-quality paper. Illustrations were included sometimes, particularly when there were many illiterate people in the audience. By the early 1500s, German printers set the type for broadsides while artists created woodcut illustrations for them. The pictures in early broadsides "often were artless and naive," according to Ingeborg Lehmann-Haupt in her article "German Woodcut Broadsides in the Seventeenth Century."[15] The same opinion could be applied to many later broadsides. Eye-catching, old-fashioned, boldfaced fonts were used in these sometimes, however. A German broadside printed for the 1932 election campaign for presidential candidate Paul von Hindenburg is a good example of such a broadside in twentieth-century politics (Fig. 1.4). It simply states: "Loyalty is the Sign of Honor! Elect Hindenburg!"

Broadsides were frequently rather large, but some of them were as small as eight by ten inches. A smaller broadside titled "Let's Look at the Record" was produced by the Democratic National Campaign Committee in 1936 in support of President Franklin D. Roosevelt's reelection drive; it focused on specific issues, including farm relief, aid to the unemployed and homeowners, and regulation of banking and investments (Fig. 1.5). Election broadsides have seldom been printed since World War II, but in localities, they are still considered useful. In 1988, for instance, a larger broadside (eleven by seventeen inches) was printed by a state labor organization, giving workers reasons to vote for the

Figure 1.5 (excerpt)

Election '88, Tuesday, November 8 . . .
Where they stand on Worker Issues

Michael Dukakis	George Bush
Lloyd Bentsen	Dan Quayle

Unions
- Knows that unions and collective bargaining are essential for keeping America strong.
- Appointed trade unionist Paul Eustace to be first Secretary of Labor in Massachusetts. Eustace is former Vice President of New England Conference of Machinists.
- Opposes "open shop" and "Right-to-Work for less". Opposes privatization of public services and jobs at Federal, State and local level.
- Committed to a fair and impartial National labor Relations Board to protect workers' rights.
- Led the fight to reform Workers' Compensation in Massachusetts, resulting in increased benefits and speedier processing of claims.

Unions
- Wants to eliminate the union shop. Supports "Right-to-Work for Less" to weaken and undermine the bargaining strength of workers and their union.
- Institutionalized union-busting and strike breaking, by firing 12,000 Air Traffic Controllers and destroying their union (PATCO).
- Wants to "contract out" a wide range of public services provided by federal, state and local governments.

Figure 1.6 (excerpt)

U.S. Democratic Party candidate, Michael Dukakis, rather than for President George H. W. Bush (Fig. 1.6). Protest groups used these modern broadsides more frequently in this period, since they did not always have the money to run off posters.

Some writings have referred to broadsides as *posters*, even in the sixteenth century, but the consensus seems to be that posters are generally more technically refined. Jules Chéret designed the first "true" posters in the 1860s, according to John Barnicoat.[16] Other authorities, however, such as Bernard Reilly, used the term *posters* when referring to "the large sheets printed for outdoor display" to promote political candidates much earlier—in the late 1840s in the United States.[17] Most authorities have considered posters by Chéret and his successors to be different from broadsides because they are dominated by pictorial elements; they are technically more polished, owing to advancements in lithography; they typically incorporate color; they are much larger than most of the earlier lithographs; and they are run off in greater numbers.[18] They also were more likely to be posted on fences and walls, rather than handed out (and, later, mailed). By the middle of the nineteenth century, small lithographic posters were printed, most often during election campaigns, and were displayed in windows of shops and homes. These became known as *window cards*. Typically, these cards were portraits of the candidates, printed in brown ink on 8 × 11-inch paper, with a slogan, such as "Reelect Roosevelt."

Also produced in the middle of the nineteenth century were political campaign *banners* that were quite similar to the posters created, except that there were much fewer made at first, since the color was added by hand. Lithographer Nathaniel Currier (joined later by James Ives) printed designs for banners (which had previously been hand painted on fabric by others) on paper for U.S. presidential candidates from 1844 to 1880. These banner designs featured draperies, as well as symbols, especially eagles, flags, shields, cornucopia, farmers and laborers, and past presidents. Some of these symbols can be seen in Figure 1.7, which promoted the 1852 Democratic ticket, headed by Franklin Pierce. Some designs

Figure 1.7

continued to be printed on cloth, and much later on vinyl for outdoor use. Many of these banners were (and still are) locally made, simple, and featured block lettering. Banners have been commonplace at rallies and parades. A print of a parade in Chicago for the

Figure 1.8

1892 Democratic Party national ticket shows a large cloth banner overhead, portraying candidates Grover Cleveland and Adlai Stevenson, as well as the Illinois governor, John Peter Algeld (Fig. 1.8).

By the mid-1890s, mass-produced, lithographic, pictorial posters were widespread in much of the Western world. A lithographic poster for the ticket of William McKinley and Garret Hobart in the U.S. election of 1896, along with the Republican Party's platform, featured a full range of colors and a variety of pictures (Fig. 1.9). Later, both glossy and

Figure 1.9

more rudimentary silk-screened posters were produced. In many countries, posters and their larger version, billboards, have been used to communicate political messages, sometimes reinforcing what has been conveyed via other more modern media such as radio and television. Figure 1.10 is an example of a bold, pro-Gaullist billboard erected in Paris during the 1962 referendum campaign to decide whether the French president should be elected by popular vote and whether the authority of the office should be increased.

Billboards have been used to advertise products and services for over one and a half centuries. P. T. Barnum promoted his American Museum in the 1840s and 1850s through billboards, as well as huge posters, and banners and handbills.[19] In 1872, billboard advertisers came together under the organizational umbrella

Figure 1.10

known as the International Bill Posters Association of North America, and, at the same time, their less organized critics lobbied to control excessive outdoor displays.[20] By the turn of the century, however, billboards (thirty-sheet posters) were frequently used in advertising, such as in the promotion of political candidates in the United States and, later, worldwide. This is because, as Nigel Potter stated, "clients are increasingly keen to take advantage of the benefits that posters provide—substantial coverage of many target audiences, near point of sale positioning, high impact, creative flexibility and—the key thing—exceptionally high frequency."[21] In fact, a driver or stroller can be exposed to an outdoor advertisement as many as twenty times in a two-week period, generating increased brand- and candidate-recognition.[22]

CR *Propaganda and Mass Persuasion.* Despite the fact that many authorities have defined *propaganda* as the dissemination of information (true, slanted, or false) that helps an organization to promote itself and its goals, the term has been defined in the negative more frequently, a development that intensified markedly in the years following World War I. It was in the aftermath of this global conflict that many people in the Allied countries, believing that they had been duped by the information campaigns of their own governments, came to view the word to mean *deceitful* information designed to mislead them; in the Axis countries, particularly Germany, the general public also viewed "propaganda" and "lying" synonymously.[23] Writers such as Harold Lasswell, whose book *Propaganda Technique in the World War* was published in 1927, contributed to this redefining phenomenon. They associated the word with deception. For example, Lasswell stated, "actual propaganda has a large element of the fake in it."[24] Dictionary definitions and thesaurus synonyms continue to reflect this change in the popular concept of the term: one meaning of *propaganda* is "deceptive or distorted information that is systematically spread" and common synonyms are "brainwashing" and "disinformation."[25]

By 1934, Lasswell referred to "propaganda" as merely a "tool," to be used either for good, bad, or amoral goals—similar to advertising or public relations.[26] The primary goal is *mass persuasion*—to convince large numbers of people "that there is only one valid point of view and to eliminate all other options," wrote David Welch.[27] Political posters, and other elements of propaganda campaigns, attempt to influence the public's opinions about candidates and causes. They also affect subsequent behavior, including votes and contributions of money and time. Clearly, the intention is that such posters should not fully inform or educate the population, although one propaganda strategy can be to include accurate information, which can increase credibility.[28] Political posters have also been designed to mislead an audience to further a movement or idea (or to damage the opposition), the goal of which is to change or solidify attitudes or ideology, and behaviors.[29] Two approaches that have accomplished this are: (1) distortion, omission, appeals to prejudice, or fabrication of events (such as in Allied posters that showed "German atrocities" during World War I, and subsequent Nazi Party election posters that included stereotypical depictions of Jews, with huge noses and obese bodies (Fig. 1.11); and/or (2) manipulation of visual images (evident in a 1976 U.S. election poster for the reelection campaign of President Gerald Ford, which used a photograph of Ford, shot from below, so that viewers would perceive him as more imposing (Fig. 1.12).

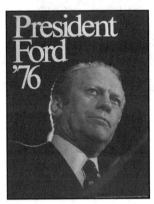

Figure 1.11   *Figure 1.12*

Other posters have been designed to try to convince an audience to accept a candidate or political position without the use of falsehoods, although simplification, as well as images, slogans, and symbols, have been employed. Examples of these can be seen in Figure 1.13: idealized drawings of President Ronald Reagan and Vice President George H. W. Bush, the façade of the White House, an American flag backdrop, and a slogan that communicates the 1984 campaign themes of economic growth and greater international respect. Nevertheless, as Oliver Thomson pointed out, patriotic appeals and symbols are propagandistic because they "play on emotions."[30] Furthermore, the themes in an election poster are magnified when posters are seen repeated in rows on a wall, displayed on many billboards, and shown in newspaper advertisements, pamphlets, and television spots. Repetition is a key technique employed by the political propagandist, just as it is by the advertising specialist.

Figure 1.13

The *Encarta*® *World English Dictionary* offers two meanings for *propaganda*: one is to cover the distribution of promotional information; the other is the spread of misleading information.[31] Thus, almost anything designed to publicize ideas, organizations, or people can be deemed "propaganda." In this book, we consider the purpose of *all* political posters to be to influence public opinion and move people toward one's point of view, party, or candidate. This can be accomplished by using a variety of methods, some of which are obviously misleading, and almost of all of which are intended to have an emotional impact on the audience and effect certain behaviors, including voting.

Changing Trends

Key developments have affected the design, content, and usage of posters produced in the political realm. These have been in the following areas:

- Technology
- Social Attitudes
- Education
- Legislation
- Advertising and Political Marketing
- Art and Graphic Design

CR **Technology.** In the 1600s, during the Thirty Years' War, the technological advance of printing from copperplates led to the increased production of broadsides, which were widely distributed by conflicting religious groups. Over the next two centuries, woodcuts and engravings, as well as lithographs, were dispensed in support of political causes and candidates. Many of these broadsides (and smaller handbills), in Europe and the United States, were set in the moveable lead type Johannes Gutenberg used in his 1440 printing press in Germany. They were generated in large numbers by higher-speed presses, some powered by steam engines by the early nineteenth century; this increased output from two hundred fifty to four hundred copies per hour in 1811, to twenty-four hundred impressions by 1815, and four thousand broadsheets per hour—on two sides—by the end of the 1820s.[32] Until the 1820s, engravers etched the fine lines of their illustrations into copperplates, applied ink afterward to fill these lines, and transferred the designs to paper. During that decade, steel generally replaced copper as the favored metal for printing plates; steel lasted much longer during the printing process, and revealed finer detail in the prints, such as the one used in George McClellan's 1864 campaign for the U.S. presidency, in which an engraving of the candidate was made from a photograph (Fig. 1.14). Within two decades, however, lithography for the most part supplanted line engraving; oil-based substances that

Figure 1.14

repelled water were employed to create images on stone (and, later, aluminum), with ink sticking to the wet stone's image areas. Wood block printing continued, but it was used much less until the late nineteenth century, when there was a brief resurgence of interest.[33]

Lithography, invented in Bavaria at the end of the eighteenth century, allowed printers to turn out illustrated broadsides more rapidly and economically. In all likelihood,

the first American lithograph was a landscape by Bass Otis in 1819. By 1850, ten thousand lithographic copies could be run off in an hour.[34] Until the second quarter of the nineteenth century, when chromolithography was invented (with separate stones for each color), color was added by hand. More refined posters were created on both sides of the Atlantic at this time as well; developments in lithography made the mass production of posters possible in the last quarter of the nineteenth century.

Figure 1.15

One such poster was generated in 1884 for the Democratic national election ticket of Grover Cleveland and Thomas Hendricks (Fig. 1.15). This chromolithograph was printed from five stones, mixing primary colors by registering two runs perfectly. One effect of all these technological innovations was to lower the cost of broadsides, which political parties could generate in large quantities while expending little money to promote their candidates.[35]

The experiments of a lithographer-engraver, Nicéphore Niépce, in the early nineteenth century, set the stage for photomechanical reproduction. Niépce was probably the first person to make possible the preservation of photographs of scenes. The images were on pewter, which had been coated with a light-sensitive substance, bitumen of Judea. More important to future poster designers was that by 1826 he was also able to duplicate existing artists' prints by transferring them to treated pewter plates. Three decades later, the photogravure process was invented, and, until the first quarter of the twentieth century, printers generally used it to reproduce on etched copperplates the photographic images of political candidates.[36] Usually these images were seen on small campaign posters, printed in sepia tones and yielding a rich, grainy quality, as is evident in the portrait of Charles Evans Hughes, the Republican candidate for U.S. president in 1916 (Fig. 1.16).

Figure 1.16

Later developments in screenprinting and computer technology affected political poster designers. These caused lithography to take a back seat, just as line engraving had earlier. By the last decade of the nineteenth century, the halftone process (the tones of photographs replicated by a printing press using different size dots in screens to dictate the image tones) made it possible for photographic prints to be widely disseminated. In 1901, the public saw a photographic portrait of Leon Czolgosz, who had recently been arrested for the assassination of U.S. President McKinley. By World War I, a few posters with photographic images appeared; these were created by a four-color printing process (cyan, magenta, yellow, and black plates were made photographically and employed to create the "impression" of full color). In this period, the invention of offset printing presses (whereby inked images were transferred from stones or plates to a roller) allowed posters to be run off more rapidly and inexpensively than ever before, leading to their increased use for political purposes. Advances in offset lithographic printing, with cutout lettering and negative reversals reproduced simply, changed advertising approaches, including those used in posters, and may have led to the birth of avant-garde design in the early decades of the twentieth century. In the late 1920s, photographic images began appearing in election posters. In the 1960s, psychedelic posters—some of them political—proliferated, owing in part to the inexpensive split fountain color method, which required only one pass through a printing press.[37] In the 1990s, the advent of computer software such as Adobe® Photoshop® and Illustrator®, and Aldus® FreeHand enabled graphic artists to manipulate images easily, and thereafter this software was commonly used in poster design. The application of computer software techniques to achieve such effects as posterization, feathering, and texturizing helped enhance the appeal of political candidates and parties in their election posters; this can be seen in another German Green Party/Alliance 90 poster from 1990 (Fig. 1.17).

Figure 1.17

In recent times, use of posters to promote political organizations and candidates, especially in Europe, Asia, Africa, and Latin America, has continued. As Susan Sontag noted, posters throughout history have been designed to be noticed at a distance in a "theatre of persuasion," a multitude of posters "competing with (and sometimes reinforcing) each other."[38] It is not surprising, therefore, that futuristic "talking posters," employing infrared sensors and speaking chips, have been developed to vie with more modern, nonprint media for attention.[39] The rise of the Internet has also brought about significant changes in political marketing, fundraising, and information dissemination. These changes have affected the ways in which posters are distributed, and have even allowed for the tailoring of their messages. Conduct a search of the World Wide Web, and you will find not only sites presenting posters of the mainstream candidates, but also sites with posters that deride them. In addition, the Internet allows activist groups with little money to raise funds by selling posters and other products online.

In the years following World War II, the importance of posters lessened, both politically and commercially, as the television medium became predominant, especially in the United States, Japan, and much of Western Europe. But the poster continued to be a useful implement in the political toolkit for election campaigns in these places. In other parts of the world, where economic and technological advances lagged, or in which political parties' use of television was limited legally, posters played an essential role. Some research indicates that billboard posters have influenced quite a few voters in Great Britain, although not as greatly as have television broadcasts.[40]

In much of the so-called developed world, with television playing the principal role in mass persuasion campaigns, posters have had diminished importance. Nevertheless, they have probably served to reinforce campaign themes and establish a "presence" for candidates in many localities. Political parties have distributed scores of campaign posters for holding up at rallies, so they can be seen, on television, in waves behind the candidates. In addition, they have learned to make "poster unveilings" into media events, covered by broadcast and print journalists. During Great Britain's 2005 elections, party leaders debuted gigantic posters—some of them one of a kind—which were attached to trailers.[41]

In rapidly modernizing countries such as India, election posters and billboards have undoubtedly lost some of their influence with certain segments of the population: those, for example, who are able to view competing political media, which include both television and Internet. Posters are still widely used, however. In countries where there are relatively few television sets, limited available public funds, a multitude of languages, and/or a considerable number of illiterate people, they are a very useful method by which governments and political parties can communicate a variety of political and informational messages.

✍ *Social Attitudes.* The extension of suffrage to additional males in many countries during the second half of the nineteenth century and first quarter of the twentieth century made it more important—for both those in power and those opposed to them—to appeal to the expanded voting populations.[42] In that period, poll taxes and literacy requirements were eliminated, and property-ownership provisions were often relaxed to enfranchise many men. Those in power, as well as groups who favored and opposed women's suffrage, displayed posters (which had taken over the central place of broadsides). As women obtained the right to vote, and as attitudes about their roles—along with those of racial minorities—in many societies changed, the ways they were depicted in posters changed too. This can be seen in posters of the two world wars: the idealized, glamorous "Christy Girl" in recruiting posters of World War I was replaced by "Rosie the Riveter" in those of World War II.

The depiction of minorities also transformed over the years. During World War II, the United States produced many more posters portraying black persons and Americans of other national origins than during World War I (although the French had done this, substantially, by 1918).[43] The "enemy," however, was often portrayed in highly negative, stereotypical ways—whether they were the Japanese in Allied posters, Jews in Nazi posters, or even blacks in Italian Fascist posters. After World War II, portrayals of workers and voters in the United States became more diverse in labor posters and subsequent election posters.

CR **Education.** In countries where illiteracy has been high, posters were—and remain—a key medium of communication. This was the case in the Soviet Union, China, and Cuba during the early periods of the revolutions there, and in other societies—past and present—in which a large segment of the populations could not read. The broadsides posted in public places could be an effective way to convey messages to illiterate people before universal education became widespread. This was because they could be read aloud by those who were literate. In addition, as Philip Meggs noted, "the proliferation of the ever-present broadside made reading desirable and increasingly necessary for Renaissance townspeople."[44] Illiteracy was high even in Europe in the 1920s—half of the Spanish population over six years of age and 15 percent of the Hungarian population were unable to read and write.[45] In post-World War II Italy, approximately 15 percent of the population was illiterate, and many only semiliterate.[46] Today, illiteracy remains high in many countries, making it particularly appropriate to employ posters with prominent visuals in them. Posters were used heavily in Afghanistan during its first presidential election, in 2004, for example; the combination of a candidate's photograph and a logo, it was thought, was quite effective, particularly in reaching those who could not read.[47] At the beginning of the twenty-first century, because of poor education systems in many countries, approximately 20 percent of the world's population aged fifteen and above (about eight hundred sixty million people), were illiterate—two-thirds of them women.[48] Posters and billboards continue to be "the mainstay of political campaigning" in countries such as India, where illiteracy persists, as Shyamsunder Tekwani noted.[49] This is particularly the case in rural areas of that country, where only 56 percent of the adult population was literate in 1997.[50]

Figure 1.18

Many governments and interest groups continue to use posters to inform citizens about occupational, safety, and health issues. These posters can cover workplace harassment and discrimination; immunization against disease; and the dangers of smoking, drugs, alcohol, and unprotected sexual activity. As David Crowley noted, posters can include more direct language and imagery than can broadcast media, and be used in places in which target audiences congregate.[51] Political parties have aligned themselves with teachers and other supporters of public education in their election campaigns to gain votes, and have positioned issue-oriented posters strategically. This was true for a 1978 election poster produced by the French Socialist Party, which featured a charming photograph of two young boys playing in the fields, with a pleasing script title, "Public School," and the message "the business of all" (Fig. 1.18).

🔖 *Legislation.* In various countries, legislation has affected the use of posters in elections. Laws in several nations led to an increased prominence of posters in election campaigns. Political parties in Belgium, Brazil, and Chile use posters more than those in many other countries, since they are allocated limited time on public television and not even allowed to purchase commercial broadcast time.[52] In Great Britain, where television time is limited as well, and no advertisements are allowed on either television or radio, there are no legal limitations on expenditures for posters and billboards;[53] therefore, they are widely used. Similar legal restrictions (paid political TV spots were often prohibited) in other countries, including Denmark, Finland, France, Germany, India, Ireland, Israel, Italy, Japan, The Netherlands, Norway, Spain, Switzerland, and Turkey,[54] have fueled the use of posters in election campaigns. In a number of countries, the use of posters to attack opposing candidates and parties has been stimulated by legislation that restricts the content of political broadcasts. For example, opposition candidates in France can be neither attacked nor disparaged on television.[55] These constraints have generally given rise to broadcasting speeches and question-and-answer segments,[56] and allowed much less time for rapidly paced, American-style video spots.[57] Posters maligning the opposition are permitted, however, and are ubiquitous at campaign time.

MOTHERS-VOTE LABOUR

Figure 1.19

Laws have had the opposite effect on poster usage in the United States. At the beginning of the twentieth century, flag desecration laws ended the practice of printing candidates' names, symbols, and slogans on flag banners. Restrictive legislation (especially antilitter laws) about fifty years later led to the heavy use of lawn signs and bumper stickers during U.S. election campaigns, while limiting the display of posters and billboards in public venues. Although posters and billboards acquired diminished status resulting from this legislation, they did not disappear. In fact, quasi-posters stuck in lawns or placed on automobile bumpers became commonplace (as well as, to a lesser extent, political ads on and in transit media), and so one could argue that the medium was still a significant factor in establishing a presence for candidates in election campaigns.

Of course, legislation that limited or expanded the right to vote to such groups as women, eighteen-year-olds, and the peasantry, affected poster campaigns, which began to target these groups. This varied by country: all adults in the Scandinavian countries achieved full suffrage by 1918; women in Great Britain obtained full voting rights in 1928; in France, women first exercised their suffrage rights in 1946; Switzerland did not accomplish this until 1971.[58] Election campaign posters in many countries targeted women, particularly in the decade after their enfranchisement. For example, a British poster in the 1930s showed a woman holding a child, with the appeal "Mothers—Vote Labour" (Fig. 1.19).

CR *Advertising and Political Marketing.* Another important development was the enlistment of advertising personnel and, later, political marketing consultants, to both plan campaign material and coordinate the campaigns. The same advertising principles applied in the design of World War I recruitment posters by the Creel Committee's Division of Advertising were later put to use in the design of election campaign posters. After the war, Albert Lasker, "the founder of the modern advertising industry," worked for the U.S. Republican Party to promote its congressional candidates.[59] According to Lasker, a political campaign was merely another advertising campaign.[60] Executives from Young & Rubicam, Inc., Saatchi & Saatchi, and other firms have been involved in politics ever since. Advertising principles, which often attempt to simplify a message for a target audience, have been effective when put into practice in the design of election posters. Slogans, for instance, ranging from "I Like Ike" to "Labour Isn't Working" have summarized an entire campaign with a few, memorable words. Repetitions of slogans and playing on emotions, as well as using popular figures, are key practices of advertising. Advertising is, of course, a form of propaganda.

It is now customary, before a poster is designed, to analyze the target audience. This can involve conducting surveys or organizing focus groups. The analysis can affect the poster's theme and graphic design, as well as the selection of symbols, slogans, icons, visuals, and type style, the determination of artistic style and composition, and whether to include certain verbal elements. Polls can reveal the leading voter concerns, which can then be translated into a simply worded campaign message.[61] Focus group comments can help decide the images chosen for a poster, or lead to modifying the poster design. Demographic research can help political strategists place billboards and posters in optimal locations,[62] and target persons in direct mail, broadside/brochure campaigns. Although audience analysis has become more sophisticated and extensive, advertising specialists recognized in the first quarter of the twentieth century that it was a critical element in the process of determining how to convince the public to buy a product, vote for a candidate, or support a dictatorial regime. One of these experts was Edward Bernays, the American pioneer in public relations, who wrote in the 1920s of the importance of using "statistics, field surveying, and the various methods of eliciting facts and opinions in examining both the public, and the idea or product ... [one] seeks to propagandize."[63]

Modern political propaganda campaigns incorporate messages designed to be most effective with targeted voting blocs, but this was the case in the U.S. election campaigns designed by Mark Hanna, who directed the 1896 McKinley effort, and Lasker, who coordinated Warren Harding's in 1920. In Great Britain, in 1922, Sidney Webb, a Labour strategist, termed this approach "stratified electioneering"; it involved identifying target audiences and positioning the party's brand to win votes.[64] In the marketing world, "stratification" was later called "segmentation."[65] Business marketers are experienced in persuading segments of the population to buy products and services, after analyzing these audiences—skills that are equally applicable in the political arena. Concepts commonly heard in business marketing, such as "brand loyalty," "product positioning," and "psychological purchase," have become commonplace in the political universe.[66] Of course, as Nicholas O'Shaughnessy noted, "consumer marketing has nothing like negative advertising, and so-called comparative advertising is a faint echo."[67] Targeted negative broadsides and posters have been seen frequently in politics worldwide.

Professional political consultants—operating outside the American party organizations—began to sell their services in the 1930s, and have influenced the messages in posters and other printed material that candidates have disseminated in their propaganda campaigns since then. The techniques employed, including audience research, segmentation, image management, and direct mail, subsequently became customary in most of the rest of the world.[68] Today, political consultants are key figures in election campaigns, particularly in countries in which the focus on individual candidates has grown in importance, and allegiance to political parties has lessened—even in party-centered systems.[69] By the 1992 U.S. election, over three-fourths of all incumbents employed media consultants and professional polling specialists in their campaigns.[70]

Furthermore, many American political consultants have been brought in by the political parties of other countries to work in their national elections in at least a score of Latin American and Caribbean countries; in a dozen European nations; and in Canada, Australia, New Zealand, Israel, Japan, the Philippines, Nigeria, and South Africa.[71] In 1975, for example, Valéry Giscard d'Estaing hired American Joseph Napolitan, a founder of both the American and International Associations of Political Consultants, to poll and devise a theme for him for his presidential election campaign in France.[72] A more recent example is the work Larry Gibson, who had been Bill Clinton's Maryland state chair in his 1992 U.S. presidential campaign, performed for Ellen Johnson-Sirleaf of the Unity Party of Liberia, who, in 2005, was elected the first female president of that country in the first democratic election held in eighteen years. After conducting quasi-focus groups (i.e., discussions with people in marketplaces), he designed several campaign posters, which featured the candidate raising her index finger, and a 1986 photograph of a young girl raising her hand. The older photograph was included because the military had overturned the election results then. Since few radio stations operated outside the capital and hardly anyone owned television sets, use of posters was a logical choice.[73]

Although research indicates that about 60 percent of the political consultants who work in other countries are from the United States, some non-American consultants have also worked overseas—frequently in neighboring nations or in those with the same language.[74] Similarities between campaigns in different countries are apparent. For instance, Gerhard Schröder's German Social Democrat Party (SPD) consulted with Tony Blair's British Labour Party and used its pledge card technique (i.e., a card with a statement that promises will be kept), slogans (such as "Be tough on crime and the causes of crime"), promises (job creation for young people), and much of its manifesto. Both the British Labourites and German Social Democrats employed market research and mass media monitoring, along with focus group testing of billboards.[75] In addition, in the 1990s, British advertising firms, as well as some other Western companies, had consulted on other continents. Saatchi & Saatchi, for example, advised parties and candidates in the first democratic elections in Russia and South Africa.[76] At the same time, political consultants from party-centered Sweden have worked in South Africa, Asia, and Eastern Europe.[77]

Of course, advertising personnel have prepared creative campaigns and posters in their own countries. In Japan, the I&S Corporation, a large advertising firm, designed innovative election posters for the Japanese Socialist Party (JSP), treating candidates like products: "Why not do this like selling a cookie? Image comes first, then policies," stated the creative director of I&S, when discussing election posters for the 1990 campaign.[78] One of its posters featured the first female JSP leader on a magazine cover, with a cherub reading the issue. Even earlier, in the 1980s, the German advertising agency Coordt von Mannstein devised effective campaigns for the Christian Democrats, with posters that spotlighted Helmut Kohl, often more than issues.[79]

American advertising and marketing techniques have influenced political propagandists in other countries for decades. Adolf Hitler was fascinated by many of these techniques, and used them in his campaigns (as is seen in Chapter Six). The Conservative Party of Margaret Thatcher hired the domestic advertising agency of Saatchi & Saatchi to aid its cause in 1979, after seeing the success of dynamic methods used to elect presidents of both Democratic and Republican Parties in the United States. In the early 1990s, the Labour Party followed suit—and British and American political marketing specialists traveled across the Atlantic Ocean to work for both Clinton and Blair. The American influence extended to France as well. U.S. consultants introduced modern polling techniques there in the 1970s, and MTV-style television segments, starting in the late 1980s. But even earlier, French consultants had developed effective coordinated media election campaigns using posters, beginning in the 1960s. Public relations personnel in many countries ensure that a sea of posters is always behind the candidates to be photographed by newspaper photographers and TV camerapersons.

Posters have remained one of the weapons in the political consultant's propaganda arsenal. Their role has changed, however, as other mass media have arrived on the scene and new marketing communications strategies have emerged, and their designs have been altered to appeal to different and changed audiences. The broadsides used by early political consultants who helped Jacksonian Democrats triumph in the early nineteenth century, evolved into impressive full-color posters by the end of that century (most notably during

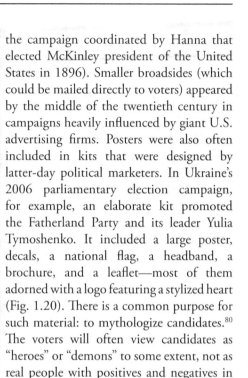

Figure 1.20

the campaign coordinated by Hanna that elected McKinley president of the United States in 1896). Smaller broadsides (which could be mailed directly to voters) appeared by the middle of the twentieth century in campaigns heavily influenced by giant U.S. advertising firms. Posters were also often included in kits that were designed by latter-day political marketers. In Ukraine's 2006 parliamentary election campaign, for example, an elaborate kit promoted the Fatherland Party and its leader Yulia Tymoshenko. It included a large poster, decals, a national flag, a headband, a brochure, and a leaflet—most of them adorned with a logo featuring a stylized heart (Fig. 1.20). There is a common purpose for such material: to mythologize candidates.[80] The voters will often view candidates as "heroes" or "demons" to some extent, not as real people with positives and negatives in their characters and records.

Front-end techniques used by political marketing consultants to design campaigns and their posters include methods (such as polling) that were used in the nineteenth century; some (e.g., focus groups) came later. Some of these practices, including image management, negative "attack ads," and distortion, have been used for well over a century; others, such as the individualization of posters via the Internet, are new. While audience analysis was always important to political consultants who had anything to do with poster designs, this process became more important and systematic in the twentieth century, resulting in simplified messages aimed at targeted segments of the electorate, and the use of graphic techniques designed to make appeals attractive to these groups.

❧ *Art and Graphic Design.* Inevitably, changes in the worlds of art and graphic design have effected changes in political poster design. In the eighteenth century, newspaper and book printers put together political broadsides.[81] Early broadsides used capital letters, and bold and large type for emphasis, and occasionally included visuals (see Figs. 2.1 and 2.4, Chapter Two). Lithographers and engravers, who operated print shops in the early nineteenth century, joined these printers. Currier ran such a shop in New York City, printing music sheets, architectural plans, portraits, and disaster and memorial prints. Since newspapers did not include pictures, Currier's illustrations appealed to the public. After Ives joined his firm, Currier expanded the list of print categories and created a wide variety of "cheap and popular pictures" (as the two men characterized the purpose of their business), including ones on sports, transportation, and hunting. Between 1835 and 1907, Currier & Ives turned out more than one million prints. These included a great many lithographic portraits of presidential candidates, as well as the aforementioned election banners. The firm employed artists, letterers, and lithographers to create these prints; when colors were needed, female immigrants added them, each worker assigned to do one color.[82]

In addition, poster houses produced woodcut posters, handbills, and broadsides by the middle of the nineteenth century. A compositor, who consulted with a client, made all design decisions, employing both wood and metal type. The color lithographs designed by Chéret were influenced by large woodcuts that advertised American circuses. The designers of these woodcuts already used text wrapped around shapes, eye-catching visuals, and a few words in large type. Political illustrators, especially Thomas Nast in post-Civil War America, created woodcut images that became symbols of political parties and even countries: the Democratic Party's donkey; the Republican Party's elephant; Uncle Sam for the United States; and John Bull for England. The lithographic posters designed in France by Henri de Toulouse-Lautrec in the final decade of the nineteenth century to promote the Moulin Rouge and other cafés were influenced by Japanese woodcuts, and featured large, flat, bright areas of primary colors and silhouettes. The political posters in the next decades sustained many of these developments, which also incorporated innovative typography.[83]

Poster artists depended more and more on compelling imagery, composition, and color, minimizing text. This was to better convey political and other promotional messages, and the new medium of film, as Max Gallo noted, "accentuated this evolution toward efforts to create immediate visual impact."[84] Influential poster designers emphasized pictorial elements. In fact, an analysis by Rune Pettersson of four posters from the 1890s (one by Alphonse Mucha, one by Chéret, and two by Toulouse-Lautrec) determined that the picture area occupied 68 percent of the posters' space, the text 15 percent, and the background area 17 percent.[85] This change can be seen in political posters, as Gallo pointed out, by comparing the posters of the French Revolution and those of World War I.[86] In eighteenth-century France, most of the larger, posted material had only lines of text (usually capitalized); during The Great War, however, powerful visuals such as soldiers, tearful widows, bloodied knives, cannons, and symbols such as John Bull, were frequently the dominant elements.

Popular American illustrators including Charles Dana Gibson, James Montgomery Flagg, Howard Chandler Christy, and N. C. Wyeth, as well as German designers including Lucian Bernhard, Julius Klinger, Hans Rudi Erdt, and Ludwig Hohlwein, worked on posters in support of the war efforts of both sides during World War I. Naturally, the realistic, artistic style favored in the popular magazines such as *Harper's* and *Scribner's* was also preferred by their artists who worked on many of the Allied war posters.[87] The posters of the Central Powers were less realistic, integrating more "symbolic imagery."[88] The brilliant German graphic designers produced posters with stylish lettering and figures. Ironically, these posters later won much critical acclaim, even though they were deemed less effective in swaying public opinion than were the opposition's posters. Adolf Hitler concurred (as is discussed in Chapter Six). The poster designs of Erdt and Hohlwein during World War I were reminiscent of the prewar work of Edward Penfield (and other graphic designers loosely classified under the Art Nouveau style) in that their illustrations were simplified by a lack of details, with a plain background, broad areas of color, and prominent, original lettering and imagery. Similar developments were manifest in the posters of other countries,

Figure 1.21

including those designed for election campaigns. A 1918 campaign poster for the Social Democratic Workers' Party (SDAP) in The Netherlands, for example, included embellished letters and a capitalist octopus with flourished tentacles, and flat color areas (particularly the red shirt of a worker fighting the tentacles of "anarchy," "war," and "famine") against a plain yellow background (Fig. 1.21).

After World War I, the ideas of the Bauhaus school, the Dada movement, and Constructivism in Europe influenced a generation of graphic designers. Photomontage, compelling color, simplified shapes, and creative typography were evident in political posters, especially in many of those created in the new Soviet Union. In Germany, the Nazi Party designed effective posters that appealed to the masses, some done in the style of Albrecht Dürer to link its movement to the past, and with striking sans-serif headlines and dynamic, diagonal lines.[89] In addition, Impressionism continued to exert an influence on political poster designers. Other art movements, such as Cubism, Surrealism, Futurism, Expressionism, Art Deco, Social Realism, and Psychedelic and Op Art, had an impact on political poster designs as well. The influence of Pablo Picasso and possibly even Fernand Léger may be seen in an Italian Communist Party poster aimed at feminists before the 1976 general election, for example (Fig. 1.22).

The main trends in poster design for most of the twentieth century were simplification and stylization. These trends were dominant in posters that advertised products and services, political causes and candidates among them. Most advertising companies sought to present their products to appeal to an audience effectively and deliver the message quickly and clearly. Accordingly, these trends were evident in

Figure 1.22

most political ads designed by the firms that became gradually more involved in election campaigns during the century. Poster designers tried to conceive distinctive styles and powerful visuals, used text sparingly, and arranged elements to attract attention. This is particularly important in a modern world in which people are "increasingly bombarded with messages," according to John Hegarty.[90] A Swedish poster merely had to say "Ford 1936" below illustrations of the new car model to advertise the product (Fig. 1.23). Sans-serif type styles became more common in posters too—another simplification that can be seen in the Ford advertisement. People on the go (in cars and on foot) could more easily read the large, unembellished lettering from a distance than they could previous styles. In this period, simpler, stylized election posters were designed as well. A good example of one of these posters is Figure 1.24, in which a man is calling his "comrades" to "vote Red" (the color of the SDAP) in the 1933 election in The Netherlands. As in the Ford advertisement, the Dutch poster boasted strong sans-serif lettering and one dominant

| Figure 1.23 | Figure 1.24 | Figure 1.25 |

image, and used diagonal lines to increase the dynamism of the composition. The dual trends of simplification and stylization became increasingly evident, particularly after World War II. A poster issued to support environmentalist Brice Lalonde's campaign for the presidency of France in 1981, for example, featured a stylized drawing of a tree and a few sans-serif capital letters (Fig. 1.25).

Promoters generally demanded simplicity and compelling visuals, text, and colors for posters advertising their products because their goal was "to get the message across quickly and convincingly to the potential market," according to art instructor George Horn.[91] As Tom Purvis, a prominent poster designer in Great Britain in the 1920s and 1930s, pointed out, "The most valuable asset of a well designed poster is its shock value. By shock value I mean its kick, strength, visibility, immediate readability."[92] Purvis' style featured flat primary colors devoid of details.[93] In addition, there was an increased use of photographic images in posters, and photorealism was predominant. Other techniques, however, were employed in political posters, including airbrushing, water coloring, color separation and shifting, block printing, silk screening, superimposition of images, high-contrast imagery, and even "ripped papers" used in montages.

Continuing Practices

Yet, some things do not change. Overall, designers have stayed with techniques that work—in different countries and historical periods. Flagg's "I Want You for U.S. Army" design in World War I, with Uncle Sam looking directly at the viewer and pointing a finger at him, was derived from a British poster produced three years earlier; in the British poster, Secretary of State for War Lord Kitchener is pointing a finger at British males, with the words "Wants You, Join Your Country's Army! God Save The King." Other countries—Italy, Hungary, Germany, Great Britain, Canada, France, the Irish Parliamentary Party, the Red Army in Russia, and later, the Republicans in the Spanish Civil War—designed similar posters. The British applied the same design idea in World War II, featuring Prime Minister Winston Churchill, instead of Kitchener, in the same pose; the U.S. Democratic Party resurrected Flagg's Uncle Sam image, including it in an election poster for Franklin D. Roosevelt. In the decades that followed, however, antiwar protest groups issued satires of Flagg's "I Want You" poster, with Uncle Sam in a variety of poses: pointing a gun at the audience; making the "peace sign," bandaged and accompanied by the slogan "I Want Out"; as a skeleton, with a target superimposed on him; and with the "bad breath" of airplanes dropping bombs on houses in his mouth.

Other techniques abound, such as the use of harsh lighting and unflattering camera angles to make opposing politicians appear to be somewhat shady and diminished in stature in a British election poster (see Fig. 5.24, Chapter Five). In addition, just as advertisements have coupled a new product with an image that is well regarded, political posters have combined images to associate a candidate or party with something positive or negative: past U.S. election posters often included portraits of George Washington and Abraham Lincoln; recent posters in Taiwan have associated candidates for president with Sun Yat-sen and Osama bin Laden (see Fig. 6.8, Chapter Six)!

Not only has image manipulation persisted in politics, but the use of visual symbols has continued as well. The goal of the political poster designer is to attract, and simplify the message for, an audience. Icons, as well as slogans, can help accomplish this. Such symbols as flags, raised fists, and birds (particularly eagles and doves) have been adopted, for generations, in many societies. For example, an eagle perched on a flag displaying the party's logo dominated a poster distributed by the victorious Soviet Revolutionary Party during the 1917 Constituent Assembly election campaign in Russia (Fig. 1.26). A poster issued by the Alliance Fatherland and Freedom Party during the 1993 election campaign in Latvia featured an oak tree, a traditional national symbol of "strength" and "unity."[94]

Figure 1.26

"Designers are all salespeople selling visually," according to graphic designer Mike Salisbury,[95] and a political candidate can be presented, using positive imagery, so that he or she will be appealing to voters. The symbols and graphic techniques that have been used in one country are often appropriated by political poster designers in others: the Statue of Liberty was featured in a Romanian election poster; in a Russian campaign poster, a presidential candidate protectively wraps his arms around a pair of children and a dog napping nearby—a scene influenced by paintings by Norman Rockwell.[96] The "V" symbol—used to signify either "victory" or "peace"—has been used in many election posters, such as in the United States by Democrats for the Humphrey-Muskie ticket in 1968; in Iran by the dominant Islamic Republic Party in the decade after that country's revolution (Fig. 1.27); and in Mexico by the Fox campaign in 2000 (see Fig. 6.45, Chapter Six).

Figure 1.27

Issues have been spotlighted on election posters through the years. This has often taken the form of slogans. The most effective election posters seem to have been "a cut above" the standard sales job, which has featured a photograph of the candidate and a slogan. Whereas a negative poster campaign may have appeal to party loyalists and depress turnout, the posters that seem to have worked well with the public have been designed creatively and have "hit" on issues that have been meaningful to many, such as high unemployment.[97] When a poster strikes a discordant note on an issue that is of real concern to voters, the negative message can influence them. This seemed true for some anti-immigrant posters that appeared in Europe in the last decade. This tactic, however, can boomerang—as seemed to be the case with poster attacks on candidates from Andrew Jackson to Tony Blair.

Political propaganda—from its inception—has been designed to educe emotional reactions. Negative advertising is one approach, and scare tactics have sometimes been employed. Attempts to increase fears and prejudice in the electorate, via the poster medium, have occurred for well over a century. This is evident in broadsides and posters from an anti-Lincoln, pro-McClellan broadside of 1864 (which warned of a new draft, increased debt, "Negro Equality," and "Universal Anarchy" if Lincoln won) to recent anti-Semitic and anti-Moslem election posters in Europe. Still, depictions in election posters of family scenes, as well as portraits of members of such target groups as college students and senior citizens, and inclusion of various symbols, have elicited positive emotions too.

Other approaches—such as trying to instill guilt, and using sexual imagery and credible figures, as well as idealistic and nationalistic appeals—have manifested in political posters. Suffragettes in the early nineteenth century, for instance, pasted posters on walls:

one large lithograph featured babies marching under the title "Give Mother The Vote: We Need It"; others showed professional women, some of whom wore caps and gowns decrying their lack of suffrage (one poster was titled "Convicts, Lunatics, and Women! Have No Vote for Parliament"). In 2002, posters printed during the Serbian presidential elections displayed photographs of former leader Slobodan Milosevic covered by the word *shame*.[98] Celebrity endorsements of candidates began with the 1920 U.S. presidential campaign, when Lasker persuaded Al Jolson, Lillian Russell, and other stars to endorse Republican Warren Harding; by 1928, sports figures such as Babe Ruth and Gene Tunney were included in election posters for Democratic presidential candidate Al Smith. In the 1990s, a researcher found that the presence or absence of a well-known figure in Belgium's election posters was the main factor that influenced voters' recognition of posters.[99]

Sexual imagery is a tactic sometimes used to attract an audience to an election poster. Other tactics are used to achieve this: displaying outrageous images (e.g., a male opposition

Figure 1.28

leader, shown pregnant or wearing a woman's hairdo); presenting nudes; or including tyrants of the past ("associated" with opposing candidates and parties). The probability that using sex will backfire is a chance some will take, particularly if young voters are the targets of an ad. Advertising executives know that there may be some objections, but the benefits often outweigh the outrage expressed by certain groups. One must be careful, however, not to "go too far." A typical approach to using sexual imagery to get attention, while not appearing to be too provocative in an election poster, is reflected in Figure 1.28: an attractive woman is touching a button on her blouse, presumably to open it, and looking alluringly at the audience in a 1953 Italian Christian Democracy Party (DC) poster. Ten years later, the DC brought in a U.S. advertising agency to design a poster campaign, applying the motivational

theories of Ernest Dichter, featuring a sexy young woman, along with the slogan "The DC is twenty years old."[100] By the German presidential election of 2002, a more stimulating poster for the Social Democrats featured heavily reddened lips, puckered for a kiss, and the slogan "That was only the foreplay. The climax is still to come. ..." The message was clear: reelect Chancellor Schröder so that he could complete his agenda.[101]

Another long-standing practice has been to include posters as part of a "media campaign package." By the middle of the nineteenth century in the United States, posters were added to the collection of badges, buttons, and banners that promoted political candidates; they, along with yard signs, have continued to hold a prominent position in twenty-first-century election campaign packages. The poster is the component of the media package that has been frequently chosen to give the critical "first impression."[102] While the broadcast media are now predominant in affecting public opinion, the poster remains an important vehicle to influence perception and behavior in political and protest campaigns worldwide. This is because posters are not only seen "on the streets," but are also viewed by millions of people on television and billboards. In developing countries, posters are used together with pamphlets, comic books, radio, and television in a variety of political campaigns.

Research Purposes

The study of the political poster as a medium of propaganda is fascinating and enlightening. The subject is immense, and this book cannot cover the posters distributed by every party, movement, and governmental agency. Rather, this book is a survey that covers the high points, and examines how and why posters—in national election campaigns of democratic countries—were designed and used, the contexts in which they were created, and their effects. Since the United States, Great Britain, and France are the oldest modern democracies, with the longest record of national election campaigning, they are covered most extensively. The most attention is given to the United States, in which occurred the first election campaigns, organized by political parties with significant power in the system. This book also examines the use of broadsides—often excluded from books on political posters.

For half a millennium, beginning with the Protestant Reformation, posters and broadsides have been used to present messages to target audiences. Posters gradually declined in popularity in much of the Western world during the second half of the twentieth century. But when broadcast media are unavailable or undesirable, political posters are used, sometimes heavily. Since the early twentieth century, the involvement of the advertising industry in the design of posters—as part of campaign packages—is of interest, as well, for advertising techniques have pervaded wartime, elections, and various political movements, and have been used to stimulate consumption of products and services. One purpose of this book is to better understand how this propaganda medium has been used to shape public opinion, and how poster messages are designed for voters. What principles that were thought to have been successful have the designers of these posters applied? What symbols have been used to convey essential meanings? How have advertising personnel and political consultants influenced the design and use of election posters?

Another purpose of this book is to examine the roles of election posters in different societies and eras. What were the conditions that led to using these posters more frequently? How, for example, have technological changes affected their use? In addition, how have the content, style, and utilization of political posters been affected by political systems, ideology, education, literacy, suffrage, financial conditions, legislation, social change, artistic movements, graphic design trends, and advertising?

The final purpose of this book is to examine evidence of the effectiveness of political posters. In general, how have they influenced public opinion and behavior? In particular, what research findings have used voting decisions as a dependent measure, and what have they revealed? This book examines studies that address exposure to political posters; recognition and recall of issues; evaluations of portrayed candidates; perceived influence of political posters and billboards; and effects on behavior.

Posters, billboards, and banners are all "tools," as Lasswell indicated, in the propaganda arsenal in an election campaign, with the goal to convince voters to support a party or a candidate over competitors. While accurate information can be included, it is presented in such a way as to favor one side over another. It is thus misleading. Other posters use distortion, stereotypes, and falsehoods, as well as emotion-laden symbols—to accomplish the goal of propaganda: mass persuasion. This book looks at a wide variety of election posters—all designed to achieve this goal.

Broadsides and Posters in Early U.S. Presidential Election Campaigns

Broadsides and posters have been used for almost two centuries in U.S. presidential election campaigns. American election managers have employed a wide variety of campaign propaganda; posters were a key political medium into the twentieth century, and their impact continued—even as radio, and then television, replaced printed matter as the paramount vehicles in politics. Posters, which have generally communicated positive messages, attempt to show the candidates in the best possible light and appeal to the interests, perceptions, and even prejudices of the public. As Cabell Phillips pointed out, "the basic script of the political campaign has changed scarcely at all in its fundamentals, only its embellishments. Its essential purpose is, and always has been, to persuade as many people as possible that the candidate is (1) wise, (2) honest, and (3) concerned about 'you.'"[1] Many posters and broadsides have achieved this over the years, by using flattering lithographic and photographic techniques, as well as establishing "eye contact" between the candidates and viewers/voters, and/or incorporating convincing slogans and illustrations to which people could relate.

In U.S. elections, posters played a key role in political communication, which Judith Trent and Robert Friedenberg declared is the core of a campaign:

> It is through communication that a political campaign begins. Individuals verbally announce their intention to run, and posters/billboards announce nonverbally that election time has begun. During the campaign, candidates and their staffs debate, appear on television, ... prepare and present messages for media commercials, take part in parades and rallies, wear funny hats, submit to media interviews, write letters and position papers, and speak at all forms of public gatherings, ... prepare and distribute literature, ... wear campaign buttons, and establish phone banks to solicit money, workers, and votes. ... And when the time comes, it is through communication that the campaign draws to a close. Candidates verbally concede defeat or extol victory, and the posters/billboards are taken down announcing nonverbally that one campaign is over even as another begins. ... Without [communication], there is no political campaign.[2]

Nonprint technologies have superseded posters, billboards, and broadsides—once probably the most important ways of communicating in American election campaigns.

This chapter examines the place of the aforementioned printed media in U.S. national election campaigns before this change transpired. The following chapters explore how the rise of broadcast media affected the application of posters, which continued to play an important role in election campaigns in many countries. Above all, the poster is still a notable means by which to establish the presence of a candidate, and to reinforce messages delivered on radio, television, and the Internet.

The United States of America was the first republic that *survived*, as Joseph Ellis pointed out, avoiding elimination by "the same kind of military dictatorship that had destroyed the Roman and English republics. ... "[3] It was also the largest geographically. Most important was that the United States was the birthplace of fully developed political parties, "with national platforms, campaigns, and conventions" emerging in the first four decades of the nineteenth century.[4] Technically, presidents are not elected directly, since those in the Electoral College actually vote for the candidates; but slates of electors, of whom most are legally obligated to vote for a specific ticket, are chosen by popular vote—a process that began in 1789, when four states used this approach. Other selection methods—most often election by state legislatures—were also employed; by 1828, however, only two of the twenty-four states did not choose electors by popular vote (down from six states only four years earlier).[5]

The 1828 election also saw a dramatic increase in the number of white males allowed to vote, and only two states retained property ownership as a qualification for voting by that year.[6] Therefore, it was no coincidence that in 1828, a major effort was undertaken to promote political candidates and parties to these new voters. Broadsides were used to both denigrate the opposition and get white working people to identify with candidates who shared attributes with the "commoners" whose votes were now so important. The first election campaign anywhere in the world in which broadsides were issued occurred in the United States in the 1820s. The use of this medium was most notable in that decade, during the epic electoral contest that pitched Andrew Jackson, a man of "humble origins," against John Quincy Adams, the incumbent and son of one of the Founding Fathers, portrayed in some broadsides as "aristocratic." The campaign was characterized by both positive and negative advertising (as are many modern contests), and broadsides played a key part. Even before this election, broadsides and large prints attacking politicians, including sitting presidents Thomas Jefferson and James Madison, were run off. During his second term in office, an anti-Jefferson broadside that included a quotation from *Hamlet* was distributed; and in a James Akin cartoon, he was represented as a prairie dog vomiting gold coins, after being stung by a hornet bearing Napoleon Bonaparte's head and hat. There were at least two broadsides printed during the election of 1824, both of which were critical of Jackson: one—the famous "Coffin Handbill"—attacked his character; the other criticized his stand on the issue of tariffs. The Coffin Handbill was reissued in 1828—the year of the first election in which broadsides were distributed widely as part of a media campaign for the masses—and is discussed shortly.

The United States is the country with the longest and richest history of political campaigning in the world. Its campaign practices have influenced those of other countries, and many of its political consultants, at least since the late 1960s, have worked abroad.

At home, numerous posters issued by official campaign committees and political parties, as well as posters and broadsides distributed by "independent" groups, have been prominent in American election campaigns, and have helped shape candidate images and voter perceptions on issues. This was true in 1828—before modern mass media were invented—and will be undoubtedly true, to a lesser extent, even in 2028. This chapter focuses particularly on key premodern presidential campaigns, beginning with the 1828 contest, when image management, negative advertising, and distortion all moved to the forefront of the propagandists' strategic plans.

The "Heroic Man of the People" Against the "Aristocrat" (1828)

In 1828, larger broadsides were used extensively, for the first time, in a full-fledged campaign.[7] Broadsides, as well as lithographic prints, were circulated both for and against Andrew Jackson. John Binns, editor of the Philadelphia *Democratic Press*, printed an anti-Jackson broadside that measured about fifteen by twenty-two inches.[8] This woodcut-with-letterpress broadside depicted six coffins containing militiamen, who, "an eye witness" alleged, had been executed wrongfully, on General Jackson's orders thirteen years earlier (Fig. 2.1). In addition, it showed another dozen coffins, representing regular soldiers and "Indians" who were put to death under Jackson's command. There was also was a drawing of Jackson on a city street, running his sword through a man's back. Coffins had been included in handbills as early as the seventeenth century in England, and were prominent in an anti-British American handbill printed in 1775, but had never been used in election propaganda before.[9]

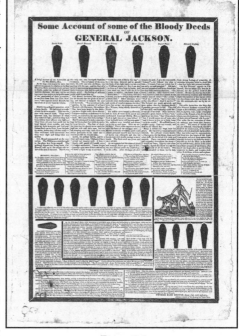

Figure 2.1

Actually, Binns' broadside was a *reprint* since he had printed it as a supplement to his newspaper during the 1824 election, in which Jackson was previously a candidate.[10] Binns claimed that "some merchants ... from Tennessee" had given him evidence that validated the charges, and then he commenced his anti-Jackson campaign.[11] In his autobiography, he described the planning, dissemination, and ramifications of the supplement:

> In order to arrest public attention and impress the public mind with the injustice and the enormity of the crime of General Jackson, in respect to the shooting of these militia men, I had six coffins cast in metal type, and on each of them the name of one of the men who had been

shot. I had supplements to the 'Democratic Press' printed, with the coffins printed on them, together with the history of the whole transaction, and had one of those supplements sent with every copy of the daily, tri-weekly, and weekly 'Democratic Press.' Thus several thousand coffin handbills were circulated through the United States. It may well be doubted whether there was a publication, which brought upon the publisher such active, general, and intense odium as those coffin handbills brought upon the writer of these recollections.[12]

On the night of the 1824 vote, according to Binns, a mob came to the house in which he had his printing office and residence. He reported that they had with them an empty coffin, and, presumably, planned to place him in it. After "demonstrating" in front of the house for two days (which included throwing stones at it), the protesters departed, and the Coffin Handbill episode died down,[13] only to be resurrected during the 1828 election.

In 1828, Binns himself was ridiculed in a satirical etching, which was printed probably by the same James Akin (also of Philadelphia),[14] who had attacked Jefferson two decades earlier. This print illustrated Binns carrying six coffins, as well as President Adams and Secretary of State Henry Clay, on his back. Jackson took Binns' charges seriously. After the Coffin Handbill first appeared, he had his "Nashville Committee" of supporters, who produced a good deal of the material for his 1828 campaign, answer them, stating that those executed had been guilty of mutiny, theft, arson, and desertion.[15] Pro- and anti-Jackson forces printed pamphlets that dealt with the charges from the previous decade.[16] The Coffin Handbill was reprinted in newspapers around the country during the 1828 campaign, and was known to many of Jackson's supporters and detractors. For example, *Our Country*, the Hagers-Town, Maryland, newspaper, featured it in its October 18, 1828, edition and added some commentary, which began as follows:

> We lay this far-famed handbill before our readers to-day. We have two reasons for doing so. Many of them have never yet seen it—this is one reason. The other is, that the Jacksonites call it an infamous bill, and pronounce its statements false. It is neither infamous nor false. If there be any infamy connected with it, that infamy should attach to General Jackson—for, however, black—however appalling this bill may appear, it presents but an inadequate representation of the still black and still more appalling acts of this violent and vindictive man.[17]

Pro-Jackson broadsides were printed too, but they lacked any shocking visuals. Instead, they extolled Old Hickory's "virtues" as "the hero of two wars" and "the man of the people." One broadside (Fig. 2.2) idolized Jackson as the hero of the Battle of New Orleans, which was fought in the previous decade, by printing the words of the popular song "The Hunters of Kentucky." Here is an excerpt:

> But Jackson he was wide awake, and wasn't scar'd at trifles,
> For well he knew what aim we take with our Kentucky rifles;
> So he led us down to Cyprus swamp, the ground was low and mucky,
> There stood John Bull in martial pomp, and here was old Kentucky.

The image of "Old Hickory," mighty in combat and a leader of "ordinary men" who performed extraordinary deeds, was communicated frequently during the election campaign. The metaphor of soldiers as "alligator horses" served to reinforce this concept and to attract voters. In addition, small, engraved prints (approximately 6½ by 8½ inches), featuring oval portraits of Jackson surrounded by the words "Protector & Defender of Beauty & Boot./Orleans," were distributed, along with campaign biographies that had similar portraits as front pieces.[18]

Figure 2.2 (excerpt)

Efforts by Democrats to portray Jackson as "manly" and for the "common man" were apparently more effective than were the campaign tactics of Adams' supporters, who attempted to depict Jackson as violent, unjust, a paramour, and even a poor speller.[19] It is quite possible that this anti-Jackson propaganda actually reinforced the positive image of Jackson as a masculine commoner—especially when contrasted with that of Adams, whom the Democrats depicted as overrefined and out of touch with much of the populace[20]—and helped him win a convincing 12-point victory in the popular vote (gaining him more than two-thirds of the Electoral College vote), as more than three times as many people voted than in the previous presidential election.[21] It is also important to note that hundreds of Democratic newspapers were started up. All of them hammered the opposition with charges of a "corrupt bargain" between Adams and Clay, which, it was alleged, had put Adams in the White House by majority vote in the House of Representatives, and made Clay the secretary of state by appointment. This occurred after the 1824 election in spite of Jackson's winning the popular vote, although he had not secured an electoral-vote majority.

As the right to vote expanded to, at least, more white males, it became more important to emphasize a candidate's "commonality," and opposition candidates as lacking qualities that the average voter possessed. This tactic was probably employed for the first time during the U.S. presidential election of 1800: Thomas Jefferson was celebrated as the "Man of the People," while President John Adams (John Quincy's father) was also denigrated as an "aristocrat."[22] Ironically, as David McCullough noted, Jefferson was the aristocratic slave owner "who lived in a style fit for a prince," whereas Adams lived much more modestly on his farm and objected to slavery.[23] Andrew Jackson, in fact, *had* been born into poverty in South Carolina. Of course, when he ran for president as a "Democrat," he was a well-to-do plantation owner, who had slaves.[24] Like so many later U.S. elections, the 1828 contest emphasized personal traits of the candidates more than issues, about which the candidates often agreed.[25] Broadsides printed during the 1828 election not only disparaged President John Quincy Adams as "aristocratic," but also insinuated that he was anti-Catholic and irreligious, and Democratic newspapers accused him of working to make naturalization of immigrants more difficult.[26] Jackson's opponents, on the other hand, accused him in their broadsides of adultery, assassination, murder, and corruption (see Figure 2.3 for an

Figure 2.3 (excerpt)

example).

The impact of good Democratic slogans, which conveyed a positive image of Jackson as a plainspoken fighter for the masses, could be seen in an increase in Jackson's appeal to citizens who had just obtained the right to vote. The image of John Quincy Adams as an accomplished intellectual could not have appealed to many of these people, especially those in the West and South; most of them viewed him as remote and aloof.[27] In addition, Adams had never served in the military. It is hard to measure the effect of the negative campaign tactics, but it became apparent by the end of the campaign that the "National Republicans" (as Adams' supporters finally labeled themselves) had been outorganized, outsloganed, outemotioned, outrallied, and outsymboled. This was recognized even by backers of President Adams, who came up with the oak as a symbol of their candidate—an icon that never successfully competed with the hickory. It was also generally acknowledged that the 1828 U.S. presidential campaign was one of the dirtiest ever: after being slandered repeatedly, the "adulterous" Mrs. Rachel Jackson died several weeks after the election; Adams was accused of having procured a young woman for the czar when he was the minister to Russia.[28] Jackson advisor Amos Kendall, in a lecture he gave more than three decades later, characterized the contest as "almost ferocious"[29]; and in his autobiography, he stated, "General Jackson was charged with every folly and crime from cock-fighting to murder. Never before nor since did a candidate encounter such a storm of obloquy or abuse."[30] The campaign was so bitter that President Adams and the members of his cabinet departed the capital before their successors arrived.[31]

Kendall was the first political consultant of note to work in an election. A newspaper editor from Kentucky, who became a member of Jackson's "Kitchen Cabinet" of advisors as well as his postmaster general,[32] Kendall was a political "public relations" specialist before there was any such field: he was concerned with news articles, speechwriting, polls, event planning, demographic analysis, and packaging ideas for targeted groups. These activities occurred during the election of 1828 in what Robert Remini called "in some respects the first modern presidential campaign," widely employing parades, songs, and slogans "to manipulate the electorate on a mass scale."[33] As Melvyn Bloom noted, Kendall "was one of the first to sense the shift in the balance of power from the traditional political aristocracy of the East to the growing frontier population and the urban working classes."[34] Accordingly, the new Democratic Party's broadsides and election tickets (i.e., very small woodcut prints, about two inches square, listing the candidates at all levels) that were produced in support of Jackson's bid for the presidency in 1828 emphasized the cause of reform—to excise the government of entrenched, privileged interests and bring in those sympathetic to the newly enfranchised workers. One election ticket, for example, had an illustration of a broom, along with the slogan "To sweep the Augean Stable," which associated Jackson with Hercules and his labor of cleaning the stables—an allusion to reform.[35]

The other main campaign advisor to Jackson was Martin Van Buren. The politically adroit New Yorker was known as "The Little Magician," and as Jackson's campaign manager, he exaggerated his candidate's rustic ruggedness and past military leadership and characterized the opposition candidate, President Adams, as weak and effeminate. An election ticket printed in 1828 exploited Jackson's appealing nickname of "Old Hickory," with its illustration of a hickory tree and the slogan "Firm united let us be, Rallying round our Hickory tree." Not only was the nickname effective in symbolizing strength and determination, but it was also the first nickname for a candidate that was used in a presidential campaign. Van Buren astutely used such imagery to appeal to the large numbers of new voters in 1828. At the same time, he led in building an effective and unified Democratic Party national organization that was instrumental in electing Jackson.[36]

Many heroic portraits of Jackson were distributed during his election campaigns, also, along with a lot of paraphernalia (hats, buttons, and vests) that would appeal to the masses.[37] Kendall and other Jacksonians organized most of the partisan newspapers (many printed only during the campaign), promoted candidates, and disseminated party propaganda.[38] Not all newspapers were pro-Jackson, however, as evidenced by the printing of the famous "Coffin Handbill" in newspapers around the country. Van Buren and Kendall coordinated the first mass political campaign on a national level. Their use of broadsides and promotional material (such as hickory poles) at the Jackson rallies that were organized, and the image manipulation and emotional appeals to the masses, were taken to new heights a few years later in the "log cabin" campaign of 1840 in the United States.

"Old Tippecanoe," "The Little Magician," and "The Log Cabin Campaign" (1836 and 1840)

The election campaign of 1828 resulted in a political communication revolution. Parties were formed, campaign tactics were developed to attract targeted groups, and printed material, particularly newspapers and broadsides, were employed to convey propagandistic messages. The campaign also witnessed a shift in the political power base from educated landowners to workingmen and the mercantile class. Van Buren, who was a senator from New York (and later, Jackson's secretary of state and vice president), had run a campaign with the theme "Andrew Jackson, who can fight" against "John Quincy Adams, who can write."[39] It is ironic that this strategy was resurrected to help defeat Van Buren himself, following his one term as president, after he succeeded Jackson in 1836.

In 1836, "Old Kinderhook" (as Van Buren was known, having been born in Kinderhook, New York) used the primary theme that had worked for Old Hickory: the "people" and "democracy" must triumph over the "aristocrats." This can be seen in two election tickets printed for Van Buren and his running mate, Richard Johnson: on one was the slogan "Liberty & Equal Rights"; on the other was "Going the whole Hog." The first slogan was designed to appeal to "the common man" and the second implied that the

Democrats would continue to push for economic growth.[40] This time it was a military hero, the main Whig candidate, General William Henry Harrison ("Old Tippecanoe"), who lost—although the Democrats were careful to balance their ticket with Colonel Johnson, who had also fought Indians. Harrison had led the American regulars and militia that defeated the Indian warriors, under Tecumseh and the Prophet, at Tippecanoe Creek in 1811. But the Democrats claimed—without any proof—that Johnson had killed Tecumseh during the Battle of the Thames in 1813, making him (at least among Democrats) "the Hero of the Thames."[41] It was the American victory over the British and Indians at the Thames River that also made Harrison—who led a force of over two thousand volunteers, including two hundred other Indians—a national hero.

The generalities embodied in slogans and expedient positions on some issues, as well as the good organization and publicity generated by Kendall and others, helped win the day for the Democrats in 1836. On the crucial issue of slavery, for example, Van Buren stated that Congress *could* abolish slavery in Washington, D.C., but that he personally objected to abolition there.[42] The Whig attacks in the broadsides of 1836 focused on the "corruption" of the Jackson-Van Buren administration and its opposition to distributing to the states surplus federal revenue for internal improvements.[43] An example of a broadside that highlighted the latter issue is seen in Figure 2.4, which was printed in Connecticut (where the Democrats had made recent gains[44]), and criticized Van Buren for opposing the allocation of this revenue. This propaganda approach (along with a magnificent drawing of an eagle) with "every Man, Woman and Child in the State" due "nearly $5," did not sway the voters. Van Buren beat Harrison by a narrow margin in the state—something that even Jackson had failed to do in the previous two elections.[45] A pro-Harrison lithograph labeled his backers "the People" and Van Buren's "Office holders & mail Contractors." Van Buren received 58 percent of the electoral vote (and 51 percent of the popular vote), sufficient to prevent the election from being thrown into the House of Representatives; only 25 percent of the electors supported Harrison, and three other candidates gained the remainder of the electoral vote.[46]

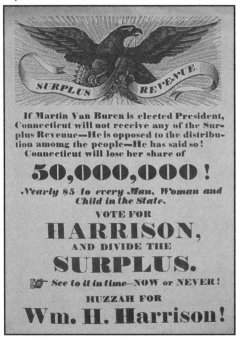

Figure 2.4

The 1840 election was a rematch between Van Buren and Harrison—this time without the other Whig candidates. In the spring of that year, President Van Buren mandated a ten-hour workday for laborers on federal projects, continued Jackson's harsh policies against the Cherokee and Seminole Indian tribes, and promised to uphold the rights of states to allow slavery (but opposed Texas' joining the Union).[47] As Wilson Sullivan stated, this resulted in Van Buren being "regarded as proslavery in the North and antislavery in the South."[48] Looming large, however, was the depression that began shortly after his inauguration, followed by policies such as cutting public spending that made the economic situation worse.[49]

The campaign may well have been as heated as the one that ushered in the Jacksonian Democrats in 1828. Lithographic prints belittled Van Buren as an antidemocratic, aristocratic, machine hack with a regal style of living, and attacked his record, which lacked military service. For example, one print satirized the policies and practices of the Van Buren administration (with Kendall shown blowing smoke and bubbles from a pipe), using verse from the nursery rhyme "The House that Jack Built."[50] In addition, illustrations that lampooned the government's handling of postal revenue ("This is the Malt that laid in the House that Jack built"), public land sales, and other issues were evident.

This time, the Whigs played up Harrison as a frontiersmen, and devised the effective slogan "Tippecanoe and Tyler too" to celebrate both their presidential candidate and his running mate, John Tyler, who had been a Virginia senator. In a broadside in which they intentionally misspelled the names of their opponents as "Van Beuren" and "Kendal," who were to go on a steamboat to "Salt River" (an expression referring to a candidate's political defeat), the Whigs also portrayed their party as protectors of "the rights of the people" against the "corrupt" Democrats. Van Buren and Kendall tried to appeal to the working class and revive memories of Jackson's victory over the Bank of the United States. These themes can be seen in Figure 2.5, a broadside with Van Buren flanked by two figures on columns: Andrew Jackson, holding his veto of the United States Bank charter, and a farmer, holding a piece of paper with the words "TEN HOURS." The Democrats spent most of their energy attacking Harrison's

Figure 2.5

war record, his age, his mental and physical conditions, and his past statements on slavery, but made less of an effort to defend their candidate.[51]

The Whigs in 1840 introduced two unique ideas to election campaigns: one was to use a potent symbol—the log cabin (often combined with soldiers and a jug of hard cider)— for candidate Harrison, depicted as a rough-and-ready, common farmer with a plough and barrel of cider (Fig. 2.6); the other was the creation of silk flag banners, which added a portrait of Harrison and the phrases "Old Tip" and "The Hero of Tippecanoe" to the

Figure 2.6

Figure 2.6a (inset)

American flag.[52] Some of the Whig rallies, with banners unfurled, drew an estimated one hundred thousand people, perhaps attracted by the seemingly endless supplies of hard cider.[53] It mattered little to most partisans that the "common man" image concocted for Harrison was false. The log cabin was used to represent Harrison's "poor" and "humble" background. His background was neither; rather, he was born in a mansion on a Virginia plantation. Regardless of the truth, the imagery and the hard cider that was distributed at the gigantic rallies undoubtedly excited voters and boosted the Harrison campaign. This is evident in the voter turnout that increased from 54 percent in 1836 to 77 percent in 1840; the Harrison-Tyler ticket won by a 6 percent margin in the popular vote and claimed 80 percent of the electoral votes.[54]

An effort was made to counter the log-cabin image management, but this anti-Whig printed material did not change public opinion. Figure 2.7 shows a broadside that warned the people of Louisiana not to fall for the *"'Log-Cabin'* trap, invented by the *bank-parlor, ruffle-shirt, silk-stocking* GENTRY, for catching the *votes* of the industrious and laboring classes ... [with] appeal to their passions, with mockeries, humbugs, shows, and parades." Yet, this log-cabin imagery, along with emphasis on Harrison's military leadership (see Fig. 1.3, Chapter One),[55] as well as the accompanying pageantry, did seem to appeal to many citizens on an emotional level, and secure their votes. The Whigs borrowed most of the Democratic Party's past publicity ideas: publishing their own newspapers; writing songs; organizing rallies and parades; printing broadsides and

Figure 2.7 (excerpt)

banners; and producing goods such as hairbrushes adorned with portraits of Harrison, ceramic dishes with his "modest" farm on them, "Tippecanoe Shaving Soap or Log-Cabin Emollient," and, above all, miniature log cabins.[56] A variety of banners were produced, some with an eagle holding a scroll with the Whig candidates' designations "Tip" and "Ty" in its beak and the slogan "Our Country is safe, in such Hands." One observer counted one thousand banners in a Baltimore parade for Harrison.[57] Horace Greeley (who ran for president himself three decades later) edited the most prominent Whig newspaper, the *Log Cabin*, which had a circulation of over eighty thousand during the campaign, and became the *New York Tribune* after the election.[58] The posters and banners promoting Harrison helped establish him as a powerful, mythologized candidate who generated great appeal to the expanded voting population in post-Jackson America.

Pre-Civil War Elections:
The Increased Standardization of Propaganda Posters
(1844–1860)

After 1840, U.S. political parties patterned their campaigns after the Whigs' "Tippecanoe and Tyler too" campaign, and they continued to appeal to the emotions in various ways. Frequently, posters in U.S. elections seemed "cut from the same cloth," sometimes using the same blocks, as can be seen in the campaign posters or paper banners for two different parties, the American in 1856 and the Republican in 1860 (Figs. 2.8 and 2.9). Most

Figure 2.8

Figure 2.9

of these woodcut-with-letterpress posters featured the symbols of the American flag, the eagle, allegorical figures of Justice and Liberty, the U.S. Constitution, and cornucopias, as well as slogans and mottos. The American Party's candidate, Millard Fillmore, is looking toward the viewers, but well into the twentieth century, this direct "eye contact" was rare. Candidates never really smiled; they were expected to present themselves as "serious." Mottos were also included in many posters. The motto for the Democratic Party, "Principles, Not Men," for instance, was featured in a poster that promoted the 1848 ticket of two generals, Lewis Cass and William Butler. It also incorporated many of the country's symbols, mentioned above, as well as oak leaves and acorns (the party's symbols), and various symbols for farmers and workers.

That same year, a beautifully drawn, multicolored woodcut was produced for the

Whigs to promote the candidacy of yet another military leader, General Zachary "Old Rough-and-Ready" Taylor, on horseback (Fig. 2.10). Riding a horse is a recurrent image in political posters in many countries and periods; in this example, Taylor is surrounded

by allegorical figures, flags, a dove holding an olive branch, and banners on which are listed his victories in the Mexican War. A more dynamic candidate-on-horseback image appears in a Republican poster to

Figure 2.10   *Figure 2.11*

promote the 1856 campaign of Colonel John Frémont (Fig. 2.11). Frémont looks almost Napoleonic here (second only to Harrison sixteen years earlier), but his regalia are those of a frontiersman—to appeal to a large segment of the American electorate.

The image manipulation during this period, which the Whigs had perfected in 1840, started with the remaking of Jefferson in 1800 and the propaganda of 1828, which portrayed Jackson as a "commoner," emphasizing his military exploits. In the years that followed the Harrison campaign, many candidates—from Colonel James "Young Hickory" Polk in 1844 to Lieutenant John Kerry in 2004—had their "humble origins" and/or "war leadership" highlighted in political material. Often coupled with these tactics was a corollary, to create an image of the opposition candidate that was highly negative—from John Adams as a "monarchist" to John Kerry as a "flip-flopping, windsurfing elitist."

Sometimes issues (or rather, information about policies or program strategies) overwhelmed character images. The most effective slogan during this period was probably the one devised in 1844 by the Democratic Party for its presidential candidate, James Polk: "Fifty-four Forty or Fight!" The slogan summarized the party's expansionist platform, which called for U.S. title to the Oregon Territory to the southern border of Russian Alaska at latitude 54°40' (as well as annexation of Texas). It helped the Democrats achieve victory over the Whigs and their presidential candidate, Henry "Old Kentucky" Clay, who opposed the annexation of Texas and whose symbol was a raccoon—hardly as effective as had been Harrison's log cabin. In addition, the issue of slavery became more important during this two-decade period. This is evident in broadsides that attacked Millard Fillmore and the Whigs in 1851 for supporting the Compromise of 1850, which included the Fugitive Slave Law (after President Taylor had opposed it). Fillmore lost his party's nomination the next year to yet another military hero, General Winfield "Old

Fuss and Feathers" Scott, an antislavery candidate who then lost the election to General Franklin Pierce (whose party's slogan was "We Polked you in 1844; we shall Pierce you in 1852").[59]

"The Rail Splitter" Becomes "The Great Emancipator," and the Politics of Race (1860 and 1864)

In 1860, the Republican Party promoted its candidate, Abraham Lincoln, as a common man of integrity and worth—the rail-splitting frontiersman. A poster for the ticket of Lincoln and Hannibal Hamlin that year, titled "The Union Must and Shall be Preserved," included a rail fence and it took care to show laborers on either side of a shield that declared "Protection to American Industry," as well as the customary eagle, cornucopias, and flags (Fig. 2.12). The motto "Free Speech, Free Homes, Free Territory" referred to the party's platform positions on the elimination of slavery in federal territories, support of the Homestead Act, and freedom to voice antislavery views (a carryover from

Figure 2.12

a slogan of the 1856 Frémont campaign).[60] The overriding issue was slavery expansion, which had finally reached the crisis stage, after decades of agitation by abolitionists and proslavery expansionists. A similar poster, published by the same firm, was produced for the ticket of John Bell and Edward Everett and it used the same basic template.

Figure 2.13

The parades, rallies, campaign newspapers and songs, and free food and drink that had been used in the past continued to be employed by all parties, of which there were four: (1) the Republicans, headed by Lincoln; (2) the regular Democrats, whose presidential nominee was Stephen Douglas; (3) the National Democrats, headed by John Breckenridge, who supported the federal government's protection of slavery in the territories; and (4) the Constitutional Union Party, which nominated Bell and, as its paper banner proclaimed, was in favor of "The Union, the Constitution and the Enforcement of the Laws." Placards and posters were essential ingredients in the rallies, as were the refreshments. For example, "an assemblage of from 20,000 to 30,000 people," according to the *New York Times,* gathered in New York City to hear Douglas and other Democrats give speeches, and eat barbecued meats, crackers, and bread.[61] This "Grand Political Carnival and Ox-roast," as the anonymous *Times* reporter labeled the event, was "extensively advertised" with a poster that contained a "monstrous blue eagle ... that stared citizens in the face from every board fence and new brick wall."[62]

Lincoln's supporters published two weekly newspapers, both called the *Rail Splitter*, which not only propagated his stands on issues, but also raised funds.[63] A broadside was printed as a supplement to the Chicago edition of the newspaper, and it included three caricatures of Douglas.[64] In addition, numerous portrait prints of the candidates were produced for rallies and parades, or simply distributed to potential voters—a practice that had occurred for some time. Many copies of Mathew Brady's photographs of Lincoln were distributed,[65] as were lithographic portrait posters of Lincoln, Bell, and Douglas (who is shown in Figure 2.13). Lithographic portraits of Lincoln by Currier & Ives, idealized from Brady photographs, were sold for twenty cents each (Fig. 2.14).[66] Some of the lithographic prints were hand-colored: a portrait of Lincoln, for example, used during his first presidential campaign, had only red added to his lips and the background curtains.

Figure 2.14

In 1860, the Republicans' presidential ticket was not even on the ballot in ten states in the South. Breckenridge gathered only 5 percent of the popular vote in the North, and Bell did more poorly, gaining less than 3 percent of the vote there. Douglas became the first presidential candidate to campaign for his own election, but despite trying to appear more moderate on slavery than Lincoln did, he won only 12 percent of the popular vote in the South and 29 percent nationally.[67] Lincoln won the election overwhelmingly in the North and West, with a popular vote north of the 41st parallel greater than 60 percent (for an easy electoral victory), and garnering about 40 percent overall.[68] James McPherson characterized the four-party campaign in 1860 as "the most fateful in American history."[69] Despite Lincoln's attempts to reassure the South, his election led to its secession and the bitter Civil War that ensued.

Limited printings of hand-colored posters were created for the 1864 Union ticket of Lincoln

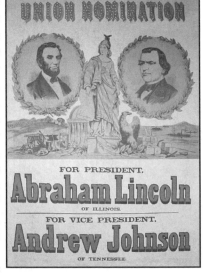

Figure 2.15

and Andrew Johnson, and positioned in shop windows.[70] Figure 2.15 shows one of these posters, with only the title and the names of the candidates colored in red to gain attention. Other versions of this poster were more fully colored, with Liberty, the eagle, cannon, and other elements in yellow, blue, green, red, and orange. A broadside distributed by the Democrats that year, however, descended from the level of propagandistic symbolism to that of distortion by including these statements: "Elect Lincoln and the Black Republican Ticket. You will bring on Negro Equality, more Debt, Harder Times, another Draft! Universal Anarchy, and Ultimate Ruin! Elect McClellan and the whole Democratic Ticket. You will defeat Negro equality, restore Prosperity, re-establish the Union! In an Honorable, Permanent and happy Peace." Thomas Nast created another misleading broadside during the 1864 campaign—this one designed to damage the Democrats. Published as a centerfold in *Harper's Weekly*,[71] it was titled "The Chicago Platform," with Democratic candidate George McClellan situated in the center of the broadside, surrounded by the party's platform resolutions, which were accompanied by derogatory illustrations. One resolution declared that the "rights of the states" should be "unimpaired," which had above it a depiction of a slave being whipped. Another anti-McClellan broadside conveyed the propaganda message more visually, showing the Democratic candidate shaking hands with the Confederate president, Jefferson Davis, who was standing before a slave auction, and Lincoln shaking hands with a workman in front of a racially integrated school scene (Fig. 2.16).

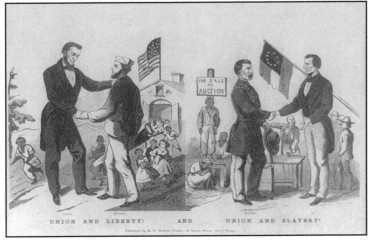

UNION AND LIBERTY!   AND   UNION AND SLAVERY!

Figure 2.16

As was the case in 1860, the North was divided. Judging by the dominant themes in campaign broadsides, this time the conflict was about the emancipation of the slaves, the prosecution of the war, and the way to deal with the Confederate states. Lincoln enjoyed a resounding victory in the Electoral College, but won by a more modest margin of 10 percentage points in the popular vote.[72] McClellan's cause was somewhat damaged by his party's platform and his battlefield record (as the Union's chief general), but his defeat has been attributed mainly to the Union capture of Atlanta before the election. The importance of the election of 1864 was obvious to Lincoln—he believed that the Democratic Party platform would lead to a McClellan administration negotiating an armistice, followed by recognition of the Confederate States of America as an independent country. Instead, Lincoln won reelection on a platform demanding that an amendment to the Constitution to abolish slavery be passed, and that the war would be pursued until the South was defeated and the Union preserved.[73]

Posters and Propaganda Strategy in Post-Civil War Elections (1868–1892)

The design and utilization of posters, broadsides, and cloth banners continued in similar fashion in the quarter century following Lincoln's victory in 1864. Parades and rallies (one of which was depicted in Figure 1.8, Chapter One) flourished as well, and voter turnout remained high, at between 65 and 73 percent for this period.[74] The first two campaigns in the postwar period pitted Republican Ulysses Grant against candidates Horatio Seymour and Horace Greeley, both of whom lost most of the electoral votes. Poster designs for Grant rendered him in uniform—to emphasize his military leadership during the Civil War—and surrounded by cannons, swords, rifles, flags, eagles, farming implements, and the allegorical figures of Justice and Wisdom. When color was added, the lettering was applied in red, white, and blue. His opponents' designs were similar—a banner for the Seymour in ticket, in 1868, adding a symbol for labor (an arm and hammer) to one for the farmers (two hands on a plow) (Fig. 2.17). Not to be outdone in the election four years later, the Grant-Wilson ticket appealed directly to workers with a banner that showed the two candidates in their past working class occupations (Fig. 2.18).

Figure 2.17

Figure 2.18

The campaigns' nastiness persisted. In 1868, Grant's "alcoholism" was implied in a poster that featured Seymour and the phrase "We Shall See More Rads 'bottled up' in November" (Fig. 2.19).[75] In contrast, an anti-Seymour broadside by Nast that year showed "The Rioter Seymour," along with three Confederate military leaders, who were

Figure 2.19 (excerpt)

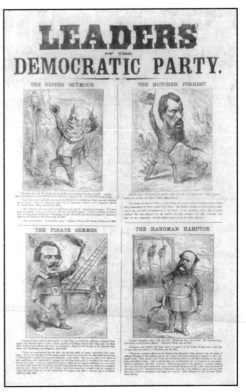

Figure 2.20

nicknamed "The Butcher," "The Pirate," and "The Hangman" (Fig. 2.20). This was unfair, since Seymour, as governor of New York, supported the preservation of the Union during the Civil War, had sent militia to fight in its army, and had declared the New York City riots of 1863 to be an "insurrection" (although he has been blamed for helping incite the riots by opposing conscription).[76] Four years later, this tactic was used again by the Republicans in a broadside—this time against Greeley: it showed him positioned next to secessionists Jefferson Davis and John Calhoun, while President Grant was placed next to Lincoln and Washington.

The 1876 campaign was heated, as usual. The Democrats emphasized the issue of corruption in the Grant administration and advocated a more lenient attitude than did the Republicans toward the former confederacy. Both parties distributed posters that were almost indistinguishable, however, and illustrated with portraits of the candidates, allegorical figures such as Fortitude and Wisdom, flags and bunting, eagles, cornucopias, and sheaves of wheat. The Democratic Party came close to gaining the presidency in 1880 by nominating a military figure, General Winfield Hancock, a hero at the Battle of Gettysburg. But he lost by a slim margin to another Civil War hero, General James Garfield. The candidates differed little on the issues, except on tariffs. Image manipulation, therefore, became more important, particularly for the Republicans, who emphasized their candidate's birth in a log cabin, childhood poverty, and hard work as a boatman in his youth (all of which were true). A broadside for the Republican ticket included portraits of George Washington and Abraham Lincoln above a picture of black and white citizens rallying around the flag, and the slogan "Devotion to the Union" (to stress that this was the party that had fought to preserve the United States of America). A racist

PLAIN WORDS TO
WORKINGMEN!
Garfield their Enemy ; Hancock their Friend.

The Republican managers, desperate at their failure to prove the hero of Gettysburg a rebel, and utterly discomfited by his plain and manly letter in regard to rebel and Southern claims—have, by a common agreement and in pursuance of an understanding lately concluded in New York arranged to charge all along the Hancock lines with the most villainous lies about the tariff and Gen. Hancock's position thereon.

Their opening gun, has now been fired in all the manufacturing towns of this State, to the effect that if Hancock is elected the present tariff will be

THESE VOTES ARE WHAT EARNED HIM THE COMPLIMENT OF AN ELECTION TO THE COBDEN CLUB.

On the 10th of June, 1866, Garfield in a debate in the House declared:

NOTHING CAN BE SAID AGAINST FREE TRADE.

Four years later, on the 10th of April, 1870, he said in the House:

"MODERN SCHOLARSHIP IS ON THE SIDE OF FREE TRADE.

In answer to Judge Kelley the noted protectionist, Garfield said in Congress:

SO FAR AS WE ARE CONCERNED, THEREFORE, ALL TALK ABOUT "FREE TRADE" IS FOLLY.

But the tariff question will probably be treated with justice to all our interests and the people by some such bill as Eaton's. I believe that a commission of intelligent experts representing both the government and American industries will suggest tariff measures that will relieve us of the crudities and inconsistencies existing in our present laws, and confirm to us a system which will be judicious, just, harmonious and incidentally protective as well as stable in its effect.

I am very truly yours,
WINFIELD S. HANCOCK.
To Hon. Theodore F. Randolph.

Figure 2.21 (excerpt)

broadside—headlined "Plain Words to Workingmen! Garfield their Enemy; Hancock their Friend"—warned New Hampshire workers "if you want to keep the horde [sic] of negroes out ... who have been invited into the State to compete with you at your mills and workshops *vote for Hancock*" (Figure 2.21). Figure 2.22 shows a strange political print,

"The Bird To Bet On!" that was published by Currier & Ives during the campaign. It displayed candidate Hancock's head on top of the body of a rooster, which sat on a hand (a play on his name). The rooster was a symbol of both the Democratic Party and toughness. The Democrats also distributed portraits of their national candidates with the requisite serious expressions, as well as a lithographic banner with the two solemn candidates, six flags, an eagle, and five mottos, including "Union is Strength."

Figure 2.22

In 1884, the Democrats finally won the presidency with the election of Grover Cleveland, who had been serving as governor of the state of New York. Despite exposure, during the campaign, of his premarital affair that had resulted in the birth of a child, and paying a substitute to serve in his place when conscripted for military service in the Civil War, Cleveland defeated Senator James Blaine of Maine by a narrow margin. Again, issues took a backseat to character, in general: Blaine was labeled corrupt, anti-Catholic, and beholden to corporate interests; Cleveland was charged with favoring the moneyed classes, in addition to fathering the child out of wedlock (to which he admitted having done, thereby mollifying many voters).[77] One particularly striking broadside caricatured "Blaine's funeral" on Election Day, with the slogan "Soap! Soap! Blaine's only Hope!" printed above a black border, probably an allusion to his alleged corrupt practices (Fig. 2.23).

Both sides issued an abundance of broadsides, designed to deliver often slanted, issue-oriented messages to targeted audiences. The Democrats, for instance, distributed a broadside addressed "To Workingmen," which told them the Republicans were responsible for decreased wages and increased inflation owing to high tariffs and taxes, and that Blaine was a "monopolist, supported by Jay Gould and Cyrus Field." The Republicans also distributed broadsides aimed at workers, some of them printed in English on one side and German on the other. One declared that if the Democrats eliminated "the protective tariff," either

Figure 2.23

unemployment would rise dramatically or pay would decrease to the "starvation wages" paid in Europe. Cloth banners continued to be relatively simple in design: one for Blaine's ticket imparted only the last names of the candidates on a cloth with three stripes (one red, one white, and one blue), and a row of stars.

By the election of 1888, the importance of posters was palpable; Democrats posted guards along the Brooklyn, New York, waterfront to prevent gang members, allegedly hired by a Republican, from tearing down the placards of President Cleveland that completely covered the wooden walls.[78] In general, however, the election campaign that year seemed to have been relatively fair and more dignified than in the past. In Cleveland's lost bid for reelection—by a slim margin—to Benjamin Harrison (who was a senator from Indiana, another Civil War general, and grandson of William Henry Harrison), the tariff was the principal issue. One anti-Cleveland broadside put it this way: "I do not believe that Free-Trade Democrats and European manufacturers combined can raise money enough to buy the votes of the honest, hard-working man that loves his family, his home and his country, and those are the ones we expect to vote for Protection in this contest."[79] Full-color portraits of Cleveland and his young wife, Frances (whom he had married in the White House), were displayed in one poster; she was deemed a "great asset to the campaign."[80] In another Democratic poster, Uncle Sam was featured with a rooster on each arm and shields emblazoned with the candidates' portraits. In addition, there was a small picture of Jefferson, with a list of positions the ticket championed, including tariff revision, labor protection, a cessation of "war taxes," and "taxes sufficient for government expenses only" (Fig. 2.24). The

Figure 2.24

Republicans also made sure to include venerated past presidents, namely Washington, Lincoln, and Grant, in their campaign posters.

In 1892, a minor political entity, The People's (or Populist) Party, did very well. Harrison and Cleveland were again matched as the main contestants. The Populists, led by James Weaver, earned 8.5 percent of the popular vote (and 5 percent of the electoral vote), probably because of the increased economic difficulties of many farmers.[81] The party's fiery platform charged that governmental policies had "bred" "two great classes—tramps and millionaires," with "the fruits of the toil of millions … badly stolen to build up colossal fortunes for a few. … "[82] Cleveland, however, won the rematch with Harrison, who undoubtedly lost many worker votes because of labor strife and high tariffs. The political parties, including the People's Party, issued conventional banner-type posters.

Broadsides and Posters in the Contest Between Advocates of "Free Silver" and "The Gold Standard" (1896)

The last U.S. election of the nineteenth century was one of the most exciting, although its consequences were not as monumental and calamitous as the contentious election that Lincoln had won more than three decades earlier. In 1896, many of the concerns voiced by the Populists were incorporated into the Democrats' platform. The most important issue conveyed was the demand for the "free and unlimited coinage of both silver and gold at the … ratio of 16 to 1."[83] The Democratic candidate for president, William Jennings Bryan,

Figure 2.25

called this "the paramount issue" because, as he stated vividly, "if protection has slain its thousands, the gold standard has slain its tens of thousands."[84] During the campaign, zealous meetings were convened to discuss the silver issue. Broadsides announced these and called for "those who believe that in silver lies the remedy for the present financial stagnation" to support the cause. As can be seen in Figure 2.25, the posters for the Democratic ticket emphasized this as well, with the word *silver* at top center and silver coins pictured directly below.

The previous Democratic candidate, President Grover Cleveland, had supported the gold standard, and had resisted the call of those, particularly in the South and West, who wanted to increase the money in circulation—even after the country fell into a depression—to lower interest rates that hurt farmers and others in debt.[85] In 1896, with farm foreclosures, and labor unemployment and discord growing alarmingly, the silver advocates took over the Democratic Party, gaining its nomination for Bryan, a dynamic congressman from Nebraska.[86] His "Cross of Gold" speech at the Democratic National Convention in July of that year compared the cause of free silver to that of the Crusades and the American Revolution, with the political fight "in the defense of our homes, our families, and posterity."[87]

The Republican nominee for president was William McKinley, the governor of Ohio, who was largely in favor of retaining the gold standard. In addition, he was the author of the McKinley Tariff Act of 1890, which was largely protectionist. His campaign manager, Mark Hanna, a wealthy businessperson who applied the principles of business of that period to political campaigns, raised anywhere from seven to thirty-two times as much money for McKinley's campaign as did the Bryan camp, which collected only about five hundred thousand dollars.[88] Hanna, as Michael McGerr noted, was the key player in changing political marketing strategy: the candidate was to be "packaged," and the message was to be simple, using slogans and symbols (while emphasizing the personality of the candidate).[89] The 1896 election occurred near the beginning of a period when posters were widely used, along with newspaper and magazine ads, to advertise a variety of products in coordinated campaigns, using similar mass persuasion techniques.[90] Some Republicans did not agree with Hanna's political marketing techniques; even McKinley's running mate, Theodore Roosevelt, declared about Hanna: "He has advertised McKinley as if he were a patent medicine!"[91] Hanna's biographer, Thomas Beer, concluded:

> This was Mr. Hanna's crime. He had openly made use of the full powers of propaganda. He had dealt with politics as if the birth of a company was being arranged. He had thrown a hundred thousand tons of advertising into the nation. ... He had made a President, and he had done it visibly. It is hard to forgive such realism. ...[92]

Overall, the Republican campaign theme was that a McKinley administration could pull the country out of the depression and return it to prosperity. This theme is illustrated in the poster shown in Figure 2.26, with the Republican presidential candidate holding a flag while literally standing on a platform of "sound money" (i.e., paper currency backed by gold). Hanna also used polling to discern his candidate's initial positions on this dominant issue, as well as voter movement; the results showed him that his campaign efforts were successful.[93] Hanna's tactics with which he associated his candidate and the Republican Party with the icon of the American flag, helped build support twenty years later to declare Flag Day an official national holiday.[94]

Figure 2.26

Figure 2.27 (excerpt)

McKinley stayed on the front porch of his home and spoke to people in groups selected by Hanna, while Bryan broke with the tradition of not campaigning actively, and became the second major candidate (after Douglas in 1860) to tour the nation extensively.[95] As Kathleen Jamieson noted, Bryan "pioneered the modern campaign," beginning the contest with an acceptance speech at the convention, and then traveling the country to deliver more speeches.[96] Bryan estimated that he gave about six hundred speeches to approximately five million people.[97] The speeches appeared to whip listeners into a fever pitch, and orations by the candidate, who had also been nominated by the People's Party, may have been considered, for the first time, more necessary in a campaign than parades, songs, cloth banners, and other "surrogate message carriers."[98] Posters, however, were still an omnipresent element, and were placed next to Bryan, along with the flag, when he spoke, even during his third run for president in 1908 (Fig. 2.27).

A "poster craze" ensued in the 1890s, when the popularity of advertising posters increased dramatically; they became more artistic, and, owing to technological advances, more plentiful. American collectors prized posters that promoted events and products as works of art, particularly those designed by artists such as William Bradley and Maxfield Parrish.[99] The artistic and technological developments also affected political posters. Printers ran off, in large numbers, a wide variety of high-quality candidate portraits and full-color posters (see Fig. 1.9, Chapter One). One of these—featuring portraits of McKinley and his running mate, Hobart, "as the advance agents of prosperity, with the National flag and illustrations of commerce"—was a gigantic forty by sixty inches.[100] Beautiful color lithographic posters, which presented the candidate and his family, as well as his "Cross of Gold" speech, "superimposed" with the motto "16 to 1," were created for the Bryan campaign also. Its somewhat idealized rendering of Bryan with his wife and children possibly softened the "radical" image the Republicans projected for him. (The campaign of Nelson Mandela, who ran for president in South Africa about one hundred years later, employed a similar approach in its poster of the candidate surrounded by children of different races.)

Both parties distributed large numbers of posters, along with other election items, but the Republican material was a deluge, sometimes reaching five million homes weekly.[101] Much of Hanna's printed material was tailored to appeal to targeted groups and printed in different languages to reach immigrants. A good example of this targeting strategy is shown in a poster titled "The Real Issue": it argued that McKinley's preference for the gold standard would benefit laborers, as opposed to the policies of his Democratic opponent, which would allegedly help only silver producers (Fig. 2.28). In another Republican poster, Uncle Sam grudgingly paid workers with silver dollars that were worth a mere fifty-three cents. Unlike many previous elections when image manipulation was the paramount tactic, the 1896 campaign was dominated by the differences over the monetary standard. This is not to say, though, that the images of the candidates were unimportant—in their printed matter, the Republicans characterized Bryan as a

Figure 2.28

dangerous "radical" while the Democrats portrayed him in posters as a family man. The population had become much larger, and even Bryan (who, it was thought, logged about eighteen thousand miles via train during the campaign) could reach only one-third of the eligible voters.[102] His Democratic-Populist campaign, and that of the Republicans, overall, did generate much excitement, and voter turnout increased from 69 percent in 1892 to 72 percent.[103] In the end, McKinley won the popular vote by a 4 percent margin and gained about 60 percent of the electoral votes.[104]

Election Campaigns Between the Depressions of 1896 and 1929

Political campaigning did not change fundamentally until the medium of radio altered strategies in the mid-1920s, although campaign speeches had surpassed parades and rallies in importance around the turn of the century. Posters, however, continued to be a significant vehicle for political operatives. In 1912, for example, the New Jersey Roosevelt Republican League issued a report on its primary campaign to defeat President William Howard Taft for the party's nomination, stating, "Banners are swung across the streets in every city and town of importance, extolling the candidates. Billboards are plastered with huge posters eulogizing President Taft. Campaign pictures of 'Teddy' [Roosevelt] and Taft look out from windows everywhere."[105] Moreover, the lithographic posters were quite colorful, with backgrounds in bright hues for greater impact. Several companies printed campaign banners (for which only a few standard designs were available) on cloth, and some of the candidates' portraits were painted by hand.[106] At the end of the nineteenth century, one could order a thirty-by-forty-foot banner with portraits at a cost of between one hundred twelve and one hundred forty dollars; without portraits, they could be purchased for eighty dollars.[107] At this time, election campaign billboards were commonplace. During the 1908 campaign, there were twenty-three thousand billboards featuring six different advertisements for William Howard Taft; his party also placed ads in movie theaters, streetcars, magazines, and newspapers.[108] In general, pictorial posters were a component of election campaign packages that often included buttons, songs, and news articles.

The Democrats nominated Bryan twice more, in 1900 and 1908. He lost both elections to Republican candidates—McKinley, again, and Taft, in Bryan's third attempt to win the presidency. Every other presidential candidate his party nominated lost in the first three decades of the century, also, except for Woodrow Wilson (in 1912 and 1916), whose rise to power was made possible by a split in the Republican Party. McKinley was reelected in 1900 by a 6-point margin over Bryan in the popular vote—a better performance for the Republican, due partly to the improved economic conditions that occurred during his term in office and to the victory of the United States in the Spanish-American War.[109] "The Real Issue" posters from 1896 (see Fig. 2.28) were reissued, with red overprints that asked "Was McKinley Right?" and declared "McKinley Was Right in 1896." A poster for the 1900 Republican ticket, with portraits of both President McKinley and Vice President Theodore Roosevelt, combined with American flags, emphasized the themes of prosperity, a dollar backed only by gold, a protective tariff policy, and pension reform to benefit Civil War widows. Portraits of the two men were displayed in another

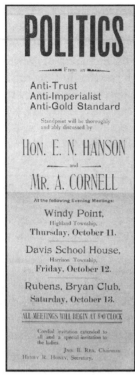

Figure 2.29

poster also, with scenes contrasting life under the Republican administration to what had occurred under the Democrats through 1896 (busy factories and farms versus shut-down plants and unplowed fields; "A run to the bank" versus "A run on the bank"; Spanish versus American rule in Cuba). Roosevelt was yet another military hero, shown in his "Rough Rider" uniform in one lithographed banner, as well as on campaign buttons.

Bryan's positions in 1896 against "the gold standard," "imperialism," and trusts could not be as popular in 1900, given the state of the economy and the world. Figure 2.29 shows a broadside that advertised a meeting of a Bryan club in rural Idaho to discuss these themes. Eight years later, it was the same story, but worse: Bryan's chances were damaged when he advocated nationalization of the railroads, which reinforced his image as a "radical" and "socialist." Bryan, who had decided not to seek his party's nomination in 1904, lost to Taft by almost a 9 percent margin in the 1908 popular vote.[110] Taft, who had been secretary of war in the cabinet of retiring president Roosevelt, was his handpicked successor.

Bryan continued to draw big crowds with his vigorous oratory and reformist zeal; Taft gave stump speeches that indicated he was progressive on many issues; and an authentic socialist, Eugene Debs of the Socialist Party, crisscrossed the country on the "Red Special" train that took him to 350 cities.[111]

At least Bryan did much better than had the previous Democratic nominee, Alton Parker, the chief justice of the New York Court of Appeals. Parker had lost to Roosevelt (who had succeeded McKinley after he was assassinated) by a 19-point margin four years earlier.[112] Neither President Roosevelt nor Judge Parker campaigned actively. The latter had no real chance to unseat a very popular and successful incumbent, who conveyed a much more dynamic image, and with whom he agreed on many issues (except for voting rights for black citizens, which Parker opposed).[113] In addition, the Roosevelt campaign cleverly made targeted appeals to groups such as organized labor. The campaign issued a poster featuring portraits of President Roosevelt and John Mitchell, the president of the United Mine Workers of America, along with two piles of coal and the caption "The World's Champions of Arbitration and Fair Play."

The election posters that were distributed during the first half of this period were similar in design and content to what had come before. In general, the format of the lithographic prints produced until 1912 included sober portraits of the candidates, eagles, flags or shields, and some cornucopias. Although there were fewer allegorical figures, an eagle was still used in a 1908 poster that promoted the Republican ticket. Actual photographic images were seen for the first time in campaign posters and postcards in the initial decade of the twentieth century, and some of the embellishments of the past were featured less frequently (only flags, party symbols, and stars were to be found). Mottos such as "Liberty,

Protection, Prosperity" and "E Pluribus Unum" continued to be incorporated in many instances, as were platform pronouncements. Of course, large albumen photographic prints, mounted on cardboard, had been used in U.S. election campaigns decades earlier.

Even the Socialist Party poster of 1904 followed the typical design: candidate portraits in ovals; a slogan; and workers and farmers (although there were more of them, and two were monumental in size). In Europe, however, the Socialist parties regularly included raised rifles in their posters. Only the rare American election poster departed very much from the above formula. A poster for the 1900 Bryan campaign, for instance, did include a portrait of the candidate, with a flag on either side of him; it also had other patriotic symbols and scenes, as well as the party's rooster symbol. Additional touches were the allegorical "Democracy" figure, which had chopped off a tentacle of an octopus that symbolized trusts, and three men holding the flags of Cuba, Puerto Rico, and the Philippines below the Statue of Liberty (Fig. 2.30). Liberal Party posters in Great Britain, produced a few years later, similarly attacked the ruling Conservatives for their imperialistic policies; and, like Bryan's, the Liberals' proposals were debunked as "socialistic" (see Chapter Five).

Figure 2.30

Campaign managers in the United States issued few innovative poster designs. Two exceptions to the usual campaign posters were distributed by the well-heeled and innovative McKinley campaign in 1896 (see Fig. 2.26 and Fig. 2.28), which focused on the issue of "sound money" and linked it to "prosperity." Several other posters followed that were quite different from the typical poster of the early twentieth century in that they used dominant visuals to convey the message. One titled "Apostle of Prosperity" was printed for Roosevelt's campaign in 1904 (Fig. 2.31). It depicted the candidate as a farmer sowing seeds in the field and included these lines from *Faust* by Goethe: "Take Spade and hoe thyself; dig on—Great shalt thou be through peasant toil." Another exception was a 1908 poster that was almost entirely dominated by an illustration of Bryan shaking the hand of Uncle Sam, featuring "fat cat" special interest and trust characters and citizens (one with a sign

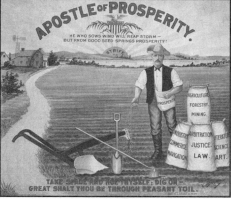

Figure 2.31

demanding "Leave Us Alone") in the background, and the caption "Uncle Sam—'Mr. Bryan, Your Enemies Are Mine Also.'" The Bryan campaign also issued a poster that year, titled "The Enthroned Hog," in which Bryan gestured toward a bloated "Trust Rex" sitting on a throne, with the question "Shall the people rule?" The same slogan headlined huge portrait posters of Bryan—with the candidate looking directly at the voters.

The election of 1912 was a watershed of sorts for U.S. campaign posters. Gone were the cornucopias and most of the patriotic symbols that had been used since the 1840s. Instead, Theodore Roosevelt's Progressive Party seized upon the symbol of the Bull Moose—which prompted the party's nickname—to symbolize the strength of the candidate and his third-party movement. The movement was formed after Roosevelt was denied the Republican nomination, and its symbol was included on posters, cloth banners, buttons, pennants, handkerchiefs, postcards, and other campaign promotions. Personality qualities were again more important than issues; all three candidates were "progressive." Slogans were also an essential ingredient: Roosevelt stumped the country calling for a "New Nationalism"; Wilson delivered campaign speeches for a "New Freedom"; and Taft generally stayed in the White House, with his banners proclaiming "Better be safe than sorry."[114] As the campaign entered its final days, Wilson concentrated his attacks on Taft and the Republican Party, which he referred to as the "Know-Nothing, Do-Nothing Party," and praised Roosevelt as a "gallant gentleman."[115] Wilson even attacked the Republican billboards, which credited the Taft administration for prosperity for farmers:

> I am sorry that the Republican Party has incorporated Providence, ... and I am sorry that those who wrote those posters do not know more about the history of their own country and the history of the world ... They say, 'You have been prosperous, therefore'—for this is their conclusion—'elect Taft.' In order to do that, what has Mr. Taft done? I must frankly say to you that I do not discover that we have had any pilot during the last four years ... Do you think that it will lend itself to your prosperity to have another four years of drifting?[116]

A series of photographic portraits of all the major candidates were issued with neither their names nor the names of their parties. Other posters did contain some of this information, but one for the Progressive ticket of Roosevelt and Senator Hiram Johnson of California included only the last names of the two candidates, their full-length photographic portraits, and the final lines of Rudyard Kipling's poem "The Ballad of the East and West" (Fig. 2.32). Roosevelt's image had come a long way since the last time he ran: in 1904, stuffed "teddy bears" were distributed, which related Roosevelt to both a huggable toy and "family values"; in 1912, he was associated more with the bull moose, with verses from Kipling fortifying the impression of strength.

The Taft campaign used the party's symbol of the elephant—which had been around for several decades, along with the Democratic donkey—on many campaign items, including a poster that displayed portraits of Taft and his running mate, Vice President James Sherman, on the animal's blanket. Undoubtedly, with Roosevelt's breakaway movement so powerful, it was important for the Taft strategists to emphasize party symbolism and loyalty. The Taft campaign conceded that Roosevelt's popularity was great. In fact, they designed a poster that contained a quote by the former president, praising Taft: "No man of better training, no man of more dauntless courage, of sounder common sense, and of higher and finer character, has ever come to the presidency than William Howard Taft." This poster also included captioned portraits of Washington ("Declined a third term"), Grant ("Denied a third term"), Roosevelt ("Demands a third term"), and Taft ("Deserves a third term"), as well as the message: "What Washington refused and Grant could not get." Taft, despite such efforts, could not compete with his vigorous and outgoing former mentor. Although Roosevelt's popular and electoral vote totals surpassed those of Taft, Wilson's margin over the former president in the popular vote was a substantial 14.5 percent.[117]

The next presidential election, in 1916, was not a "cake walk" for Wilson. The Republican Party was united again, with Roosevelt back in the party's camp,

Figure 2.32

and it nominated New York's moderate former governor and sitting U.S. supreme court justice, Charles Evans Hughes, who appealed to both the progressive and conservative elements in the party. Unfortunately, Hughes' public persona was that of "a bearded iceberg," as Roosevelt called him, appearing distant and stern (see Fig. 1.16, Chapter One).[118] Another problem Hughes faced was that his campaign was not well organized, compared to that of the opposition. The Publicity Bureau of the Democratic Party was particularly effective in printing and distributing material to a variety of targeted groups, which included labor and the foreign-born. Pro-Wilson posters in Italian were displayed; they included both the American and Italian flags, as well as a photographic portrait of the president. The Republicans also tried to appeal to laborers with a series of broadsides: the Michigan Central Committee of the party issued several, which used quotations from Wilson's past writings and speeches to cast doubt on his pro-labor positions. Figure 2.33 shows one of these broadsides, which contained part of a 1905 speech, in which Wilson criticized unions for rewarding "the shiftless and incompetent at the expense of the able and industrious." All indications, however, were that many more workers voted for Wilson than for Hughes.[119] In addition, Wilson's reelection campaign also greatly utilized direct mail for the first time in a national election; as a result, the Democratic Party received about three hundred thousand contributions from one letter it released.[120]

George Creel (whom Wilson would appoint a year later to head the wartime U.S. Committee on Public Information) worked in the Democratic advertising campaign that helped keep Wilson in power in 1916. Looking back at what Hanna's campaign for McKinley had accomplished twenty years earlier, Creel might have been influenced

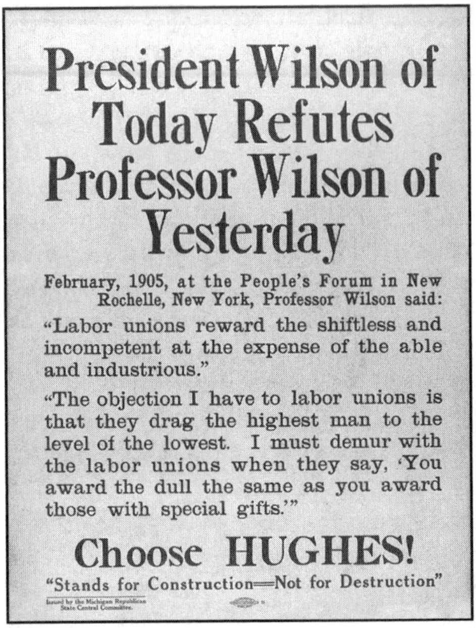

President Wilson of Today Refutes Professor Wilson of Yesterday

February, 1905, at the People's Forum in New Rochelle, New York, Professor Wilson said:

"Labor unions reward the shiftless and incompetent at the expense of the able and industrious."

"The objection I have to labor unions is that they drag the highest man to the level of the lowest. I must demur with the labor unions when they say, 'You award the dull the same as you award those with special gifts.'"

Choose HUGHES!

"Stands for Construction—Not for Destruction"

Issued for the Michigan Republican State Central Committee.

Figure 2.33

to help choose slogans for Wilson that were as simple and direct as they had been for the Republican candidate: "America First!" and "He Kept Us Out of War." A national poster for President Wilson's reelection bid in 1916 was similar in style to many of the American posters, whose designs were governed by advertising principles, that would soon be produced to promote World War I. Much more captivating than past election campaign posters, it was dominated by a large graphic image of the candidate, with the flag draped behind him—all in bold color. The poster conveyed two brief verbal messages: the title "America First"—a reference to the Wilson administration having kept the country out of the war in Europe; and the slogan "Wilson, That's All!" The slogan had been employed previously in advertisements for a brand of whiskey.[121]

Although this poster design was simpler than previous ones, other poster designs in the Democrats' national campaign were even less complex, composed of only a solemn portrait of the candidate and the words "For President" at the top of the paper and "Woodrow Wilson" at the bottom. The slogan "He Kept Us Out of War" was seen everywhere—on billboards, electric signs, streetcars, and magazine and newspaper ads that promoted the Wilson candidacy[122]—and surely had great appeal to the majority of American voters who wanted to stay out of European conflicts. Yet, another slogan used in the Wilson campaign was "Peace With Honor," which was included on a poster that featured a lithographic portrait of Wilson, along with the ubiquitous "He Kept Us Out of War." Most of all, Hughes blamed the concerted "He Kept Us Out of War"/"America First!" propaganda effort that so heavily exploited vivid pictorial posters and billboards for his defeat:

> The Democratic appeal was driven home during the latter part of the campaign by spreading throughout the country enormous picture-posters, giving a lurid display of the carnage of war, while on the side-lines stood a mother and her children looking on, —with the legend underneath—"He has protected me and mine. ... " I still should have been elected had it not been for the effectiveness ... of the Democratic slogan—"He kept us out of war. ..."[123]

When the final votes were tallied, it was apparent that many bull-moose progressives had voted for Wilson, instead of returning to the Republican Party tent to vote for Hughes. Wilson increased his percentage of the popular vote from 42 percent to 49 percent in four years and had a 3-point margin over Hughes, but still only squeaked through by a small margin in the Electoral College.[124] Amid charges that the Republican State Central Committee of California had not used money given to it by the national committee to spend on posters for Hughes, the Republican candidate lost the state—and the electoral votes that would have given him a victory—by about four thousand votes (out of almost one million cast).[125] Eighty-four years had elapsed since a Democratic president had been elected to serve a second consecutive term in office, the last one being Jackson.[126] There would not be another national Democratic victory until the 1932 election, after the Great Depression had started. A string of three Democratic Party defeats occurred following the public's disillusionment with Wilson's foreign policy, after World War I was won, and when the United States voted not to join the League of Nations. A broadside titled "Keep Faith With Our Dead" was disseminated in support of the 1920 Democratic Party ticket and the League, but the Republicans trounced Wilson's party at the polls.

The Republican national campaigns in the 1920s were awash in money, with the Democratic Party having far less to spend (about one-fourth of the Republican total in 1924, for instance); it was also less organized overall at the national level.[127] In the early part of the decade, much of this money was spent on campaign paraphernalia, including lithographic portraits, billboard posters, electric signs, pamphlets, and buttons, as well as newspaper advertisements.[128] It was reported that the Republicans ordered fifteen million buttons promoting their candidate for president, Senator Harding of Ohio, and five million posters that included portraits of Harding and the vice-presidential candidate, Massachusetts governor Calvin Coolidge.[129] It was estimated that in 1924 the political parties (including the Progressive Party, headed by Senator Robert La Follette of Wisconsin) allocated about 20 percent of their national campaign funds to books, buttons, and lithographic portraits; 20 percent to speakers and radio; 10 percent to advertising; 10 percent to press bureaus and services; and the rest to headquarters, trains, and miscellaneous expenses.[130]

So important in many past elections—and still crucial—was the image component concerning character, which a candidate would project or have conveyed for him. It was often a more significant factor than his program plans. Images of the candidates—using words and pictures—were devised to win votes: Hoover was "efficient"; Coolidge (who ran for president, in his own right, in 1924) was "Honest Cal"; and Harding looked "presidential." Advertising executives had much to do with the creation of these images. The most important participant was advertising executive Albert Lasker, who played a key role in the Republican national campaign that elected Harding in a landslide in 1920. He coordinated public relations and advertising, and posters and billboards were a fundamental part of the campaign. Lasker's style of advertising, which often advocated the purchase of one product over another, worked very well in politics, with newspaper and billboard ads promoting politicians rather than products. It was a small leap for him to come up with a slogan for Harding, "Let's be done with wiggle and wobble" (a reference to a Democratic policy that seemed first to have been isolationist, then interventionist), after concocting such slogans as "Keep that Schoolgirl Complexion" and "A Cow in Every Pantry" for products.[131] Lasker's slogan was seen on billboards across the country at a cost of four hundred thousand dollars (while the Democrats did little with this medium)—and that was only 7.5 percent of the Republican National Committee's total expenditures.[132] Even comic strip characters, called "Uncle Wobble" and "Uncle Wiggle," were part of

Lasker's coordinated media campaign.[133] The "wiggle and wobble" slogan strategy contrasted Lasker's candidate with the outgoing president: Harding was a solid, steady leader with small-town values, who would return the country to "normalcy"; Wilson, on the other hand, had promised to keep the country out of the Great War, and then had led it into the conflict. Later in the century, the two presidents named George Bush used a similar strategy for their respective campaigns, when they characterized their Democratic opponents as "flip-floppers."[134] The idea was to use slogans to label one's opponent as possessing, as pollster John Zogby stated, "the antithesis of leadership."[135]

Lasker's advertising campaign, however, emphasized the personable and down-to-earth qualities of his candidate, in a mainly positive and dynamic campaign. The campaign package consisted of billboards, millions of posters, pamphlets, magazine advertisements, motion picture newsreels, phonograph records, still photographs of Harding's front-porch speeches, candidate portraits, and celebrity testimonials.[136] More than two hundred thousand dollars was expended on lithographic portraits of the Republican presidential candidate alone.[137] In addition, a speaker's bureau coordinated orators, drawn from a list of more than fifteen thousand names, in support of Harding and his party.[138]

The visual images that were sometimes fashioned for the posters and billboards were imposing: a good example is Howard Chandler Christy's idealized rendition of Harding with the candidate dramatically raising one hand and waving an American flag with the other (see Fig. 2.34). There were only two words accompanying the image: "America First!" This was the same slogan that was used in the Wilson poster in the previous election campaign, and, amazingly, the slogan that was included in some Democratic posters in 1920. An advertisement for Palmolive soap (Fig. 2.35), commissioned by Lasker, had also

Figure 2.34   *Figure 2.35*

featured artwork by another prominent illustrator, Coles Phillips. In the ad, Cleopatra dominated the design as much as Harding did, along with another slogan: "The Oldest of Toilet Requisites"; the name of the product, displayed in large, distinctive type, conveyed that "the beautiful of Ancient Egypt … chose Palm and Olive Oils [as] their most important toilet requirements" (just as Harding chose "America First!"). Campaign posters started to become more stylized and simplified, as had posters that advertised products such as automobiles and motion pictures, and services such as railroads and electric utilities. Most of the election posters were quite simple indeed, showing a photogravure, photographic, or drawn portrait of the candidate, and a few well-chosen words: a 1928 poster for Smith, for example, included his photograph and the caption "Honest • Able • Fearless" (Fig. 2.36).

Figure 2.36

Some broadsides, particularly in 1928, were designed to appeal to the prejudices that existed: Smith was "loyal to the Vatican," the printed material alleged. Figure 2.37 shows this in a cartoon in which Smith is seen kneeling beneath a cardinal. The anti-Catholic broadsides that were distributed by groups opposed to Smith were vicious. One presented "Alcohol Smith's Platform." In it, Smith ("My platform is wet and I am too") is associated with Jews, "ignorant wops," and the Pope (who would "rule" him). Another broadside stressed that Hoover was a Quaker. Comparing him to Smith, who had learned his religious lessons "from the rabid priests, … " it concluded that "choosing between Hoover and Smith [is] like choosing between Jesus and Barabbas." Consequently, Democratic organizations issued posters that attempted to counter the anti-Catholic, anti-Smith slander. In Oklahoma, the state organization issued a poster of Uncle Sam clenching his fists; it was captioned "Sectarian Poison Spreaders Exposed," along with an accusation leveled against the Republican party that they were spreading religious bigotry.[139] Posters and broadsides functioned as they had in past elections to help further negative and positive stereotypes, and combat lies and innuendoes.

Figure 2.37

Millions of campaign portraits were usually run off in only one color (typically black or brown) to cut printing costs, and were intended to be displayed primarily in windows.[140] The cost for each of these lithographs, in the 1920s, was about four cents.[141] One of these portraits featured James Cox, the Democratic candidate for president in 1920, with the slogan "Peace-Progress-Prosperity" at the top; another one, printed for the 1928 Hoover campaign, included the slogan "This Home is for Hoover" (Fig. 2.38). These so-called window cards were not new. They had been used in U.S. election campaigns since, at least, Lincoln's second run in 1864 (see Fig. 2.15).[142]

Figure 2.38

The Republican candidates of the 1920s seemed not only to have the best images concocted for them, but also the best slogans. Not only was the Harding campaign's nostalgic "Back to Normalcy" devised in 1920 to best promote its candidate in the face of rapid urbanization and a postwar environment, but also the party followed that in 1924 with "Keep Cool with Coolidge," a plea to stay with an administration that had brought prosperity to most citizens, and then, in 1928, the Hoover campaign featured two: "A Car in Every Garage and a Chicken in Every Pot" and "Let's Keep What We've Got" (both were appeals to keep the "good times" going).[143] Cloth banners for the Hoover campaign reinforced the message, proclaiming that a vote for the Republican ticket was a vote for "Four More Years of Coolidge Policies." In 1928, political radio spot ads were employed for the first time.[144] The Republicans placed "boilerplate advertisements" in newspapers that hammered home one theme, "Let's keep what we've got. Prosperity didn't just happen. Hoover and happiness or Smith and soup houses? Which shall it be? Hard times always come when the Democrats try to run the nation. ..."[145] All media repeated this propaganda; the scare tactic was an obvious one to choose for the party in power during good economic times. The Republicans won by huge margins, ranging from 17 to 26 percent of the popular vote, in the decade's three national elections.[146] The Progressive Party in 1924, with La Follette's campaign poorly funded (having less than one-fourth of what even the Democrats had to spend), poorly organized, and underreported by the press, did remarkably well, gaining about 17 percent of the popular vote.[147] A poster for the La Follette ticket was traditional in design. At the top was the Liberty Bell, an eagle, and the words, "The People's Choice"; gracing the bottom was a quote by the presidential candidate, "Each generation must wage a war for freedom," and two descriptors: "Fearless" and "Incorruptible."

Women voted for the first time in 1920, but their turnout was low, as was the case for the population overall: the percentage of eligible voters had declined to 44 percent, from 56 percent in 1916.[148] This was, perhaps, because people were certain about the outcome of the election or because the excitement of past contests was missing (gargantuan personalities such as Bryan and Roosevelt were not in the race). The political parties did target women with special appeals. Lasker arranged to have Republican publications that targeted women, blacks, and other groups printed and distributed.[149] By 1928, the Republican Party's campaign organization had not only a women's division, but a homemaker's subgroup as well.[150] Posters (along with postcards and pamphlets) were still important in their appeal to female voters and "the rallying cry of this drive [was] 'A picture of Hoover in every kitchen.'"[151] The Democrats used house-to-house canvassing and town-to-town caravans to reach out to women, and they decorated automobiles with posters and banners for Smith.[152]

In the century that passed since Jackson's election as president in 1828, America's advertising personnel had brought their methods into the political arena. Slogans had generally replaced nicknames, although there were exceptions; for example, in 1928 Smith was referred to as "The Happy Warrior." Candidate image management was still largely more important than issues in most election campaigns. This can be seen in the posters that were printed. They became simpler, spotlighting the candidate in a usually appealing portrait with a brief slogan designed to be remembered. Accordingly, although symbols such as the flag were still incorporated into many posters, others, such as eagles, cornucopias, and allegorical figures, were not. Broadsides, often locally and anonymously produced, were still used more than posters to attack and even defame opponents. Later in the period, some of these were sent to potential voters in the form of direct mail.

CHAPTER THREE

U.S. Presidential Election Posters in the Age of Mass Media

With the advent of radio as the main method of communication, fiery stump speeches grew to be less common, when it became apparent that candidates who employed a lower key, more conversational speaking style were more effective during radio transmissions.[1] By the election of 1924, political parties were budgeting substantial funds for their candidates' radio broadcasts, as well as for buttons, pamphlets, printed speeches, banners, and posters.[2] Four years later, Democratic presidential candidate Al Smith was telling radio listeners that he would "talk intimately" to them "as though [he] were sitting with ... [them] in ... [their] own home. ... "[3] The lithographic poster was once a key element in U.S. political campaigns, since, as Crowley stated, it "was a mature and established form of graphic communication."[4] But in terms of the proportion of the funds expended, it became a secondary component; whereas radio, with its popularity having increased, was used more frequently. It should be emphasized that although more of the available campaign money was spent on radio, a greater number of election posters were actually printed in the 1920s (and also in the next two decades); this was due to the development of less expensive, thinner paper stock in smaller sizes, and low-cost, high-volume printing methods.[5]

This chapter focuses on posters, broadsides, and banners used in U.S. national election campaigns beginning in the 1930s, and the media trends that transpired, as well as the changing roles that posters played as political advertising dollars moved into new media. By 1928, funds that candidates were spending on radio broadcasts had increased.[6] It was the first election year in which more than half of the Republican Party's publicity money was dedicated to radio.[7] The Republican presidential candidate, Herbert Hoover, secretary of commerce under Harding and Coolidge, who made only occasional public appearances during the campaign, and seemed aloof, wordy, and lifeless in his speeches, generally came across as a "high-minded statesman" in his nationwide radio addresses.[8] Smith performed better in person, despite his awareness about the need for "intimacy" on the radio, where his New York accent and nervousness diminished his performance.[9] How one communicated on the radio—and later on television—could be critical to one's electoral chances: pronunciation, tone, accent, and smoothness in delivery became important factors in politics. So, too, were the visual images that were communicated on posters and other printed material.

Franklin D. Roosevelt's Four Campaigns
(1932–1944)

Theodore Roosevelt's Democratic cousin, Franklin Delano Roosevelt (FDR), emerged as a viable presidential candidate in 1932. He had been the party's nominee for vice president in 1920, when he was an assistant secretary of the navy. Elected governor of New York in 1928, Roosevelt was nominated for president in the midst of a depression that saw terrible human suffering, which was probably at its worst point when he was selected. The election of 1932 was held amid massive unemployment, bank failures, bankruptcies, foreclosures, homelessness, and hunger. President Hoover, despite efforts to stimulate the economy, was perceived as rigid, insensitive, and ineffectual; FDR, on the other hand, was seen as more caring, optimistic, and confident, as well as having gained approval for promising aid to various sectors of the economy.[10] Arthur Krock encapsulated the parties' themes nicely when he wrote, "The people of the United States [were] being urged by the Democrats to make a change in the Presidency, and by the Republicans not, as Mr. Hoover is supposed to have said, to 'change toboggans on a slide.'"[11] When the votes were counted in 1932, Americans chose to ride on a new "toboggan."

Hoover—like Van Buren in 1840 and the Democrats in 1896—went down to defeat after a severe economic depression. In 1932, FDR handily won his first presidential campaign, and he won again in 1936, 1940, and 1944, achieving huge electoral majorities each time.[12] The Socialist Party ticket (which gained over 2 percent of the popular vote in 1932[13]) was headed by Norman Thomas, and it issued a poster with dark brown portraits of Thomas and James Maurer, who was the nominee for vice president, together with the slogan "Repeal Unemployment." Thomas attacked both major parties: the Republicans for their "failures" and the Democrats for their "promises."[14] Neither party, he stated, addressed the failure of the capitalist system to alleviate unemployment or eliminate poverty.[15]

The Democrats, after Smith had been defeated, started up the first publicity bureau for a political party, under Charles Michelson in June 1929 (the Republicans launched a similar unit shortly thereafter).[16] After the Stock Market Crash in October of that year, Michelson's material became quite negative, referring to the shacks in which the unemployed lived as "Hoovervilles."[17] The Republican publicity bureau's strategy was to depict Hoover as a "martyr" who was trying valiantly to solve the nation's problems, like the much-criticized Lincoln during the Civil War (an analogy Hoover himself made during a radio address that he delivered from the Lincoln Study of the White House during the campaign).[18] In the Depression years, both parties continued to print much material, as well as distribute campaign films and provide speakers, but it was radio that was favored.[19] A huge number of radio listeners—sometimes as many as sixty million per broadcast—heard Roosevelt's "fireside chats."[20]

By 1932, radio had become the key medium of political communication: in June of that year, there had already been over two thousand *Amos 'n Andy* broadcasts over the radio; by 1935, radio ownership had increased tenfold since the 1924 election; by 1939, more than 85 percent of all American homes had a radio set.[21] By the start of the 1932 election campaign, both the Republicans and Democrats were prepared to spend millions of dollars on radio broadcasts.[22] The Democratic slogan "A New Deal" was quite effective, in that it implied that there was hope for a better American economy, which would be brought about by a change in policies. The slogan was taken from the last paragraph of Roosevelt's acceptance speech at the Democratic Convention on July 2, 1932:

> I pledge you, I pledge myself, to a new deal for the American people. Let us all here assembled constitute ourselves prophets of a new order of competence and of courage. This is more than a political campaign; it is a call to arms.[23]

FDR's acceptance speech was heard by radio listeners, and considering his ability to communicate very effectively on the medium, it must have had quite an impact on them. In fact, a week later, John Carlile, the production manager of the Columbia Broadcasting System, acclaimed Roosevelt's voice as "one of the finest on the radio, carrying a tone of perfect sincerity and pleasing inflection."[24] He said that Hoover's voice, on the other hand, was too "deliberate."[25] Moreover, Hoover's rhetoric in 1932 could be overblown. During a radio broadcast of a speech he gave in New York, for example, Hoover avowed that the "inchoate new deal ... would destroy the very foundations of our government and crack the timbers of the Constitution."[26]

Although radio campaign spending increased, it was still viewed by many political advisors as a supplement, albeit a more intimate one, to "large posters on barns, pictures in store and home windows, and ... printed matter disclosing the history of [presidential candidates'] careers, their economic policies, their principles of government, philosophies, hobbies and friendships," according to a report in the *New York Times*.[27] The Republican campaign treasury was about two million dollars richer than was that of the Democrats; this enabled the Hoover campaign to purchase more radio time than the opposition, as well as distribute large quantities of posters, buttons, and pamphlets.[28] Most of the Republican posters were traditional, dominated by portraits of the candidates, and sometimes the slogan "Keep Him On The Job" was added. The party disseminated several unusual posters, however, that did not present the candidates at all. One of these full-color posters, which was also produced as a sticker, displayed a large cartoon of the Republican elephant pushing a truck labeled "US & Co." toward the rising sun, while the Democratic donkey was illustrated running away. The title of the poster was "It's An Elephant's Job—No Time For 'Donkey Business'!" Another such poster, titled "Vote for Hoover, Don't Change Now," featured a cartoon in which Uncle Sam rode an elephant in deep water with an angry donkey behind them. The Republicans also commissioned Christy again to design a monochromatic poster for Hoover, with the slogan "Stand By Your President," and titled "The Dawn of Victory"; it presented an eagle and a revealing rendering of "Liberty" holding a cornucopia. In 1992, George H. W. Bush—another incumbent, who did not even approach Hoover's beleaguerment—used a similar slogan (but only with a portrait of himself) (see Fig. 3.28). The party's treatment of political subjects in an almost frivolous manner could very well have been a counterproductive strategy in those harsh economic times.

The use of broadsides continued in the election propaganda wars. A particularly pointed broadside was headlined "Public Sale!" in large type, followed by "Closing Out Sale of the Grand Old Party" (Fig. 3.1). It called for the sale of all Republican property on Election Day, November 8, 1932. The following are some the items listed in it:

1 political machine, 1921 Model, badly in need of repair.
1 moss grown platform, with all its Farm Planks broken.
11 million dinner pails. All empty.
21 thousand miles of bread lines without vacant space.
700 rum running vessels, just learning to swim, but all dives.
14 million moonshine stills, all operating.

Both parties printed broadsides that targeted various groups. A broadside for Hoover was designed to be mailed and then unfolded to eleven by seventeen inches. This broadside, headlined "You Should Re-Elect President Hoover," was directed at workers, and it listed how the president had been "Labor's Friend" for three years ("despite propaganda to the contrary" and "hard pulling for everyone"). Whereas broadsides had been around for centuries, there was one innovation in 1932—a poster intended to cover an automobile's spare tire (which, during this period, was placed at the rear or side of a car).[29]

Figure 3.1

In 1936, the Republicans nominated Governor Alf Landon of Kansas for president, and hoped that a new "humanized" advertising drive would help unseat President Roosevelt.[30] This plan was marked by both negative and positive campaigning to convince individuals that the "New Deal" posed a threat to them, with higher taxes, worse economic conditions, and an increase in unemployment on the horizon; and, conversely, appeals about Landon and his "common sense" approach to problem solving.[31] A poster for the 1936 Republican

Figure 3.2   *Figure 3.3*

ticket, captioned "Deeds ... *Not* Deficits" summarized this approach (see Fig. 3.2). There was also a concerted effort to capture the rural vote: the Republicans handed out Landon sunflower buttons, and distributed portrait posters of the candidate, headlined "From a Typical Prairie State" (Fig. 3.3). The Republicans spent almost five million dollars more than the Democrats did—a gap that was even greater than that of 1932.[32] Some of the Republican money paid for the first spot announcements on radio, but at least one hundred twenty-five million pieces of campaign literature, including broadsides with specific appeals to labor, which were posted in factories, were printed. These lamented the Social Security Act's payroll deduction, declaring "You're Sentenced to a Weekly Pay Reduction for All Your Working Life."[33] The Democratic National Committee (DNC) highlighted issues on broadsides that targeted specific voting blocs—farmers, homeowners, workers, and civil servants—either alone or in combination (see Fig. 1.5, Chapter One). The slogans of FDR's campaign in 1936 were "Carry on with Franklin D. Roosevelt," seen in this simple poster featuring a photograph of the president (Fig. 3.4) and "Forward with Roosevelt."

CARRY ON WITH

FRANKLIN D. ROOSEVELT

Figure 3.4

Similar posters, without the slogans, were sized smaller so they could be displayed in windows. It should be noted that some posters from the 1936 campaign were reissued in 1940 and, again, in 1944.[34]

In 1940, Roosevelt defeated Wendell Willkie, a New York City lawyer and president of a utility company, with liberal views on social programs, and an internationalist whose opinions did not differ appreciably from FDR's. Willkie was an attractive candidate, who had been a Democrat until he differed with Roosevelt over the Tennessee Valley Authority, and he won the Republican nod as attendees at the convention chanted, "We Want Willkie!"[35] The chant was chosen for many of his posters, along with the slogan, "For Peace, Preparedness and Prosperity." Small black-and-white photographic portraits of Willkie, looking out at the viewers, with "Republican Candidate for President," were distributed during the campaign. The Republicans, in their campaign material, tried to depict FDR as weak on national security and were highly critical of him for seeking a third term.[36] Posters for Willkie declared, "This Preparedness Business is a Job for a Business Man" and "For Unpreparedness France Dismissed Daladier, England Replaced Chamberlain, Why Should America Keep Roosevelt?"; a sticker averred, "No Crown for Franklin." The Republicans also tried to attract laborers to the Willkie side. In one red-white-and-blue poster is a blue-collar worker with an oilcan, and the slogan "Work With Willkie," as part of the campaign to accomplish this shift (Fig. 3.5). With the economy lingering in the doldrums and Europe engulfed in World War II, Roosevelt was not as popular, but he, nevertheless, won by a respectable margin. Smaller cloth banners (typically colored in red, white, and blue) were popular campaign items in 1940, displaying mottos and slogans, such as "God Bless America," as well as drawn portraits of the candidates.[37] Figure 3.6 exemplifies a banner from this period (from the 1944 campaign), depicting FDR with

Figure 3.5

Figure 3.6

Washington and Lincoln, using key words the designer wanted voters to associate with these presidents and Roosevelt. It also connected the president with the war effort in a most patriotic way.

Four years later, the Republicans nominated Governor Thomas E. Dewey of New York, who did not greatly criticize the New Deal's ideas, but instead stated that the government was incompetent in administering its domestic programs. As for foreign policy, Dewey would not go on the attack in the middle of a war, which the country had entered almost three years earlier. Roosevelt devoted most of his time to his duties in office, but used his powers of radio communication to good effect late in the campaign. A slogan on FDR's posters was "A Gallant Leader," one of the slogans from his past campaigns. In 1944, Democrats produced radio advertisements of short duration to replace much lengthier broadcasts, with celebrity endorsements, brief statements about ordinary people, and background music in the clips. Campaign material for Dewey rarely featured slogans (the most memorable one being "Dewey • We are DUE for a change"), and the posters issued by the Republican National Committee were simply small black-and-white photographic portraits of Dewey.[38]

Roosevelt's allies, particularly labor unions, helped his cause by issuing pamphlets and posters to increase voter registration.[39] Blue-toned photographs of FDR and his candidate for vice president in 1944, Senator Harry S. Truman of Missouri, dominated posters that were headlined "Register and Vote Democratic" and had "Lasting Peace • Security for All" printed at the bottom. Some posters with this slogan even included the Democratic rooster (which was still around, in competition with the donkey). As was often the case, words were printed in red and blue inks on a white background to strike the right patriotic note. Another poster featured a photograph of a smiling Roosevelt in an open car in the rain, looking directly at the audience, with the simple slogan "Rain Or Shine" above him. The three words conveyed a feeling of confidence for many in his steady, optimistic leadership, which had taken the country through harsh economic and military times.

A poster designed by artist Ben Shahn, titled "Our Friend," portrayed President Roosevelt, with hands of different races raised around him. Both poster and billboard versions were produced during the 1944 presidential election campaign by the Political

Action Committee of the Congress of Industrial Organizations (CIO-PAC).[40] The CIO-PAC also issued a poster, dominated by a headshot of the smiling Roosevelt, which appealed to workers to donate "a dollar you won't miss to elect a man you can't afford to lose." Other organizations opposing a fourth term for FDR, worked against him. Some farmer groups, for instance, that believed the New Deal had hurt their interests "spent a lot of money for posters and radio time for Dewey."[41]

Several 1944 campaign posters—besides some by Shahn—were in the style of those produced during the two world wars. In fact, a poster for the president's campaign in 1944 was painted in watercolor by artist James Montgomery Flagg, and included his famous Uncle Sam pointing a finger at the viewer (from his 1917 poster), along with a portrait of Roosevelt and the words "I Want You F. D. R. … Stay and Finish the Job!" It was used on billboards and in campaign literature.[42] Naturally, there were people who objected to the Democratic Party's exploitation of a national symbol.[43] Another poster even included a portrait of Roosevelt, surrounded by American flags, and battleships in the background. It practically declared "Re-elect Our Leader During The War."

Posters at the Dawn of the Television Era
(1948–1956)

The significance of posters lessened with the advent of radio, and it was further diminished with the arrival of television in many American homes. By 1955, almost two-thirds of all U.S. households had a television set.[44] Nevertheless, the poster continued to be a valuable propaganda tool in the country's election campaigns.

In 1948, the election posters for President Truman (who had served more than three years of FDR's term, following Roosevelt's sudden death) focused on the economic accomplishments of the New Deal, his prudent and forceful foreign policy, and his identification with the Roosevelt administration's fight against fascism. One Democratic poster presented former president Hoover, with the admonition "Don't Monkey with the Donkey in '48 or Sell Hoover Apples in '49"; another promised "Homes for All"; and yet another declared "Count Your Blessings."[45] Organized labor also produced posters for the Truman ticket, which warned workers: "If you stay home on Nov. 2, You will be voting for higher prices; tougher anti-labor laws; housing shortages; boom, bust and breadlines." Another poster that unions distributed was titled "Your Right to Vote Cost Many American Lives"; it pictured a blue-toned Truman against a brown background, with the Mount Rushmore Memorial and the flag raising at Iwo Jima. "Secure the Peace" posters for Truman's 1948 election campaign emphasized his international leadership. One poster, considered particularly persuasive, showed Truman in his World War I captain's uniform, along with the phrases "Nobody Wants War" and "Harry S. Truman Knows Why!" implying that the president was both "strong" and "peaceful"[46] (Fig. 3.7).

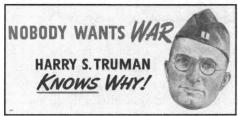

Figure 3.7

It was important to stress Truman's foreign policy accomplishments, since his predecessor as vice president, Henry Wallace, was running against him on the Progressive Party ticket—Wallace was highly critical of what he perceived to be Truman's anti-Soviet stance. Another branch of the Democratic Party, led by Senator Strom Thurmond of South Carolina, departed to form the States Rights Party, which resented the efforts of the federal government to force a change in race relations.[47] Thurmond's new party distributed broadsides that decried the "invasion of states rights proposed by Truman, Dewey and Wallace" and predicted the creation of "a police-state."

Posters could have a political impact, but in this period before television became widespread, newsreels were probably more noteworthy: in 1948, more than fifty million people viewed a newsreel-biography of Truman in movie theaters; however, the campaigns of both presidential candidates in 1948—Truman and Dewey—did purchase television time to air their speeches.[48] Truman's campaign was ultimately successful, as he traveled around the country by train (logging more miles than Bryan did in 1896) and tailored radio broadcasts, to deliver "hard-hitting and frequently folksy and entertaining" addresses while appealing to both liberal and conservative voters, as well as black citizens.[49] Truman also focused on local issues and tried to associate his campaign with the interests of the ordinary person. This was in opposition to "special interests," which he attempted to link to the Republican Party, while blaming the Republican-controlled Congress for failing to enact needed legislation. Dewey generally stayed above the fray, preferring to be more statesmanlike and avoiding specifics. Wallace lost much of his popular support when he refused to renounce the Communist Party, which had endorsed him.[50] Thurmond's appeal to continue racial segregation was limited mainly to the Deep South. Contrary to most pollsters' predictions, Truman won the election with a clear majority of the electoral vote, gaining only 1.5 million popular votes fewer than had FDR four years earlier. His margin over Dewey was more than 4 percent; Wallace and Thurmond performed poorly, each receiving slightly more than 2 percent.[51]

Although in 1948 some political operatives were aware of how their candidates should appear on television, there were television sets in fewer than five hundred thousand homes that year.[52] By the election of 1952, however, this number had mushroomed to almost nineteen million—greater than one-third of all American households—and almost as much political-campaign money was spent on television as radio.[53] Personality and image management became more essential, as the new medium developed into a powerful factor in politics; advertising personnel played an ever-increasing role, beginning most notably in the two presidential campaigns of the 1950s, particularly on the Republican side.

In 1952, the Republicans nominated General Eisenhower, allied commander in Europe during World War II, and then president of Columbia University; the Democrats nominated Governor Adlai Stevenson (grandson of Cleveland's running mate) of Illinois. Eisenhower had been asked to run by segments of both parties for four years, and he appealed to a significant number of Democratic, Republican, and independent voters.[54] Many of the posters for Eisenhower did not note his party designation, since there were about three million more registered Democrats than Republican registrants, and millions of independents.[55] The exclusion of the party's name on Eisenhower's posters may have become more pronounced, but this had been the trend for a half century. Nearly all of the

Republican campaign paraphernalia in 1952—and in Eisenhower's reelection campaign against Stevenson four years later—failed to even mention Stevenson, but instead either attacked the record of the Truman administration or praised the Republican ticket.[56] One poster showed photographic portraits of Eisenhower and his running mate, Senator Richard Nixon of California, with the slogan "Let's Clean House with Ike and Dick," and an Eisenhower poster asked the public to "Vote for a Man You Can Trust." Implied here was a blanket condemnation of the Democratic administration, which the Republican platform's preamble charged with "a long succession of vicious acts, [which] so undermined the foundations of our Republic as to threaten its existence."[57] Broadsides with similar visuals and themes were printed too. One included a photograph of the triumphant Ike and Dick at the convention podium, under the headline "Vote the Winning Team in November!" Five themes were delineated in this broadside: "End the Korean Slaughter," "Kick Out the Commies," "Clean Up Truman's Mess," "Stop Crazy Spending," and "End Our Hit-Or-Miss Foreign Policy." As in the past, because they conveyed themes with more detail and gusto, broadsides were often chosen over posters as the means by which to communicate negative messages.

Eisenhower was yet another military leader nominated for president, but his campaign staff clearly understood that two of his main attributes as a candidate were his folksiness and positive, smiling persona, which he conveyed through posters and television.[58] Many advertising firms assisted the Eisenhower campaign, most notably Batten, Barton, Durstine & Osborne (BBDO), which wanted to present Eisenhower as "warm" and "friendly"—partly to overcome the public's image of Republicans as opponents of New Deal social programs.[59] Rosser Reeves (of Ted Bates & Company), another advertising executive who worked in Ike's campaign, believed that Eisenhower's military experience, along with his desire for "peace," should be emphasized repeatedly. Reeves was an advocate of emphasizing "one strong concept" in an advertisement that was unique and would set apart a product from its competitors.[60] Just as ads for M&M's® candy (designed by Reeves' firm) included the slogan "Melts in your mouth, not in your hand,"[61] the political advertising for Eisenhower represented him as the personable "Ike" who had led the country to victory in the recent war. Stevenson, also, was shown smiling in some of his posters, with his party designation either inconspicuous or not present at all (Fig. 3.8). This was the first U.S. national election campaign

Figure 3.8

that displayed both candidates smiling, and in which posters de-emphasized their party affiliation. It became a trend both at home and abroad.

The Stevenson campaign stressed twenty years of achievements by the Democratic administrations of Roosevelt and Truman, and decried the state of things under Hoover, who had preceded them. This strategy can be seen in the 1952 party platform, which noted that "unemployment [was] … less than 3 per cent of the labor force, compared with almost 25 per cent in 1932";[62] by statements of outgoing President Truman, who referred to Eisenhower as "the candidate of the 'depression party'";[63] by one of the few Democratic TV spots, "Sh-h-h-h. Don't mention it to a soul … the Republican Party was in power in 1932 … 13 million people were unemployed. … ";[64] and by a poster issued by organized labor, titled "WHICH will be SAFER for YOU?" It took a similar approach to that of a Republican poster of 1900 that had visually contrasted the economic distress under the Democratic government of Cleveland to the relative prosperity during McKinley's administration. The Stevenson poster used visuals, not unlike the 1900 poster, to illustrate its points about the harsh times under "The Party of Hoover/1932" as compared to the good times continuing under "The Party of Roosevelt/1952": it contrasted scenes of breadlines, the homeless, and closed banks to depictions of better homes, and workers receiving higher wages and social security checks. Color was used to emphasize the contrast—scenes from 1932 were tinted blue, and those from 1952 were multicolored. Portraits of FDR, Truman, and Stevenson were displayed in oval frames. No foreign-policy issues were part of the 1952 design, a departure from the 1900 campaign poster. Another poster distributed by organized labor included a cartoon of a "Republican" horse-drawn streetcar, with its destination "Depression"; photographs of the Democratic ticket; and the title "Don't Transfer to a Horsecar!" Domestic issues were again emphasized, specifically "Full Civil Rights," "Increased Aid for the Aged," and "High Wages, Steady Work." Yet another Stevenson poster asserted "Let's Talk Sense to the American People," a clever bit of wordplay meaning straight talk on economic matters.

Not only did the Democrats try to resurrect images from the Great Depression to remind voters of past Republican economic failures, but they also tried to tie the Eisenhower campaign to "big business." Truman campaigned for Stevenson, and was particularly adamant about making the connection, declaring that the "big-money boys" had to be "licked" again.[65] The Republican National Committee did have well over twice as much money to spend as did its Democratic counterpart (a ratio that also held for the next election); however, Truman's warnings, that "a return to Republican policies" (heavily influenced by special interest groups, he claimed) would lead to a new depression, were in vain.[66] This was not surprising, since he was quite unpopular at that time.[67] Equally ineffective were the posters of Stevenson and *his* running mate, Senator John Sparkman of Alabama with the slogan "for all people."

Domestic issues were secondary to international concerns in 1952. In particular, the Korean War was the campaign's dominant issue. The Democratic platform proclaimed, "the Communist aggressor [has] been hurled back from South Korea";[68] the Republican platform, on the other hand, asserted, "with foresight, the Korean War would never have happened" and, the "hampering orders" of the Truman administration had "produced stalemates and ignominious bartering with our enemies, and they offer no hope of victory."[69] While the Democrats sought praise for the economic and social benefits of the New Deal, the Republicans linked the war to increased military spending and taxes, and inflationary prices.[70] In late October, Eisenhower promised, "I shall go to Korea," which appealed to the considerable number of people who were frustrated by the war.[71] The Eisenhower "peace and personality" campaign in 1952 proved to be the most effective approach—he won by a margin of about 11 percent in the popular vote and overwhelmingly in the Electoral College.[72] Running as an incumbent in 1956, with the nation at peace and fairly prosperous, Ike again bested Stevenson—this time by 15 percent in the popular vote and another electoral landslide (despite the Democratic Party's increased publicity efforts, which included many televised spot advertisements).[73]

Although television had become a significant factor in national political campaigns, in 1952, the two presidential candidates set records for traveling the country—predominantly by airplane—to deliver speeches, and their combined total mileage was over sixty-five thousand (which was about equally divided).[74] About one-tenth of Stevenson's speeches in his first presidential campaign were nationally televised,[75] and the medium was credited with helping establish him as a personable candidate in the minds of the American public.[76] Almost all of Stevenson's time on television was dedicated to political speeches. In one study, 96 percent of the Democrats' TV time was devoted to speeches and only 4 percent to programs that had been produced.[77] Both campaigns had to divert money budgeted initially for billboards and other traditional advertising methods, as well as for travel, to pay for TV broadcasts and spots.[78] Eisenhower—already widely known—was probably the most admired person in the country; although he was often perceived more positively in person, his television appearances seemed to humanize him, giving the impression that he was sincere and cheerful.[79] In addition, the multitude of TV spots with which the Republicans saturated the airways in the final two weeks of the 1952 campaign appeared to have had a positive effect on the voters.[80] The strategy of the advertising executives who labored in Ike's campaign clearly worked to enhance his already positive image. The idea was to expose the public to the Republican candidate frequently, briefly, relatively inexpensively, and with total control over image and words. Posters reinforced the image of a confident, smiling presidential candidate who was ready to face all problems, and above petty party concerns. An existing commodity was presented to the public with little modification—in the best possible light.

The publicity divisions of both parties' national committees continued to churn out printed material, including posters, during the 1952 campaign. One poster was dominated by a full-color photograph of Ike in civilian attire, with the slogan "America Needs Eisenhower for a Durable Peace." In his campaign posters, Eisenhower was never presented in a military outfit. It was important to show that he could be an effective leader for peace, and negotiate an end to the stalemate in Korea, even though he had been a wartime commander. By 1956, as the popular incumbent, Eisenhower's campaign needed only to reinforce his positive image. His consultants did so in a coordinated promotion that used all media approaches, including a package that accompanied a televised musical "Happy Birthday, Mr. President" tribute narrated by Jimmy Stewart, two weeks before Election Day (Fig. 3.9).[81] The package contained two identical posters (Fig. 3.10); a sheet offering suggestions for other displays; and cake decoration ideas, letterheads, model news releases, and publicity advice. Television continued to play an important role in the 1956 campaign, with Young & Rubicam, Inc. scripting "Citizens for Eisenhower" programs.[82]

Figure 3.9   *Figure 3.10*

A concern for Stevenson in both campaigns was his divorce; therefore, the Democrats circulated a poster in 1956 that showed their presidential candidate hugging a young girl, and urging people to vote for him as an advocate of school construction and child welfare. Such posters, as well as TV spots, probably did little to prevent the defection of voters who viewed divorce as a moral failure.[83] A problem for the Republicans in 1956 was Eisenhower's health, after he had been stricken by a heart attack a year before the election, followed by a period of recuperation. The Democrats dispersed posters that declared, "America Needs A Full-time President," but most Americans did not appear to be too troubled about the possibility of an incapacitated or dying president. In one group interview, several people suggested that Ike "had become so firmly established as a 'father-image' that he had a certain political invulnerability. 'You don't hear much about the health issue,' one observer said, 'because in the family nobody ever talks about Daddy dying.'"[84]

Of note is that campaigns for Eisenhower, and, previously, Truman, portrayed them as down-to-earth, plainspoken men from the heartland (like Jackson, Harrison, Lincoln, and others before them), but neither candidate's posters showed them as "common" folk. This continued the general nineteenth-century practice of depicting the candidates rather formally. The posters for Eisenhower occasionally used his nickname of "Ike," however, and implied his affability by revealing him grinning; conversely, the posters for Truman had him conservatively dressed and bearing a serious facial expression. In addition, Truman's strategists, to impart a "serious" image, had him wear his eyeglasses; Eisenhower's team, on the other hand, had him remove his eyeglasses, to increase the informality of his image. Of course, when it was appropriate, Eisenhower was pictured with a serious facial expression, which can be seen in a reelection poster with the title "Keep America Strong."

The adhesive bumper sticker was another campaign device that was developed in 1956. Beginning with the second Eisenhower-Stevenson election, the campaign poster relinquished its role to the bumper sticker as the primary printed medium of display in U.S. elections.[85] Bumper stickers professed "I Still Like Ike" and "For Ike 1956," and pro-Stevenson stickers were overprinted "I've Switched to Adlai" in red on "I Like Ike" in white. Even earlier—in the 1920 campaign—both the Republicans and Democrats handed out window stickers for automobiles initiating the age of the "moving political advertisement." As Roger Fischer noted, the advent of antilitter laws reduced the amount of political advertising: previously, campaign posters could be plastered on telephone- and power poles, and street lampposts, but this practice became more restricted; the use of billboard space for political purposes lessened as well.[86] Besides controls imposed on billboard advertising, two other factors contributed to limiting the utilization of billboards in U.S. election campaigns during and following the 1950s: diversion of funds to more modern media, and the political communication consultants' realization that there were more effective and economical ways to build name recognition for a nominated presidential candidate.[87] Less costly posters could still be distributed at campaign rallies, however, and positioned in suburban windows and lawns to establish a presence in a neighborhood.

Posters in the Era of Television Dominance
(1960–2004)

The most memorable event of the 1960 election campaign was the first of four televised debates between the Republican nominee, Vice President Nixon, and his Democratic opponent, Senator John F. Kennedy (JFK) of Massachusetts (another war hero and a Roman Catholic). By that year, 88 percent of American households owned a television set.[88] The importance of "image" was mentioned right away in newspaper articles. For example, two days after the first debate, a piece in the *New York Times* stated that viewers had made "frequent mention of how drawn and weary the Vice President had looked" and how his "grimness was shocking," but many thought that Senator Kennedy had projected a "mature image."[89] The editorial writers, on the other hand, concentrated more on the discussion of the issues. The *Boston Traveler* stated, "For through TV, the twentieth century is truly providing what our founding fathers in the eighteenth century hoped for—an informed electorate, equipped with the comparative knowledge to make the best choice."[90] Of course, the campaign managers realized that perception of their candidate's visual image was a factor, and for television they had Kennedy wear a dark gray suit, replace his white shirt with a blue one, and Nixon wear a blue-gray suit and a light blue shirt.[91] Furthermore, the concerned Nixon advisors were aware that the background needed to be made darker, the lighting on their candidate had to be adjusted to lighten his eye shadows, and facial makeup needed to be applied to cover his "five o'clock shadow."[92] It was estimated that about 65 percent of households turned on the first debate, and that an audience of more than seventy-three million watched it—in a year when fewer than sixty-eight million people voted.[93]

As for the importance of visual image, surveys revealed that for those who heard all the debates on radio, there was no significant difference between how listeners thought the candidates presented themselves; for television viewers, however, Kennedy was thought to have won.[94] A national survey further indicated that the debates influenced 57 percent of voters, with 6 percent attributing their decision only to the debates; this group broke for Kennedy over Nixon by 72 percent versus 26 percent.[95] Image management, also, was a factor in the posters designed for the 1960 campaign. Nixon, who had somewhat of an image problem—and whom Eisenhower, *both* times, had almost dumped from the Republican ticket[96]—was shown smiling and establishing "eye contact" in the photographs used in his posters (alongside his running mate, United Nations Ambassador Henry Cabot Lodge of Massachusetts). The posters featured the slogan "Experience Counts," alluding to Nixon's eight years as Eisenhower's vice president and Kennedy not having served in a national executive office (Fig. 3.11). The Kennedy campaign also designed posters that showed its candidate smiling—but not always looking directly at the viewers—and included the slogans "Leadership for the 60's" and "A Time for Greatness," which pointed to a change from the allegedly ineffectual record of the Eisenhower Administration (Fig. 3.12). In

Figure 3.11   *Figure 3.12*

addition, Kennedy's advisors, aware of the "experience" perceptions of the two candidates, fashioned a more "conservative" image for him—the candidate was convinced to get a less "boyish" haircut and wear more conservative clothing for his poster photographs and public appearances.[97]

At the local level, posters were a central element in the campaign. The fifteen hundred members of the National Federation of Republican Women, for example, were issued a campaign kit that held "posters, banners, film and speeches adaptable for use at local meetings of any size."[98] Similar kits, containing photographs, buttons, lapel tabs, "talking-points" cards, and posters, went out to self-financed "Nixon clubs" across the country, whose purpose was to appeal to Democrats, independents, and Republicans who did not wish to work within the party organization.[99] The Kennedy poster designs were also used on fliers, bumper stickers, buttons, and even matchbook covers.

Both parties ran aggressive campaigns—particularly in the last days of October—that attacked or defended the economic and foreign-policy records of the past administration. Nixon told an audience at the end of October, "America has never been more prosperous. You know that Jack [Kennedy] may have more dollars than you have but you have more sense."[100] Nixon, thus, defended the record of the administration, but he had also attempted to place himself alongside the common folk and Kennedy among the wealthy elite. Not only did the speeches become more aggressive, but so, too, did the posters that the local Republican organizations circulated, one of which carried the slogan "Kennedy Means War."[101] The Republican efforts came up short. Kennedy defeated Nixon in one of the closest elections in U.S. history—at least in the popular vote, winning by less than one hundred fifteen thousand votes—and he barely achieved a majority of the electoral votes.[102] It was also the first and only time (to date) that a non-Protestant was elected president, despite the dissemination of an estimated twenty million pieces of anti-Catholic printed material during the campaign.[103]

The year following Kennedy's assassination in 1963, his vice president and successor, Lyndon B. Johnson (LBJ), ran in his own right. He did so after securing passage of the Civil Rights Act that Kennedy failed to push through Congress, as well as the Economic Opportunity Act declaring "war on poverty" and the Gulf of Tonkin Resolution giving Johnson the authority to retaliate against North Vietnam for alleged aggression.[104] The election campaign of 1964 proved to be perhaps the most ideologically polarized battle of the twentieth century in American politics. Johnson's Republican opponent, Senator Barry Goldwater of Arizona, was the party's ultraconservative leader. He had proposed to eliminate the graduated federal income tax, educational aid, agricultural subsidies, and mandatory Social Security; had opposed civil rights legislation; and called for empowering military commanders to deploy tactical nuclear weapons.[105] Johnson labeled the Republican nominee a "radical" and a "preacher of hate."[106] Many viewed Goldwater as an extremist. The Republican candidate did not alleviate concerns with his phraseology as the campaign began: in his acceptance speech at the convention, he sealed his fate when he declared, "extremism in the defense of liberty is no vice! And ... moderation in the pursuit of justice is no virtue!" as he reached the conclusion of his remarks.[107]

Television continued to be quite important, with a set in well over nine out of ten households.[108] President Johnson refused to debate Goldwater, but his advertising people televised spot ads, along with other media, which conveyed the image of the Republican nominee as a dangerous reactionary, applying the classic techniques of advertising propaganda: exaggeration and distortion. Posters did not impart this propaganda; rather, they were quite traditional in design and message. Their use continued in the same ways as in the prior decade, with many of them dispensed to supporters for displaying at rallies.[109]

The Democratic National Committee, however, did not include money for print advertising in its budget, and they eliminated all spending for billboards.[110] Consequently, almost all posters and other printed material were issued by citizen groups, state committees, and labor organizations. The Republicans generally followed this practice also. Two posters printed for the Goldwater campaign used a template that had been employed by the 1936 Landon campaign, substituting the 1964 slogans "A Choice ... *Not* An Echo" and "In Your Heart ... You Know They're Right" (Fig. 3.13) for "Deeds ... *Not* Deficits"

Figure 3.13

(see Fig. 3.2). Other than the presence of different halftone photographs, candidate names, and slogans, these were the same posters—even though they were distributed in elections that were twenty-eight years apart. Local organizations that supported the Republican ticket issued less elaborate posters that included two photographs and the title "Victory for America in 1964" or, even more simply, "Goldwater for President," with the senator's photograph. A Democratic Party poster design featured a confident Johnson "in" a map of the country (and a variation of this poster also featured his smiling running mate, Vice President Hubert Humphrey, beside him). The slogan "Johnson [Humphrey] for the USA" was added in the usual red-white-and-blue color scheme. For those voters who were partial to initials and rhyming, there was also a poster with the slogan "LBJ for the USA." The Liberal Party of New York State produced two posters: placed at the top of one was a quote by Johnson, "Let Us Continue … " —a vow to continue the policies of his slain predecessor—which was subtitled "a Better Deal for You and America … "; the other was more pointed, declaring "Vote LBJ the Liberal Way … " and "Defeat Goldwater and His Right Wing Extremists."

The Republican budget for political advertising was almost five million dollars; all but about 4 percent of that was earmarked for "peace through strength" TV spots and programs, which also criticized LBJ's foreign policy.[111] The Democrats planned to spend almost as much, most of it on television and radio commercials critical of Goldwater's positions and ones that credited Johnson for "peace, prosperity and legislative progress."[112] Johnson's campaign did not duplicate Wilson's "He Kept Us Out of War" theme, but the candidate did reject an enlargement of the conflict in Vietnam, in opposition to Goldwater's advocacy of such a move. Johnson's TV spots—and most of his campaign—were quite general. Goldwater's, on the other hand, was more specific: TV spots proposed a reduction in government spending and bureaucracy.[113] Like Wilson, Johnson authorized military deployment after his election victory, and helped seal the fate of the Democratic Party in the next national political campaign. A few months after winning by more than a 22-point margin in the popular vote, LBJ began to escalate the Vietnam War militarily.[114]

The 1964 presidential election campaign was marked by increased media expenditures for TV spots, and audience attentiveness to them.[115] According to Larry Sabato, ten thousand TV spots were aired in the largest seventy-five media markets during the election.[116] Doyle Dane Bernbach (DDB) developed a memorable spot for Johnson, calling it "Peace, Little Girl."[117] A DDB media specialist, Tony Schwartz, conceived the spot, after doing commercials that included children for Ivory Snow®, Johnson's® Baby Powder, Polaroid cameras, and other corporate products.[118] Schwartz believed that by combining the right images, words, music, and sound effects, an ad could strike an emotional "responsive chord" in a consumer.[119] The "Daisy Spot" commercial opened with a young girl picking a daisy, and a narrator counting down from "ten." The girl plucks off the petals as the countdown continues, the camera simultaneously zooming in to an extreme close-up of the girl's eye. An atomic explosion erupts, and Lyndon Johnson is heard saying, "These are the stakes—to make a world in which all of God's children can live, or go into the dark. We must either love each other, or we must die."[120] Although the Republicans tried to counter the tactics manifested in this (and a similar) commercial with their own TV spots—the theme of which was "we are the party of peace through strength" and which were highly critical of the Democratic administration's "failures at the 'wall of shame in Berlin,' the Bay of Pigs in Cuba and in Vietnam"[121]—Goldwater's already hawkish image had become so negative for so many people that the deleterious consequences of the Democratic propaganda could not be undone. Even though the "Daisy Spot" ran only once, an estimated fifty million viewers saw it, and after the Republicans protested its airing, many more read and heard about it.[122] While it is likely that, without the efforts of the advertising firms, Eisenhower in 1952 and Johnson in 1964 would have won the U.S. presidency (as well as—later—Nixon, Carter, Reagan, and Clinton), their margins were probably increased substantially by the campaigns. In addition, later campaigns, in several countries, employed and modeled various techniques used in the United States; in closer races, they very well could have made the difference between victory and defeat.

Interestingly, Johnson's advertising campaign did not have posters reinforcing the theme that "Goldwater [was] an extremist who could blow up the world," even though a radio spot, a printed ad, and brochures were devised that accomplished this.[123] There were targeted brochures, also, issued by both parties, which employed "fear" appeals. One, titled "why older people FEAR GOLDWATER!" featured a cartoon of Johnson's Republican opponent kicking an elderly man's crutch. A handbill issued by Citizens for Goldwater was titled "Who Will Dictate?" and had a photograph of Johnson with black civil rights leaders. Interestingly, one Democratic TV spot, designed by DDB, *did* include traditional posters—from the failed Republican campaigns of Governors Nelson Rockefeller, George Romney, and William Scranton—which were seen littered on the floor of the convention hall in which Goldwater had been nominated, just as their party had discarded their moderate views.[124] The announcer's voiceover concluded, "If you're a Republican with serious doubts about Barry Goldwater, you're in good company."[125] DDB's and others' propaganda campaigns did two significant things: (1) they created a convincing image of Goldwater as an "extremist" "product" and (2) they softened the image of Johnson as a "crass wheeler-dealer," making him seem almost avuncular—virtually a "peace and love" advocate of the 1960s—in comparison to his "bellicose" opponent.

It is remarkable that presidential slogans summarizing the themes of their campaigns and subsequent administrations—Theodore Roosevelt's "Square Deal" and "New Nationalism," Wilson's "New Freedom," Franklin Roosevelt's "New Deal," Truman's "Fair Deal," and Kennedy's "New Frontier"—rarely showed up on posters, although some of these were present on buttons, postcards, and other campaign paraphernalia. One interesting poster that was issued by the United Auto Workers (UAW), however, paired FDR's 1932 slogan and JFK's 1960 slogan, and was distributed during the latter's campaign: the design featured red-toned drawings of both men against a yellow background, and the phrases "Franklin Roosevelt's New Deal," "John Kennedy's New Frontier," and "In the 1960's as in the 1930's." LBJ's "Great Society" was included at least twice in two UAW campaign posters in 1964: one titled "let's keep building the Great Society," asked people to vote for Johnson, who was shown beneath Democrats Roosevelt, Truman, and Kennedy (Fig. 3.14); another featured a photograph of Johnson, with Kennedy in semifocus in the background, and the message "Let Us Continue to Build the Great Society" (Fig. 3.15).

Figure 3.14	*Figure 3.15*

Four years later, an anti-Johnson poster showed the Great Society overwhelmed by the Vietnam War.

By the 1968 election campaign, the country was in turmoil. The Great Society had achieved many worthwhile goals, but race riots, high crime rates, student unrest, and radical protests disturbed many citizens.[126] However, the Vietnam conflict dominated the political scene. The mainstream media, particularly television, transmitted vivid images—usually within hours—of burning villages, executions, and corpses. This heavily influenced American public opinion, even if the military situation on the ground was often communicated inaccurately to the public, and the political and strategic issues were not always fully addressed.[127] Support for the war declined dramatically after the Tet Offensive in January of 1968, which made it appear that there was not really "light … at the end of the tunnel," as the public had been led to believe.[128] Antiwar sentiment increased markedly, President Johnson withdrew from the race for his party's nomination before its convention, and Vice President Humphrey stepped in to seek the presidency. Humphrey believed that he had to take a relatively hard-line stance on the war to retain Southern support for the Democratic nomination.[129] Nevertheless, he lost every state of the Confederacy except Texas in the general election, and lost other votes when antiwar protests erupted into a riot, when police brutally clubbed demonstrators in the streets outside the Democratic National Convention in Chicago.

The Republicans again nominated Nixon, who had failed in his bid to become governor of California two years after his narrow defeat to Kennedy in 1960. After telling news reporters that they had witnessed his "last press conference" and that they would not have him "to kick around anymore," Nixon moved to New York to practice law.[130] Six years later, he reemerged as the "New Nixon," his image developed with the aid of his advertising people. It did seem though that Richard Nixon had matured, and was no longer enraged at the press and others who "belittled" him. As Theodore White wrote, "here was a man who in 1960 had been attacked as vicious, untrustworthy and unstable. … Now, in 1968, he was being attacked as dull, smooth, and programmed."[131]

There were no debates again, when third-party candidate George Wallace, the former governor of Alabama, insisted on being included, and Nixon refused to participate with Wallace present; however, Nixon spent two dollars for every one that Humphrey spent on television time.[132] On the major issue of Vietnam, Nixon was quite vague, stating that he had a "plan" that would "bring peace with honor."[133] The Republican campaign primary slogan "Nixon's the One!" was concise and confident; it was displayed in posters that showed a smiling Nixon, looking directly and assuredly at the viewer—sometimes alone, sometimes with others surrounding him. A simpler, but striking poster design comprised a

Figure 3.16

large, stylized "N" and "Nixon" printed in script, and a red-white-and-blue color scheme (Fig. 3.16). Humphrey supporters, not to be outdone, designed a poster with a large "h" on it, donkeys in the background, and a blue-black-and-white color scheme.

The campaign designed for Nixon in 1968 was a marvel of image management. Nixon's image with many Americans was so negative that he was referred to routinely as "Tricky Dick." The Nixon strategists viewed television as the primary medium in U.S. election campaigns, and the candidate was instructed by J. Walter Thompson advertising executive Harry Treleaven to use words that "show[ed] his *emotional* involvement in the issues" in nonstudio TV spots that would appear to be natural and warm.[134] The shift from black-and-white television sets to color (and better shaving practices) also helped to soften Nixon's image.[135] To counter the warmer image of the often ebullient Humphrey, Republican posters included photographs of Nixon smiling under warm lighting, or featuring him in flattering artists' portraits. The Republican advertising team also designed enormous full-color portrait posters of the candidate and additional "Nixon's the One!" posters and plastic banners, which were included in a sixteen-page catalog, along with paraphernalia such as buttons, flags, cartop signs, bumper strips, T-shirts, and stuffed elephants.

Another slogan, "This Time, Nixon," was equally simple, and was used in a month-long, thirty-sheet billboard campaign.[136] The Democrats never devised as good a slogan as the two Republican ones. Among the several that were created for the Humphrey campaign was "Some talk change. Others cause it." This was at the top of a poster that also presented Humphrey—a "bold man of action"—making direct eye contact with the voters, hoping that they would recall his progressive domestic record. A similar poster—with a similar purpose—simply stated "Humphrey; You know he cares." above a photographic portrait of the candidate, smiling and looking at the viewers. Supporters of Humphrey, who called for a halt to the bombing of North Vietnam, issued a words-only poster that called for support of the Democratic Party's ticket; it declared, "Two you can trust to bring peace to Vietnam." A different poster showed Humphrey pointing a finger at an audience during a speech (but, unlike Uncle Sam, not making eye contact), with the nation's colors behind him and the word "Unite." The Humphrey-Muskie "Student Coalition" also appealed directly to college students to support the ticket, with a poster titled "We're Coming Back!" and the message "Admit it … the Stakes are too high … "; the "V" hand sign, a gesture originally symbolizing "Victory" but popularized in the 1960s to mean "Peace," was incorporated into the poster, as well, to draw on antiwar sentiments.

Wallace, the American Independent Party candidate, who advocated "law-and-order," "states' rights," racially segregated schools, and victory in Vietnam, won forty-six electoral votes in the Deep South.[137] Wallace, who, polls indicated, had the support of over one-fifth of the voters five weeks before the election, wound up with 13.5 percent of the popular vote.[138] Despite all of Humphrey's disadvantages, he rose from 28 percent in the polls to almost 43 percent of the popular vote in that five-week period (but still received only 36 percent of the electoral votes).[139] The gain was probably the effect of a Humphrey speech that called for a halt to the bombing in Vietnam; his compelling attacks on both Nixon and Wallace; an infusion of monetary contributions; and the (late) backing of the supporters of the antiwar candidate, Eugene McCarthy, and McCarthy himself.[140] And, as Theodore White pointed out, the assistance organized labor gave to the Humphrey campaign was significant, with 4.6 million voters registered, one hundred fifteen million leaflets and pamphlets distributed—twenty million aimed at peeling off laborers from Wallace—and well over one hundred thousand workers engaged in "get-out-the-vote" drives.[141] Posters also targeted black voters: one poster, titled "Voting is Beautiful," featured a large black-and-white, close-up photograph of two young black persons, one of whom looked directly at the viewers; below the photograph was the message "Be Beautiful— Vote! Humphrey-Muskie" (Senator Edmund Muskie of Maine was the Democratic vice-presidential nominee). The Wallace campaign raised a great deal of money by selling campaign paraphernalia that was usually given away,[142] including posters that called on citizens to "Stand Up for America!" and laminated posters that were mounted on poles and carried at rallies.

In a landslide vote, Nixon was reelected in 1972. His opponent was Senator George McGovern of South Dakota, who received less than 38 percent of the popular vote and the electoral votes of only Massachusetts and the District of Columbia.[143] It was later discovered that a Nixon operative, Donald Segretti, had sabotaged the candidacy of Muskie (a potentially stronger Democratic candidate than McGovern). The "dirty tricks" that were played on McGovern and Humphrey (his primary opponent) hurt McGovern's campaign in the fall. This was followed by the break-in at the Democratic National Committee headquarters in Washington's Watergate Hotel, the cover-up of White House complicity, and the eventual resignation of Nixon before he could be impeached for obstruction of justice, abuse of power, and failure to comply with congressional subpoenas.[144] In any event, with the nation more peaceful domestically and fewer American troops stationed in Southeast Asia, McGovern would have lost, in all likelihood. Nixon was seen as a relatively successful incumbent, and, as Bloom stated, he ran as "the President," not as a "candidate," so "the media had no campaign style to criticize, or campaign blunders in which to catch him."[145] Most of Nixon's posters, in fact, referred to him as "President Nixon," or sometimes just as "The President."

Both campaigns advertised heavily. The McGovern campaign primarily utilized television for endorsement and concept spots, telethons, speeches, interviews with cutaways, a panel discussion, and a biography of the candidate broadcast. The Vietnam

War once again was the key issue, and McGovern, who had opposed U.S. involvement there since 1963, ran ads in various media that decried the human, economic, and strategic costs of the conflict. Although Nixon had not ended the war as he had promised four years earlier he would, and continued massive bombing, he had withdrawn all American ground combat forces and terminated the military draft. Consequently, the McGovern campaign was unable to convince a large segment of the public that its candidate could achieve peace more successfully than could Nixon; on the contrary, a poll taken less than one month before Election Day showed Nixon with a 32 percent margin over McGovern in handling Vietnam.[146] Organized labor, in one of the posters they issued, did try to use a Nixon quote against him, from a speech he delivered in the previous election campaign: "Those who have had a chance for four years and could not produce peace should not be given another chance." The poster also featured a caricature of the Republican candidate on a soapbox. Independent groups who opposed Nixon's reelection issued posters that showed civilian casualties.

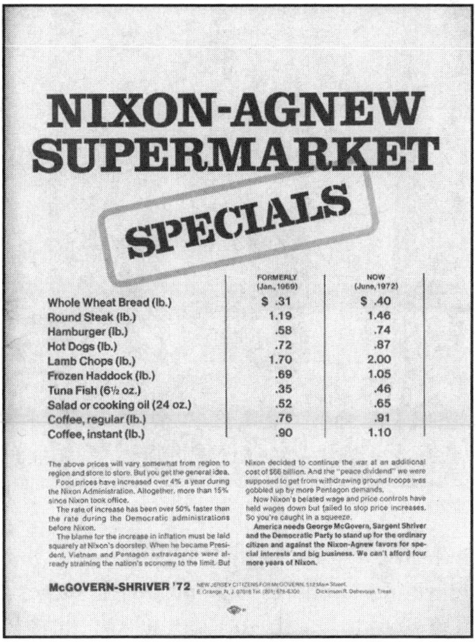
NIXON-AGNEW SUPERMARKET
SPECIALS

	FORMERLY (Jan., 1969)	NOW (June, 1972)
Whole Wheat Bread (lb.)	$ .31	$ .40
Round Steak (lb.)	1.19	1.46
Hamburger (lb.)	.58	.74
Hot Dogs (lb.)	.72	.87
Lamb Chops (lb.)	1.70	2.00
Frozen Haddock (lb.)	.69	1.05
Tuna Fish (6½ oz.)	.35	.46
Salad or cooking oil (24 oz.)	.52	.65
Coffee, regular (lb.)	.76	.91
Coffee, instant (lb.)	.90	1.10

The above prices will vary somewhat from region to region and store to store. But you get the general idea.
Food prices have increased over 4% a year during the Nixon Administration. Altogether, more than 15% since Nixon took office.
The rate of increase has been over 50% faster than the rate during the Democratic administrations before Nixon.
The blame for the increase in inflation must be laid squarely at Nixon's doorstep. When he became President, Vietnam and Pentagon extravagance were already straining the nation's economy to the limit. But Nixon decided to continue the war at an additional cost of $66 billion. And the "peace dividend" we were supposed to get from withdrawing ground troops was gobbled up by more Pentagon demands.
Now Nixon's belated wage and price controls have held wages down but failed to stop price increases. So you're caught in a squeeze.
America needs George McGovern, Sargent Shriver and the Democratic Party to stand up for the ordinary citizen and against the Nixon-Agnew favors for special interests and big business. We can't afford four more years of Nixon.

McGOVERN-SHRIVER '72

Figure 3.17

Little was said of the military service of either candidate, contrary to what had been the case in past (and future) U.S. elections, even though McGovern had won medals in combat as a pilot during World War II.[147] Although the focus was mainly on America's involvement in Vietnam, groups opposed to Nixon, and his vice president, Spiro Agnew, also distributed broadsides on domestic concerns. An example is shown in Figure 3.17, "Nixon-Agnew Supermarket Specials," which pointed to the rise in food prices during Nixon's four-year term. Another broadside protested his "broken promises" to extend "good health care … to all our citizens."

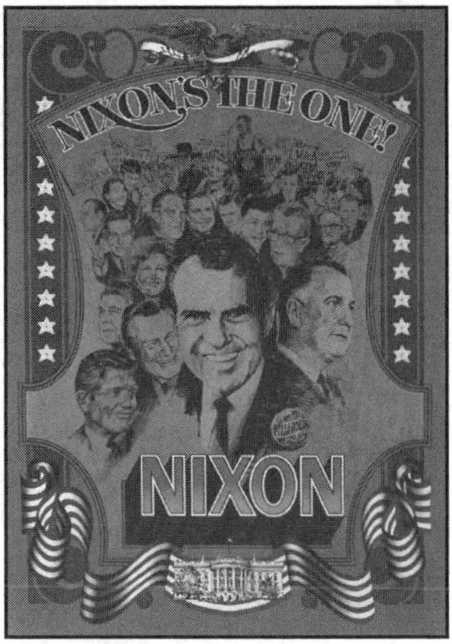

Figure 3.18

Two groups, the Committee to Re-Elect the President and Democrats for Nixon, created a multitude of advertisements, including appeals designed for younger voters, since the voting age had been lowered to eighteen two years earlier.[148] Even before this change, in 1968, when posters were becoming popular again, particularly with high school and college students, the National Youth for Nixon-Agnew distributed a "Nixon's

the One!" poster that was calculated to appeal to younger voters, even if it was hardly "with it" (see Fig. 3.18). The campaign planners hoped to attract them and win their votes by surrounding a smiling Nixon with celebrities such as actors Clint Eastwood and Paul

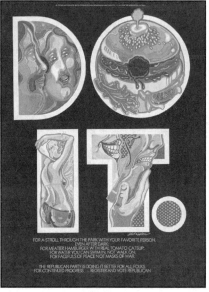

Newman, basketball player Wilt Chamberlain, and the youthful mayor of New York City, John Lindsay; incorporated were some graphic embellishments, such as zoom shadows on the candidate's name and an orange-and-red color scheme. Symbols of patriotism and power were added: stars, stripes, an eagle, and the White House.

By the 1972 election campaign, posters were even more popular among youth, who were pinning posters of music and entertainment artists on their walls—some of them wildly imaginative; and some of the Republican posters that targeted this group were risqué and graphically stylish. At least one Pop Art, voter-registration poster for Nixon included a scantily clothed woman, inside the "I" in the message "Do It!" (Fig. 3.19). The Nixon campaign in 1972 merely followed the practices of the advertising

Figure 3.19

industry, by associating brands with sex when appealing to young adults to buy products. Other Republican posters—designed to appeal to "middle-American youth"—were more stylistically conservative.[149] For example, one was patterned after a movie poster from the 1930s;[150] another was dominated by a sepia-toned, genial Nixon in the center, bordered by scenes of him speaking with young people, walking on a beach with his wife and wearing a turtleneck shirt, and participating in diplomatic missions. Here was a poster that used warm colors and photographs (as well as outlined lettering in a slight wave) to convey an image of a more "humanized" Nixon, even though he wore formal attire in all but one photograph. Young Voters for the President, who collected one dollar for each one circulated, issued this poster. The group distributed another poster that portrayed Nixon talking to a young boy. It highlighted the administration's themes and accomplishments, such

Figure 3.20

as ending the draft and supporting education. Relevant visuals were included, as was the slogan "Now More Than Ever," in casual, sans-serif letters. A statement by Nixon graced the top of the design: "For the first time in 20 years we are spending more on human resources than on defense!"

Some of the McGovern posters were also intended to appeal to younger voters. N. Schneider designed a series of posters for the McGovern for President Committee, all of which were colorful, exuberant, and stylized: one was dominated by a drawing of a leafy tree, accompanied by the phrase "A time to grow in a world of permanent change"; another showed the sun breaking through the clouds, along with the slogan "A little light in a cold world"; one illustrated a hand making the "V" peace sign; one more featured doves, each labeled with a positive, peaceful message (Fig. 3.20). Another group issued a poster that used abstract color patches as a background for one of the McGovern campaign's slogans, "Come home America." The candidate was nowhere to be found on any of these posters. A photograph of McGovern was included in a poster that appealed directly to "young Americans" to work and vote for him: it stated simply, "It's Your Campaign. He's Your Candidate."[151] Not to be outdone, the Nixon campaign produced a poster with the same goals, headlined "This is Your Country ... and your country needs Nixon-Agnew ... and YOU!"

A single photograph of McGovern was the principal element in most of his campaign posters, and the wording was brief. Figure 3.21 is a good example of one of these: the title says merely "McGovern • President '72"; however, the design is atypical of most campaign posters in that, like a Kennedy design from 1960, it showed the candidate in profile—rather than addressing the voters directly or looking out at an audience. McGovern is shown with his jacket missing and his tie loosened in an attempt to convey informality (as opposed to Nixon's suited stiffness). A Republican poster that year broke tradition by presenting Nixon in a full-length profile (Fig. 3.22). In this poster, the viewers see much less of the face than in the McGovern or Kennedy posters (see Fig. 3.12 for the latter one). President Nixon is seen gazing out of a White House window contemplatively, accompanied by the following quotation:

The nation needs coolness more than clarion calls;
intelligence more than charisma;
a sense of history more than a sense of histrionics.

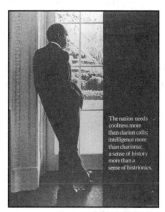

Figure 3.21   *Figure 3.22*

This was an effective summation of a campaign theme, which was appropriate for a nation that seemed to desire tranquility and social order over street protests and social unrest. Most of the posters of both parties continued the trend to avoid or downplay the party affiliation of the candidate—an approach that, overall, had been followed for at least three decades. Not only had visual images taken a more central role over the years than positions on specific issues, but a lack of connection to one's political party had developed as well.

Less than one year after the huge Republican victory, Agnew was forced to resign, because of charges of corruption, bribery, and tax evasion while he was the county executive of Baltimore, governor of Maryland, and vice president. Gerald Ford, Minority Leader of the House of Representatives, replaced Agnew, and then became president when Nixon resigned in late summer, 1974. An "outsider" from Washington politics, Jimmy Carter of Georgia—former governor, naval nuclear engineer, and peanut-farm manager—won the presidency over Ford by a narrow margin of 2 percent in the popular vote and by 11 percent in the electoral vote.[152] Ford, the consummate "insider," had been damaged by his pardon of Nixon and by his claim during the first televised presidential debate since 1960 that Poland was not under Soviet domination. Carter ran a populist campaign that opposed the influence of the "rich" and "powerful" in government, and "big shot crooks" avoiding prison time for their crimes while the poor were punished.[153] His television commercials reinforced these themes, and decried the high unemployment rate, while building his populist image by showing him in work clothes on his Georgia farm and pulling weeds in the field.[154] Some of Carter's posters enhanced this persona, although much more subtly, by depicting him in an open-collared work shirt leaning on a bin of peanuts, smiling and looking directly at the audience. Another Washington insider, Senator Walter Mondale of Minnesota, was Carter's running mate, but was not shown on many of the posters.

According to Jamieson, both the Democrats and Republicans concentrated their spending more on mass media advertising than on traditional campaign paraphernalia;[155] 30- and 60-second TV commercials that focused on "character" rather than issues were generally favored once again.[156] As John Deardourff, one of President Ford's advertising advisors, noted, "Our studies show that there is no correlation between how the voter feels about an issue and the candidate of his choice," and researcher Daniel Yankelovich confirmed this, stating that "personality" and "credibility" were more important than issues.[157]

The Democratic Party also mounted successful drives to register black and Hispanic voters.[158] The 1976 Democratic Presidential Campaign Committee issued a leaflet that opened into an $8\frac{1}{2} \times 11$-inch poster titled "Leaders, for a Change," which was circulated in black neighborhoods. On the back of the poster/leaflet, the issues of racial equality, housing, welfare, and the economy were highlighted. Other groups were targeted also, and the Democrats even designed a similar poster in French that they distributed throughout New Orleans. Perhaps the most attractive poster of the campaign was presented as a montage of line drawings of Carter at various stages of his life (specifically, as a peanut farmer, naval officer, and candidate), and showed him with family members and Martin Luther King, Sr., with an American flag backdrop (Fig. 3.23). The slogan again emphasized change, leadership, and patriotism: "A New Vision for America."

The Ford campaign strategized that its candidate could win by "acting presidential," and by attacking Carter's lack of national qualifications and his liberal beliefs in a way that would cast doubt on him.[159] The Ford slogan "He's making us proud again" was used on a poster that depicted him, conservatively dressed in a suit and tie, looking serious, but staring away from the viewers (unlike most of Carter's posters). The photographer shot the portrait of Ford from below (as was done in the poster shown in Figure 1.12, Chapter One, with Ford formally dressed as well), so that he would seem more visually commanding. However, Ford's campaign slogan, as Jamieson noted, boomeranged, because it reminded some voters of his pardon of Nixon and the former president's shameful actions.[160] The president also appeared in a poster with his running mate, Senator Robert Dole of Kansas, but again

Figure 3.23

Ford (and Dole) was conservatively dressed and profiled against a blurred background of trees. Later, Ford's television commercials started to represent him "as a dependable father figure who quietly inspire[d] feelings of serenity," Joseph Lelyveld wrote in the *New York Times* during the campaign.[161] These spots showed Ford, sans tie, to be a more mature version of Carter, a down-to-earth, family man who could be trusted. During this phase of the campaign, Betty Ford appeared for the first time next to her husband in a poster.[162] Nevertheless, the changes in Ford's advertising campaign could not overcome the political problems and perceptions that beleaguered it.

Carter's term as president was only about a year old, when a group opposed to his Panama Canal treaties issued a poster that urged his defeat in 1980; to raise money for their campaign, they sold each copy for $1.75. This poster was dominated by a photograph of the cigar-smoking dictator of Panama, General Omar Torrijos, who had negotiated the treaties that would turn over the canal to his country. United States conservatives condemned the treaties for giving up rights of sovereignty and for undermining security. Ronald Reagan, who had recently retired as the governor of California—and had almost gained the Republican nomination over President Ford in 1976, with the canal a core issue in the Californian's campaign—criticized Carter on Panama, even before the negotiations on the treaties concluded. Reagan stated that the Carter administration had a "double standard" on human rights, disapproving of violations in Chile, Argentina, and Brazil, but ignoring them in Panama and in Communist nations, and that the United States should not relinquish ownership of the canal.[163]

The accords with Panama were ratified, despite Reagan's determined opposition, and were followed by Carter's successful diplomatic efforts in the Middle East, which resulted in a peace agreement between Egypt and Israel. A year before the election, however, extremists took over the U.S. embassy in Tehran, Iran, holding more than fifty Americans hostage there throughout the entire 1980 election campaign. All efforts by the Carter administration to free them failed. On the domestic front, raging inflation, gasoline lines, and increased unemployment hurt Carter's political standing. By late 1979, President Carter's approval rating in the Gallup Poll had descended to 29 percent.[164] The leading question, which pinpointed the feelings of many about the state of the nation, was posed by Reagan to more than one hundred million viewers during the second televised debate with the president: "It might be well if you would ask yourself, are you better off than you were four years ago?"[165] A majority of the country's voters answered that question with a "No," and elected Reagan by a 10-point margin in the popular vote (with moderate third-party candidate Congressman John Anderson of Illinois capturing about 7 percent).[166] Four years later, Reagan was reelected by almost double his previous margin.[167] In both elections, the Democratic ticket received only 41 percent of the vote and lost in the Electoral College by overwhelming margins.[168]

The Re-Elect Carter-Mondale campaign in 1980 apparently failed to pretest their basic poster design (Fig. 3.24) with focus groups, which was unfortunate because, unlike the

ticket's main poster design four years earlier, it was not very good. Rather than being presented smiling confidently, the candidates looked almost grim; instead of facing the voters, they were gazing away; in place of the hopeful slogan about leadership and change was "A Tested and Trustworthy Team." Many voters might have agreed that they had been tested, but had they passed? Another poster design for Carter was an improvement: the president and vice president were shown behind a podium smiling and looking out toward the audience, but the podium posed an "obstacle" between the candidates and the voters. In addition, the slogan "Keep them working for you" was probably also not beneficial to the campaign, considering some of the problems that had developed during the Democrats' term of office.

Figure 3.24

Reagan's team, on the other hand, authorized the distribution of poster designs that were excellent, both for the 1980 campaign and for Reagan's reelection campaign four

years later. A full-color photograph of Reagan in a cowboy hat and open workshirt was prominent in one 1980 poster. Like Carter in 1976, Reagan was presented as an "outsider" in touch with "the common folk," and here he was smiling and looking directly at the viewers, faded drawings of the Statue of Liberty, farmland, New York City, Washington, D.C., and the American flag in the background (Fig. 3.25). The slogan was short and patriotic, associating the candidate with the nation: "America, Reagan Country." The patriotism was reinforced by the word *America*, in which the bottoms of its letters were filled with red-and-white stripes, the tops were filled with blue, and the dot of the "i" was represented by one star.

Figure 3.25

Other 1980 Reagan posters displayed the flag behind the smiling, direct candidate, with the slogans "Let's make America great again" and "The time is now," or simply "Reagan."

Although Reagan was the favored candidate of the right wing of the Republican Party, his posters avoided the "in-your-face" tone of many of those produced in the Goldwater campaign sixteen years earlier. Both parties in the 1980 campaign used television commercials extensively, but the Republicans employed them most effectively, with Reagan (known as "The Great Communicator") addressing television viewers directly—just as he did in his posters—much of the time.[169]

In a poster for his successful 1984 campaign, Reagan was shown with his vice president, George H. W. Bush, the flag flying prominently behind them and the White House in front and to the side of Reagan. Again, Reagan (now in suit and tie) was seen smiling benignly at the voters, as "The President" (see Fig. 1.13, Chapter One). This poster is similar in style to a Carter-Mondale poster of 1976 in some ways, in that both posters used the flag and White House comparably, together with artistic drawings of smiling candidates. There were two differences: eye contact (Carter and Mondale were shown looking away in the earlier poster); and the style of the slogans (the 1976 poster stated "Challenging Leadership for Challenging Times" while the 1984 design used the much simpler "Bringing America Back!"). Of course, the Democrats in the earlier campaign *were* the challengers; Reagan and Bush were the incumbents in the latter election. Another simple, yet appealing Reagan-Bush '84 poster displayed full-color photographs of the smiling duo in a circle, with the ubiquitous flag behind them, and the same three-word, conservative slogan, with the addition of "Prouder, Stronger, Better." Reagan's campaign theme was similar to that of Ford (again, whose slogan was "He's making us proud again") in 1976, but much more effective. There were also posters that included Reagan and Bush smiling and gazing directly, and the slogan "Leadership you can trust!"

The 1984 election result was never in doubt, with Reagan a very popular incumbent in a period of relative peace and prosperity—a situation similar to that of Eisenhower in the 1956 campaign.[170] The Democrats nominated former vice president Mondale, who selected New York Congresswomen Geraldine Ferraro as the first woman to run for a national office on a major-party ticket. Posters of the trailblazing ticket showed them waving from the convention podium or Ferraro smiling and Mondale tenaciously clenching his fist while making a point (the imagery perhaps echoing the Democrats' slogan—used in other ads—"Fighting for the Future"). Special interest groups, such as the National Education Association and various unions, distributed brochures, which unfolded into large posters, and promotional packages. One such package, containing twenty items, was produced and distributed by the United Food and Commercial Workers International Union (UFCW). It included not only a full-color Mondale-Ferraro poster, but also a twenty-eight-page analysis of Reagan's National Labor Relations Board, a sample campaign speech, five press releases, a bumper sticker, three illustration clipsheets, a brochure, a peel-off sticker, a union magazine that covered the Democratic convention, and other material. Unfortunately, the UFCW poster was dominated by a photograph that cast the candidates in, literally, a "bad light," since it was taken in bright sunlight, effecting deep shadows around their eyes, which were almost obliterated; it captured Mondale and Ferraro with grim facial expressions, as well.

The biggest problems in Mondale's campaign, however, were his call for higher taxes to cut the budget deficits that had accumulated under Reagan; the fiasco that resulted from not hiring anyone to produce television advertisements until the early fall and the lack of a solid theme in these commercials; the questionable financial dealings of Ferraro's husband (which she tried to laugh off); and the challenger's failure to decisively best Reagan in their second debate. All of these hurt his cause and contributed to the magnitude of the Democratic defeat.[171] In addition, Mondale was associated with the Carter administration's record, which certainly hurt him in the 1984 campaign. For example, in a poll of voters who indicated that inflation was one of the two most important issues, only 17 percent favored Mondale.[172] One group, Students for America, issued a satirical "movie poster" for "The Return of Walter Mondale (Rated 'R' for 'Rip-Off')," which told of the "malaise," "boredom," and "runaway inflation" that would be seen in such a production. Besides the attacks on Mondale by outside groups, the Reagan people ran a television campaign, "Morning in America," which effectively communicated the theme "America is back"[173] (i.e., back to a better economy and positive feelings about the country and its leadership); that idea was also conveyed in some posters.

Vice President Bush succeeded Reagan as president in 1988. Bush defeated the Democratic Party's candidate, Governor Michael Dukakis of Massachusetts, by 8 percent of the popular vote and by a large electoral margin.[174] Visual media images were prominent in the 1988 campaign, some successful with the public and others backfiring: Bush shaking hands with Russian president Mikhail Gorbachev and Polish leader Lech Wałęsa; Dukakis, riding atop a tank and wearing an army helmet; Bush's visit to a flag factory; shots of garbage in Boston Harbor (in Dukakis' home state); and the face of an angry black man, Willie Horton, imprisoned for murder, but furloughed under a program signed by Governor Dukakis, only to commit violent crimes while out of prison. The power of television to influence voters was demonstrated not only by spot ads that used the Willie Horton case, but also by Dukakis' reply to the initial question of his second debate with Bush, in which he was asked whether he would be in favor of the death penalty for someone who raped and killed the Democratic candidate's wife. When Bush showed more passion in his response to the question (as well as favoring the death penalty) than did Dukakis, who stated, "I've opposed the death penalty during all my life" and "I don't see any evidence that it's a deterrent,"[175] it confirmed for many viewers that the Democrat was an unfeeling, "knee-jerk liberal," who was too "easy" on criminals.

Republican strategists and media advisors, working for Bush, put together a devastating political marketing campaign, which focused on the Horton furlough, designed to tarnish Dukakis. The campaign consisted of four components: televised spots (the most effective being one that included stark, black-and-white shots of a guard near a prison fence and inmates moving through a revolving door with bars around it), a radio commercial, a newspaper ad, and a direct mail flier. Horton was featured in the flier (a modern broadside) that was easily tacked on bulletin boards. It contained a menacing photograph of the prisoner, and various headlines in different states, such as "Will Dukakis Turn Gun Owners Into Criminals … While Murderers Go Free?" and "Gov. 'gave pardons to 21 drug dealers.' How Serious Is Dukakis About Crime?" The Horton flier (along with a brochure that showed a photograph of the Republican vice-presidential candidate,

Senator Dan Quayle of Indiana, standing next to his "friends," the Ayatollah Khomeini of Iran and General Manuel Noriega of Panama) was among the direct mail deluge during the election.[176] In New York State alone, the Horton direct mail campaign reached several hundred thousand people.[177] Although fundraising was the primary objective of these mailings, direct mail attacks on the opposition were now more prevalent, Dukakis sustaining most of the damage.[178] The Democrats issued their own fliers (which could also be displayed), but they paled in comparison to those used in the Republican assault. One, for instance, asked "working families" to "take a close look" at Bush's "experience" as head of a trade commission with Japan, stating,

> Bush came back from Japan saying that US-Japan trade relations were superb.
> *Superb for Japan Maybe.*
> *Superb for Japanese Workers.*
> *Bad News for American Working Families.*
> Michael Dukakis Stands Up to Foreign Competition.

Large and small broadsides were printed, too, by state labor organizations in support of the Democratic presidential candidate. One, distributed by the Pennsylvania AFL-CIO, was positive, giving "12 good reasons to vote for Michael Dukakis … "; another compared the positions of Bush and Dukakis on such issues as plant closings, the minimum wage, and workplace safety and health (see Fig. 1.6, Chapter One). The latter used an unflattering photograph of the president and an appealing one of his challenger. Nothing, however, could match the Horton package. The damage inflicted on Dukakis from this media campaign was marked: with less than a month to go before Election Day, his lead in the polls was gone.[179] The TV spot and direct mail campaign had clearly played upon the racial fears of white voters. As Herbert Parmet stated, "The Willie Horton issue became a classic example of how to exploit racial divisions. … It was a prison furlough issue, which had sufficient political implications in itself but, making it far more sensitive, a matter that was more upsetting to the public's psyche, the specter of murderous blacks turned loose."[180] After Dukakis was soundly defeated, Gordon Reece, who had coordinated victories for the British Conservative Party, and was another advocate of emphasizing emotions over issues, declared that the Dukakis campaign had made "mistakes of absolutely heroic dimensions."[181] The Democratic political marketing communications team failed to deliver timely and effective responses to counter the attacks on its candidate, and the image of a "weak, liberal governor" was ingrained in the minds of many voters.

Unions distributed a great deal of printed material, including posters. One produced by the UFCW showed a full-color photograph of the Democratic candidate speaking next to an American flag, with a crowd (in black-and-white) in the background. The only words visible from a distance were "Dukakis" and the union's initials

Figure 3.26

(Fig. 3.26). Another poster, distributed by the American Federation of State, County, and Municipal Employees (AFSCME) also lacked a slogan, and depicted only the smiling Dukakis and his running mate, Senator Lloyd Bentsen of Texas, photographed from below against a blue sky, and the candidates' names and "'88." An AFL-CIO poster featured a color photograph of a serious-looking Dukakis gazing far away, to his right (suggestive of George Washington crossing the Delaware River), with the flag behind him.[182] Few Dukakis posters, however, featured any visuals or portraits of the candidates on the ticket. One poster, issued by the Democratic National Committee, was a collage of buttons, DNC passes, bumper stickers, promotional photographs, and campaign comic books, but there was neither text nor photographs of the candidate, other than what were included on the paraphernalia themselves. Another poster distributed by the Dukakis for President Committee looked like a giant bumper sticker, and said simply "Mike Dukakis for President '88." The Democratic state-run organizations issued similar posters to promote the ticket. These were simply printed on cardboard to be used in rallies, for such placards had been employed since the Nixon campaigns. The Dukakis campaign in 1988, by all accounts, started a trend by national campaign organizations to use only words in most of the posters they produced. Although American political parties had issued similar posters for at least two decades, most of those distributed incorporated visuals.

The Bush campaign printed a similar poster, but the national organization designed several visually dominant ones. The Republicans produced a poster that featured a

photograph of Bush and Quayle together in the convention hall, waving and smiling, with the slogan "Leadership for America." There was also a black-and-white line drawing of the two, looking more serious. In addition, a poster—presenting Bush in his U.S. Navy bomber jacket—was printed to reach at least three audiences: pro-military voters, veterans, and the voters who "raise the family, pay the taxes, meet the mortgage" (Fig. 3.27). The back of the poster was used to compare Bush to Dukakis, akin to that of the Dukakis broadside (although from the other side of the political fence). The first statement in the Bush column was "As President, will not raise taxes—period." Unlike in the McGovern campaign, the Bush strategists widely publicized their candidate's valor in wartime, during which he won the Distinguished Flying Cross. To appeal more concretely

Figure 3.27   to the family-minded voters, the Republicans issued a horizontal poster that showed Bush and his wife, sitting on his lawn, with seventeen members of his family, including sons, future president George W. and future Florida governor Jeb.

Much negative advertising, however, marked the campaign. A poll indicated that a healthy majority of the public did not like the increased negative campaign tactics, but polls also suggested that these tactics worked to sway opinion.[183] Undoubtedly, the Horton ads both reflected and shaped public perceptions: 19 percent of respondents in a national survey maintained that "public order" was the most important problem facing the country (up from only 4 percent in 1984)—which was second to "deficit/government spending" at 32 percent.[184] Billboards, by this time most commonly used in state and local races, were also utilized to paint a negative picture of Dukakis as a "liberal" who would be tougher on citizens than on criminals. These were used in targeted areas such as regions of Texas, and billboards declared that the Democrat would prevent people from owning guns.[185]

Outgoing president Reagan, in the waning days of the 1988 campaign, wrapped up many of the Republican arguments against Dukakis that had damaged his image so much: the Democrat was against the death penalty, and his state furlough program for prisoners was, as Reagan claimed, "the most liberal prison program since Billy the Kid sprung the Lincoln County jail."[186] It certainly helped Bush that the nation was at peace; unemployment had gone from 7.5 percent to 5.2 percent during the Reagan-Bush administration; the prime interest rate had decreased from 15.5 percent to 10 percent; and the rate of inflation had plummeted to 4.2 percent from a catastrophic 12.5 percent.[187] The images created for Bush—and, earlier, Reagan—clearly resonated with many voters, and were instantly recognizable in their posters. Reagan was portrayed as a "cowboy" in touch with the country and its people in his 1980 posters; Bush was depicted as a "war hero" who had been a player on the world stage diplomatically in his 1988 ads. But the strategy that ensured Bush's reelection that year was the decision of his advisors to use negative advertising, while continuing to manage his image.

Bush's pledge of "Read my lips: No new taxes"—recited during his acceptance speech at the Republican convention on August, 18, 1988[188]—came back to haunt him and helped lead to his defeat when he ran for reelection in 1992 against Governor Bill Clinton of Arkansas. Bush believed that he had to break his pledge to cut the budget deficit when the economy fell into recession.[189] Again, image management (or "character," as the strategists liked to say) was important. Clinton, who was being accused of "dodging" military service during the Vietnam War (and, later, being dishonest about his avoidance efforts), appeared on television speaking at the American Legion annual convention, at which he admitted that he had not wanted to serve; the Republicans tried to use the phrase "family values" to evoke images of Bush and Quayle as solid, moral leaders, who stood for the traditional parental unit and against abortion and single motherhood (as opposed to Clinton, who many perceived as a philanderer and untruthful).[190]

Bush had his own image problem concerning honesty, particularly late in the campaign, when information about his awareness of the Iran-Contra dealings while he was vice president was circulated by a special prosecutor, after Bush had denied knowledge about trading arms to Iran to release American hostages it had held (with some funds also going to antigovernment rebels in Nicaragua). This disclosure surfaced a few days before Election Day, when one poll showed that the president's numbers had caught up with Clinton's. It eliminated Bush's best line of attack—on his opponent's trustworthiness—and he lost about 5 percentage points in the polls.[191]

Television was the venue by which much of the campaign was contested, with three debates and a mix of positive and negative ads; it was radio, however, that was the medium frequently chosen to convey the most negative messages.[192] Nevertheless, the primary share of the major parties' monies went for television advertising: the Bush campaign spent about three-fourths of its funds on these ads; the Clinton campaign about two-thirds.[193] Brochures, newspaper ads, and other printed material were used in the various political campaigns, but less than had been the case four years earlier—the same recession that damaged Bush's reelection chances also reduced the amount of funds available to the party for print endeavors. The recession also accelerated political communication strategies that employed computer technology to deliver the message to targeted groups, rather than using more expensive and often broader advertising methods. Interestingly, orders for posters and yard signs were stable, since they were viewed as "essentials" (as opposed to bags, refrigerator magnets, pencils, and other paraphernalia).[194]

The Republican National Committee released a patriotic poster that asked voters to "Stand By The President," bombarding them with a multitude of blue stars and red stripes on a white background (Fig. 3.28). Clinton allies, particularly those in organized labor, distributed posters, with a portrait of him either, like Bush, smiling and looking at the viewers (Fig. 3.29)—or interacting with students, or people at a union-sponsored campaign rally. Fewer posters, however, included photographs or artwork. More frequently,

Figure 3.28   *Figure 3.29*

major and minor parties issued campaign posters that solely featured large logos that were also used on bumper stickers, buttons, letterheads, and other material. The Clinton posters—and more significantly, his television commercials—not only emphasized his "competence" and "leadership," but also called for "change." His hairstyle was similar to that of John F. Kennedy, and his TV spots included a clip of him as a young man, shown, in slow motion, meeting President Kennedy, inferring that they had comparable campaign themes and were preferable to their more "experienced" opponents.[195]

The trend of "logo posters" was evident in the campaign posters of a third-party candidate, Ross Perot, a billionaire Texas businessperson, who received 19 percent of the popular vote:[196] most of his posters simply featured his last name and stars and stripes in red, white, and blue. Perot's showing was second only to Theodore Roosevelt's in 1912 for an independent candidate in the twentieth century, even though the Texan had withdrawn from the race in the middle of the campaign and then reentered it. His primary issue was the growing budget deficit. It was also one, along with the general economic situation, that Clinton emphasized. A sign in Clinton's main headquarters summed up the main campaign theme that won the presidency for the Democrats: "The economy, stupid."[197] Of Clinton's TV spots that were issue-oriented, 80 percent concerned the economy; of Bush's issue-oriented spots, only 8 percent mentioned the economy.[198] Clinton's winning margin was 5.5 percent, and he garnered more than two-thirds of the electoral vote and became the first Democratic president elected since 1976 (when Jimmy Carter, another Southern moderate, won).[199]

Perot ran again in 1996, but Clinton won easily over Dole, who had run with Ford twenty years earlier, and the Texas independent candidate. This time, Perot was supported by only about 8 percent of the electorate, and Clinton's popular-vote margin expanded to 8.5 percent (with about the same margin in the Electoral College as in his previous victory).[200] One way this election year differed from 1992 was that the incumbent benefited from a good economy and a lower budget deficit. Clinton's reelection seemed inevitable; peace and prosperity were, once again, the two key ingredients for reelection. The only surprise was that he did not win by a larger margin in the popular vote against a fairly weak Republican opponent, particularly after the president seized the long-standing Republican issues of welfare reform and deficit reduction and made them his own. It was more difficult than in the past to brand the Democratic presidential candidate as a "liberal," since, as one of Dole's advertising advisors put it, "now … there [were] two Republican parties"; instead, it was the Democrats, in their television ads, who successfully labeled the opposition as "extremists."[201] It did appear that Clinton lost some support in the final weeks of the campaign, after some of his fundraising techniques were criticized.[202] Dole's slogans on his posters, "A Better Man for a Better America" and "Trust Dole," tried to make character and morality the key issues in the campaign, but these themes did not seem to resonate with enough Americans to get him elected.[203] Clinton's campaign slogan, "Building Bridges to Our Future," which appeared on some posters, ignored his opponent and was more forward-looking.

Political advertising on television again was the dominant means of trying to influence the voting public; though it increased from four years before, it had begun earlier (the first Clinton-Gore TV commercial was seen in June 1995).[204] One significant development was the rise of the Internet as a political force in national election campaigns. Approximately one-fourth of the voting public had access to the Internet, but all major parties and candidates had Web sites.[205] This was only the beginning of the role the Internet plays in presidential politics, with a mere 8 percent of voters reporting that they had been to a "politically oriented" Web site.[206] Nevertheless, after Dole mentioned his Web site in the first presidential debate, it registered two million hits in the next twenty-four hours.[207] Dole's site was the first to allow users the opportunity to create their own buttons and posters, and Clinton's site provided the means to print bumper stickers. Traditional posters and lawn signs seemed to be produced in large quantities, but the former were used mainly at rallies to provide a good backdrop for the candidates when they were shown briefly on the television newscasts. It was not necessary, therefore, to include a portrait—or, for that matter, any distracting picture—on them. In fact, when Paul Ekman, an expert on "reading" human facial expressions, was asked to analyze portraits of the 1996 presidential candidates in their campaign posters, he stated "they're not making posters with pictures these days."[208]

The 2000 election was one of the closest and most controversial in the nation's history. The Democrats nominated Clinton's vice president, Albert Gore, and the Republicans selected Governor George W. Bush of Texas (the son of the man Clinton defeated eight years earlier). Gore, who had much experience on the national stage in the executive and legislative branches of the federal government, as a senator and congressman from Tennessee, ran television commercials that asked whether Bush, who had no such experience, was "ready to lead America."[209] He also selected as his running mate Senator Joseph Lieberman of Connecticut, an experienced moderate, who was the first Jewish nominee on a national ticket. In past elections, however, Washington "outsiders" often seemed to have an advantage; ironically, the last "insider" to win the presidency was Bush's father in 1988. In the twentieth century, Clinton, Reagan, Franklin Roosevelt, Wilson, and even Nixon all had defeated politicians perceived to be based in the nation's capital. On the other hand, 2000 was a year that saw overall peace and prosperity, both of which usually favored the incumbent's party. It was ironic that Bush's father was the last vice president to win the presidency in his own right during a period of peace and prosperity.

Gore's advertising campaign was both positive and negative. It emphasized his "experience, vision, values" and the economic record of the Clinton administration, together with his service in Vietnam as an army reporter-photographer; but it heavily criticized Bush's plans for some privatization in the Social Security System and withdrawal of military forces from the Balkans, as well as his record as governor.[210] Bush's ads, on the other hand, attacked Gore as "untruthful" in some of his statements, specifically those about the cost of a prescription drug, raising campaign funds in a Buddhist temple, and "creating the Internet." They also focused on presenting the Republican's "no child left behind" program in education and his plans to help the elderly, along with his desire to reform Social Security.[211] One study found that whereas almost two-thirds of the Gore campaign's spot ads were negative, about the same proportion of Bush's spots were positive.[212] Again, most of the posters produced did not show the candidates themselves; instead, the practice of using names and symbols continued: Republican posters included a stylized American flag, and sometimes a slogan in English or Spanish, such as "*Un Nuevo Día*" (A New Day) (Fig. 3.30); the Gore-Lieberman ticket circulated posters that displayed a shooting star and the year.

Figure 3.30

The New York State Council of Black Elected Democrats did issue a poster that included photographs, but not any that featured the candidates.

The reality was that there were no dramatic differences on the issues and that, once again, as communication professor Tobe Berkovitz remarked, "image, persona, has become … important as a criteria: Who is this person, what is his character, does he care about people like me?"[213] This is where Gore did not seem to do particularly well. Proportionately, the Gore campaign produced significantly more TV spots that focused on issues than did the Bush campaign, which designed more "image" spots that focused on personality attributes, researchers found.[214] Content analysis of these television spots also revealed that Bush smiled and made eye contact much more frequently than Gore did in his commercials, and that the Bush ads used significantly tighter camera shots.[215] One negative TV spot issued by the Gore campaign alleged that Bush had given preferential treatment to oil interests in Texas, ending with "By favoring the few, George W. Bush would hurt the many."[216] Bush's spots, by contrast, depicted him as a "compassionate conservative," who cared about education and prescription drugs for senior citizens. Bush's more positive, direct, and character-oriented ad campaign may well have been the difference in this close election, in which the odds favored his opponent.

More than 50 percent of American voters now had access to the World Wide Web.[217] All the presidential candidates had Web sites that successfully raised monies for their campaigns. The Bush campaign's Web site even posted all spot advertisements, including one that promoted the Web site itself. It greatly expanded what the 1996 Dole Web site allowed, in that Bush supporters could not only print posters, but also download other graphics, including wallpaper and screen savers. Gore's Web site was noted for its high-technology features, such as its ability to telecast live the candidate campaigning.[218]

Gore did not seem to "connect" with enough voters to win, despite the advantages he had as a member of a successful administration. He clearly was not as good a campaigner as Clinton (from whom he tried to distance himself, after the president was impeached), seemed ill at ease during televised debates, and came across as "phony" when he followed advice on how to behave and what to wear. On the other hand, Bush generally surpassed expectations with his campaigning style, and many people perceived him as likeable and having integrity.[219] In addition, as Kenneth Goldstein speculated, Gore appealed to the left in his campaign to sway people from voting for Green Party candidate Ralph Nader, which probably cost him votes with independent and undecided voters. He also had to spend millions of dollars on television commercials in typically Democratic states to ensure that votes for Nader did not throw them into the Republican column.[220]

The outcome of the election was not decided until the evening of December 12, 2000, when the Supreme Court ruled by one vote that disputed ballots in Florida could not be counted.[221] Bush's margin in Florida was determined to be only five hundred thirty-seven votes out of almost six million that were cast in that state, and minor party candidates Nader and Patrick Buchanan of the Reform Party received, respectively, about ninety-seven thousand and seventeen thousand votes there.[222] Florida's twenty-five electoral votes went to Bush and with them the presidency. Gore had won the national popular vote by a margin of one-half of 1 percent, and he became the first candidate since 1876 to win the popular vote, but lose a disputed election in the Electoral College.[223] As for the popular vote, it was the closest election since 1960, when there was a 0.17 percent difference between Kennedy and Nixon.[224] Personality and expectation factors—along with the slimmest possible majority of the highest court in the nation—had seemingly played a large part in the election result: the candidate of the challenging party had gained power from the candidate of the ruling party, with neither major military conflicts nor economic problems on the horizon. That was to change very soon.

On September 11, 2001, al-Qaeda terrorists slammed passenger jets that they had hijacked into the World Trade Center buildings in New York City, the Pentagon in Washington, D.C., and into a field in Pennsylvania. About three thousand persons lost their lives on "9/11," and by early October, the United States was at war in Afghanistan (where al-Qaeda training camps existed). Republicans again nominated George W. Bush at their convention in New York City almost exactly three years later, and most of the defining words from his acceptance speech, "We will build a safer world and a more hopeful America," had already been printed on a large banner in the hall.[225]

With the economy ostensibly recovering from recession, Bush's main themes of "security" and "hope" proved successful in the 2004 election, but he won less than a majority of the popular votes, with a war in Iraq not going well, according to many commentators. Upon receiving his party's nomination, Bush strongly defended the U.S. invasion of Iraq and the toppling of its dictatorial leader, Saddam Hussein. He also attacked his Democratic opponent, Senator John Kerry of Massachusetts, for voting against funds for troops in Iraq and Afghanistan and for advocating the "tax and spend … policies of the past."[226] Kerry, in his acceptance speech, began by alluding to his military service in Vietnam by saluting and saying that he was "reporting for duty."[227] Soon, he was being condemned in independent TV ads, paid for by a group called the "Swift Boat Veterans for Truth," for allegedly making untrue statements about his military accomplishments and about events that he said had occurred during the Vietnam War, which he subsequently opposed. Kerry called the election "the most important … of our lifetime," with "a global war on terror" to be won.[228] Although many American voters agreed that terrorism was a dominant issue, they did not want to "change horses in the middle of the stream"; with voters uncertain that the war was going badly, the incumbent was returned to office by a narrow margin of 3 percent in the popular vote and 6 percent in the Electoral College.[229]

The campaign featured a multitude of attacks by both parties, embodied in the many 30-second TV spots. The Republicans accused Kerry of changing his position on the war in Iraq several times (showing him windsurfing to the left and right, for example). They even charged him, along with "the Liberals in Congress," with making the country more vulnerable to terrorist threats because of their statements. One spot included a pack of wolves waiting to strike, and another ad featured scenes of the devastated World Trade Center, the flag, masked terrorists, and a child's face. The Democrats charged that Bush had misled the nation about the existence of weapons of mass destruction in Iraq, that he did not have a plan to extricate troops from that country, and that he also planned to reinstitute the military draft and eliminate the Social Security System.[230] Emotional ads supporting both candidates that incorporated statements by relatives of 9/11 victims supplemented negative TV spots on these issues.[231]

There were also positive TV spots that showed both candidates, without their jackets and ties, appealing to various groups, including farmers, laborers, housewives, and Latinos. These ads were, typically, in the form of short video clips of members of these groups, often with music in the background, which were obviously influenced by Music Television (MTV). Although both Bush and Kerry had similar "patrician" backgrounds, it was the former candidate who came across as having the "common touch," especially when he was shown in televised commercials, wearing a work shirt on the porch of his ranch. To increase the "contrast" between the two candidates' images, a conservative group, Citizens United, devised TV ads that focused on Kerry's seventy-five-dollar haircuts and his "four lavish mansions and beachfront estate."[232] When the dust settled, three times as much money had been spent on television and radio advertising for the 2004 presidential race than had been expended during the previous national election campaign.[233]

Also launched were direct mail and handbill attacks on Kerry's "record on terrorism," featuring photographs of the burning World Trade Center buildings; leaflets criticizing his gun-control votes, with pictures of a French poodle dressed in a Kerry sweater and the caption "That dog don't hunt"; and brochures that supplemented the Swift Boat Vets' TV spots, attacking Kerry's service in Vietnam. Groups supporting Kerry, on the other hand, mailed fliers that included an old "photograph of a firefighter blasting a black man with a hose," captioned "This is what they used to do to keep us from voting. Don't let them do it again." Anti-Bush brochures, featuring a picture of a hand pocketing piles of cash, along with the caption "He won't be in the pocket of big oil," were mailed as well. About six *billion* pieces of direct mail were dispatched during the 2004 presidential

Figure 3.31

and congressional campaigns, much of it negative, with consultants believing that targeted negative campaign tactics were more effective than were positive ones. The Republicans distributed an innovative direct mail piece in the form of a DVD: "George W. Bush: Faith in the White House"; it promoted the image of the president as a devout evangelical Christian to fundamentalist congregations.[234] Market research before the U.S. presidential election in 2004 identified rising drug costs and Medicare premiums as a primary concern for senior citizens. Therefore, direct mail and other media campaigns were designed in a way that would likely appeal to seniors. For example, The Campaign Network, a strategic communication company specializing in direct mail for Democrats, put together a piece titled "Bad Medicine," which unfolded to a poster that detailed how Republican presidential candidate George W. Bush "broke his promise to New Hampshire's Seniors" (Fig. 3.31).

Posters again complemented the mass media and direct mail campaigns. Kerry's attempt to show that he would be tougher against terrorism was summarized in one of his slogans, "A Stronger America," which was the basis of his main poster. Added to it was a patriotic logo for his ticket, which he shared with the former senator from North Carolina, John Edwards (Fig. 3.32). The basic poster design (see Fig. 8.1, Chapter Eight) for the Republican ticket, headed by Bush, and the renominated vice president, Dick Cheney, were not only quite similar to those of the opposition, but used the same design

Figure 3.32

as the one used four years earlier (see Fig. 3.30). The only differences were that the American flag did not protrude into the "H" in "BUSH" (instead being lined up with the right side of that letter) and the letters were slightly slanted to the right. Scott Dadich, a graphic artist, declared the Bush-Cheney logo to be superior in design: "It's brash and snazzy: a field of powerful, militaristic navy blue punctuated with the four letters of his surname spelled out in white in what appears to be Folio Extra-Bold Italic letters."[235] He further noted, "the rightward lilt of the ... letters reinforces Mr. Bush's ideology while at the same time portraying a buoyant sense of forward movement, energy, and positive change."[236] It is obvious when comparing the two poster designs that the Republican one was stronger and simpler, since it used bold type, capital letters, and a powerful flag icon with fewer stars and stripes than the more realistic one in the Democratic poster. The projection of relative "weakness" goes for the latter party's choice of color as well: the paler blue background was inferior to the Republicans' richer dark navy.[237] Finally, the names of the Democratic nominees are the same size; but "Bush" is larger than "Cheney" in the Republican poster. The latter approach is more in line with American political realities. Most labor unions continued to support the Democrats and produce their own posters. The International Brotherhood of Electrical Workers, for example, distributed a poster that showed the smiling Kerry and Edwards campaigning—with the ubiquitous principal design behind them (Fig. 3.33).

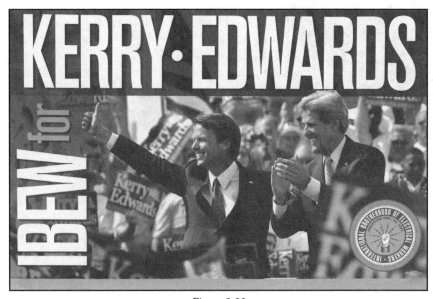

Figure 3.33

Several posters that supplemented the main poster design appeared in the Bush campaign. One said simply "Reelect the President in 2004" and had a black-and-

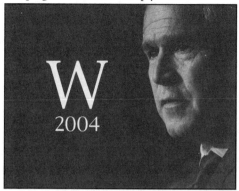

white photograph of Bush with a look of determination; the other was even simpler, with just the letter "W" and "2004" and a color photograph of the president, again bearing a serious facial expression, looking toward the text (Fig. 3.34). The latter poster was sold on party Web sites to raise funds. The use of a "W" with serifs was a very modern and corporate tactic, since, as Dadich pointed out, "Americans are conditioned to equate visual brevity with success and power."[238] This is not only true of Americans, since people worldwide have

Figure 3.34

positive attitudinal and emotional associations with the logos for Mercedes, Nike, Apple, and Honda.

In 2004, the Republican Party improved the way posters were printed via the Internet. People could create and print their own personalized posters on the Bush-Cheney '04 Web site, using a template that allowed them to select their state and the name of a coalition group (see Fig. 8.1, Chapter Eight). At one point, there was a "fill-in-the-blank" option, but anti-Bush partisans used that feature to create posters that debunked the Republicans, inserting such phrases as "A Miserable Failure," and the option was removed from the Web site.[239] Internet advertising, including blogs, saw increased spending of political revenue over that of the year 2000 (from 0.1 percent to 0.9 percent), placing that vehicle ahead of billboards (which declined from 1.1 percent to 0.7 percent).[240] As had been the case for half a century, broadcast television grabbed the lion's share of the political-advertising money (56.1 percent), with cable and satellite television increasing its share (from 1.6 percent to 2.9 percent), and radio's percentage declining dramatically (from 10.6 percent to 7 percent).[241] However, neighborhoods continued to be dotted with lawn signs, many similar to the posters produced, as well as posters displayed in windows; to some were added pointed slogans such as "Bush Must Go" and "Kerry is a Flip-Flopper," which undoubtedly increased the sense of urgency for partisans. This is an example of what election posters were probably designed to do—establish the presence of a candidate and to reaffirm the commitment of that candidate's followers.

CHAPTER FOUR

Politics and Posters in France

While election campaign posters first emerged in the United States, they soon appeared in other countries, the most notable being France and Great Britain—the two other oldest and largest modern democracies. Developments that made the poster a logical medium in U.S. election campaigns were important in Great Britain and France, and worldwide. For example, in the nineteenth century, suffrage was extended to a large number of male citizens (and later female ones) in much of Europe, as well as the Americas. In addition, the leaders of political movements who appealed to the working classes believed that the distribution of posters and broadsides were quite effective in gaining and retaining support in elections. Consequently, they were used often, particularly in France (beginning with the revolutions at the end of the eighteenth century). A wide variety of strategies, including appeals to nationalism, the class struggle, and ethnic prejudices, as well the application of symbols and slogans, can be seen in the posters and broadsides produced. Other international trends delineated (which are explored in this, and the next two chapters) are the importance of billboards, the impact of major technological developments (especially in printing and photography), the effects of legislation, and the influence of movements in art and graphic design.

The role of political marketing consultants in many countries subsequently became quite significant. They employed posters as part of their campaign strategies; and image and issues management, media planning, and distribution were crucial. Such practitioners have been active in French election campaigns since 1965: prominent French political consultants have been Michel Bongrand, who worked for Jean Lecanuet in 1965; Jacques Séguéla, for François Mitterrand in the 1980s; and Thierry Saussez, for Giscard d'Estaing and Nicolas Sarkozy in the same decade (and later).[1] Television has had less impact in France than in the United States, owing primarily to legislative restrictions. Nevertheless, French politicians, particularly Charles de Gaulle and Georges Pompidou in the 1960s, and Mitterrand in the 1980s, have effectively utilized television in campaigns, sometimes with the aid of professional consultants' image management. In addition, televised propaganda strategies, particularly "fear of the left" tactics, appeared to have been successful. These were used, also, in political poster campaigns, and continue to manifest in printed propaganda at election time.

Broadsides and Posters in the Emergence of Representative Politics in France

In fifteenth-century France, delegates were chosen for the Estates-General, a national assembly representing three orders—the church, provincial nobles, and mainly urban merchants. The delegates typically exercised little power or influence when they met sporadically between 1302 and 1789. The commoners, through a system of indirect election, selected the members of the body.[2] In French communities by the end of the fifteenth century, the common people who paid taxes nominated representatives to meet with neighboring electors to designate delegates to electoral assemblies, which in turn chose the delegates to the Estates-General. The initial selections occurred at meetings in the parishes; there were no declared candidates nor was there campaigning. This process ended under the absolute monarchy, and the Estates-General did not meet between 1614 and 1789, when Louis XVI, faced with an immense financial crisis, was forced to convene it.[3]

The crisis deepened, and by 1791, the Estates-General (renamed the National or Constituent Assembly) had created a constitutional monarchy with a legislative body that had supreme powers. The indirect electoral system continued, with the franchise and the right to serve in the legislature restricted to certain taxpayers. The new Constitution called for only one round of elections, to be held in the summer of 1791. One departure from the tradition of not conducting a campaign occurred when some local political clubs (including the Jacobin societies at Beauvais, Lille, Toulouse, and Tulle) printed candidate slates for voters to select as well as lists of electors to avoid. The revolutionary forces eliminated the constitutional monarchy the next summer, and the king was subsequently tried in the elected National Convention and executed in January 1793. Election of members of the National Convention took place with greatly expanded suffrage: males were allowed to vote at age twenty-one, if they had a profession (other than being a domestic servant), provided they had lived in a canton for at least one year. This resulted in an increase in the number of voters to approximately six million, or about 25 percent of the total population.[4] A referendum to approve the new constitution of 1793 was then held, and the document was overwhelmingly favored (by a margin of 99 to 1).[5] It was never put into practice, however, as France became involved in war abroad and dictatorship and executions of "enemies of the Republic" at home.[6]

By 1794, the "Reign of Terror" had ended, and a more moderate, bourgeois leadership formed another republic, with the Constitution of 1795 allowing six out of every seven Frenchmen to vote—excluding about one million nontaxpaying males.[7] A referendum again took place, and about 95 percent voted to approve this constitution.[8] The return of democratic elections to France in 1797 resulted in a short-lived republic, albeit one ruled by a five-man Directory. The voters elected a large number of constitutional monarchists to the national legislature, after they waged an effective eighteen-month propaganda campaign, which employed newspapers that supported declared royalist candidates (as well as ones that promoted republicans), broadsheets with titles such as "Prevent Anarchy," and slogans such as "It is not five rulers we want, just one." The Directory invalidated the election when the royalists won, instituted repressive measures, and attempted to rig new elections in 1798. This was the first French election in which placards—which covered walls throughout Paris—were used extensively, and the Jacobins, royalists, republicans, and Catholics, all electioneered in some form. When the Jacobins won the election, the results were again invalidated. In 1799, the Directory tried for a third straight year to manipulate the elections; opponents of the regime were threatened with death, little campaigning was evident, and there was a much lower voter turnout in many departments. It was all for naught, and the Directory called on Napoleon Bonaparte and the army, later in the year, to "restore order" under a dictatorship, with democratic trappings (such as a popularly elected legislature, which had no real power).[9]

French election laws in the early nineteenth century severely restricted the right to vote. The assessment of poll taxes granted the franchise, almost exclusively, to landowners, professionals, officials, businessmen, and successful artisans—a very small percentage of the population.[10] Restrictive legislation outlawing printed political "drawings" (including broadsides) was passed, after the lithographic process came to France in 1819.[11] A decade and a half later, artist Honoré Daumier was jailed, under these laws, for his lithographs, one of which depicted the king as a pear and another as Gargantua.[12] By 1847, however, dissatisfaction with the monarchy (which, after Napoleon's defeat at Waterloo, had been restored to power three decades earlier) intensified during an economic crisis; this led to the republicans insisting on and, the next year, achieving universal male suffrage.[13]

The Second Republic and Second Empire Under Louis Napoleon Bonaparte

Revolutionary agitation in Paris in February of 1848 effected the formation of a republican government, which expanded suffrage dramatically. The legislation that was enacted was "the broadest election law the world [had] ever seen," according to Priscilla Robertson, "even including classes like domestic servants that had been excluded in 1789."[14] Those eligible to vote grew from two hundred fifty thousand to more than nine million.[15] With the expansion of the voting population came a large number of workers' groups and political clubs, together with the production of many broadsides, pamphlets, and newspapers. No official party organizations existed, and there were no legislative controls on poster displays. The election propaganda in the spring featured massive deception on the part of candidates: broadsides declared (usually untruthfully) that candidates had been workers, peasants, or republicans, or had been delegates to the 1792 Convention, when they were actually monarchists. Despite all the radical claims, the more conservative elements— often landlords, nobles, clergy, merchants, and bankers—were better organized and boasted higher status in localities. In particular, they carried out more effective propaganda campaigns, and broadsides featuring the word *order* (along with *liberty, equality,* and *fraternity*) were used extensively. On April 23, 1848, more than 80 percent of the voters turned out, and elected a greater number of conservative representatives than reformers and militants to the Constituent Assembly: more than four hundred monarchists won seats, whereas about three hundred fifty republicans, radicals, and socialists were elected. Only eighteen workers gained seats.[16]

Subsequent protests and repression led to restrictions on political activities, and to a constitution that bestowed great power on the office of the president. By summer, Bonapartist newspapers were propagandizing for the installation of Louis Napoleon

Bonaparte (the nephew of the emperor), who professed that he was a socialist, as the nation's ruler. Small posters, along with songs, medals, buttonhole flags, and Bonapartist newspapers, promoted his candidacy in the June by-elections. Posters and speeches that supported him as "the symbol of order" were evident during the supplementary election campaign for the Constituent Assembly in the fall. In December, Louis Napoleon Bonaparte was elected president with 74 percent of the vote—a margin of fifty-five points over his opponent, General Louis Eugène Cavaignac, who had put down the revolt.[17] Those suspected of being republican militants were arrested and newspapers were soon closed; eligibility to vote was reduced by about 30 percent due to an 1850 election law requiring citizens to have paid taxes and lived at an address for three years.[18] Voters overwhelmingly approved the takeover in the plebiscites of 1851 and 1852. The votes of Frenchmen were not secret, however, since the paper ballots were color-coded. The Bonaparte regime's candidates distributed posters and circulars, and were covered by the press; opposition candidates, on the other hand, lacked much of this support. Some republican candidates who did manage to win seats in elections in the 1850s were unseated when they would not take a loyalty oath; other republicans did pledge allegiance to the new emperor and served in the legislature. There appeared to be a great deal of popular support for the Second Empire of Napoleon III during this period, with almost 90 percent of voters supporting the regime's candidates in 1857.[19] Distributed to the public were many copies of engravings of Napoleon III, the empress, and the prince, all surrounded by commoners and with Napoleon I on his horse faintly illustrated in the background.[20]

In legislative elections, many of the candidates hailed from the moneyed and aristocratic classes.[21] Louis Girard wrote that "most of the candidates for the 1869 elections were notables dependent on their local influence, with a secure electoral base in the particular locale in which their land, château, or factory was located."[22] Many voters were illiterate or could barely read. The use of posters was one of the means to gain their support. Support for the Bonaparte regime declined in the 1863 and 1869 elections, particularly in the latter balloting, which occurred a year after the reemergence of freedoms of the

Figure 4.1

press and meeting; however, many workers (who had put up pro-regime posters) continued to back the emperor, often because of fears of renewed violence, instability, and economic problems. Bonapartist newspapers stoked these fears, comparing one moderate candidate, Jean David, to Jean-Paul Marat, and characterizing another, Jules Favre, as "the man of 48, of disorder, of the 45 centimes."[23] The last was a reference to an unpopular tax.

In addition to newspaper propaganda, the "image management" intensified with the distribution of lithographic portraits of both the first Napoleon—and the mythology surrounding him—and his nephew, and voters displayed these portraits in their homes. The new methods of lithographic printing made it possible to produce tens of thousands of these portraits each day. There were also hand-colored photomontage prints of Eugène, the imperial prince, holding the banner of the Bonapartist Party, *l'Appel au Peuple* (The Call to the People) (Fig. 4.1). The regime introduced measures that were more liberal, including the reinstitution of universal male suffrage (called for in Figure 4.1). The expanded electorate, of whom a significant number became agitated by the regime's problems in Mexico and elsewhere, elected many more liberals to the legislature in 1869. Votes for opposition candidates rose to 42 percent of the total votes cast.[24] In a plebiscite in May 1870, French voters approved liberal reforms by a margin of almost 5 to 1.[25] Four months later, however, the Franco-Prussian War ended with the defeat of the French army and the capture of Napoleon III. Moderate deputies announced the establishment of the Third Republic.[26]

The Third French Republic

After the new French government and the Prussians agreed to a truce, an election was held in early 1871. The republicans campaigned to continue the conflict and the conservatives favored peace. Some notables even demanded the dissolution of the legislature in the election. An election broadside called on voters to send author Victor Hugo to the National Assembly, even though he wanted it disbanded (Fig. 4.2). Conservatives did far better in the vote count, and one of them, Adolphe Thiers, formed a government in which the moderate republicans were well represented. Peace was negotiated with Prussia, and the army put an end to the brief rule of the Paris Commune (or parliament), consisting of a majority of elected delegates of a radical or socialist bent, with ten thousand to thirty thousand Commune supporters and innocent civilians killed, as well as four hundred soldiers, in street battles.[27]

Figure 4.2

Nevertheless, by the 1876 election, only France and the United States offered meaningful universal male suffrage.[28] The expansion of the right to vote was, probably, one reason why the republicans won the general elections of 1876 and 1878 by substantial margins over the conservative-monarchist forces, with the former faction's propaganda persuading most citizens—particularly peasants—"that the Republic was the best guarantee of firm, stable, and moderate government," as James McMillan stated.[29] Another explanation was that the forces opposing the republicans were often divided, and proffered their own candidates, splitting the nonrepublican votes.[30] Posted printed matter addressed the voters ubiquitously. According to a newspaper account at the time, the elections, particularly in Paris, were "picturesque," with "all the walls being covered with colored handbills, containing electoral addresses, or large posters, with the names of the candidates in fine bold type."[31] In the 1876 election campaign, the government used white paper for its posters, and opposition candidates employed blue, yellow, and other paper.[32] Posters of candidates were often pulled down right after they were put up: one "billsticker" noted that eighteen of the twenty posters he had just put up were torn down when he looked back on a street.[33] One reason for the increase in posted printed matter was that the Third Republic's legislators passed new laws repealing past censorship decrees and facilitating the growth of small businesses (which included small lithographic print shops).[34]

France now had a bicameral parliamentary system that was similar, in many respects, to that of Great Britain: most laws began in the Chamber of Deputies and a Senate acted as a "safeguard against radical legislation."[35] Unlike the British system, the members of both bodies were elected; but there was a Council of Ministers, led by a premier, which stayed in office only if a majority in parliament was maintained. The primary difference between the two systems, as Jeremy Popkin pointed out, was that "the French did not have a strongly rooted two-party system like the British."[36] There were many independent deputies, and shifting coalitions and majorities led to many governments, but the Third Republic persisted in France until the German army invaded the country in 1940.

This is not to say that there were no political crises. In 1885, for example, when economic problems worsened, Radical Republican and rightist candidates gained a substantial number of seats in the Chamber of Deputies. This created both a legislative body with no stable majority and a situation that nearly led a general, Georges Boulanger—who appealed to both the left and right—to seize power. In the 1893 election, about fifty socialists replaced some republicans as deputies, after a series of scandals, but moderate-conservative republicans also did well.[37]

At this time, many political liberals in France started to believe that lithographic posters, which had become easier and less costly to produce in bulk and which were often more colorful and pictorial than before, could become a real force for political and social change. Reinforcing this belief was the success of huge posters illustrated by Chéret, Toulouse-Lautrec, Mucha, and other artists. These were used to promote events, business establishments, factory-produced goods, books, movies, and even train travel to resorts, and were wildly popular during this period. The posters appeared to boost attendance and sales, and aid the careers of singers and entertainers. Imaginative posters, printed in eye-catching colors from lithographic stones, were used for a wide variety of political purposes. For example, a poster for a "republican, anti-clerical" newspaper titled *La Lanterne*, printed at the end of the century, depicted a monstrous, birdlike religious figure clutching what appears to be a church, with the slogan "Behold the Enemy."[38]

As the nineteenth century ended, there were several squabbling socialist political parties, as well as the Radical Party, which formed "something akin to a modern party electoral organization," according to Roger Price.[39] This party triumphed in the 1902 election, after which the Radicals fashioned a legislative coalition with some moderate republicans and socialists. In 1905, the various socialist parties merged into one political party, the *Parti socialiste unifie* (or, the *Section française de l'Internationale ouvrière* [the French Section of the Workingmen's International]), but internal arguments over ideology and tactics continued to divide the party, which was generally committed to working within the democratic system. During this period, there was a good deal of propaganda—much of it by Socialists, aimed at the working class. Posters and placards promoting candidates for deputy slots, lined walls on many streets; antimilitaristic, anticapitalistic skits were performed; and socialist songs were sung in workingmen's music halls. Political prints often featured workers raising rifles on the barricades, and large, provocative lettering. In the 1914 elections, as war with Germany loomed, the Socialists increased their total of deputies to 102, and were able to form a new government supported by an additional 240 leftist candidates.[40] It was led by an independent socialist, but was controlled by Radicals. Despite the left's ideological stance against an "imperialist war," however, nothing was done to prevent it, and after the assassination of Austrian Archduke Franz Ferdinand, war was declared in 1914.[41]

Elections for parliament did not take place again until the end of 1919. The Socialists—many supporting the Bolshevik Revolution in Russia—made it clear in their campaign that they would refuse to deal with the Radicals in the Chamber of Deputies. One of the consequences of this position was that the more conservative forces won most of the races, with the Socialist Party gaining only sixty-eight seats (although its percentage of votes increased from 17 to 21).[42] The Socialists were also penalized by the Chamber's new system that rewarded parties that joined coalitions. The Radicals had no qualms about joining with others, and looked to the right to form a coalition with the conservatives, known as the *Bloc National*. Many of those who rejected this approach went down in defeat, and after the election, center-right parties controlled four hundred fifty of the six hundred sixteen seats in the Chamber.[43] The election propaganda disseminated by these parties transformed the barbarous "Hun" of the war into the wild-eyed, unkempt Bolshevik revolutionary—shown in a poster with a knife between his teeth (Fig. 4.3). The attempt

Figure 4.3

to associate the French Socialist Party with Bolshevism appeared to be somewhat successful with many voters, who were sensitive to past revolutions and worker strikes in their own country.

Many of the election posters, beginning in the postwar period, followed the principles of advertising advocated by French pioneers in the field. The advertising poster was viewed as a "stimulus machine" that had to gain the attention of the audience (i.e., in the political sphere—the voters), and motivate people to buy the product (i.e., to vote for a party, typically); and, to achieve these goals, color was used liberally in more simplified designs, which often had a background devoid of details.[44] The anti-Bolshevist poster was such a design, devised to attract attention, interest the voter, arouse his emotions, and persuade him to vote accordingly. Of course, there was no reference to the "product" (as there would be in a commercial poster), and the imagery was designed to evoke negative sentiments (the opposite of a Cappiello poster for Cinzano® vermouth, for example).

The postwar period was a difficult one for France. The franc and fixed-income bonds lost much of their value, the military was deployed to occupy part of Germany, and only a small number of people possessed power, education, and wealth. By the election of 1924, the Socialists had changed their stance, deciding to enter a coalition with the Radicals, known as the *Cartel des Gauches*. The *Cartel* won three hundred twenty-eight (or 58 percent) of the seats in the Chamber of Deputies; the Socialists secured almost one-third of them, which was double what they had after the previous election.[45] Over the next two years, myriad domestic and foreign problems brought down the *Cartel*. Among these were both the Socialists' continuing inability to work with the Radicals and the opposition of the new Russian-controlled French Communist Party, which disseminated posters, aimed especially at renters, attacking the "oppressive" bourgeoisie. Conservative Raymon Poincaré formed a new government, naming six former premiers cabinet ministers. Some of the conservative campaign posters in the next election—1928—pinned the responsibility for inflationary prices on the Socialists and Radicals by showing downcast people looking at meat and produce with high price tags (Fig. 4.4). The Poincaré government, supported

Figure 4.4

by a Radical-conservative coalition in the Chamber, had enacted measures that helped increase the franc's value and trim the budget deficit, and his coalition retained power in the election.[46] The perception was that the economy had been stabilized and that conditions had improved. "One sometimes hears the sigh 'Poor France' from a Frenchman's lips, ... but it is not any longer said tragically," reported P. J. Philip during the election campaign.[47] In the months preceding the voting, posters were plastered on walls, with conservatives focusing their attacks on Bolshevism. In general, the posters were large, and were placed on temporary "bill boards" (with their size prescribed by law) on the sidewalks. The better times ended in 1931, when the Great Depression began in France.[48]

The policies of the Radical-conservative coalition governments to combat the declining economic conditions were failures. As in the United States, the voters in 1932 shifted to the left (as was seen in Chapter Three), and a Radical-Socialist partnership gained power. When the votes were counted, 157 Radicals, 129 Socialists and 230 conservatives had been elected.[49] Once again, however, the Socialists and Radicals were not able to cooperate, and a succession of conservative-led governments followed. By mid-1935, the French Communists, Radicals, and Socialists moved toward the formation of the Popular Front in anticipation of the next year's election. However, among the three front parties, there was considerable disagreement on tactics and issues, which manifested in the campaign.[50]

As for media employed in the 1936 election campaign, party radio broadcasts and posters were dominant. Posters were prolific, and many of them

Figure 4.5

focused on the threat of war and fascism, and were designed to appeal to the workers and the middle class (as can be seen in Figure 4.5). The right, on the other hand, warned in some of its posters that "The Popular Front Means War." Other posters noted that the election victory in Spain for the Socialist-Communist Popular Front had resulted in "civil war and misery" (Fig. 4.6). In addition to their attacks on fascism, the parties of the left produced posters that attacked the Bank of France, insurance companies, and armament manufacturers, calling for their nationalization. One poster, for instance, depicted a caricatured group of financiers looking at bank statements and a declaration that they were working in the national interest, with a laborer—whose shoulder carries a party emblem—towering over

Figure 4.6

them (Fig. 4.7). The Popular Front parties also distributed anti-Bolshevist, antifascist, anticapitalist broadsides, some of which incorporated medieval warriors behind the text. The Popular Front coalition was victorious in the election: the Socialists and the Communists increased their representation dramatically, and the Radicals lost many seats. Under a two-ballot system, candidates needed a majority-plus-one of the votes on the initial ballot to win and much-disciplined vote-switching on the second.[51]

The day after the election, shares of Bank of France stock fell to less than one-half of their value from the previous year, and a decline of almost one-third from the week before the elections. However, Léon Blum, designated to be the Popular

Figure 4.7

Front's premier, was able to stem the financial panic by indicating that he would not move to nationalize the Bank, but rather to reform it. Blum's government, which lasted two years, was able to achieve some banking reforms, as well as others such as the inclusion of women in the government as undersecretaries (although they were not destined to obtain the right to vote until 1944). It failed, nevertheless, to end the depression and industrial strikes, or even come to the aid of the Spanish Republic, which was fighting the forces of fascism; and the Radicals subsequently formed a new government. On the other hand, the French Communist Party—for almost the next half century—became *the* political party for many workers, who had been radicalized during the decade. But after Soviet dictator Joseph Stalin signed a nonaggression pact with Nazi Germany, which then invaded Poland, the Moscow-controlled Communist Party in France abandoned its antifascist and pro-military preparedness positions, and instructed its members to oppose war with Germany.[52]

There was no election in 1940, as that year German tanks and mobile infantry units quickly overwhelmed French forces, invalidating the military's defensive strategy. The Chamber of Deputies soon voted for the draft of a new constitution that dissolved the Third Republic.[53] The new "Vichy Regime" collaborated with the German occupiers of France, and revoked prior reforms, such as free secondary education.[54] It also distributed posters trumpeting its "national revolution." This was a proclamation of a stable France, supported by "Work, Family, Fatherland." Depicted was a crumbling nation, enveloped in black clouds, which the previous regimes had allegedly allowed to be damaged by the forces of radicalism, communism, and capitalism, and, by Jews, to name a few enemies of the state.

Charles de Gaulle and the Fourth and Fifth Republics

The next democratic election for Frenchmen did not occur in France proper. It was held on the Caribbean island of St. Pierre at the end of 1941. In a plebiscite, 650 males voted in favor of a "Rally to Free France" option, and 10 chose "Collaboration with the Axis Powers." Undoubtedly, the margin would have been even more lopsided if the approximately one hundred fifty men from the island, who had joined Charles de Gaulle's Free French army, had been there to vote. There was not much need to campaign, but a reporter did note that a poster was displayed, stating in part, "People of St. Pierre: Don't forget that your vote is going to decide your future. … Do not listen to the Vichy-ards who will go away from St. Pierre and leave you here in the soup. … Everybody vote for Free France."[55] De Gaulle had been a critic of the French military's defensive strategy in the 1930s, and (supported by the British) had vowed to carry on the war against Germany, after the French defeat. In late August 1944, de Gaulle's army and the American forces entered Paris, and a month later, liberated most of France.[56]

In late October 1945, 96 percent of the men and women who cast their votes in a referendum were against a return to the political system of the Third Republic.[57] At the same time, voters elected a Constituent Assembly, with seats distributed proportionately. The Communists received about 26 percent of the vote, the Socialists 23 percent, the *Mouvement Républicain Populaire* (MRP, or Christian Democrats) 24 percent, conservatives and independents 16 percent, and the Radicals and *Union démocratique et socialiste de la Résistance* 10 percent.[58] The Communists did particularly well because they positioned themselves in the campaign as heroes of the Resistance and united with the Soviet Union, which had valiantly fought Nazi Germany after being invaded, while controlling most of the French trade unions. Many of the party's posters showed workers with construction occurring in the background, and included past leaders such as Robespierre. They also railed against governmental corruption, and appealed directly to pensioners (Fig. 4.8). Many of the Socialists' leaders had been active in the Resistance, and had the support of scores of voters who favored the restoration of democratic institutions and increased egalitarianism. Resistance leaders were prominent in the Christian Democrat Party too, but the MRP was more conservative and Catholic than the parties of the left were. General de Gaulle, who was Head of State, continued to serve in that post, but resigned a few months later, following disputes with

Figure 4.8

ministers, and when he anticipated challenges to his authority in the new political system. However, an initial referendum, which proposed a unicameral legislative system that many perceived as favoring the interests of the Communist Party, was defeated by a margin of about 7 percent in May 1946.[59]

A revised constitution, written by a new Constituent Assembly, now dominated by the MRP, which had done better in the next election in June, was put to the electorate in October, and passed with a 53 percent majority, even though de Gaulle called for a "no" vote and millions abstained.[60] The Fourth Republic, which was barely different from the Third, had finally been established, with a bicameral legislature, the Chamber of Deputies having

Figure 4.9

the most power, and a president (with much less authority).[61] The national campaigns to elect these assemblies to construct a constitution, as well as those on the referenda themselves, were marked by posters and broadsides, which were plastered on walls throughout France. The Socialist Party's posters, in particular, were quite striking: one was dominated by a laborer's silhouette and showed the erection of buildings behind the ruins; another presented a long line of marching workers holding red flags with demands on them, and appealed to workers to vote for the party: "For the Rebuilding of France" (Fig. 4.9).

The postwar period saw nationalizations of many industries, restoration of the right to unionize, and several social reform measures, one of which created a national healthcare system. Nevertheless, in May 1947, the Communist ministers in the government of Socialist Prime Minister Paul Ramadier were removed from office, after they had refused to increase wages for Renault workers in the nationalized automobile industry. About the same time, de Gaulle's *Rassemblement du Peuple Français* (Rally of the French People [RPF]) was formed; its goal was to have France adopt a presidential system. Posters were produced, calling on citizens to join the general's party, using symbols such as Marianne holding a shield emblazoned with the Lorraine cross (Fig. 4.10). The MRP, Radicals,

Figure 4.10

and Socialists stood in opposition to de Gaulle's movement, as did the Communists. By 1948, strikes and fighting between workers and police were widespread (the winter coal strike cost the country more than two hundred million dollars). De Gaulle called for elections, and the RPF organized a poster campaign to achieve the goal. The posters were financed by the sale of stamps, and "express[ed] confidence in M. de Gaulle."[62]

All parties conducted a propaganda war in France at the end of the decade. The highly professional Communist Party's AgitProp Committee coordinated its campaigns. The Committee was run, as Joseph Barry of the *New York Times* wrote, "not [by] information officers or newspaper men on temporary leaves of absence," but rather by "lifetime" staff members, who efficiently printed party newspapers and magazines that targeted women, young people, and other groups.[63] Its propaganda seemed so pervasive that Barry "counted nineteen posters and stickers and newspapers of Communist origin ... on one fifty-foot stretch of fence. ...."[64] The prominent word in these posters was "peace" and the dominant symbol was the "dove"; the main themes were opposition to both the Marshall Plan, which would result in the United States' "colonization" of France, and the Atlantic pact, which would, supposedly, bring about a war with the Soviet Union.[65] The Communist Party implemented an extensive billboard campaign that included a drawing of a dove by Pablo Picasso.[66]

The Communist propaganda campaign was countered by an organization known as *Paix et Liberté* (Peace and Freedom), which was founded in 1950 by Jean-Paul David, the mayor of Mantes, who was a Radical deputy. The group produced posters, which changed images from the Communist Party's posters into anti-Communist icons. For example, *Paix et Liberté* transformed Picasso's dove into a tank adorned with a hammer and sickle in a poster titled "The Dove that Makes Bang." In 1950, the organization distributed two hundred thousand copies of this poster. Another powerful image designed was a boot, with its sole covered with hammer-and-sickle symbols, about to crush a French village with flames everywhere in the background (Fig. 4.11). Other *Paix et Liberté* posters were more traditional in design. One included a photograph of a family and text that read, "In the U.S.S.R., children belong to the State. Protect their liberty by voting!" The group also issued targeted broadsides such as one embellished with patriotic streaks of

Figure 4.11

blue and red at top and bottom that appealed to soldiers to vote against the dictatorship of Communism and "for a strong France and a free Republic" (Fig. 4.12). The RPF mounted an anti-Communist propaganda campaign as well, headed by novelist André Malraux, who circulated newspapers and posters, with the middle class as the primary targeted population and the workers the secondary target. Although the Communist posters were more abundant, the RPF concocted a clever campaign: the Gaullists placed on them stickers featuring a caricature of Stalin, saying, "This poster is mine." Other factions used their posters to attack de Gaulle. An anti-Gaullist, anti-Communist group, for instance, debunked the general by depicting him carrying Maurice Thorez, a Communist who had been a member of his cabinet.[67]

Figure 4.12

The election finally occurred in 1951, after France had seen a succession of weak coalition governments, comprising Radicals, Socialists, and Christian Democrats. The Communists and the Gaullists (i.e., the RPF) rejected the existing political system (i.e., the Fourth Republic), and became more alienated when the Chamber of Deputies changed the proportional representation method to help the in-parties gain more seats. Consequently, the coalition retained power in an unfair election. The Communist and Gaullist parties received far more support at the polls than did the Socialists, Radicals, and the MRP. Yet, they both emerged with only a few more seats (and, compared to the Socialists, far fewer) in the National Assembly than the other parties did. The Gaullist party was particularly bitter, since it had increased its percentage of the vote by about 50 percent.[68]

The Communists' primary campaign theme in 1951 was "Americans, go home" (a reference to the "occupying" forces after the war), which appeared on its posters, along with images of the "American octopus" and the admonition: "Don't let France become an American colony." The Gaullists sounded the same theme, warning about subordinating France to the United States and criticizing the government for allowing American airbases in French Morocco. Economic and colonial-military problems, most notably the war in Vietnam, plagued the subsequent coalition governments. The disastrous battle at Dien Bien Phu in 1954 brought the Radical Pierre Mendès-France to power as prime minister. Mendès-France ended the war and tried to relate to the public in radio "fireside chats," but his government was soon brought down, partly because of a split in his party. By the election of 1956, Algeria had replaced Vietnam as a threat to France's economy and military forces. The many political parties flooded the country with printed propaganda. The Socialist Party, in particular, targeted various voting blocs, including young people, wavering Communists, miners (with printed material in Polish), and North Africans (in Arabic), with handbills, as well as posters. A profusion of posters with photographs of the party leaders, and broadsides listing candidates and issues, also were circulated. After the election, the Socialist-centrist government that was formed would not grant the Algerians full independence, the violence in Algeria increased, and the economy deteriorated.[69]

By 1958, the country's state of affairs were so grave that four prime ministers had gained and lost power in a year's time, and French generals in Algeria planned to topple the government in Paris using their paratroopers and other forces in the capital. The plot was averted and the Fourth Republic ended when 60 percent of the deputies in the National Assembly agreed on June 1 to return de Gaulle to power for six months.[70] A poster campaign helped bring about this change. The posters declared, "Call De Gaulle ... And

Figure 4.13

France Will Be France" (Fig. 4.13). The Fifth Republic was constituted, with several important new provisions in the political system: an electoral college of about eighty thousand officials would elect the president; that person would then appoint the prime minister; the president could order referenda on crucial issues; and he or she could call states of emergency, taking special powers, including the dissolution of the National Assembly. The bicameral legislature and the prime minister, dependent on National Assembly support, were retained. In September 1958, the voters of France approved these changes in a referendum by a margin of almost 4 to 1.[71] A massive poster campaign by the Gaullists undoubtedly helped increase the margin. Blue-white-and-red posters with the slogan "OUI a la France" were omnipresent, and pamphlets designed to affect different segments of the electorate were plentiful. Public relations specialists, who had become more active in French politics, wrote many of them. The printing of posters was often funded by government agencies.[72]

A parliamentary election was soon held. Candidates of the Gaullist-conservative party, the *Union pour la Nouvelle République* (Union for the New Republic [UNR]), and other supporters of de Gaulle emerged with about 70 percent of the seats in the National Assembly, even though they received about 45 percent of the votes.[73] This was due to another unfair representation system, with a runoff round that had been decreed. Most of the other parties—even the Communists—tried to co-opt the themes of the Gaullists in the campaign, but to no avail. The Communist Party, for example, distributed posters that included such Gaullist verbiage as "the grandeur of France" and "national independence." After the 1958 election, the legislative majority would provide support for de Gaulle, in what became a presidential system, and the general exerted control over foreign and military affairs. In December, the Electoral College voted overwhelmingly for de Gaulle (who was supported by almost 80 percent of its members), and a few weeks later, he had Gaullist Michel Debré establish a government.[74] France's Electoral College system was not abolished until 1962. That year, the voters approved a referendum (about 62 percent were in favor), which provided for the direct election of the president.[75] The Gaullists campaigned actively for this change, erecting huge billboards in Paris and other cities. One of them used the familiar finger-pointing technique that had been prevalent in World War I, and thereafter (see Fig. 1.10, Chapter One). During this referendum campaign, as well as others to follow, political party propagandists continued the practice of using authorized smaller, standing billboards on sidewalks reserved for their parties, on which they posted broadsides and posters, some with simple graphics and many with only words. It was common, however, to circumvent the law on postings during election campaigns: political parties could paste posters anywhere before the official campaign period; stickers were frequently placed on opposition posters; or posters were put up illegally with no consequences.[76]

The Gaullists tried to convey that their party's reason for being was to support the general, and that his aims and those of the party were the same. They initiated this strategy in the 1958 campaign for the National Assembly. The message was communicated via the slogan "UNR=DE GAULLE," which was prominent on many campaign posters. After the election, however, party members and deputies appeared to exercise a degree of independence. Albin Chalandon, the UNR's secretary-general, for example, would not support the economic policies of the new government later in the year. By the early 1960s, the more extreme rightists in the party departed, became more moderate, or lost influence; the UNR developed into an efficiently modern center-right party, led by Pompidou; and television and nonideological concerns dominated campaigns. In fact, the 1965 presidential election has been called the first "television election" in France, as television-set ownership had increased markedly during de Gaulle's presidency from 10 percent of households to 40 percent.[77] Socialists, Communists, and Radicals supported de Gaulle's opponent, François Mitterrand, a small-town mayor, who had been a deputy in the National Assembly and a cabinet minister. He received equal television time, but lost by 10 percent in the runoff round of the election.[78]

The Role of Posters in French Elections in the Mass Media Age

It should be noted that, since the 1960s, all radio and television slots have been provided free to political candidates in France (as has been the case in Great Britain) and apportioned on the basis of representation for National Assembly campaigns.[79] De Gaulle did little campaigning in 1965, while his opponents used a TV attack strategy to keep the president from attaining a "majority-plus-one" on the first ballot. But, by the second-round campaign "an aroused de Gaulle demonstrated that he still had no master in the art of broadcast propaganda," wrote Jeremy Popkin, and the general won the election.[80] De Gaulle, instead of making the one appearance on television he had planned just before the election, decided to use all of the time allocated to him as a candidate—two hours on television and seventy-five minutes on radio.[81] Television had become an important factor in French politics, since there were now six million television sets owned and many more rented (rentals increased more than threefold during the campaign).[82] One effect that television had in France, as Philip Williams noted, was that before the 1960s, posters focused more on the views of candidates, but with the development of television as a significant mass medium in political campaigns, posters became, mainly, a way to establish candidates' presence and "remind" citizens to turn out to vote for them.[83] The same trend was apparent in many other countries, particularly in the United States. The day was gone when posters served as a primary source of information for voters. Poll data from 1958 had ranked posters third (behind the press and radio/TV) as a means of information used by voters during French election campaigns; in election years thereafter, they fell to seventh through ninth place.[84] This is not to say that posters became unimportant in France. Posters, as Jean and Monica Charlot pointed out, convey the theme of a campaign, summarized in a slogan, which is seen repeatedly communicated on televised news broadcasts that cover rallies.[85]

The power of television to boost the popularity of candidates in France was made clear by the success, in 1965, of Senator Jean Lecanuet (and leader of the MRP). Lecanuet had been virtually unknown nationally, but in a two-week period projected such a positive television image (handsome, vibrant, frank, and mentioning U.S. President Kennedy), combined with attacks on some of de Gaulle's policies, that he received an unexpectedly high 16 percent of the vote in the first round of voting in 1965.[86] Furthermore, his employment of the same public relations company that promoted the James Bond films, and the use of market research to help "package" the candidate, probably helped him at the polls. The Lecanuet campaign was the first French political campaign run by a professional political consultant, Michel Bongrand, who later became the first president of the International Association of Political Consultants, and all key election campaigns in the years that followed were managed by such advisors, using opinion polling to help determine image and issue management.[87]

In 1968, in an election called after the French student revolt in May, the Gaullists and their allies again swept to victory in the parliamentary elections. They captured almost 45 percent of the vote (versus only about 20 percent for the Communists, 16.5 percent for the Socialists and Radicals, and a mere 3.5 percent for rightist parties) and won more than 60 percent of the seats.[88] French university students, artists, and workers ran off thousands of silk-screened and lithographic posters deriding de Gaulle, some comparing him to Hitler for the repressive actions of the government and the police. One showed a boxing glove aimed at a caricature of the president, with the slogan "The fist of no return"; others referred to de Gaulle as "the bed-soiler," after he had stated, "Reform, yes, bed-soiling no!" as a response to the revolt. Within a year, de Gaulle resigned, when his referendum to reform the Senate and the regions was rejected by 53 percent of the voters.[89]

The general's resignation did not substantially alter the political landscape though, as Pompidou was elected president in June 1969, with 44 percent on the first ballot and over 57 percent on the second, defeating the centrist president of the Senate, Alain Poher, in the runoff.[90] Four years later, the Gaullist coalition garnered 36 percent of the vote and about 55 percent of the seats in the National Assembly, even though the Communists and Socialists had formed an alliance and won about 42 percent on the first ballot.[91] The alliance came apart before the second ballot, however, when votes were split in many districts between candidates of the two parties—a trend that continued in future elections. Television was used even more effectively, as Pompidou delivered fear appeals, stressing "the threat to freedom and to people's homes and property that would immediately follow a victory by the left." Fear of the left, thus, continued to be a potent factor in French politics, particularly in the aftermaths of the student rebellion in France and the Soviet invasion of Czechoslovakia in 1968.[92]

The far right became marginalized in France during and after the de Gaulle period, usually winning less than 5 percent of the vote in the elections in the 1960s and 1970s.[93] The far left had its problems too. As Charles Hauss noted, "the collapse of communism and the *de facto* end of any sort of radical democratic socialism as a viable rallying point … sapped the left of much what it used to offer voters."[94] The mainstream left party, the Socialists, won the presidency in both 1981 and 1988, and Mitterrand finally assumed the office. Mitterrand, who had lost the runoff round to President Giscard d'Estaing—the Gaullist-centrist candidate, following Pompidou's death—by a margin of only 1.4 percent in 1974, won the second round in 1981 by a difference of 3.6 percent over d'Estaing.[95] He was helped by the support of Communist candidate Georges Marchais (who gained 15 percent of the votes—down from the 23 percent for the party's candidate in 1969). The conservative-right, however, did not come together in support of d'Estaing in the second round as satisfactorily as the left did for Mitterrand. After coming in a poor fourth in the first round, Jacques Chirac (the mayor of Paris), the candidate of the *Rassemblement pour la République* Party (Rally for the Republic [RPR]), refused to back d'Estaing in the second round.[96]

Mitterrand's propaganda campaign in 1981 seemed to be most effective, since it managed his image to best match the expectations and leadership conceptions of many French voters. It depicted "him as *la force tranquille*, the guardian of established values as well as the proponent of sensible and moderate reform … in marked contrast with the aggressive approach favored by Marchais and Chirac and the studied ambiguities of Giscard," according to Price.[97] This can be seen in a poster produced for Mitterrand's campaign that showed him with a slightly benign smile and a peaceful farm in the background. The slogan "*La force tranquille*" appeared in bold, serif type above the design. There was also a poster of a wise-looking Mitterrand, shown in an extreme close-up, with the slogan "When one cares for the rich better than the poor: I, François Mitterrand, say that it is not just'" (Fig. 4.14). The Socialists also printed negative posters, with one showing d'Estaing in an unflattering view from behind, headlined "1 unemployed every 3 minutes." The Young Socialists used an edgier photomontage approach to attack Giscard and his state education minister, Alice Saunier-Seite, who were dressed as punks and labeled "the real thugs of the university" (Fig. 4.15). They also produced a poster with a drawing by Jean-François Batellier of a prison cell and notches sketched on the wall for each month of d'Estaing's seven-year term (Fig. 4.16). Giscard's *Union pour la Démocratie Française* (Union for French Democracy [UDF]) team produced a series of positive posters, with the slogan "We need a strong France," which showed him with young boys playing soccer, rolling green hills, a factory, and a world map in the background (Fig. 4.17). Tried-and-true symbols such as the flag were visible again on the major parties' posters. The UDF campaign, however, did not seem as effective as that of the Socialists. Mitterrand emerged as the winner in the second round of voting, defeating Giscard by 52 to 48 percent.[98] All parties continued to distribute broadsides; some candidates used them as a way to thank voters for their support after the first round of the election.

Mitterrand and his Socialist-centrist coalition, following his election as president in 1981, won the parliamentary elections later that year, after campaigning to radically "break with capitalism."[99] The Socialist coalition received an impressive 38 percent of the vote, which resulted in 58 percent of the seats in the National Assembly.[100] Although Communist posters emphasized their candidates as being from "the United Left Party" ("Presented by the Communist Party" appeared in very small type), they lost almost half their seats and gained only a 16 percent share of the vote.[101] Nevertheless, Mitterrand appointed four Communists to his cabinet as junior ministers in an attempt to garner the support of their party.[102] The decline of the Communist Party in national elections in France continued, however, with the party receiving roughly 10 percent of the vote in

Figure 4.14

Figure 4.15

Figure 4.16

Figure 4.17

National Assembly elections in the 1980s and 1990s, and less than 5 percent in 2002.[103]

Mitterrand advocated granting immigrants the right to vote in local elections, a position that was criticized by many on both the right *and* left. The increase in the number of immigrants and Arabs with French citizenship, and such positions by the parties of the left (and avoidance of the immigration issue by Chirac and his party), helped resurrect Jean-Marie Le Pen's party, the *Front National* (FN), which had received little support since Le Pen helped found it in 1972. The party has often been described as anti-Semitic, anti-immigrant, demagogic, and antiestablishment. Le Pen had served in the National Assembly in the early days of the Fifth Republic, opposed de Gaulle's policy of independence for Algeria, and consequently lost his seat in November 1962 as the Gaullists swept the legislative elections, with the rightist parties receiving less than 9 percent of the vote.[104] The decades that followed the ouster of Le Pen from his seat in the legislature saw the extreme right moribund until the mid-1980s, when it gradually extended its appeal to mainstream voters by stoking fears and prejudices about foreign workers and Jews, and promoting nationalistic and anti-European positions. A 1988 Le Pen poster, showing the smiling candidate looking directly at the audience, listed key positions of his campaigns, including favoring the death penalty, employment preference for French citizens, giving income to mothers who stayed home with their children, reduction of the number of immigrants, and popular referenda. Public opinion polls have confirmed that some of Le Pen's strident positions have resonated with a large number of French citizens. A *Le Monde* poll in 1991, for example, revealed that 32 percent of the sample agreed with his stands on immigration, law and order, and the upholding of "traditional values."[105]

In addition to the usual speeches and posters, Le Pen received much exposure on television, particularly with interviews on political shows, which helped him communicate his messages more effectively, beginning in the 1980s. In the 1986 legislative elections, the percentage of votes gained by the FN increased from 0.3 percent in 1981 to 9.6 percent (about the same as for the Communists); by the 1993 National Assembly elections, its share was 12.5 percent, and it rose to 14.9 percent four years later.[106]

Although it had gained support, the FN was still a minority party. In 1984, the Communists left the ruling coalition, when they disagreed with the Mitterrand government's economic austerity measures undertaken during the recession the previous year. There was also dissent concerning his move more toward the middle of the political spectrum by putting a halt to the previous emphases on nationalization, nuclear disarmament, and the class struggle.[107] In 1986, Mitterrand appointed Chirac prime minister, when the latter's Gaullist-conservative party won a majority in the National Assembly that year, after his RPR, the UDF, and their allies won 43 percent of the vote (compared to 32 percent for the Socialists and their allies).[108] The FN won representation for the first time, with its thirty-five seats comprising 6 percent of the legislative body.[109] The themes of the RPR, UDF, and the FN were similar: law and order, and concern about immigration and unemployment.[110] The ruling Socialists' strategy was evident on billboards that were seen throughout France, on which a shocked, crying face was shown looking backwards, along with the phrase "Help! The right is coming back."[111] This scare tactic proved, obviously, to be ineffective.

Chirac held the office of prime minister until 1988, when, again, as the candidate of the RPR, he lost the presidential election to Mitterrand, who increased his margin of victory in the runoff to 8 percent.[112] In the first round, Raymond Barre (the UDF candidate) came in a weak third (with 16.5 percent of the vote—more than three points behind Chirac), owing, partly, to his refusal to employ the modern political marketing specialists that the other candidates used.[113] However, Le Pen did quite well (receiving a share of more than 14 percent of the first-round votes), using fiery speeches before large crowds and on free television broadcasts, and distributing posters that linked high unemployment with immigration and portrayed him as "the outsider." The message of protecting white French citizens against the waves of immigrants was summed up on a Le Pen poster with the slogan "Defend our colors." Chirac's defeat was attributed to the languishing economy, since he had been primarily responsible for domestic matters while Mitterrand focused on foreign and defense concerns. One of Chirac's slogans, *"Nous irons plus loin*

Figure 4.18

ensemble" (We will go farther together) (Fig. 4.18), was not as positive as a slogan in his victorious campaign seven years later: "*La France en grand, La France ensemble*" (France is great, France together). Mitterrand, who advocated moderation in a generally nonideological campaign, helped his own cause with some successful image management, depicting Chirac as "risky and impulsive."[114] Mitterrand's image was enhanced further—as a president of *all* the people—by posters that were issued before the campaign began, which acclaimed the "Mitterrand Generation" and featured a baby with an aged, helping hand reaching toward it. On the other hand, some of Chirac's posters probably reinforced a damaging image of him, showing the prime minister as almost frenetic, with another slogan "Go Chirac! Go France!" The slogan on Barre's posters conveyed the opposite image—but was hardly helpful for a dull candidate, characterizing him as "Serious, Solid."[115] A photograph of the Socialist candidate smiling warmly and holding a young girl from the French overseas territories in a campaign poster in all probability did not help him gain votes with the many voters who were upset about unemployment and immigration, even if the poster was used outside of France (Fig. 4.19). The opposition would have ensured it was seen at home too.

Figure 4.19

The emphasis on personality—over issues and parties—in modern French national election campaigns is a strategy that has apparently affected voter perceptions and preferences. Exit-poll data has supported this conclusion: after the first ballot in 1988, voters indicated that they favored a candidate for his personal qualities more than for the candidate's stand on issues or party affiliation, in general.[116] Of course, it mattered enormously who the candidate was, as Barre, Chirac, and Mitterrand were backed foremost for their personalities, but Le Pen was supported mostly for his stand on an issue, not his personal qualities.[117] The influence of professional political marketing consultants, with their emphasis on image manipulation, has been evident as well. Both of Mitterrand's slogans "The Tranquil Force" and "Generation Mitterrand" were devised by

Jacques Séguéla, a creative advertising executive, who stated that there was no significant difference between advertising for a soap powder, an automobile, or a president of the republic.[118] The concept developed for the "product" (i.e., Mitterrand) was to portray him as both strong and calm, and connected to the French people and their hopes and dreams, which he could help bring to fruition. The above slogans, along with another one shown on posters during the campaign, "A united France is on the march," delivered the message of the importance of unity for progress under the president. This theme was also conveyed via TV spots in which shots of voters were combined with text. The words "solidarity," "protection," and "security" were prominent, and Mitterrand called "Frenchmen to unity," warning that partisan conflicts would hurt the nation and relating it all to French history and culture—as visuals of the French Revolution, art, the five-week vacation, and celebrities were aired.[119] The emphasis on image over issues was evident in the posters for all the candidates and parties, except the Communists, "who continued to explain their positions in detail in handouts and posters, with the result that their efforts ... appear[ed] surprisingly dated and verbose," according to Kay Lawson and Colette Ysmal.[120]

After the presidential election of 1988, Mitterrand had Chirac initiate legislation to limit campaign expenditures and provide government financial assistance to candidates who received at least 5 percent of the vote on the first ballot (with additional financial support if they qualified for the second round).[121] These regulations were added to the ones that existed. Candidates in France were already forbidden to use commercial billboards during the official campaign period; rather, they were given access to billboard space provided by the government, and each candidate was allocated the same number of equal spots. The temporary billboards thus became even more important in political campaigns, giving parties and candidates "one of few places ... to sell their virtues to voters," according to Alan Riding.[122] The National Commission for the Control of the Electoral Campaign regulated the official posters for these sites, controlling their size and colors. The colors of the French flag could not be used, for example, so that candidates could not try to imply that they were the "patriotic" choice.[123]

Although television broadcasts certainly have an influence, posters "hold a special weight" in France, with "heavily muscled and occasionally armed squads ... pasting up posters for their own candidates and defacing or tearing down those of rivals," reported Gail Russell Chaddock.[124] There are several reasons why the poster is still an essential medium in election campaigns, probably more so in France than in the United States. One reason is that the French government does not allow paid political advertisements on television or radio.[125] This leaves printed political material, including posters, as a fertile medium to sow campaign propaganda, which includes the denigration of the opposition, in countries such as France (as well as Spain and Great Britain). Another factor is that many citizens guard the "privacy of their homes," and thus do not want to contend with political telephone calls and canvassers (not that the parties have many volunteers to perform these tasks).[126] One more is that since postage is so costly, direct mailings rarely occur beyond the official packet, containing campaign literature on behalf of all candidates and sent out by the government at election time.[127] In 1988, for instance, only Mitterrand had his own direct mail campaign, posting three million letters (each more than forty pages in length!).[128] Unlike in the United States, this direct mailing (which also was published in newspapers) did not target segments of the population on specific issues or attempt to raise campaign funds; rather, it spelled out Mitterrand's plans for the entire nation.[129]

In addition to posters, the role of newspapers has become more noteworthy, with frequent planting of negative stories about opposition candidates. This practice occurs before the official campaign period begins, at which time government-provided funds can be spent on campaign material and media spots. *Unofficial* campaign activity can occur at any time, however, and, as Lawson and Ysmal pointed out, nonpublic monies can be spent before the official period. It is common, therefore, for an abundance of posters of every size, and with any color used, to appear on commercial billboards, walls, utility poles, and kiosks before the official campaign periods commence (i.e., three weeks before the first-round voting and two weeks between the two votes).[130]

Chirac finally won a presidential election in 1995, and was in office for a dozen years. His success was due, in no small measure, to support from an effective RPR political organization and prominent Gaullists in the government. Chirac's pledge in the first-round campaign to "break with the past," by reducing taxes and deficits and by promising to increase spending for education and welfare programs while lessening crime and immigration, in the second-round campaign, resulted in a victory in the runoff by a margin of 5 percent over Lionel Jospin, the Socialist candidate and a former minister of education.[131] Le Pen surpassed his 1988 percentage in the first round, with a 15 percent share of those who voted.[132] His campaign was marked by a call for the removal of three million immigrants to "solve France's unemployment problem."[133] This was made clear in a *Front National* poster, which stated, "Three million unemployed, that is three million immigrants too many!"[134] Another FN poster included a silhouette of an airplane in front of the setting sun, with the slogan "When we come in … They go out!" Later in the campaign, when three FN party members attacked rappers who walked past some FN posters, shooting to death the son of an immigrant from Africa, Le Pen would not condemn the homicide. Moreover, the *Front National* chairman stated that the killing was a case of "self-defense."[135]

By 2002, the Socialist Party was down to 24 percent in the National Assembly elections.[136] Its leader, Jospin, whose party—along with other parties of the left—had taken control of the National Assembly five years earlier, resulting in his appointment as prime minister, did not even make the second round in the presidential election in 2002. Le Pen, who received almost 17 percent of the votes, edged him out by slightly more than half a point.[137] One of Le Pen's posters depicted Chirac and Jospin as liars with long noses, with the former politician stating, "I've never met Mr. Chirac," and the latter saying, "I've never been a Trotskyist."[138] This Pinocchio imagery was so compelling that it appeared the next year, and again in 2005, in posters produced by the British Conservative Party (as is seen in the next chapter). Another FN poster showed a head-and-shoulders photograph of a stern-looking Le Pen, with the slogan "France and the French First" (a reference to his anti-immigrant stance). A poster featuring a similar photographic portrait of Chirac (albeit smiling), headlined "*La France en grand, La France ensemble*," struck the theme of a greater, unified nation, under his leadership. Despite Le Pen's efforts, he gained only an additional 1 percent support in the runoff, and Chirac won overwhelmingly, gaining 82 percent of the votes.[139] In the subsequent legislative elections a little more than one month later, however, Le Pen's FN party won only 11 percent of the votes and no seats in the National Assembly. This happened as Chirac's new united conservative party for the presidential majority, the *Union pour la majorite presidentielle* (UMP), won three times the FN's share of the popular vote and almost two-thirds of the seats. The divided Socialist Party lost more than one hundred seats in the National Assembly. Support for Le Pen and the FN, due in large part to its anti-immigration stance, had increased over two decades, in general.[140] In other European countries, parties with similar positions (and posters) had recently performed even better, as is seen in Chapter Six.

In addition to the regulation of television and radio time, the prohibition of political advertising on these media, and the restrictions on campaign funding, posters are now banned on commercial board fences or "hoardings" during the four months preceding any official election campaign.[141] Although television time is restricted and most of it is occupied by candidates' broadcasts, it can sometimes be used very creatively. In 1988, for example, the Mitterrand broadcast was preceded by a 90-second MTV-style, multi-image segment (alluded to previously), designed by the Séguéla team, which showed rapidly changing visuals, "recalling the historical tradition of the left and situating the candidate within the history of France," according to Charlot and Charlot.[142] Again, it was the job of Mitterrand's political consultant to design propaganda that would appeal to swing voters' emotions, especially their patriotism. Polling data have indicated that the percentage of such "floating voters" in France has fluctuated between approximately 25 percent and 40 percent since the mid-twentieth century.[143]

In the 2007 presidential election, François Bayrou of the UDF, seemed to position himself to appeal to these voters with the centrist idea "to create a pro-Europe, pro-market, social-democratic parliamentary bloc: a party … that would draw its membership from progressives on the left and the right," according to Jane Kramer.[144] Bayrou came in third in the first round, with more than 18 percent of the votes. The winner of the runoff election was Minister of the Interior Sarkozy of the UMP, a conservative who promised sweeping economic reforms (with tax incentives and training to reduce unemployment). He won the runoff election by a 6-point margin (after receiving 31 percent in the initial voting) over legislator Ségolène Royal (26 percent in the first round), a Socialist—who would have been the first woman to be president of France. Le Pen did not perform as well as he had in the previous election, gaining about 10 percent of the votes.[145] Le Pen sounded the same themes, but an FN poster did include a black woman from the Antilles. Slogans continued to be carefully chosen. One of Sarkozy's was "*a rupture tranquille*," which took Mitterrand's past slogan and made it "a tranquil break"; another, translated, was "Together Everything Becomes Possible." Bayrou's "France with all our forces" reflected his campaign strategy, to attract voters from both sides of the political spectrum, and Royal's was simply "Change." The imagery on most of the campaign posters was quite conventional: the top three candidates all dressed conservatively and looked at the voters, warmly, but without smiling broadly. In France, presidential candidates seem to be expected to have relatively serious facial expressions on their posters. In the campaign itself, style, image, and personality appeared to be more important than ever, and character traits such as "toughness" were discussed at length.[146]

Broadsides, together with posters, have been an important political medium in France for more than two centuries, beginning with the French Revolution. Image management has been evident in even earlier prints and posters. Kings were mythologized, as were candidates in French elections. Owing to legal restrictions on the use of television in election campaigns, posters have been more prominent in France and used to attack opponents—something that is not allowed in the broadcast media. France has a rich tradition of political satire and artistic expression (with Daumier, Toulouse-Lautrec, and others influencing poster designers). This has been reflected in some of its election posters. In the last third of the twentieth century and into the next, political consultants have been hired to carefully choose the themes and slogans in these posters. Two of the themes (also apparent in British politics) have been "fear of the left" and "the evils of capitalism"— propaganda strategies manifest in printed propaganda at election time. Economic concerns have been prominent, along with the issues of war and peace, militarism, colonialism, immigration, nationalism, fascism, and corruption, but more and more the focus has been on *leadership*, and the images of various politicians—from de Gaulle to Chirac—who claimed that they could provide it.

Broadsides and Posters in British Election Campaigns

C andidates who sought support from the masses, most of whom could not cast ballots, used broadsides in election campaigns in England in the late 1600s. Posters became indispensable during election periods in Great Britain in the second half of the nineteenth and early twentieth centuries, when many more people were enfranchised, especially after the Labour Party was established in 1906. The campaign tactics practiced in America have greatly influenced those in Great Britain, beginning with reformer William Gladstone of the Liberal Party in the final quarter of the nineteenth century; he emulated American politicians' stumping and advertising approaches, including the use of posters. Later, U.S. political consultants were brought to Great Britain to advise its parties. In addition, homegrown political marketing teams were active. While Saatchi & Saatchi's work done for the British Conservative Party is probably the most noteworthy example of the involvement by an advertising firm in politics beyond American shores, other examples abound in Great Britain. The most recent is Boase Massimi Pollitt's (BMP) promotion, carried out for the resurgent Labour Party, whose personnel also crossed the Atlantic to work in the United States. Several were involved in Bill Clinton's campaign for the presidency in 1992, and their recommendations contributed to Tony Blair's successful marketing plan (evident in the posters created), which helped the latter candidate's party take office in 1997.[1] As in France, the role of television in Great Britain is a lesser one than it is in the United States, due primarily to legislation. In both these European countries, political parties are not allowed to attack the opposition on television, but they can do so in their election posters; consequently, imagery and slogans have grown in prominence compared to issues.

The Genesis of Representative British Politics and the
First Broadsides in Great Britain

In 1265, Simon de Montfort, Earl of Leicester, convened the first English parliament that included commoners.[2] Simon, who wrote a constitution called the *Mise of Lewes*, while ruling England briefly (after the barons successfully revolted against Henry III), wanted to gain the support of the common people for the new order.[3] Knights and nobles were asked to attend this parliament, along with elected representatives, to be dispatched by the citizens of various cities, boroughs, and counties.[4] Landowners in England gained the right to vote by the early fifteenth century, with members of the House of Commons elected to enact legislation concerning finances.[5] The appointed body, the House of Lords, or monarch, could veto such laws, however.[6]

There were no political parties until the seventeenth century. The British Liberal Party is the world's oldest party, born in 1679 when anti-Catholic members of parliament assembled to work against the succession of the Duke of York to the throne. The British Conservative Party, which favored the duke's claim, was formed soon afterward. The former group became known as the *Whigs* (a derisive term for Scottish horse thieves as well as nonconformists) and the latter group became the *Tories* (a term for Irish cattle rustlers), until the party changed its name to *Conservative* in 1830. About a decade later, the Whigs' adversaries began to call them Liberals, to suggest that they were morally lax; in time, the obloquy was embraced and adopted.[7]

By the end of the seventeenth century, the well-to-do class in Great Britain was involved in propaganda campaigns—dominated by broadsides, pamphlets, newspapers, engravings, and other print material—during elections for their Tory and Whig candidacies for seats in the House of Commons, to garner support from the populace, many of whom were not allowed to vote. Voters were offered food and drink as early as the sixteenth century, and bribery appeared to be common in the seventeenth. After political parties were formed, elections were held frequently. Sixteen general election campaigns were conducted between 1679 and 1717, and most electors voted a straight party ticket in constituencies that had two members of parliament (which was most of them).[8] It would be an overstatement to call elections around this time "democratic" since, for much of the eighteenth century, only about one in fifty people were allowed to vote, and only about two in five members of the Commons were actually elected.[9] However, there were some boroughs (in which resident householders were enfranchised) where well over half of the adult males could vote. One account stated that in 1715 about 23 percent of all adult males were eligible to vote in England and Wales; other accounts put the percentage much lower, barely breaking 10 percent—well into the nineteenth century.[10] Most of the contestants for parliamentary seats focused on local issues, but national concerns were sometimes raised, including ones involving the church, military actions, peace negotiations, naturalization of Jews, abolition of the slave trade, the crisis in the American colonies, and political reform.[11]

Propaganda campaigns were fought with ever-increasing pamphlets, broadsides, handbills, and letters, and the role of newspapers as an important advertising medium continued. In addition, canvassing, meals, meetings, marches, and speeches (complemented with food, alcoholic beverages, bands, ribbons, flags, and banners) were organized in the boroughs. A huge number of printed pieces were circulated. In a 1749 by-election in Westminster, for example, a candidate ran off almost two hundred fifty thousand electoral letters, broadsheets, and other advertisements—aimed at only about ten thousand voters.[12] Often, broadsides were tacked up in inns, clubs, shops, churches, committee rooms, and other public meeting places. In the latter part of the eighteenth century, a greater number of independent parliamentary candidates emerged to challenge the power of the elite in many election contests, in which there was competition for about three of every five seats. Sometimes these challenges proved successful, with pamphlets and other printed propaganda stating the case against the landlords. The 1810s and 1820s witnessed mass meetings (accompanied by banners, petitions, pamphlets, broadsheets, music, and newspaper support), which were usually organized by members of the upper and middle classes, and called for the reform of the political system. Rallies drew gigantic crowds—some numbering as many as two hundred thousand people, many of them from the working class. Broadsides, addressed "To the Working Men," announced Chartist (and other) demonstrations, and called for fair wages and the right to vote. Political parties, particularly the Whigs and Tories, maintained central election funds, some of which were used for printing and distribution of propaganda during election campaigns. In the early nineteenth century, a significant amount of money was also expended on cabs, both to transport voters to the polls and display placards, as well as for meals, beer and whiskey, lodging, and stabling for voters' horses.[13]

The Role of Election Broadsides as the British Electorate Expanded

The Whig Party gained power in parliament at the end of 1830, and about one and a half years later, the Reform Act of 1832 created a more representative districting system for elections, and expanded the franchise to adult males who lived in houses of a certain value. The House of Lords failed to stop the passage of this act, thus demonstrating that it lacked the power of the Commons. The working class, both men and women—still without the vote—would continue to agitate for it in the Chartist movement, as well as in later socialist and union groups, eventually leading to the formation of the Labour Party.[14]

The Whigs and Radicals!

Composed by John M'Lean, Coal-miner, and Poet Laureate to his Baccanalian Majesty.

Come voters now, come every one,
Vote for Campbell as fast's you can ;
Don't let a Tory into the chair,
For he'll lead you into a snare.

Figure 5.1 (excerpt)

Elections for seats in the House of Commons in the nineteenth century were often fiercely contested, and broadsides were abundant. The broadsides frequently included attention-grabbing visuals, such as soldiers on horseback, and were often in the form of poems and songs. Crowds chanted or sang them, trying to influence electors (voting before the secret ballot was mandated). The broadsides also provided slogans to be shouted.[15] John McLean, "Coal-miner, and Poet Laureate to his Baccanalian Majesty," wrote the following verse for an illustrated broadside (Fig. 5.1) supporting a Whig candidate for a seat in Edinburgh, Scotland, in the 1834 by-election:

> Come voters now, come every one,
> Vote for Campbell as fast's you can;
> Don't let a Tory into the Chair,
> For he'll lead you into a snare.

The by-election was called when a House member, who had been appointed a senator in the College of Justice, resigned.[16] The candidate promoted in the 1834 broadside was Sir John Campbell, who was a moderate Liberal in favor of such reforms as not imprisoning debtors except in the case of fraud.[17] The broadside also declared Radical candidate James Aytoun, a lawyer and manufacturer, and a Chartist who advocated free trade,[18] "fit enough for a Parliament-man." It asked people to vote for either anti-Tory candidate in the election, which was won by Campbell (who received 1,932 votes) over the Tory John Learmouth (who had 1,401) and Aytoun (with 480).[19] After the election, Campbell wrote of the widespread bribing of voters:

> The incipient danger of corruption I found to arise from publicans and keepers of beer-shops, who were electors, and, without any notion of receiving bribe or voting-money, were eager to have their houses opened with a view to the profit on the sale of liquor, and I fear would be thereby influenced in their votes.[20]

The Chartists used placards liberally: some featured imagery from the French Revolution (e.g., the Cap of Liberty) and others focused on specific subjects (e.g., one issued during the Irish potato famine in 1848 stated "Irishmen resident in London, on the part of the democrats in England we extend to you the warm hand of fraternalization … ").[21]

The pressure exerted by the Chartists, and the movements that preceded and followed them, helped lead to the enactment of reform acts in 1832 and 1867. Even so, by 1869 as few as one-third of the adult male population of England, Wales, and Scotland could vote. The Reform Act of 1867, however, led to an increase in the number of voters from approximately seven hundred thousand to more than two million in Great Britain from three decades earlier, and people began to identify more with political parties. Consequently, portraits of party leaders—typically Benjamin Disraeli (of the Conservative Party) and William Gladstone (of the Liberal Party)—were frequently displayed, usually in homes. Many male laborers were granted the right to vote in the Reform Act of 1867. Naturally, as occurred in the United States a generation earlier with the Jacksonian Democrats and Harrison's Whigs, the British political parties devised tactics to target these newly enfranchised voters. This included disseminating news magazines and newspapers that emphasized worker concerns. Election campaigns on a national level began at the end of the 1870s, and meetings, canvassing, and newspapers focused more on national issues.[22]

The bribing and imbibing of electors (along with other corrupt practices) and a lack of information to workers regularly characterized elections. This continued until reforms were enacted in the nineteenth century, culminating with the secret ballot in 1872, controls on campaign spending in 1883, extension of the franchise to householders and lodgers in 1885, redistricting in 1886, and the earlier elimination of newspaper duties in 1861 (which made the medium more accessible to the working class). Gladstone, who had been a prime mover for these reforms, became the leader of the Liberal Party, and based his campaign on those of some American politicians by giving speeches at railroad stops, winning audiences with captivating oratory. He also looked at the United States and saw the value of advertising to its economy. It is not surprising, therefore, that the Liberal Party used advertisements, including posters, to promote itself in the election campaigns. British elections in the nineteenth century were quite different from American ones, however, in that about half the seats were uncontested, and that local issues dominated many of the contested ones. In 1867, the number of uncontested seats declined significantly (by almost 50 percent) from nine years earlier, although some of the contests were between members of the same party; by the election of 1880, they had been reduced by about half again when compared to that of 1868.[23]

The political parties increasingly focused their advertising on their leaders, who, in turn, emphasized generally one national issue during the election campaign, although local candidates were given much leeway in message design.[24] Gladstone, for example, as H. J. Hanham noted, stressed "the disestablishment of the Irish Church in 1868, the abolition of the income tax in 1874, the Turkish atrocities in 1880, and Home Rule for Ireland in 1886."[25] Anti-Catholic broadsides were common before the 1868 election, and suspicion was cast upon papal "agents" and those who "imprisoned" women in convents. Other broadsides smeared Gladstone: one, titled "The Queen or the Pope?" posed the question in 1868, "Will you permit Gladstone to take away the supremacy of your Sovereign, and hand it over to the Pope?"[26] Prints and posters of the period also slurred Disraeli, whose parents were Jewish; some depicted him with an enlarged nose in cartoons. Customarily printed in Conservative blue, posters and broadsides that were distributed during the election of 1880 attacked Gladstone for being a "radical." Liberals that year issued election posters, usually printed with yellow ink, reproaching the Conservatives for increased unemployment from 1875 to 1879 (although the economy as an issue was secondary to foreign affairs). This helped them regain power in 1880 in an overwhelming victory—after six years as the opposition—winning more seats (three hundred forty-seven) than did the Conservatives (two hundred forty) and Irish Nationalists (sixty-five) combined.[27] Some of the Liberals' posters depicted the past prosperity, when their party was in power, as rays of sunshine, in contrast to the gloomy economic situation under the Conservatives. These posters foreshadowed the posters produced for the Labour and Conservative Parties in 1923 and 1929 (see Figs. 5.11 and 5.14). How much was expended on broadsides and posters before the Corrupt Practices Act of 1883 placed limits on campaign spending? A good indication is in the breakdown of expenditures, totaling 1.7 million pounds, for the 1880 election for House of Commons' seats: about 23 percent were for printing and advertising; 50 percent for compensating agents, clerks, and canvassers; and 27 percent for transportation.[28]

Gladstone's Liberal government was brought down in 1885 when its budget was defeated. In that year's campaign, the Conservatives undoubtedly believed that they had a good chance to regain power: the country had fallen into depression; and Gladstone had been discredited in the eyes of many when he first imprisoned Charles Parnell, the leader of the Irish Nationalists in the House of Commons, and then released him, negotiating the "Kilmainham Treaty" with him. These two themes can be seen in a Conservative poster comparing the lower spending by the previous Tory government (with bars in blue) to the higher expenditures by the Liberals (with bars in red); it also claimed that "Peace with Honour" (i.e., diplomatic victories over Russia in 1878) had occurred on the Conservative watch, but that "Surrender with Dishonor" (i.e., problems in Africa

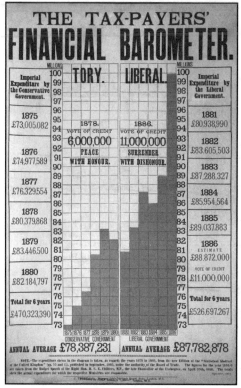

Figure 5.2

and Asia, and in Ireland) had disgraced the nation under the Liberals (Fig. 5.2). Gladstone's hopes for a moderate solution in Ireland, with the Irish wishing to stay in the United Kingdom, were dashed as the "Home Rule" movement gathered steam. Nevertheless, the Liberals won again in 1885; however, they lost twelve seats in the Commons, whereas the Irish Nationalists gained twenty-one and the Conservatives picked up nine. Furthermore, their popular margin over the Conservatives was only about 4 percent.[29]

By 1886, the two recently enacted reform acts resulted in an electorate that had expanded from 3 million just three years earlier to 5.5 million.[30] Even though there were many more voters, and districting was considerably fairer, this did not benefit the Liberals. Although the Liberal Party targeted newly enfranchised farm laborers, and issued proposals that were designed to appeal to them, the Conservatives won the votes of many middle-class town and city dwellers dismayed by some of these proposals that threatened property rights. The Conservatives also claimed to be more fiscally competent, and advertised that their governments under Lord Beaconsfield (i.e., Disraeli, who had been made an earl during his term in office) had helped localities, previously, with grants-in-aid, in large broadsides and handbills issued during the election that year. The General Election of 1886 saw the Conservatives and their allies, the Liberal Unionists, who had departed the Liberal Party owing to opposition to "Home Rule" in Ireland, achieve a margin of more than 6 percent over the Liberals in the popular vote and a two hundred-seat margin over the Liberals in the Commons.[31]

The Conservative Party had become more powerful, as it grew to be simply "the party of property" rather than "the party of landed property."[32] The Liberal Party, on the other hand, became weaker as a split developed between the Whigs (the more conservative aristocratic members) and the Radicals (those who proposed seizing property) in the party and as "the Irish question" caused further devastation to its ranks.[33] The Conservatives printed posters that targeted the working class: in 1895, for example, they issued two posters: one, titled "Under the Gladstonian Government" and subtitled "Misery," which illustrated a depressed laborer and his family adjacent to an empty cupboard; and another, titled "Under the Unionist Government" and subtitled "Happiness," which depicted a prosperous working class family with good food on the table. The Liberals, in their posters, tried to portray the Tories as "for the wealthy and privileged," and themselves as "for the people," but their campaigns failed to win another national election until 1906. In addition, during this period, worker-employer strife and unionism intensified, resulting in the birth of the Labour Party in the first decade of the new century.

Posters, the Rise and Fall of the Liberals, and the Growth of the Labour Party

The Labour Party originated in 1899, when a local branch of the Amalgamated Society of Railway Servants voted to call on the Trades Union Congress to hold a conference on ensuring the representation of labor interests in the House of Commons. At this meeting, a motion was passed to form the Labour Representation Committee (LRC) to support candidates and to develop a new political party, which would introduce legislation to protect unions—something both the Liberals and Conservatives would not do. The LRC did not achieve much success until 1903, when its secretary, Ramsay MacDonald, concluded an agreement with the Chief Whip of the Liberal Party, Herbert Gladstone, a son of William Gladstone (who had died five years earlier) ensuring that the two groups' official candidates would not run against each other. The LRC won twenty-nine seats in the 1906 election, and upon entering parliament, they announced that they were members of the Labour Party. In that election, labor candidates received about 5 percent of the popular vote, as the Liberals finally regained power by obtaining more than 49 percent (a 6 percent margin over the Conservatives), giving them 60 percent of the seats in the House of Commons.[34] With more than 2.5 million trade union members in the United Kingdom (a sixfold increase from 1882), labour interests had become a force to be reckoned with.[35]

How did the Liberals regain power—in such a convincing fashion—in 1906? The Liberals "rebranded" their party as one that was more in favor of social reform, and "New Liberals" such as Lloyd George advocated for legislation to protect and help children, workers, and the unemployed. At the same time, the ruling Conservative-Liberal Unionist coalition had not succeeded in passing any social reform laws, was held responsible for the death of Boers in South African "concentration camps," and for the appalling working conditions of Chinese laborers in the South African gold mines. Some also condemned it for having passed a law that granted public funds to Anglican schools, and its split over free trade and taxation (leading to import duties and, ultimately, inflated food prices). In fact, Joseph Chamberlain, who had proposed the tariffs, resigned from the government over this issue, but continued to advocate for protectionism. The pro-tariff Conservatives gave both the Liberal and Labour Parties an issue, with the latter blaming all Conservatives for wanting to burden workers with higher prices and taxes, since the government seemed to favor *some* tariffs.[36]

Some of these factors were manifest in the posters circulated during the election campaign. The issue of "Chinese slavery" was illustrated in Liberal Party posters such as the one shown in Figure 5.3, which criticized the Tory government for allowing the importation of laborers from China to the Transvaal, after soldiers had fought and died in the Boer War. Prominent figures in the colorful lithograph are a sleeping John Bull, Tommy Atkins (representing the dead soldiers), and a caricature of a well-to-do man who

Figure 5.3

Figure 5.4

is probably Jewish.[37] Another Liberal poster portrayed a gentleman in a top hat (labeled "tariff reform") rolling the "taxation" barrel over an irate laborer. On the wall is tacked a proclamation by Chamberlain that states, "If you are to give a preference to the colonies you <u>must put</u> a tax on food." The same theme was addressed in a different way in the "Substance and Shadow" poster (shown in Figure 5.4), which promoted free trade and "cheap food" for the laborers (embodied by a bulldog dressed in a worker's clothing), rather than supporting tariffs to boost wages and work (presented as an illusion in the water).

The Conservatives also issued attractive posters, but the issues they emphasized were not as compelling for voters. They distributed a poster, for example, that extolled the alliance negotiated between Great Britain (symbolized by the ubiquitous John Bull) and Japan (personified by a soldier) (Fig. 5.5). The Conservative-Unionist forces continued to hammer the

Figure 5.5

Figure 5.6

Liberals on the Irish issue, as seen in Figure 5.6, with politicians made to put up with the stink of "Home Rule" cigar smoke, advocated by the Liberal Party's leader, Henry Campbell-Bannerman (H. C. B.). In addition, the Conservatives produced posters that attacked the Liberals' economic policies as "socialism." In one poster, titled "The Fraud Exposed!" John Bull can be seen rubbing down a horse, labeled "Liberal Budget," only to reveal the word "Socialism" beneath the paint. Another poster portrayed Campbell-Bannerman, clad in a frock and apron in a kitchen, mixing a "Radical Programme" in a bowl, with John Bull refusing to taste it. The Conservatives also attempted to counter the Liberals' propaganda on "Chinese slavery" by conveying its "benefits." One poster exhibited Campbell-Bannerman speaking to a well-dressed British worker outside a South African mine, with cartoonish Chinese workers in the background. The Liberal leader is sympathetic about the British worker losing out on a job, but is met with disagreement, as he is told "For every nine collies, there's a white man gettin' £1 a day to boss 'em." The emphasis on these issues, particularly the Liberals' charge that the Conservatives would levy a "tax on bread," helped ensure victory for the Liberal Party and resulted in a voter turnout of about 83 percent (up from 75 percent in 1900).[38] Also produced were hand-colored posters that included symbols such as flags of Scotland and the United Kingdom, Britannia, and the crown, leaving spaces for parliamentary candidates' lithographic portraits together with their names. These were similar to the "banners" printed in the United States in the 1800s (discussed in Chapters One and Two), which followed a formula with American flags, eagles, and allegorical symbols. The British banners, like their U.S. counterparts, bore slogans such as "Good Government and National Prosperity." At the end of the nineteenth century, it was also common to represent various party leaders at different ends of the political spectrum as Saint George on horseback, or as a dragon-slaying knight (often the illustration had only to be altered by substituting the head of one politician with another and changing the labels on the mythical animal).

By the next elections, two of which took place in 1910, the novelty of the mass-produced, multicolored, lithographic pictorial posters for such advertising purposes as political propagandizing seemed to wane a bit in Great Britain. The lack of available funds was also a factor in the design and production of fewer posters. The elections of 1910, according to contemporary accounts, saw a reduction in the number of all printed campaign material, since, as *The Times* of London noted, "all parties seem[ed] to have realized the costliness of this method of propaganda."[39] The distribution of posters continued, however, and some of the expenses—at least for those printed by the Labour Party—were financed by union members. It also appears that more funds were devoted to smaller posters. For example, the Liberal Publication Department's policy was "to furnish their customers with relatively small posters capable of being displayed on hoardings in such a way to form a pictorial picture gallery."[40] This tactic also ensured that viewers could be exposed to a multitude of issues at once. Around this time, horse-drawn "Conservative Vans" were engaged to display rows of posters and broadsides. Another interesting development was that the most compelling pictorial designs from the previous election were reissued. But the political parties still distributed large broadsides devoid of illustrations, as well as massive quantities of pamphlets and leaflets. The Conservative Party dispensed an estimated fifty million printed items; the Liberals disseminated more than forty million items during the two campaigns; and the Labour Party circulated five million leaflets, as well as eight hundred thousand manifestos and fifty thousand posters.[41] In addition, the Conservatives sold gramophone records filled with propagandistic messages. The Liberal Party's broadsides were often designed to attract attention by posing provocative questions such as "Which will you be—Peers' Men or Free Men?" or statements such as "Tariff Reform would let off the Rich in order to Tax the Poor!" It also seemed common at this time for the opposition to deface posters or cover them with their own declarations, sometimes resulting in the issuance of summonses and even outbreaks of violence.[42]

As for themes, the Irish "Home Rule" contentiousness continued in 1910, intensifying after the first election in January of that year. That is when the Liberals won only two more seats than the Unionists (i.e., Conservatives and Liberal Unionists), giving the balance of power to the Irish Nationalist Party, led by John Redmond, a moderate who favored allowing Ireland to remain in the United Kingdom. The Liberal Party was forced to work with the Irish Nationalists to try to pass a bill that would prevent the House of Lords from blocking legislation—most particularly "Home Rule" and new taxes.[43] The thwarting of the "will of the people" had been an issue in the January campaign. Posters on walls featured caricatures of the Lords and depicted free trade as deleterious to the working class. One Liberal poster had John Bull (standing on a map of the UK), ready to fight a "Tory peer," wearing hunting clothes, an ermine-trimmed robe, a monocle, and carrying a shotgun. The poster's caption was "Vote Liberal and back up John Bull." By the second election campaign of 1910 (with voting scheduled for December), the Conservatives and Unionists were having a field day ridiculing the Liberals as Redmond's lackeys. The Irish leader was featured in many of the cartoon posters distributed by the National Union of Conservative and Constitutional Associations: one showed Redmond holding chains attached to the noses of Liberal leaders Herbert Henry Asquith, Lloyd George, and Winston Churchill, and carrying the green flag of Irish independence (in a poster titled "Their Irish Master"); another pictured John Bull (with the headline "Halt!") arresting Redmond (shown with a bag of dollars, presumably from Irish American supporters); a third illustrated Redmond training a Radical parrot, with the head of Asquith (now the prime minister), to "Say, 'Home Rule'"; a fourth once again lampooned Redmond, this time portrayed as a gramophone, with a terrier labeled "the Liberal Party."[44]

Perhaps the biggest issue, however, was that of Chancellor of the Exchequer George's "People's Budget," proposed in 1909, which included a land-sales tax, higher and somewhat progressive income taxes, increases in death duties, and alcohol and tobacco taxes to pay for pensions for the retired, roads for the new automobiles, and new warships.[45] The Conservatives attacked these taxes with relish. In one poster, two umbrella-carrying foreigners observed marching British workers, bearing banners that read "Unemployed" and "Tax the Foreigner Not Us." The caption states: "Genial foreigner: — 'How they must wish that Mr. Lloyd George had taxed us instead of them.'" Another Conservative poster had Robin Hood telling George, "I took from the rich and gave to the poor—you rob from both!" George, on the other hand, made speeches preceding the election that attacked "dukes" and "landlords," and Liberal Party posters issued during the election campaign continued the propaganda. One poster, for example, captioned "Vote for Liberalism and Fair Play," had Asquith atop an anxious horse (labeled "British Constitution") outside the parliament buildings. Seated behind the prime minister is a peer, who is controlling the horse with reins represented as "Financial Control" and "Legislation." Another Liberal poster illustrated a peer unwilling to do anything to help Britannia pay for some of George's programs (Fig. 5.7).

Figure 5.7

Political strategy was another factor. George, in pushing for radical reforms, shifted the Liberal Party more toward the left to prevent the new Labour Party from mounting an effective challenge to his party and gaining support for its socialist agenda. In the elections of 1910, this strategy was largely successful, with Labour winning only two-score seats and 7 percent of the popular total in December, whereas the two main parties between them divided 90 percent of the popular vote.[46] Furthermore, the Conservative-Unionist attacks on tariffs—as detrimental to the workers—helped it win few seats in its areas, while the Liberals picked up seats in some bigger cities, including the slums of London.[47] For the time being, the Liberals stayed in power with the aid of the Irish Nationalists and, sometimes, Labour.

Although it was not yet a truly national party, and attracted far fewer votes than did the Tories and Liberals, the Labour Party did publish several posters that were recognized as works of art at the time. The posters were also appealing and simple in design, to attract viewers and help them grasp the message quickly and easily. The Times of London singled out several of the Labour posters of 1910 for their "striking" design, noting the interesting concept of displaying all three together as a panel:

Figure 5.8

Three of these are of exceptional merit as artistic productions. They are printed in colours, and the designs are of such a character as to arrest the eye and rivet the attention of the passer-by. One of them shows an advancing host of workers, beneath it being the words, "Forward! The day is breaking!" Another is a picture of two figures, of which one is a woman standing with a babe in her arms, the other a crouching figure in shadow. A third poster shows a group of men and women huddled together on the embankment of a river. It is labeled "Workless!" These three pictures are intended to be exhibited as panels, the first, which is the largest, being flanked by the other two.[48]

The theme of unemployment, as David Crowley pointed out, has been a powerful and commonly used one in political posters.[49] The out-of-work laborers in the "Workless" poster of 1910 (Fig. 5.8) were placed in a bleak urban setting by artist Gerald Spencer Pryse, their shadowed features barely distinguishable, in the social-realism style employed by many artists of the period. The same theme was handled quite differently in the later Conservative "Labour Isn't Working" posters, in the 1978–1979 period (see Fig. 5.25): the unemployed were still depicted as anonymous, passive figures, but they

Figure 5.9

were shown in great numbers in a queue from a birds-eye view. Another arresting poster image from 1910 was the young party's "Labour Clears the Way" (Fig. 5.9), which took the opposite approach visually, presenting workers as activists, rather than victims, demolishing the House of Lords (perhaps symbolically, since it had been an obstacle to reform).

Regardless of the heat generated by the second campaign of 1910, however, the results were almost identical to those of the election held in January (no party gained or lost more than two seats), with the Liberals and Unionists each winning two hundred seventy-two seats, the Irish Nationalists eighty-four, and the Labour Party forty-two.[50] While retaining their tenuous hold on power, nonetheless, the Liberals were able to pass a law that reformed parliament (with the House of Lords' veto over legislation having ended), as well as enact unemployment- and health-insurance laws within a year.[51] Notwithstanding the great advances in social reform legislation, including the institution of both old-age pensions and trade boards that could set minimum wages,[52] the Liberal-led government was unable (or unwilling) to enfranchise women nationally. Female ratepayers already possessed the right to vote in local elections, and the women's suffrage movement had been quite active in Great Britain since the 1860s,[53] and several groups produced posters in the first years of the twentieth century. Most active was the Women's Social and Political Union (WSPU), whose massive demonstrations and protests attracted much attention, particularly when its members heaved stones at Prime Minister Asquith.[54] By 1913, the government passed the Prisoners (Temporary Discharge for Ill Health) Act—commonly known as the "Cat and Mouse Act." The act provided for the release of hunger-striking suffragettes, only to later reimprison them.[55] Subsequently, one suffragette poster had a vicious cat holding in its teeth a woman wearing a WSPU sash, with a caption that implored electors to cast their votes against "The Liberal Cat."

Lloyd George blamed the "militancy" of some in the movement, which he stated had moved the public from "indifference" to "hostility," for the failure to achieve women's suffrage when members of parliament, listening to their constituents, according to George, turned against the cause.[56] What George did not say was that many Liberals feared many women would vote for the Conservatives, at least initially; his government, therefore, never supported any women's suffrage bill.[57] Whereas the antagonism toward women's suffrage certainly was a moral failure on the part of the Liberal Party leadership, it does not explain why the Liberals never again won a national election, and were replaced by Labour as the party of the working class and reform, in general. While the Labour Party supported some Liberal bills in parliament, it continued to attack the Liberal government, focusing on the failure to pass a right-to-work amendment to the Unemployed Workmen Act. MacDonald and other Labour leaders issued a manifesto, published in the form of a broadside, decrying increased unemployment and calling for demonstrations.

The demise of the Liberal Party, as one of the two major parties in Great Britain, began with World War I, which the nation entered with little dissent, even by most Labourites and Irish Nationalists in parliament. Redmond, for example, called for Irish volunteers to fight in the conflict, after war was declared in 1914. In less than a year, the Liberals joined with the Unionists and pro-war Labourites in a coalition government. Asquith continued as the prime minister and Liberals headed most of the ministries. The British government's harsh treatment of the Irish, after the Easter Rising of 1916, pushed most Catholics in that country away from the moderate stance advocated by Redmond, and toward the extreme Sinn Féin position. Conscription of Irishmen exacerbated the problem for the government, as did the failure of Asquith to push hard for the Home Rule pact that George had negotiated with the Irish Nationalists and Ulsterites, which resulted in its defeat in parliament. In addition, enthusiasm for the war waned after several years. In the postwar period, the deaths of over nine hundred thousand soldiers of the British Empire seemed senseless to many citizens, who came to believe that they had been misled by the propaganda issued by their own government, led by the Liberals.[58]

By the end of 1916, the Liberal Party started to break up, and George formed a coalition government. Conservative-Unionists held most of the ministry positions. Within two years, George pushed through legislation that gave the right to vote to many women over age thirty and most men over twenty-one (except for soldiers, who could vote at nineteen). Legislation also called for redistricting the country more fairly: most constituencies had one member of Parliament (MP) and equal populations. It should be noted that residency and household requirements made women, and some men, ineligible to vote. Nevertheless, the number of enfranchised citizens increased almost threefold— actually, about the same increase as that which had occurred after the Reform Act of 1867. The percentage of the adult population that could vote had grown from 28 percent at the start of the decade to 78 percent by its final year.[59] While it was the right thing to do, the expansion of the right to vote hurt the Liberals, apparently, as more new voters favored the Conservatives and Labour.[60]

The fortunes of the Labour Party also took a turn for the better, ironically, after Arthur Henderson, the leader of the party, was compelled to resign from George's coalition cabinet in 1917, because he favored sending a delegation to a socialist conference in Sweden to explore ways of ending the war. Henderson proceeded to move his party away from the Liberals, and reorganized it to be more of a national party with a broader appeal. In the General Election of 1918, the opposition Labour Party increased its percentage of the popular vote, since the last balloting, from 7 percent to 22 percent and won twenty-one more seats in the Commons. By this first postwar election, the split between Asquith and George had grown wider, and George had formed a separate party of Liberals, with its own organization and funding. This Coalition Liberal Party won 13.5 percent of the popular vote and one hundred thirty-three seats—more than double Labour's sixty-three. The Coalition Unionists, however, won almost 33 percent of the popular vote and three hundred thirty-five seats. The Asquith Liberals did almost as well as George's group with the voters, gaining 12 percent of the popular total, but only twenty-eight seats. The Conservatives were now dominant, as they were in postwar France and in the United States. However, one ominous development for those who favored Ireland remaining in a united kingdom

Figure 5.10

was that although Sinn Féin won seventy-three seats in the election, compared to the Irish Nationalists' seven, they refused to be seated in the British Parliament, and soon formed the Irish Republic, with Éamon de Valera, who had been elected as an MP, as its president.[61]

By the autumn of 1922, Conservatives' disagreements with Lloyd George had grown, a large majority of the party leaders voted to terminate the coalition, and George resigned as prime minister. In the subsequent election, the Labour Party fielded more candidates, and attacked the Liberals vigorously. This can be seen in a Labour poster, in which the paraphrase of Lloyd George's words, stated at the end of World War I, was used against him four years later: George had said, "What is our task? To make Britain a fit country for heroes to live in" (Fig. 5.10). Three years later, however, Great Britain saw increased unemployment in the cities and countryside, wage reductions, unionism,

and strikes. In the General Election of November 1922, Labour won enough seats (one hundred forty-two) to become the main opposition party to the Conservatives, who gained three hundred forty-four seats and 38 percent of the popular vote. The Conservatives' campaign theme of a return to "tranquility and stability both at home and abroad" echoed that of Harding's "Back to Normalcy" in the U.S. election campaign two years earlier[62] (as was noted in Chapter Two). The National Liberals (who were pro-George) and Liberals (pro-Asquith) *combined* won only one hundred sixteen seats and received fewer popular votes than did Labour, with both groups gaining slightly more than 29 percent of that total.[63]

In the next decade, "tranquility" characterized the campaigns and policies of the Conservatives, led by Stanley Baldwin, acknowledged as a master of political communication, as radio, newsreels, and speeches were used effectively. This theme would often resonate with voters, who were worn out by the maneuverings of George and the contentious Liberals or frightened by the Labour Party's issuance of socialistic manifestos. Nevertheless, support for Labour was strong, particularly in formerly Liberal areas, and in the 1923 General Election, the party received over 30 percent of the popular vote and one hundred ninety-one seats, leading to a short-term Labour minority government, under Ramsey MacDonald. By this time, many in the middle class viewed the Labour Party with suspicion, but quite a few workers and intellectuals were willing to vote for it, over the Liberals, now that the anti-war aura surrounding it had dissipated. A Labour poster titled "Greet the Dawn: Give Labour It's Chance" showed a man (whose wife and baby are behind him) imploring the electorate to give his party the opportunity to implement measures that would reform the economic system (Fig. 5.11). Other posters continued this theme: "To-morrow—When Labour Rules," for example, showed a crowd of working people moving toward a literally brighter future (Fig. 5.12). Despite the temporary setback of 1923, which occurred because the Conservatives won less than a majority of the seats in the Commons, even though they achieved a 38 percent share of the total vote, the voters returned Baldwin and his party to power by the end of 1924.[64]

The 1924 General Election witnessed the extinguishing of all realistic hopes that the Liberals might have had to resurrect their party as a major political player in Great Britain. In the span of one year, the Liberals' share of the popular vote declined from almost 30 percent to under 18 percent, and the party won only forty seats in Parliament (down from one hundred

Figure 5.11

fifty-nine). The Conservative Party, on the other hand, won 48 percent of the popular vote and four hundred nineteen seats (or 68 percent of the Commons).[65] Posters and pamphlets were produced in huge quantities. Labour Party officials stated that they printed forty million pamphlets and fliers in 1924, and during the campaign, the *New York Times* headlined, "Britain is Flooded with Party Posters." As was the case in the U.S. election campaigns, British

Figure 5.12

politicians traveled everywhere, delivering stump speeches; MacDonald, for one, delivered twenty-two speeches in one day during the campaign. Unlike U.S. campaigns at that time, however, British electioneering was less costly. Party spending was limited to a set amount, based on the number of voters in counties and boroughs, and prohibited were American practices such as paying for vehicles to transport voters to the polls, giving out flags and ribbons, and hiring bands.[66]

The 1924 campaign was acrimonious, much of it trying to depict Labour as "Bolshevik." One Conservative poster, using a photogravure reproduction of Hubert von Herkomer's widely known painting "On Strike," added the caption "The Socialists promised me work, I've not got it." Other Tory posters employed "bewhiskered, blood-stained Bolsheviki of the usual caricature type," according to the *New York Times;* one poster, featuring a "Red" returning to Russia with bundles of banknotes, turned out the lyrics "Bolshevik, Bolshevik, where have you been? Over to England, where the 'Reds' are still green?" Similar images had already been used in French posters (see Fig. 4.3, Chapter Four). Posters for Labour,

SAFETY FIRST!

STANLEY BALDWIN
THE MAN YOU CAN TRUST !

Figure 5.13

trying to portray itself in the mainstream, showed a football player heading a ball, along with the caption "Use your head and vote Labour." In addition, during this period, concerned English citizens wrote letters to the editor, decrying pictorial advertising's spoiling of public places and complaining about the lack of good poster design. While they focused their wrath mainly on commercial posters, one can only imagine the dismay some of them felt, while taking a Sunday stroll, when they were subjected to posters that besmirched favored candidates or when the rain had dulled the sheen of posters put up by their own parties.[67]

Baldwin continued to lead the Conservative Party, and appeared prominently on some of its posters in 1929, the year of the next election campaign, along with the slogan "Safety First" (Fig. 5.13). This slogan was already familiar to the public, since the Conservatives had used it in a "drive carefully" campaign, as well as in 1922, when they stressed the need for moderate policies in government.[68] Generally, Baldwin's government *had* been moderate: it extended pension coverage, abolished taxes for agricultural property and many industries to stimulate business growth and employment, pushed through an unemployment bill, and pursued a policy of "peace and reconciliation" in foreign affairs.[69] It also lowered the voting age for women to twenty-one, despite Conservative politicians' fears that these "flappers" would be more likely to vote for the opposition parties.[70] Many of the Conservative government's accomplishments were trumpeted in its 1929 propaganda. A good example is the poster "The Conservative Sun-Ray Treatment," which presented many of these achievements, including "equal franchise," as rays of the sun (Fig. 5.14). In subsequent elections, posters targeted women more frequently. Two years later, for instance, a Conservative Party election poster simply showed an elderly woman, above the statement, "We must think of our savings and our home. That's why I'm voting for the National Government" (in which the Conservatives would be dominant).

By the 1929 election, however, unemployment had increased as the economy worsened, and both the Liberals and Labour picked up support among the newly enfranchised and swing voters who had supported Conservative five years previously. Labour continued to use many of their posters to try to

Figure 5.14

Figure 5.15

reach out to a broader segment of the populace, an approach that can be seen in the more diverse people shown in Figure 5.15 and the more inclusive slogan "Labour Stands for All Who Work." In broadside-style, nonpictorial posters, the Conservative Party propagandized that (1) joblessness was worse under Lloyd George in 1921 than under Baldwin five years later (which was true); (2) union unrest was responsible for an increase in unemployment (also true); and (3) there were more people employed in 1929 than was the case five years earlier (which was true, but misleading) (Fig. 5.16). In addition, the party warned of the dangers of Labour socialism, implying that benevolent "New Conservatism" was the only way (Fig. 5.17). One development in 1929 was that the

Figure 5.16   *Figure 5.17*

Conservative Party began to produce and paste on billboards much larger posters—up to sixty-four sheets in size[71]—emphasizing social reforms (such as the extension of pensions and public-health measures) and housing construction. The party also attacked socialism with slogans such as "The Socialists will be Liberal with your money!" and "Who will pay for Socialist schemes? You! You! You!" In the campaign, Lloyd George and the Liberal Party called for a Keynesian program of public works to alleviate unemployment, to be financed with deficit spending—an idea that was well in advance of its time. The Liberals did obtain substantially more popular votes in 1929 than in 1924 (increasing their share almost 6 percentage points), but they won only nineteen additional seats in the Commons.[72] Labour's publicity heavily emphasized the unemployment issue, stressing that the party would alleviate the problem by increasing efficiency and eliminating wastefulness in industries that could be nationalized gradually—promises that were stated in the forty-three million pieces of printed material the party produced.[73] The Conservatives fell back to a 38 percent share of the total vote and won twenty-eight fewer seats than the Labour Party did, even though the latter obtained 1 percentage point less of the popular vote than Baldwin's party did.[74] Consequently, MacDonald was able to form another minority government.

Above all, it was deemed necessary to hire advertising personnel to design the posters and leaflets for the Conservatives in the postwar years. Political marketing began in Britain around the time Lasker was using advertising techniques across the Atlantic to help Harding.[75] By 1929, the *New York Times* reported that "American methods of appealing to the voters [were] gaining headway in Great Britain. There [was] no lack of 'slogans,' posters, [and] broadcasting. ... "[76] The Conservatives spent more than one hundred fifty-five thousand pounds on publicity that year, over one-half of the total campaign budget, the lion's share expended on posters and leaflets; approximately five hundred thousand copies of the former were distributed and over eight million copies of the party's manifesto were printed.[77] The Benson agency, which handled the Guinness® account, was responsible for the slogan "Safety First," which was blamed, in part, for the party's narrow loss in 1929 election.[78] Given the economic hard times, fewer British voters were swayed by the Conservatives' scare tactics. After the war, the British Labour Party had launched the first publicity and press department, using many wartime propaganda techniques in its election campaigns.[79] The Tories also reaped the benefits of the propagandists' wartime experience. This was noted in a memorandum written by J. C. C. Davidson, the Conservative Party chairman in the second half of the 1920s: "The first job on which I set my mind was to apply the lessons of the Great War to the organization of political warfare."[80] One of the propaganda techniques the Conservatives employed was writing letters to the editor under different pseudonyms; another was putting candidate portraits and slogans on cigarette cards.[81]

The unemployment numbers increased while MacDonald was the prime minister, as the Great Depression developed. The Labourites in power mainly followed a conventional approach to righting the economy, with little or no commitment to socialism, nationalization, and deficit spending. The result was that the Labour Party alienated their traditional union and left-wing allies, and by 1931, other forces, including influential persons in banking and journalism, were calling for a "national government" to deal with the economic crisis. What soon followed was that MacDonald asked four Conservatives (including Baldwin), three other Labourites, and two Liberals to join the government; the General Election of 1931 was held within a few months. In the campaign, both MacDonald and Baldwin made vague statements on what their policies would be, and the Labour Party, again under Henderson, advocated nationalization and taxes on unearned income. Labour was depicted, frequently, as being directed by radical socialists and concerned more about the working class than the nation as a whole. This was implied in some of the National posters, portraying an unemployed man and the headline "What Have the Socialists Done for Me?" Others displayed Union Jacks with the slogan "Our Country First." Some posters were designed to appeal to women ("Smokeless Chimneys and Anxious Mothers!"), or farmers ("Back to the Plough"), or hinted at protective tariffs to prevent the loss of jobs ("Better 'Punch In' than be 'Knocked Out' by the foreigner"). The propaganda strategy was wildly successful, and workers and Liberal voters deserted their parties to support the National Government forces. Labour lost a 6.5 percent share of the popular vote and two hundred thirty-six seats in the House of Commons, and the five parties that comprised the National Government coalition attracted 67 percent of the total vote and an astounding 90 percent of the seats in the Commons; the Conservatives gained 55 percent of the votes and 77 percent of the seats.[82]

In the months leading up to the General Election of 1935, the strategy of the National Government coalition forces, now headed by Baldwin, was to emphasize positive news and ignore opposition charges, in general. Hence, posters, broadsides, and newsreels were designed by the National Publicity Bureau to emphasize decreased joblessness and unemployment compensation, lower taxes, higher farm prices and wages, improved trade figures, better housing, and peace and security.[83] One 1931 poster was incorporated into a new one produced for the National Government coalition, which communicated the message that the employment situation had improved, but that voters needed to return the coalition for this to continue. The first poster was placed on the left side, under "1931," and presented a frowning man with an outstretched hand, pleading, "Mates! help me get a job"; on the right side of the newly issued poster, under "1935," was a smiling man with one hand reaching out and the other giving the "thumbs up," saying "I got the Job—help me to keep it."

Some of these messages were national in scope; others targeted regions. One billboard—with the headline "Saved Scottish Agriculture from Collapse"—was displayed obviously in rural areas in Scotland; another one, aimed at all voters, showed three soccer players, with the slogan "It's team work that counts. Support National Government." Other poster and billboard campaigns targeted seaside vacationers and Underground passengers. Images of citizens, rather than the leadership, were standard in most of the posters, although Baldwin was quoted and George was referred to in several. Designed to give the appearance of tabloid newspapers, broadsides were used heavily, and up to five million complimentary copies were distributed. These contained illustrations that were selected to attract attention or provide "human interest" appeal, and included features aimed at women voters, sports enthusiasts, and crossword puzzle fans.[84]

The massive publicity campaign, coupled with good economic growth, the imposition of import duties, nationalization of London's mass transit system, and an acquiescence to the pacifism of the times, resulted in another huge victory for the National Government in the 1935 election. Several Labour posters attacked the Conservatives as "warmongers"—one, titled "Stop War," even featured a baby wearing a gas mask. Nevertheless, the Conservatives maintained their dominance politically, again winning over one-half of the popular vote and seven of ten seats in the Commons; the Liberals lost many of their voters and most of their seats to Labour, winding up with only twenty MPs compared to the Labour Party's one hundred fifty-four (an increase of one hundred two seats). Labour's 38 percent share of the popular vote, however, was still far removed from the Tories' 54 percent.[85] There was not to be another election in Great Britain for ten years. The country moved toward involvement in World War II, under Neville Chamberlain—who had replaced the retired Baldwin as party leader and prime minister in 1937—as head of a mainly Conservative government. Ramsey MacDonald also retired from public service and died shortly thereafter.[86]

The Role of Posters in British Elections in the Mass Media Age

In the British election campaigns during this period, radio was the medium of choice from the 1920s until the 1959 General Election, when television was effectively employed for the first time. The British Broadcasting Company (BBC) was formed in 1922, and presumed to be politically impartial. During the 1924 election campaign, it arranged for each major party to address the voters. After delivering what he called a "heart-to-heart talk," Baldwin was judged the most effective radio speaker because, according to a *New York Times* reporter, he "seemed to realize that he was not addressing a meeting of his own supporters only, but was speaking into the homes of many people hostile to him."[87] Two years later, the BBC was granted a monopoly in radio broadcasting, since it was a national, public corporation, and most observers thereafter considered it neutral in its political coverage. The political parties were not allowed to propagandize on the BBC, so they turned to other media to do so. Posters and other printed material proliferated because of this prohibition. In addition, newsreels (with an estimated audience of twenty million each week in the latter part of the 1920s) were used to convey political messages to the voters, particularly by the Conservative Party, which established a film section. When theater managers objected to the showing of party propaganda in their establishments, the Conservatives organized "cinema vans" that ran their newsreels—laced with patriotic references—before the presentation of a feature film, to a large number of voters. In the 1935 election campaign, for example, about 1.5 million people viewed them this way.[88] An estimated 12.5 million people listened to a Conservative Party radio broadcast by Baldwin.[89]

By the end of the 1930s, three out of four British households owned a radio.[90] The emergence of this mass medium of communication affected politics: there was less stumping and more emphasis on the parties' individual leaders, particularly on those who were adept at addressing the public via the new media. This emphasis on the leadership was evident in the posters that began to emerge in the 1920s, which included idealized, almost "heroic" portraits of men such as Baldwin, according to the newspapers of the time. One contemporary reporter, Ernest Marshall, wrote in 1929 that although "Baldwin has been described as the homeliest man in a conspicuous position in British politics, … [his] facial lineaments are now displayed on posters all over the country as an attractive appeal to the voters, … [with his] features … rounded out almost to John Bullish fullness."[91] The same artistic license seemed to be applied to other political leaders. For example, Lloyd George, in a Liberal poster, wrote Marshall, "has been poetized and etherealized[,] … his eyes gazing at the dawn, which is breaking over his Welsh hills."[92] The Conservative Party also practiced "image management" during this period in its newsreels. Baldwin was advised by the party's publicity people how to project "reassurance" to the public, using brief speeches, favorable camera angles, and an informal style that had been perfected in radio broadcasts.[93] Apparently, Baldwin was the "FDR of Britain" giving "fireside chats" (discussed in Chapter Three); or rather, since Baldwin preceded Roosevelt, FDR was the "Baldwin of the U.S." He also was not the first "homely" candidate to be idealized in campaign portraits, since this process had transformed, earlier, plain-looking or unattractive politicians, most notably Abraham Lincoln in the United States.

One of the greatest media politicians, Winston Churchill, was soon to take center stage in Great Britain. Chamberlain's mainly Conservative government failed to meet the challenge posed by Hitler, marked by the prime minister's refusal to work out an anti-Nazi pact with the Soviet Union in 1939. By the next year, many in his own party abandoned him, and he was forced to resign. Churchill became head of a coalition government, which included the leader of the Labour Party, Clement Attlee, and the Liberal leader, Archibald Sinclair (both of whom had refused to join a war cabinet under Chamberlain). Churchill presided over the BBC in the 1920s, and during the 1930s, he was recognized as a compelling radio broadcaster. His stirring radio transmissions during the early portion of World War II did much to rally the spirit of the citizens of the United Kingdom, after France fell to the German army and during the Battle of Britain.[94] Wartime posters featuring the resolute and charismatic prime minister, with planes and tanks in the background, enhanced his image.

After the war was won, however, Prime Minister Churchill and the Conservatives, in a coalition with the National Liberals and the National Party, were roundly defeated in 1945, soon after the Labourites and Liberals departed from the wartime coalition government. A photograph of Churchill, who clearly was more popular than his party, appeared on election campaign posters, with the prime minister smiling and looking directly at the voters, and a slogan appealing, "Help Him finish the Job" (Fig. 5.18). Another portrait poster was captioned "You followed through the trials of war. Follow him into the triumphs of peace." There were also portraits—captioned "Coming my way?"— of Liberal Party leader William Beveridge, who authored a governmental report during the war that proposed a "cradle

Figure 5.18

to the grave" social system. The use of the portrait in an election propaganda poster was atypical of Great Britain's national campaigns, with their emphasis on parties and issues. But it made sense to the strategists in these instances, considering Churchill's prestige as a leader during the conflict and the prominence of the "Beveridge Report." Most of the posters that were produced by all parties, however, did not feature the leadership. During the campaign, Churchill delivered four of the Conservative coalition's radio addresses, whereas all ten of those aired by the Labour Party featured different leaders. These radio broadcasts probably had an impact on the voters, since the average audience was about 45 percent of the electorate.[95] Unfortunately, the prime minister, in one of his addresses, compared his Labour opponents—who had just served in his victorious cabinet—to the Nazis. This boomeranged, and a nation that had experienced many socialistic policies during the war, along with about a 40 percent increase in trade union membership, gave Labour 48 percent of its vote (and Churchill's National Party received only about 40 percent), providing the Labour Party a majority of almost two hundred seats in the House of Commons.[96]

Posters issued by the National Party in 1945 tried to link the victory in the war to domestic concerns. One, for example, showed a farmer driving a tractor, along with the slogan "They did not fail us. ... We must not fail them. For a prosperous countryside VOTE NATIONAL." The Labour Party also tried to associate the victory of the British soldiers with the need to "win the peace" (Fig. 5.19). The National Party relied on scare tactics in their posters, with slogans such as "Britain fought for freedom. See you get it. Vote National." However, as domestic issues such as housing took precedence after the defeat of Nazi Germany, and as Labour leaders, such as Attlee, were trusted by much of the populace, Labour benefited at the polls.[97] The Labour Party's awareness that domestic issues were dominant was reflected in the slogans of its posters, which included "Labour for prosperity" and "Let's build the houses quick! Vote Labour" and featured average citizens. In all, the party printed four hundred thousand posters (eight times as many as in 1910), but only five hundred thousand manifestos (almost 40 percent fewer than thirty-five years earlier).[98]

Figure 5.19

The Conservatives hired the firm of Coleman, Prentis & Varley to design the party's issue-oriented advertising campaigns, which ran before the elections of 1950 and 1951, but "image-building" was not yet in vogue as the dominant propaganda strategy.[99] The firm also chose to employ pictures of "ordinary people," rather than those of the political leaders (as it explained in a memorandum), to "help the average reader to identify himself or herself with them. This campaign deals with the facts and figures of political propaganda but expresses them warmly and in terms of human feelings."[100] The Labour Party did likewise, with posters of mothers and children, workers with shovels, and grandparents. In these years, as well as in 1955, nearly all of the election posters featured photographic and drawn portraits of family members, workers, children, or just slogans such as "healthy thanks to Labour" (Fig. 5.20) and "Make Britain great again. Vote Conservative," featuring a bulldog that symbolized the party (Fig. 5.21). The Conservatives even issued a poster

| Figure 5.20 | Figure 5.21 |

that was dominated by a graph illustrating how unemployment had risen under "Socialist Governments" during the 1920s and 1930s, and had declined under Conservative rule during these decades. It should be noted that legal restrictions on campaign expenditures adversely affected the number of posters printed. However, newspapers such as *The Times* of London printed examples of the posters issued by the three largest parties, thus giving them free and broader exposure. The elections themselves were close. The 1950 contest gave Labour a majority so slim that another election was called for the next year. Perceived negative developments—communal violence in India, inflation, insufficient housing, a lack of spending on consumer durables, and a desire to unnecessarily nationalize industries—counterbalanced, for many, the accomplishments of the postwar, Attlee-led Labour government—particularly full employment, the establishment of the National Health Service, and decolonization. Naturally, Conservative posters spotlighted these negatives and Labour posters focused attention on the positive moves. One Conservative poster, for instance, was headlined "Had enough high prices, house hunting? Then let the Tories have a go." A Labour poster declared "It's never happened before—six years of full employment!" In addition, an antinationalization advertising campaign, featuring the character "Mr. Cube," targeted women voters, and probably lost votes for Labour.[101]

The Conservatives barely won a functioning majority in the Commons in the 1951 election; the Tories benefited from the failure of the Liberals to attract many votes; and Churchill returned to power as prime minister. The Conservatives generally accepted the elements of the welfare state that their predecessors had bequeathed to them, but, under Minister for Housing Harold Macmillan, did much better than Labour in stimulating a consumer economy and in housing construction. Posters and other printed advertising approaches dominated the 1951 election campaign, which witnessed the first public education broadcasts (PEBs), with one 15-minute segment allocated to each of the three major parties.[102] When Churchill resigned in 1955 because of ill health, Anthony Eden succeeded him. He called for an election for the following month, and was returned as prime minister with a sixty-seven-seat advantage over Labour, still led by Attlee, in the House of Commons (having won 3 percent more of the popular vote).[103] By the 1955 General Election, the average audience for party radio broadcasts had declined to 15 percent of the electorate; the average for the television broadcasts was 14 percent.[104] Posters continued to be widely exhibited, often in rows, with most of them devoid of pictures, but with slogans such as "Better value for your money with Labour" and "As Promised—A Million Houses. Vote Conservative." The displays were occasionally interrupted by a portrait of Eden, looking determined, along with the slogan "Working for Peace"; or, the opposition leader, seen smiling, with "You Can Trust Mr. Attlee" under his photograph.[105]

A key election year was 1959. Television became a more important medium to British political campaigns, since homes with TV sets had doubled to more than 70 percent since the last election in 1955, and consequently, party television (and radio) broadcasts doubled also. But television's audience was the larger of the two media: 61 percent of the voting public saw at least one party TV show, whereas only 27 percent listened to one on radio.[106] It is notable that political time on the broadcast media (first radio, then television) was regulated by legislation: minutes for PEBs were determined by proportion of votes, and paid TV political advertising was prohibited. Instead, parties were provided free television and radio time. Campaign spending at the national level, however, was not controlled in any way at this time.[107]

Advertising and public relations consultants became more heavily involved in British politics, at least on the Conservatives' side, and image management—more for the party's "brand" than for any candidate—was paramount. Since the Conservative Party was more "pro-business" than was Labour, it had far fewer reservations about employing modern advertising techniques to advance its interests. Labour leader Hugh Gaitskell, in fact, referred to advertising as "somehow false."[108] The Tories again hired Coleman, Prentis & Varley, and spent a record amount for advertising: one hundred thirty-five thousand pounds for posters and one hundred thirteen thousand pounds for press ads, largely to shape their image in general, not to emphasize issues.[109] The themes of "prosperity" and "opportunity" were devised, and associated with the party.[110] "During the campaign," as D. E. Butler and Richard Rose stated, "the term 'party image' was continually invoked, almost as if it represented a magical new force."[111] The consultants worded the party's thematic propaganda simply to increase the likelihood that voters would easily grasp the messages and view them as relevant.

When the Conservative political marketing campaign commenced two years before the election, a Gallup poll showed that the Conservative Party was 7 percentage points behind Labour and less than one-third approved of the government and leadership of Macmillan, who had replaced Eden.[112] The Conservatives' costly advertising continued full blast—at the same time an effective antinationalism business campaign ensued, with brochures such as *They've Got a Little List. Steel and the Nation—Labour's Plan.* The party removed the posters when the government called the election, so that they (and the newspaper advertisements) could not be labeled "election expenses." One could say, though, that unofficial campaigning continued because soon afterward, U.S. President Eisenhower paid Macmillan a visit, and subsequently appeared with him on British television. Seven years earlier, the election campaign for the conservative Eisenhower had been the first to use television effectively, and now it seemed fitting that he was part of the medium's early employment in British politics.[113]

In addition, a massive poster campaign helped return the Conservative Party to power in 1959. The majority of the posters neither showed Macmillan, nor listed the issues the party advocated; instead, they included illustrations of the "good life" under Conservative rule. In fact, only 31 percent of the one hundred ninety thousand posters issued by the Conservative Central Office portrayed the prime minister.[114] One poster showed a family eating a sumptuous meal, a TV set behind them; another portrayed a family washing a car. The slogan used in this poster series was designed to motivate voters to feel good about the party in power, and make them fearful about damaging the economic good times: "Life's Better with the Conservatives. Don't Let Labour Ruin It." (Fig. 5.22). Other Conservative posters lacked pictures altogether; the slogans were sometimes positive ("Earnings up—Living better!") and were sometimes designed to invoke mild fearfulness ("It's Full Employment. Keep it so!"). The Labour Party's posters were more issue-oriented (e.g., headlined "Stop H-Bomb Poison Now" [Fig. 5.23]) or were directed at targeted

Figure 5.22

Figure 5.23

groups such as senior citizens. One poster showed a concerned-looking couple, with the slogan "Labour will never forget the old folk." Another showed Gaitskell smiling at the voters, with the lengthy caption "We want a Britain where production expands year by year and the growing wealth is fairly shared throughout the nation." The Conservatives, however, appeared to get much of the credit (as incumbents usually do) for the country's general peace and prosperity, and when the votes were counted, they had won by a margin of more than 5 percent.[115]

The age at which one could vote in Great Britain was lowered in 1969 (one year ahead of the United States) from twenty-one to eighteen.[116] Labour, led by Harold Wilson, had narrowly won power five years earlier and retained it by a wider margin in 1966.[117] The ruling government had been in trouble, but pulled slightly ahead in the polls by the end of April 1970.[118] By May, though, the Gallup Poll found the Conservatives had a 7-point lead among voters, reversing what had been a 5 percent margin for Labour in the previous

month.[119] Subsequently, a clever Labour poster titled "Yesterday's Men," released in May, may have cut into this lead. The idea was to depict key Conservative leaders as incompetent businessmen who "previously ran the firm to the point of bankruptcy."[120] The poster and its slogan "They failed before!" represented Conservative Party leader Edward Heath (who was front and center) and other party leaders as clay figures, not real people. Furthermore, "sinister" lighting from below, dark colors, and malevolent facial expressions were used to show them in a highly unflattering manner. The poster was also designed so that the viewers would see these men from above, looking down on "diminished" figures (Fig. 5.24). Another factor was that this poster, with these haughty, aging politicians, was intended to help the Labour

Figure 5.24

Party with the younger voting population. Although the "Yesterday's Men" poster was so popular that it was sold for a decade to the party faithful in fundraising campaigns, some media commentators and party activists objected to the derisive advertising techniques used, and David Kingsley of Kingsley Manton Palmer (KMP) was never again employed by Labour after his campaign failed to lead to victory.[121]

"Yesterday's Men" probably did advance the Labour cause, but a targeted marketing campaign for the Conservatives, coordinated by the advertising firm of Davidson, Pearce, Barry, and Tuck, seemed to aid the Conservatives in overcoming the Labour lead in the polls, and they won the 1970 election by a margin of 3 percent.[122] A Conservative poster (circulated in 1968) showed a dignified Heath, gazing thoughtfully into the distance, and the label "Man of Principle." The Conservative Party's Central Office resolved to emulate American political TV spots that avoided the use of "talking head" speeches, and it authorized political advertising personnel to produce two such spots (broadcast in 1968 and 1969) that were designed to "humanize" the prime minister, pictured in a pub and at a football game. While these propaganda strategies may have improved Heath's image, his approval rating at the time of the election was only 28 percent, compared to Wilson's 51 percent.[123] His party regained power, however, as Scottish, Welsh, and other minor parties picked up votes that had previously gone to Labour, when many supporters of immigration opponent Enoch Powell voted Conservative, and when inflation accelerated and poor trade figures were released shortly before the voting.[124]

As was typical, more than ten times as much printed campaign material was produced at the local level as at central headquarters.[125] Parliamentary candidates often had three-fold pamphlets that included a photographic portrait (as well as one of the candidate's family), some policy points, a biographical sketch, and perhaps some photographs of those giving testimonial statements. There were fewer posters printed than in previous years, but they were targeted (at least by the Conservatives) in "critical seats" and major intersections. The election law prohibited the display of political posters in railway areas, however. All the allowed billboard posters included the slogan "For a better tomorrow vote Conservative." The most utilized designs had an overflowing wastepaper basket (and the title "Remember Labour's broken promises") and one that showed decreasing monetary values (titled "The £ in your pocket is now worth … ."). Only 6 percent of the Conservative posters included Heath, whereas the wastepaper and diminished-pound posters accounted for 73 percent of those displayed.[126] Labour, on the other hand, featured its leader, Prime Minister Wilson, and the three posters the party issued during the 1970 election campaign all involved him.[127] Another added his wife and a group of children, with the slogan "Their health, their education, their opportunity—when it comes down to it aren't you voting for your children's future as well?" It has been more common for opposition leaders to be lampooned in election posters. "Yesterday's Men," which was released by the Labour Party right before the 1970 election was called, is a good example of this strategy, but Gladstone, Disraeli, George, and others were ridiculed in negative posters that preceded this campaign.

By the time of the 1979 election, Great Britain had seen a succession of governments that were led mainly by the Labour Party in the previous fifteen years. The 1979 campaign was noteworthy for the aggressive and innovative advertising campaign devised by Saatchi & Saatchi, and for its effective "Labour Isn't Working" posters. The creative ads designed by the huge English firm for corporate clients such as Gillette, British Leyland, and Schweppes drew the interest of Reece, who had just been appointed the director of communications of the Conservative Party. Impressed by American advertising techniques, with their "hard-sell" approaches, and by the innovative, negative propaganda ads designed for Johnson and Nixon in the 1960s, Reece hired Saatchi & Saatchi to devise an imaginative, tough campaign for his opposition party, led by Margaret Thatcher. The firm's Tim Bell (whom Thatcher later knighted for his efforts) was given the account. It was Bell who decided to emphasize emotions, not issues, which would appeal to voters—an approach, as we have seen, that was hardly new.[128] In 1979, high inflation, strikes, joblessness, declining market shares in many industries, monetary devaluation, and skyrocketing oil prices plagued the Labour government. In fact, many of the same problems beset U.S. President Carter at the end of the decade. As a result (and with effective political marketing specialists aiding the conservatives in the two countries), both Carter and Labour lost power to Reagan and Thatcher (see Chapter Three for the former leader's campaign). The faltering British economy and the Tories' advertising strategy clearly convinced many voters to side with Thatcher's party, which increased its share of the vote from 36 percent in the previous election to almost 44 percent (while Labour's share declined from 39 percent to 37 percent).[129]

Bell asked that members of targeted groups be interviewed. Two of the findings revealed were that most voters did not perceive the ruling Labour government's record

Figure 5.25

on unemployment to be worse than that of the Conservative government that had preceded it, and that Conservatives were thought to be better at dealing with issues that affected people.[130] One can see how the billboard posters "Labour Isn't Working," issued in 1978, and "Labour Still Isn't Working," disseminated in 1979, embodied these themes. Both showed a long, snakelike line of people at the unemployment office, and the caption "Britain's Better Off With The Conservatives" (Fig. 5.25). The slogan was quite similar to one from two decades earlier, which stated, "Life's better with the Conservatives" (see Fig. 5.22); but the design of the latter poster was stark, emphasizing the plight of the multitudes (viewed from above), as opposed to a warm family scene (shot at ground level with people smiling). In both, the message and mood was stated simply and clearly. As Maurice Saatchi said years later, "in great advertising, as in great art, simplicity is all … [with] simple themes, simple

messages, simple visual images."[131]

While the Conservative Party's advertising campaign in 1979 ran relatively smoothly, Labour's did not. Conflicts between its politicians and the creative advertising and marketing people resulted in some poorly designed posters with counterproductive slogans such as "Keep Britain Labour and it will keep on getting better" (which was displayed during a series of strikes). One of the disagreements between the two factions in Labour's planning sessions was whether to show the party's leader, James Callaghan, on posters, with the advertising people favoring a more leader-dominated campaign. The Conservative strategists had no such divisiveness with which to contend, and its main posters emphasized party image and issues. Among the party's other creative posters used on billboards during the 1978–1979 campaign was one depicting a line of people outside a hospital, with the headline "Britain Isn't Getting Any Better"; another, in a child's handwriting, read "Educashun Isnt Wurking." The Labourites also disagreed about the use of television. Some of its broadcasts were more traditional and poorly produced, whereas their opponents' televised broadcasts were of better production quality and geared more to younger voters.[132]

It also did not hurt that the Conservatives had twice the amount of money to spend on their broadcasts as the Labour Party had, as well as having the financial resources to outspend their rivals for polls, posters, and other advertisements. In fact, the Conservatives spent twice as much on posters, as well. Saatchi & Saatchi was also innovative in its ads for television and movie theaters, breaking away from the general practice of presenting politicians in TV ads, and instead using actors, unseen narrators, film clips, and appropriate background music.[133] These spots (as did the posters) focused on distinctions on issues and parties, not Conservative party leader Thatcher.[134] The two-and-a-half-minute "Labour Isn't Working" TV spot featured a worker and his wife, an industrialist, and a small-business person lamenting high prices, unemployment, and taxes, and speaking positively about Conservative economic policies.[135] One reason the Conservative Party was more financially endowed was that small and large businesses reacted favorably to the creative advertising campaign coordinated by Saatchi & Saatchi, and thus contributed even greater amounts. "Thatcherism," with its promises to reverse some features of "the welfare state," stem the power of labor unions, and reduce government spending, also proved attractive to donors.[136]

Many observers acknowledged that the "Labour Isn't Working" poster was crucial in the campaign, resulting in the Conservative victory.[137] Strategic communications and public relations specialist Kevin Goldman cited the poster as one of Saatchi & Saatchi's great successes: "The ad ran at only twenty sites, but the message was startling and pervasive."[138] The "Labour Isn't Working" poster and press advertising campaign ran in August 1978 on billboards and as an ad in movie theaters.[139] Some evidence suggests that this campaign was effective. Various polls taken in September revealed that the Conservatives had a nationwide lead that ranged from 2 to 7 percent, and that the party benefited more in marginal seats that were targeted in Saatchi & Saatchi's campaign.[140] In July, however, polls indicated that the parties had been dead even.[141] Perhaps the primary reason why posters had such prominence in the 1979 election campaign (and subsequent ones) was that British law limited each main party to the five television broadcasts, each to be ten minutes long; minor parties were allotted fewer transmissions, based on their proportion of the votes in the previous election.[142]

Thatcher and her party won again in 1983 and 1987. After the British victory over Argentina in the Falklands War, and with improved economic conditions, the Conservatives won decisively (by popular-vote margins of almost 15 and 12 percent, respectively, over Labour—which, in turn, had only single-digit margins over a resurgent Liberal Party).[143] Saatchi & Saatchi's campaign for the Conservatives, in 1983, featured a poster that compared the Labour Party's policies to those expressed in the Communist Manifesto. The poster's headline read "Like Your Manifesto, Comrade." In addition, a poster series in 1983 attempted to depict the Conservative Party as the champion of immigrant integration, while attacking Labour for treating them differently. These posters showed a young immigrant, with the slogan "Labour says he's black, Tories say he's British." A content analysis study of 1983's campaign advertising, including posters, concluded that negative advertising was the dominant method used by the Conservatives, but not by Labour or the Social Democratic Party-Liberal Alliance. Furthermore, although issues were more prominent in political advertisements than were personality attributes, the authors of this study reasoned that there had been "little in-depth treatment of issues and potential solutions."[144] In other words, there was some evidence that the "Americanization" of British election campaigning was taking hold.

In 1987, a Saatchi & Saatchi creative team designed posters and press ads for the Conservative Party and the incumbent Prime Minister Thatcher, carrying the campaign line "Britain is Great Again. Don't Let Labour Wreck It," giving voters the general idea that a vote for Labour was to court disastrous consequences. The slogan, as David Butler and Dennis Kavanagh noted, was merely a restatement of the one on the poster that helped elect Harold Macmillan and the Conservatives in 1959: "Life's Better with the Conservatives. Don't Let Labour Ruin It."[145] Other posters were more specific, focusing on voters' concerns (uncovered in polls) that Labour was weak on the issue of defense (see Fig. 5.26), and that the Conservative Party position on crime and economic growth was

Figure 5.26

better. One poster, for example, depicted dogs, growing larger and more powerful as viewers scanned from left to right, with the slogan "Now we've the fastest growth of any major economy in Europe"; another illustrated a criminal grabbed by a hand attached to an elongated arm, bearing the slogan "10,500 more policemen are helping the police with their enquiries." A poll found that voters reported that *all* the Conservative posters and billboards had a slightly negative effect on them in 1987.[146] Another poll determined that posters were the third most viewed campaign medium, behind leaflets and PEBs.[147] In contrast to U.S. elections, it was clear, once again, that British voters put less emphasis on the leader of the party. In a 1987 exit poll, voters were asked to indicate "the most important reason which decided their vote," and only 6 percent replied that it was the party's leader.[148] It is not surprising, therefore, that British posters in the 1980s often excluded Thatcher and the opposing leaders (while U.S. posters showed Reagan, Bush, Carter, and Mondale).

While it is true that, because its political system is parliamentary, there is more emphasis on parties than there is in the United States, Great Britain's campaigns became "presidential"—in many ways—in the 1990s. This "presidentialization" was stimulated, in part, by the concentration of broadcast and newspaper reporting on party leaders; decisions by the parties themselves to focus attention on these men and women as message deliverers also factored.[149] Even earlier, in 1987, the Labour Party brought in American political consultant Joseph Napolitan. Napolitan, who had worked for Humphrey in his American campaign in 1968 and for Giscard d'Estaing in France in 1975, helped design a PEB, as well as a poster, for Labour leader Neil Kinnock, which emphasized his background and personality.[150] It was in the 1980s that the Labour Party (seeing how political marketing techniques had proven to be successful for the Conservatives) began to move away from its reluctance to employ "modern" strategic political advertising and promotional methods and began to embrace them.[151] This transition accelerated in the early 1990s, under Blair's leadership. The "Americanization" (i.e., more emphasis on personality and image, simplification of problems to a few emphasized issues, targeting of voters, and negative and/or emotional messages) of the campaigns conducted by the Labour Party was manifest in the inclusion, on posters, of photographs of Blair and five "Labour's pledges" such as "more jobs for the young." Blair's idea to make these pledges was reminiscent of the U.S. Republican Party's "Contract with America" that was issued a few years earlier. The Conservatives continued to use market research to select what were likely to be the most effective issues, and highlighted their leaders in ways that would resonate with the working class. Both parties' posters were often calculated to play on the emotions of voters.

Since British political parties are not permitted to broadcast commercials,[152] posters and billboards have been used more frequently than in many other countries and, when designed with dominant issues in mind, have seemed to impact voters. As big advertising became involved in political campaign communications in British elections, the posters' messages grew to be more negative and controversial than in many other countries. Pretesting of approaches contemplated for posters in focus groups revealed that negative attacks would work well with many British citizens, although voters in other nations apparently were of different mind-sets. A Conservative Party poster in 1997, for instance, portrayed a diminutive Labour leader Tony Blair sitting in the lap of German chancellor Helmut Kohl, under the headline "Labour's Position on Europe." German citizens, when asked about the advertisement, opined that this approach would not be applied in their country because, as one German stated, "it's very polemical and we don't like that."[153]

Political poster advertisements on billboards were used extensively during the earlier British General Election of 1992. Surveys of the electorate indicated that in the week before the election, 43 percent had seen a Conservative billboard poster; 36 percent, one for Labour; and 13 percent, one put up by the Liberal Democrats. The percentages for Conservative leaflets and television broadcasts were only moderately higher.[154] The 1992 voting public, in fact, witnessed a dramatic increase in such large political poster displays, owing to recent legislation that limited parties' campaign expenditures. Since the Conservative Party had more than twice as many billboards as Labour and nine times as many as the Liberal Democrats, it was not surprising that more people spotted its billboard ads, with slogans such as "You Can't Trust Labour" (with the "L" in Labour a red symbol for a learner-driver) and "Five Years Hard Labour," featuring giant balls (chained to a citizen) that were labeled "Taxes Up," "Mortgages Up," and "Prices Up." Thousands of smaller posters and "window bills" were displayed, also, in 1992. The poster campaign for the Conservatives cost an estimated six million pounds (four million for design).[155] A report by the Home Affairs Committee indicated that the Conservatives spent millions of pounds more on posters than did Labour—even though both parties' total expenditures were similar—and that more money was spent on posters by the Conservative Party than on any other category (including press advertising, producing television broadcasts, and publications).[156] Of course, the free television and radio election broadcasts were worth millions of pounds—making them the primary means of political communication for the parties.[157]

One poster in the Conservatives' 1992 campaign showed the smiling Prime Minister John Major surrounded by happy schoolchildren, with the slogan "Vote for recovery. Not the start of a new recession" (Fig. 5.27). Another (also with a photograph of Major) targeted workers, with the question, "What does the Conservative Party offer a working class kid from Brixton?" along with the answer, "They made him prime minister." This imagery was echoed by television broadcasts that showed him traveling from Brixton to 10 Downing Street.[158] Labour posters included a grim Major and the headline "Sorry, but we're going to have to let you go," as well as the fact that "since Mr. Major got his job, 850,000 have lost theirs." One clever Labour poster/billboard personified Chancellor of the Exchequer

Figure 5.28

Norman Lamont as "Vatman," warning that a vote for the Conservatives meant an increase in the value-added tax (VAT) from 17.5 percent to 22 percent (Fig. 5.28). Surveys after the election, however, suggested that Labour billboards contributed to the shift of votes to the ruling Conservatives, due to distrust of the former party's policies on taxes and the economy, even during a recession. Coincidentally, the election results were similar to the aforementioned percentages of potential voters who had seen each party's billboards. The British electorate in 1992 divided their votes as follows: 42 percent to the Conservatives; 34 percent to Labour; and 18 percent to the Liberal Democrats.[159]

Figure 5.27

Extensive poster campaigns continued in the 1997 election in Great Britain. Although during the campaign the Conservative Party still displayed a larger number of posters than did Labour, the gap between the two parties was much narrower (a 40 percent difference) than in the previous election campaign. This was despite the former party's expenditures for posters were almost eleven million pounds and those of the latter were almost six million.[160] In the year preceding the vote, both the major British parties spent much more on posters than on press advertisements.[161] The number of newspaper pages purchased by these two parties decreased to a combined total of thirty-nine (from one hundred thirteen in the 1992 campaign and three hundred nineteen in 1987).[162] Stuart Weir and David Beetham described the election campaign as "a year-long heavyweight poster battle," with the two major parties "spending some four-fifths of their advertising budget on posters."[163] The Liberal Democrats, with less money to spend, organized "posters on wheels," and deployed vans to targeted areas. A poll revealed that more British voters were exposed to a political poster than they had been five years before, with 55 percent indicating that they had seen a Labour poster, 53 percent a Conservative one, and 16 percent a Liberal Democrat poster. The percentages were higher for all three parties, particularly for Labour.[164] Window bills resurfaced, with a Gallup poll finding that 13 percent of Labour voters, 11 percent of Liberal Democrats, and 2 percent of Conservatives had placed them in their homes.[165] A new development was the political video promo—sent to targeted voters gratis. The Referendum Party, primarily, employed this medium; it distributed an estimated five million copies of its anti-European Union video (received by 22 percent of British households), and subsequently gained about 3 percent of the vote.[166]

Major's Conservative government was in trouble. Its large advertising campaign in 1997 did not prevent the Labour Party from assuming control for the first time in almost two decades. This was despite Conservative attempts to position the opposition (led by Tony Blair, who was advocating more moderate economic policies than Labour had previously advanced, characterized by the slogan "New Labour, New Britain") as "New Labour, New Danger." In addition to this slogan (used in a poster that depicted Blair with demonic, red eyes), others in the campaign included "New Labour, New Taxes" (which had a purse with red eyes (Fig. 5.29); "New Labour, No Britain" (featuring a white flag); and "Britain is Booming, Don't Let Labour Blow It" (a boldfaced, capitalized text message that screamed from hoardings). The mainly negative campaign strategy was interrupted by several poster messages that were somewhat positive, such as one that showed Major beaming directly at the voters, captioned "You can only be sure with the Conservatives."

Figure 5.29

However, although the economy was distinguished by lower inflation, interest rates, and unemployment, the Labour Party campaign exploited voters' unhappiness with the ruling government on health and educational issues while minimizing the differences it had with the Conservatives on economic matters. One slogan on Labour's posters, "Britain Deserves Better," said much of this in three words. Focus group research had pointed to two themes for Labour to emphasize: (1) Major's "weak" leadership, and (2) resentment about tax increases.[167] These manifested in a poster that showed a "two-faced" Major turning to the statements "<u>1992</u>. 'Tax Cuts Year on Year'" and "22 Tax Rises Since <u>1992</u>." The Labour campaign slogan followed: "Enough is enough." Blair's "contract with the people" emphasized that education was the top priority, the National Health Service (NHS) would be rebuilt, and income tax rates would remain the same. A Labour broadside advertisement titled "Another 5 Years? Another Fine Mess," which was published in the campaign's final week, stressed some of these key issues. It portrayed Major as comedian "Stan Laurel" and warned that a Conservative victory "could mean VAT on food, schools that fail to educate your children, and the tearing about of NHS." This time, large segments of the British electorate could not be scared away from Labour, by fears of higher taxes and prices, and lost jobs. A pledge not to increase direct taxes accompanied a photograph of Blair (along with his signature) on a poster that was issued in the last week of the election campaign. Labour also broadcast a "presidential" PEB, which showed Blair as a very human and dynamic leader, and another that presented a plaintive "angel" complaining about the opposition party's performance while in power.

In addition, Labour used a technique, which Clinton had employed in the United States, of co-opting the opposition's symbols and issues: one of its advertisements, for example, featured the typically Conservative bulldog. Blair's move toward the center and the BMP-orchestrated marketing campaign—particularly adverts that countered the Conservatives' attacks—helped produce an overwhelming Labour victory in the popular vote, with a margin of 12.5 percentage points more than the Conservatives, about twenty-six points over the Liberal Democrats, and almost forty-one points more than the Referendum Party.[168]

The results were about the same in 2001: Labour won by a 9 percent margin in the popular vote over the main opposition party.[169] The Conservatives' "You Paid the Tax" campaign in 2000–01 employed a series of posters that targeted women, the elderly, railway passengers, and other population segments. One poster illustrated an anxious female carrying grocery bags on a dark, deserted street, accompanied by the slogan "You paid the tax. So where are the police?" Another featured a worried, older woman clutching crutches, with the slogan "You paid the tax. So where is your operation?" A few months later, Labour countered with a poster that warned, "Tory cuts. Tories' 16 billion cuts will hit hospitals"; replacing a "Y" at the end of "Tory" was a pair of gigantic scissors. The Conservatives gained thirty-two seats in the House of Commons in the 2005 General Election, but Labour still held a majority of 356 to 198. Although there was only about a 3 percent difference in vote share between the two parties, some Conservative Party operatives were very critical of the Tory campaign's lack of direction and skill.[170] Much of it was negative and ineffective. On the other hand, a Labour propaganda campaign that year appeared to resonate with many voters. Its slogan "Britain is working" (a reference to the good economic times, which reversed the 1979 Conservative catchphrase "Labour Isn't Working") was tested in the local elections the previous year. Focus groups indicated that the economy was a key issue that would work for the Labour, as opposed to the war in Iraq, which would not.[171] The slogan was used on a series of posters, with the additional one "Don't let the Tories wreck it again," one of which showed past and present Conservative leaders, including Major, Thatcher, and Michael Howard.

Researchers have found that billboards can influence one-tenth of the British electorate (see Chapter Seven). Owing to the legal prohibition of TV and radio spot ads, however, the influence of billboards and posters is probably, in reality, greater in Great Britain, since the negative advertising in them is prevalent in television news broadcasts and discussed in newspapers. The parties and their consultants understand this, the result of which is the generation of clever, eye-catching billboards and posters, designed to be covered by the mass media. Examples from Labour's 2001 campaign include "The Repossessed. No home is safe from spiraling Tory interest rates," which showed Conservative leader William Hague and shadow chancellor Michael Portillo as zombies in a horror film," and "Economic Disaster II. Coming to a home, hospital, school and business near you" showing the same two leaders starring as Mr. Boom and Mr. Bust (a takeoff on the film *Reservoir Dogs*).[172]

Not to be outdone, the Conservative Party, two years later, unveiled a poster of Blair with a long nose, and the quotation "We have no plans to increase tax at all," along with statements about the business tax and taxes in general having been increased dramatically. The "lying" theme continued in 2005, with the Conservatives producing a poster campaign that included an unflattering photograph of Blair, and the statement: "If he's prepared to lie to take us to war, he's prepared to lie to win an election." The prime minister in another poster again had a long nose made to look like a fighter airplane, and the slogan "Bliar! Bliar! Iraq's on Fire"—a reference to his "deception" by involving the country in 2003 in the conflict initiated by the U.S. administration. These posters were placed on a dozen advertising vans, and were intended to be put up at thousands of poster sites around Great Britain. Nevertheless, the latter did not happen, as tracking polls indicated they had backfired on the Tories.[173] Although there seems to be a trend toward more negative campaigns, it is important to realize that they are not always effective. Negative campaigning was not limited to the major parties. The Liberal Democrats, for example, launched a poster campaign in 2004 comprising portraits of Blair and U.S. President Bush, and the declaration, "The environment. Some people wish it would just go away."

Although there have been some complaints about the "Americanization" of British election campaigns, the American-influenced advertising techniques, employed by Saatchi & Saatchi and other firms, have often succeeded. The Conservative's television broadcasts in 1992 contained a higher proportion of attacks than those of the other two parties that year. This aggressive approach, particularly in its poster and billboard campaigns, probably helped the party achieve success: the Tories won by a margin of more than seven points,

Figure 5.30

even though Labour had been slightly ahead in the polls before the election. The U.S. influence was obvious in the 1992 election campaign, as Margaret Scammell and Holli Semetko noted: a billboard poster designed for the Conservatives by Saatchi & Saatchi featured an American slang expression, "Labour's double whammy," an attack on the opposition party's tax plans and a play on fears of higher prices[174] (Fig. 5.30). Even earlier, in the election campaigns from 1979 through 1987, the Conservatives copied techniques used in U.S. political rallies and party conferences, putting celebrities from the entertainment world on stage with British candidates, and utilizing lasers and balloons.[175]

Many of the poster campaigns in British elections, unlike those in the United States, have not featured the candidates themselves. In fact, Margaret Thatcher did not appear in most of the poster advertisements in her three campaigns.[176] Past election posters sometimes featured party leaders, including Baldwin, Churchill, Attlee, and Wilson. More often than not, British election propaganda campaigns have emphasized issues more than the leaders, even popular ones. Party leaders, however, have appeared on posters more frequently in the past two decades. British voters have seen Kinnock, Major, Blair, and others on many more "presidential" outdoor displays. Slogans have accompanied most of the portraits. Although Saatchi & Saatchi created several effective slogans, they were not the first to have done so. A Labour poster in 1935, for example, vowed that the government would engage in "Not Wanton War but War on Want."[177]

Posters in Britain seem to function similarly to lawn signs in the United States, to establish a presence in a neighborhood for the party and perhaps to boost party workers' morale.[178] The trend in electioneering, though, seems to be the display of fewer political window cards, as people are less willing to declare their partialities. Voters are now more likely to receive material in the mail and on their computers. The major causes of these developments are more effective online political advertising along with the perfection of direct mail and data management techniques, with digital printing producing material quickly and inexpensively for targeted voters.[179] Most important is that mass media can pick up a striking poster and give it extensive coverage. As a result, fewer poster prints are needed.

There is one difference to note between American and British poster campaigns: in Great Britain, posters are much more likely to show the opposition leader (exhibiting a negative facial expression), and in the United States that has happened very infrequently (although that has not been the case in TV spots). In the 2005 British election, for example, the Conservatives distributed a poster that had Blair arguing with his chancellor of the exchequer, Gordon Brown, and the words "How can they fight crime when they're fighting each other?" The Labour Party employed the same strategy in its billboard poster that was dominated by a sleeping Howard, with a copy of the "Tory Hidden Agenda" buried under his pillow, dreaming of "Cuts to schools and hospitals," with the warning "Vote Labour. Or wake up with Michael Howard"; a Conservative billboard showed Blair grinning, with the slogan "Imagine 5 more years of him. Are you thinking what we're thinking?" (see Fig. 5.31 for both billboards). One can routinely find billboards in Great Britain that deride an

Figure 5.31 (excerpt)

opposing party. During the 1997 campaign, for example, Labour paid for billboards that stated: "Be warned. Same old Tories. Same old lies." Posters are often a key component of negative advertising during British election campaigns. Such ads cannot be placed on TV (as they often are in the United States). American posters are much more positive and they focus on the parties' candidates, not their opponents. Yet another difference is that British political parties sometimes run poster campaigns even before elections are called. For instance, Labour distributed posters in 2000 (in anticipation of an election that seemed likely the next year) that stated, "If you voted for change in 1997—thank you."[180]

British election posters, more than PEBs, are frequently negative. The attacks are often amusing (unlike most in the United States), and advertising consultants for both parties get to try out creative, outlandish visual and verbal ideas. Not only was Blair pregnant in a 2001 Tory poster, but he was also coupled with the slogan "Four Years of Labour and He Still Hasn't Delivered." The imagery was borrowed from a famous advertisement for the Family Planning Association (with the man's head in the social-marketing ad replaced with Blair's). Another witty, but hardly compelling Conservative poster, in 2005, simply said, "La La La La La La La ... Labour isn't listening." In general, television advertising in Great Britain has declined somewhat, while outdoor advertising has increased, with political parties booking as much as 15 percent of the sites.[181] Legislation limiting election campaign spending, however, has resulted in fewer hoardings booked, so far, in the twenty-first century.[182] British political parties all employ focus groups to uncover ideas for their advertisements.[183] The result has been a bevy of slogans on posters and billboards, such as the Conservatives' "It's Not Racist to Impose Limits on Immigration" in 2005. Today, the major British political parties are firmly committed to comprehensive political marketing. One Labour politician, Adrian McMenamin, stated this reality succinctly: "The way people absorb politics has changed. We have to be able to engage with what the consumers, in this case the voters, are thinking."[184] While billboards and posters continue to be an important part of the marketing in the country's elections, telemarketing and direct mail approaches are playing a larger role, targeting undecided voters.[185]

Recent British election campaigns have been marked by both positive and negative party election broadcasts—a certain number of which are allocated to each party free of charge, and which are now slightly under three minutes to almost five minutes in length.[186] Just like many of the posters, PEBs concentrate on a single theme, with simple slogans and imagery. A 2001 Conservative PEB, for instance, attacked Labour for two rapes that were committed by two men who were out of prison under an early release program.[187] The program was similar to the Willie Horton ads used by George H. W. Bush in the 1988 U.S. election campaign (yet another example of the American influence). As the incumbent party, Labour was more positive in its PEBs, which contained celebrities, such as the Spice Girls (a Lasker technique), and many images of smiling schoolchildren, laborers, hospital patients, and pensioners.[188] The imagery used in British election posters is sometimes borrowed from past campaigns in the United Kingdom. In 2000, for instance, the Conservatives reused the image of the long line of people outside a hospital from more than twenty years earlier, again to criticize the ruling Labourites, this time on National Health Insurance, with the slogan "Britain's still waiting ... 264 more people have joined the queue for the NHS every day ... for a 1000 days." The visual ideas from commercial advertisements (pregnant Blair), as well as those of other countries (the wild-eyed Bolsheviks), also are recycled.

Broadsides and posters were important propaganda vehicles in British elections in the nineteenth century. In the past century or so, posters were, and remain, valuable in political campaigns. They are useful in focusing attention on an issue, building the image of a leader or party, and attacking the opposition. The legislative limits placed on political broadcasts have made the poster the medium of choice for negative advertising. Posters such as "Yesterday's Men" and "Educashun Isnt Wurking" create potent images of failure by the rival party and its leadership. In the mass media age, televised news shows and newspapers cover the unveilings of (and controversies surrounding) these posters, and large numbers of voters are exposed to their messages.

The broadsides of nineteenth-century Great Britain used imagery, rhyme, and hyperbole to muster support for candidates. The posters that followed in the next century continued to include imagery (more dominant and pointed) and exaggeration. When reforms in the nineteenth century led to the expansion of the voting franchise, posters targeted the many new voters and issues of importance to them. Poster attacks on the opposition intensified, and religious issues, class, and the "extremism" of other parties and leaders were included more often. The new Labour Party, in particular, targeted the laboring class and issued posters such as "Workless" and "Labour Clears the Way," which depicted workers as either victims or activists. Later, as advertising personnel entered the political arena, themes were more carefully chosen, initially by the Conservatives, and catchy slogans employed. Although the party leaders, particularly those who were charismatic and/or effective in mass media broadcasts, were sometimes featured in election posters, *party* image management in Great Britain was of paramount importance in modern times. The posters were designed accordingly. They often included visuals of members of targeted groups of all classes and focused on themes that it was hoped would resonate with them: a mother and son who were "healthy thanks to Labour"; a family eating a nice dinner because "life's better with the Conservatives"; and lines of people at the unemployment office because "Labour isn't working."

CHAPTER SIX

Posters in Election Campaigns Around the Rest of the World

While posters were an essential component of the political marketing packages in campaigns of the three long-standing democracies, they also had a considerable role in elections in other countries. As in the United States, Great Britain, and France, posters and broadsides were most significant before the proliferation of more modern media in these nations also. In addition, in countries where political parties were not flush with funds or where legal restrictions were in place, they played a central role. In Western Europe, at the end of the twentieth century, for instance, campaign consultants rated the street poster as a more important medium of political communication than radio and magazines.[1] German and Austrian political parties, at the turn of the twenty-first century, spent 35 to 40 percent of their advertising funds on street posters.[2] Survey data in Japan revealed that election posters were influential for millions of voters (see Chapter Seven).

By the early 1930s, radio had become a prominent electioneering medium in many parts of the world. One example of this was the use of spot advertisements in Australia's 1931 campaign.[3] Campaign television advertising (which began in the United States in the 1950s) became a valuable political-communication tool in most of Western Europe and Latin America, and in Japan, Australia, and New Zealand by the 1970s, and, even later, in other democracies. In fact, many European nations did not have commercial television stations until the 1980s and most Indians were unable to receive any televised broadcasts until the 1989 election.[4] By the 1990s, however, the dominant share of political party funds in most countries was being used to purchase television time during election campaigns, especially where strict legislative limits on such spending did not exist. In the 1990 Australian election, for example, 50 to 70 percent of the parties' media funds were spent on television;[5] in Greece's 1993 election, 94 percent of the advertising expenditures went to television.[6] While American political consultants have been brought in and TV commercials have become commonplace, the spot campaigns have frequently differed from those in the United States. A cross-cultural content analysis by Lynda Lee Kaid and Christina Holtz-Bacha revealed that spots aired outside the United States between 1988 and 1992 focused more often on issues—rather than image—and were more positive in tone.[7]

As was the case particularly in Great Britain, the propaganda tactics evident in American election campaigns affected those of other countries. American campaign professionals were active in Germany (as well as in France) as early as the 1970s. U.S. consultants were instrumental in the defeat of Slobodan Milosevic in the Serbian presidential election in 2000, perhaps "the first poll-driven, focus-group tested revolution," according to Fritz Plasser.[8] External consultants have been imported—sometimes secretly, because of nationalistic concerns—into Latin American countries. One 1998–2000 survey indicated that almost 60 percent of campaign managers in Argentina, Chile, Colombia, Mexico, and Venezuela had recently cooperated with a U.S. consultant. This survey further revealed that the percentage was the same for South Africa, considerable for East Central Europe (40 percent) and Western Europe (30 percent), but low for East Asia (4 percent). In addition, it was reported that many foreign consultants had a strong orientation toward American political campaign tactics: For example, this applied to 38 percent of East Asian campaign professionals; 30 percent of political practitioners in Australia and New Zealand; 25 percent of those in Western Europe; and 24 percent in the five Latin American nations listed above. The percentages were much higher, however, when the foreign consultants were asked about the possibility of implementing American-style campaign practices: 88 percent in the five Latin American countries; 80 percent in East Asia; 78 percent in Brazil; 68 percent in South Africa; and 52 percent in East Central Europe.[9] The professional, modern campaign techniques employed by American consultants (and those influenced by them) comprised the following: strategic communication, coordinated political marketing, image management, focus-group and polling research, segmentation, negative advertising, event planning, Web campaigning, and hard-hitting TV spots. In many countries, the use of posters remains a key media element of the integrated political marketing campaigns that are conducted, especially where legal constraints on expenditures and use of mass media are in force. Professional consultants have provided "special know-how for the conception and production of [these, and other] political advertisements," wrote Plasser.[10]

Figure 6.1

Imagery has been prominent in political posters around the world for generations. For example, an election poster, issued by the Anti-Revolutionary Party of The Netherlands in 1925, featured its leader, Hendrikus Colijn as "'s LANDS STUURMAN" (The Country's Helmsman), steadfastly steering the ship of state through the stormy political seas (Fig. 6.1). Other symbols common in the campaigns that political parties have conducted throughout the world include snakes and octopi, to be combated; lighthouses and the Sun, to denote "a better tomorrow"; the cross, to represent a party's religious values or "martyrdom"; raised fists, to demonstrate "defiance"; as well as a plethora of eagles and other animals, "V"s for "victory," and, of course, flags. While the artistic styles of these posters are frequently traditional in their graphic design, styles that are more radical have been employed too. Carlo Piatti, for instance, designed a 1971 Swiss poster in a quasi-Futurist style (somewhat reminiscent of Marcel Duchamp's "Nude Descending a Staircase") that depicted "immigration" as a kinetic six-armed, six-legged man. Political parties in Italy and Canada, in the 1960s and 1970s, imitated the rock-concert posters of such American "psychedelic" artists as Wes Wilson, and employed Op Art techniques. Art Nouveau, as well as symbolism, was evident in such posters as Albert Hahn's post-World War I "Vote Red!" (see Fig. 1.21, Chapter One) and Expressionism, in Nico Schrier's 1933 poster with the same message (see Fig. 1.24, Chapter One). The influence of the 1920s Dutch art movement known as *De Stijl* (The Style) is apparent in this latter work in its asymmetrical design and use of straight lines, primary colors, and sans-serif capital letters.[11] By the late 1920s, several political parties were featuring photographs in their election posters. Among them was a German Communist Party poster designed by John Heartfield in 1928 that was dominated by a hand and accompanied by the text "The hand has five fingers; with five you can grab the enemy."[12] Use of photography in election posters

increased worldwide, and often integrated simple, sparse designs that were similar to corporate advertisements.[13] Sometimes these posters were part of an integrated "corporate identity" campaign, such as the ones graphic artist Michele Spera designed for the Italian Republican Party for three decades (beginning in 1965).[14] Spera's Op Art imagery evoked Olivetti's advertising, and was used in an array of political items, including brochures, the party newspaper, and stage settings for campaign events.[15]

Figure 6.2

Virtually every art style can be found in election posters. Gunhild Terzenbach's primitivism, for instance, was displayed in a 1975 Socialist poster in West Germany (Fig. 6.2).

Political advertising on television has generally been restricted much more outside the United States than in American campaigns. Naturally, other media (particularly posters) have been used when parties have not been allowed an unlimited number of broadcasts. This has been the case in France and the United Kingdom, and much of the rest of Europe, as well as in Brazil, Chile, India, Israel, and Japan. For example, in The Netherlands, in which paid political broadcasts are prohibited, the Dutch Labor (PvdA) Party and the D66 party spent more money on printed material (including posters) for the 1989 election campaign (about one-third of their budgets) than on any other category, including other advertising and research.[16] When the Italian Parliament enacted legislation in 2001 that banned paid television campaign advertising, the two main political parties dramatically increased their spending on posters and billboards during the official campaign, devoting over two-thirds of their budgets to these media.[17] In some countries, legislative prohibitions against defacement of public places have led to the display of posters mainly in stores and homes or on designated wooden notice boards. This is often the case in India, where, for example, party headquarters distribute posters, banners, flags, handbills, and stickers to localities for display by owners of private establishments. Posters have been prominent in marches and rallies in India and other nations during election campaigns, helping gain attention from onlookers, advertising meetings, and attracting media coverage.[18]

Many modern election posters simply show a photograph of a smiling candidate and a slogan. For voters in many countries, the effect of seeing nondescript posters with smiling politicians may be minimal or even negative, lowering turnout. One South African graphic designer, commenting on the posters displayed during the 2004 elections in his nation, stated, "When do you ever see a politician smiling? Only when they want something from you."[19] Most U.S. election posters in the last decade have not even included candidate photographs. Other Western political parties, however, have bucked this trend. In The Netherlands, for instance, the PvdA went from minimalist posters in 2002 that showed the head of the party and its name, to posters in 2003 that presented the party's new leader surrounded by citizens.[20] In countries such as Afghanistan, in which there are relatively few televisions or even radios, a multitude of languages, and large numbers of illiterates, posters are a very useful way to communicate with voters. During the European Parliament elections of 2004, some parties printed posters that presented their policy views. In Sweden, for example, the issues addressed on the campaign posters included terrorism, trafficking of women, organized crime and drugs, welfare, globalization, and bureaucratization.[21]

This chapter explores key election campaigns—and the way in which posters, broadsides, and billboards were used in them—in Africa, Asia, Europe, and Latin America.

Africa

Democratic elections have not been held with great frequency in Africa. Only two countries in Africa were "fully democratic," according to World Audit, a not-for-profit company that ranks nations on such factors as public corruption, freedom of speech, and human rights: Mauritius (which ranked 35th in the world in May 2007) and Ghana (36th). South Africa (which ranked 35th toward the end of 2006) fell to 42nd six months later as a consequence of "all too much big-time corruption and some highly questionable legal decisions."[22] South Africa thus dropped into the category of "qualified freedom," alongside Botswana (41st), Namibia (43rd), Mali (45th), Benin (49th), Lesotho (56th), Senegal (60th), Niger (75th), and Kenya (76th), all of which were considered "free," but with some problems affecting segments of their populations.[23]

Even in countries that have not been classified as "democratic," election posters are omnipresent preceding voting day. In Algeria, for example, there are so many posters displaying portraits of the candidates that they pose a problem for automobile drivers: "It's a mess. People are getting lost because road signs are covered with election posters," claimed a taxi driver.[24] While the Internet is being used in Africa more often for political purposes, posters continue as a primary communication vehicle during election campaigns, even in South Africa, in which only about one-eighth of the voters have regular access to television and one-third to radio.[25] Accordingly, 54 percent of South African campaign managers rated street posters as "exceptionally important"—second only to the medium of radio (88 percent).[26]

ℭ *South Africa: Nelson Mandela and the ANC Victory (1994).* The minority white population, descended from English and Dutch colonists, dominated South Africa for eight decades. During this time, exploitation and prejudicial treatment of the native African population, along with Chinese and Indian laborers, led to the formation of several organizations dedicated to resist these actions. Among these organizations was the Native National Congress (which later became the African National Congress [ANC]). Elections were held in the Union of South Africa, at that time part of the British Commonwealth, but none of the parties campaigned against white supremacy. In 1960, the ANC—along with the Pan Africanist Congress—was banned, although it continued its struggle in which it utilized posters and other printed material.[27]

In 1961, South Africa left the British Commonwealth to become a republic. The system of apartheid continued, however, instituted by the racist National Party between the late 1940s and during the 1950s. The apartheid legislation provided for the registration of "whites," "Coloureds," "Indians," and "African" groups; separate facilities; and the prohibition of mixed marriages and sexual relations. The National Party further enacted legislation to deprive Coloured and African persons of the right to vote. Election contests between the National Party and the similarly pro-apartheid Conservative Party often became a debate, as Roger Thurow wrote, "to prove which party [was] whiter," with posters lamenting the end of white-rule in neighboring Rhodesia.[28] The killings of protestors, the escalation of resistance tactics from nonviolent actions to armed methods, the arrests and life sentences of Nelson Mandela and other leaders, the ostracizing of South Africa internationally, and labor strikes during the three decades after the ANC was banned eventually culminated in an end to apartheid, following Mandela's release from prison in 1990.[29]

Posters were a key medium of communication for the resistance, in addition to newspapers and Freedom Radio broadcasts, and the ANC smuggled its messages from neighboring states. The campaign that led to the first free election vote began more than a year in advance of the April 1994 date designated for the balloting. The National Party reversed course, appealing to black voters for their support, as well as campaigning in relatively sympathetic Indian and Coloured areas. When the votes were counted, the ANC—a militant national-liberation movement—had won a huge victory, gaining 63 percent of the total vote (and the parliamentary seats); the National Party had achieved a share of only 20 percent. In addition, the Inkatha Freedom Party, representing the Zulus (who had announced a boycott of the election), agreed to participate and won 10.5 percent of the vote, after campaigning for only five days.[30]

Another factor in the ANC's victory and Mandela's election as president in 1994 was the work of American political consultant Stan Greenberg. Greenberg, who had helped with Bill Clinton's presidential election in the United States two years earlier, organized a Clintonian "war room" for Mandela's campaign to facilitate information sharing, communication, and strategy. He also utilized focus groups heavily to determine the campaign's main theme—that the ANC was an "agent of change," not a "liberation movement." In addition, Greenberg advised Mandela to soften his image. This image management can be seen in a poster of Mandela surrounded by children of all races—the smiling, grandfatherly change agent who would work to help all the people look forward to a brighter future for their children. Along with the image manipulation, however, came specific goals: "2.5 million new jobs and 1 million new housing units within five years."[31] One poster depicted a black hand marking the ballot for the ANC and Mandela, and the slogans "A better life for all. Working together for jobs, peace, and freedom," accompanied by text that noted a plan "to create jobs, to ensure 10 years free, quality education for all our children, and to provide the homes and infrastructure our country needs." The ANC billboards reiterated these themes. The ANC's two main slogans, "A better life for all" and "Now is the time!" summed up its effective campaign, which both reached out to nonblacks and emphasized its leadership to gain political power for the black majority.

The National Party brought in Saatchi & Saatchi.[32] Its election campaign attacked the ANC for being "communist" and charged that it had intimidated black voters, fermented violence, and would be unable to govern the townships (Fig. 6.3).[33] The ANC and National Party each emphasized that they had changed: the former for protection of everyone's rights; the latter for integration of the races.[34] The ANC posters were not all positive. One presented photographic portraits of five former Nationalist leaders, and listed offenses committed during the party's rule (Fig. 6.4). It was an effective piece of

Figure 6.3   Figure 6.4

counterpropaganda, used to combat the National Party's attempt to gain black votes.

By the next election in 1999, campaigns were generally being run by South African consultants. They frequently chose posters to convey their messages, since paid TV spots were prohibited during parliamentary election campaign periods. The result was "a war of political posters": posters disparaging opponents and many torn down in some provinces. In addition to posters (often seen at rallies), radio spots and newspaper advertisements were used.[35]

Asia

Three countries in Asia were "fully democratic," according to the World Audit assessment, conducted in May 2007: Japan (31st), Israel (32nd), and South Korea (33rd). Further down the list were Taiwan (39th), India (47th), Papua New Guinea (50th), Mongolia (51st), Turkey (58th), the Philippines (68th), and Indonesia (73rd), all of which were classified as "qualified" democracies. A military coup occurred in Thailand in 2006, which substantially lowered it out of this latter category to 95th the next year. Taiwan (which was 22nd in November 2006) plummeted to 39th place six months later; the downgrading was due to corruption charges and extreme political "mudslinging." Election campaigns in Asia have often followed the trends in other areas of the world: personality stressed over issues, and employment of negative tactics.[36]

In many countries, election posters offer only photographs of the candidates, party logos, and slogans. A study of over nine hundred election posters in Japan from 2000 to 2001 revealed that almost 99 percent included a candidate's photograph (93 percent having a head-and-shoulders shot). Furthermore, 53 percent of the posters showed a candidate smiling, 89 percent included a slogan or statement, and between 23 percent and 90 percent of candidate posters of various parties incorporated a logo (the Communist Party using identifiable color blocks instead of a logo). Smiling also varied by party: in Japan, only 36 percent of candidates of the Clean Government Party smiled in campaign posters, in contrast to the 80 percent of Communist candidates who did.[37] Some Japanese candidates shown unsmiling in their posters have used reliable attention-grabbing techniques, such as finger-pointing and appearing in karate attire. Many also established "eye contact," with their photographers having them look directly into the camera for their poster shots. The posters displayed in Figure 1.1, Chapter One, show typical poses (in accord with the survey findings) of candidates in Japan in 2000. During the same period, candidates in other Asian countries were invariably shown smiling and sometimes waving.

The imagery in election posters is sometimes enhanced by the addition of beaming children. A poster issued by a Thai Rak Thai Party parliamentary candidate in Thailand in 2005, for example, depicted him surrounded by joyful youngsters, while he smiled and gazed upwards, along with the slogan "Let us build up Dindaeng [a district] to be a land of paradise." This approach was reminiscent of the Mandela "A better life for all" poster. Of course, the use of children's images has been popular for decades in election posters in many countries. Occasionally, the smiling candidate will be shown with a celebrity to try to improve his or her image. Thai Rak Thai candidates in the 2005 election campaign were seen in posters shaking hands with foreign leaders Koizumi, Bush, and Chinese Premier Wen Jiabao.[38]

Sometimes issues *are* highlighted. In India, for instance, many parties have employed specific issues, such as communal violence, in election posters. The Bharatiya Janata Party, for the 2004 national elections in India, for example, printed posters that included the image of a burning train, in which fifty-nine people died because of terrorism. Many Indian political consultants have reported that there has been a recent increase in emotionalism and negative campaign tactics in the country's election campaigns. The street poster is a medium to which many Indian campaign managers turn. A survey found that 25 percent of them rated posters as "exceptionally important" as a political advertising medium, behind rallies and daily newspapers (both 50 percent), public television (45 percent), and radio (41 percent). Private television (17 percent), direct mail (3 percent), and magazines (0 percent) trailed badly.[39]

Posters are at least as popular in many countries in Asia during election periods as they are elsewhere. Survey data from 1992 to 2000 in Japan revealed general popularity

ratings similar to those in Europe. Rows of posters, usually on sanctioned notice boards, are ubiquitous in Japan; during the 2000 House of Representatives' election in that country, over thirteen thousand such boards were placed in Tokyo (see Fig. 1.1, Chapter One). In India, billboards dotting roads, and posters tacked on walls, taxis, and buses, advertise films all year, making these media logical choices to promote candidates during election periods. Large political billboards also are evident in Thailand (Fig.

Figure 6.5

6.5), but are not permitted in Japan.[40]

∽ *Japan: A Traditional Society Moves Toward Image Management in Politics in 2001.* Posters and other printed material have been political staples in Japan for two centuries.[41] The influence of the West in the late nineteenth century, along with pressure exerted by social-protest movements, resulted in the constitution of 1889. The constitution established the Diet (or parliament) with two chambers, the House of Representatives and House of Peers, whose members voted on legislation initiated by the emperor. Males over the age of twenty-five who paid a tax of at least fifteen yen elected the members of the former body. This provision allowed about 1 percent of the total population to vote. The small number of voters, allegedly, led to vote buying.[42] The Universal Manhood Suffrage Law was enacted by the Diet in 1925, eliminating poll taxes and enfranchising all men aged twenty-five and older. The percentage of the population that could vote was expanded to 22 percent.[43] The next year, the Labor-Farmer, the Japan Labor-Farmer, and the Socialist People's Parties were established.

In 1928, elections for the House of Representatives were called, and the suffrage law banned door-to-door and telephone canvassing. Election posters were allowed, but could not be printed in more than two colors. Nevertheless, they could be large and placed in any location, when an owner's permission was given. Because of the relative lack of restrictions, posters were the dominant form of electioneering, with candidates averaging thirty thousand.[44] In addition, the expansion of the electorate resulted in an explosion of printed propaganda appeals, particularly posters. The Japan Labor-Farmer Party produced a compelling poster, which featured three red flags, a red sun, and the slogan "Bread, Justice, Freedom." One of its candidates printed a poster that illustrated a red, torchbearing, shield-carrying man and slogans calling for full employment and universal suffrage for

Japanese citizens who were at least twenty years old. An election poster for the Japanese Socialist People's Party featured a gigantic, muscle-bound laborer and the slogan "Less tax for the worker, more tax for the rich!" Several candidates included photographs or drawings of themselves in their posters. Some of these portraits confronted the viewers directly and most had several exclamatory slogans, such as the one shown in Figure 6.6: "Guarantee Land to Working Farmers! Give Food and Work to the Laborers! Give Freedom to All!" The government issued a poster that appealed to the males to vote, with a red sun and rays dominating the design. However, the election was not entirely fair, and the regime engineered the defeat of some farmer-worker and leftist candidates, several of whom printed their names in red on actual newspapers, which were subsequently posted.

Figure 6.6

Elections were held in 1930 and 1932, but following the prime minister's assassination in the latter year, military leaders and bureaucrats replaced party representatives in the cabinets.[45]

Later in the decade, the Japanese mobilized for war. It was not until Japan was defeated that party politics recommenced, with the establishment of the Socialist, Liberal, Progressive, and Cooperative Parties, as well as the legalization of the Communist Party. In 1946, elections for the Diet took place again, and for the first time women were allowed to vote; at the same time, the voting age for men was lowered from twenty-five to twenty.[46] While no party succeeded in gaining a majority of the seats, the top two parties—the Liberals and the Progressives—were able to form a coalition. The conservative Liberal Democratic Party (LDP) was founded in 1955 as an "anti-socialist" force, as unions demonstrated for wage increases. The party's name indicated the two existing parties that merged. In the next election, in 1958, the LDP won 44 percent of the total vote (and 287 seats in the House of Representatives), a large margin over the runner-up Japan Socialist Party's (JSP's) 25 percent (and 166 seats).[47]

The Liberal Democrats' control of the reins of government continued for the next thirty-five years, as Japan experienced great economic growth, and overall social and political stability. As early as 1960, more than 70 percent of the adult population considered themselves to be "middle class" and 45 percent of nonfarming homes had black-and-white television sets (compared to 8 percent only three years earlier).[48] Color photographs of smiling citizens, often in family scenes, dominated the election posters of every political party. The LDP issued one poster, for example, showing a joyous, adoring mother holding her laughing baby. The only exception to this strategy was seen in the posters distributed by the Communists, who mounted a pictureless poster attack on corporate monetary contributions to parties. The posters were relatively positive and innocuous partly because an election commission had to approve their content. The commission outlawed direct attacks, and enforced limits on print runs, number of variations, size, funding, and positioning. In 1996, for example, in a House of Representatives' district of over three hundred thousand voters, only one thousand posters could be displayed separately, and an additional five hundred were allowed on wooden boards, for each candidate (but not a party) during a twelve-day campaign period.[49]

The legal restrictions have continued, although by the 1990s, content approval was no longer mandated and negative campaigning was permitted. Nevertheless, few election posters include negativism, with only about 1 percent of one sample found to contain even mildly negative slogans or words.[50] It would appear that such campaign tactics are still usually frowned upon in the Japanese culture. A few small billboards are permitted, also, as is the placement of posters on houses, restaurants, and public baths (if owners grant permission). The number of radio appearances, and newspaper and television ads for candidates, is limited and regulated as well. Political parties, however, have had few restrictions imposed on them since campaign legislation was enacted in 1975, and an unlimited number of television, radio, newspaper and magazine ads, and direct mail pieces, and other printed matter can be disseminated, if candidates' names are not included.[51]

Although it stayed in power during this period, the dominant party had some minor vicissitudes. Several bribery scandals led all the way to the prime ministers. Consequently, they were forced to resign and Diet members split to join existing parties or form minor ones. The opposition socialists remained divided, however, and votes went to both the JSP and the Democratic Socialist Party (DSP). The Liberal Democrats retained power, owing to the divided opposition, with support from the rural areas, corporations, bureaucrats, and moderate-conservative citizens who had benefited from economic booms. From 1963 to 1990, the Liberal Democrats' share of the vote in House of Representatives elections ranged from 30 to 39 percent; the Japanese Socialist Party's best performance during this period was 20 percent, and its percentages ranged from 12 to 20 percent. The vote totals typically translated into majorities for the LDP in both houses of parliament, the House of Representatives (i.e., the lower house) and the House of Councillors (i.e., the upper house). In 1986, for example, the party received 59 percent of the seats in the lower house and 57 percent of the seats in the upper house.[52] Displaying the candidates shown in head-and-shoulders photographs, most of the posters issued during these campaigns were traditional. The only change over the decades, in general, was that there were many more smiles, rather than "serious" facial expressions, exhibited in later posters. Widespread corruption resulted in the loss of the LDP majority in the upper house to the JSP in the 1989 elections. An election poster that showed JSP leader Takako Doi with a red crayfish above her head, to symbolize public disgust with the corruption, probably helped boost support for the party. The Japanese Socialist Party's share of the vote improved from 12 percent to 18 percent in the lower house elections the next year, but the Liberal Democrats maintained their majority by garnering 34 percent of the total vote.[53] The JSP again used innovative poster advertising in its campaign, with its symbol, the rose, transformed into a running person, shown with the slogan "Japan is moving." Most of the election posters, however, continued to be relatively conventional. For example, Prime Minister Toshiki Kaifu of the ruling Liberal Democrats was shown sitting cross-legged with happy children nearby, along with the slogan "A vital life, a happy life"; and a Democratic Socialist poster presented a young woman hugging a dog and verbiage about a "better life."[54]

It would take more than creative advertising and somewhat negative news to dislodge the Liberal Democratic Party's hold on the voters. The more damaging news arrived in 1993, when yet another political scandal broke, followed by the failure to pass all proposed constitutional reform legislation. The House of Representatives passed a no-confidence motion that was supported by thirty-nine LDP members.[55] The body subsequently dissolved, and dozens of Liberal Democratic MPs departed for new parties that were formed. These parties (most prominently, the Japan Renewal Party and the New Harbinger Party) participated in the lower-house elections that occurred a month later, and the LDP failed to gain a majority of seats (after it obtained only 25 percent of the vote). Subsequently, eight opposition parties put together a coalition government, led by Morihiro Hosokawa, one of the LDP defectors who founded the Japan New Party (JNP), which received only 6 percent of the vote (the JSP topped the opposition parties with 10 percent).[56] In less than one year, however, the Liberal Democrats regained power, without an election, when the ruling coalition fell apart.[57]

In the next few years, other defections occurred and parties were formed or realigned, but the Liberal Democratic Party continued in power, passing bills with the aid of other parties' members. In the 2000 elections for the House of Representatives, it gained 49 percent of the lower house.[58] However, the party's leader, Prime Minister Mori Yoshiro was forced to resign the next year, and Junichiro Koizumi (who was very popular with the public) was chosen to succeed him. Koizumi, a former cabinet minister, promised economic and governmental reform—some of which he accomplished. He also cultivated a dynamic, positive image as the "Lionheart" (with his flowing, silver "mane"), and called his party "the new LDP" (similar to Tony Blair reimaging his party as "New Labour"). Koizumi's popularity helped the party improve its segment of the upper house in elections held in 2001. Koizumi was included in the photographic portions of many candidates' posters, even in those distributed by critics (who nevertheless pledged to work with him in their slogans). "Reform" was the dominant word on LDP posters, and was included in 44 percent of them.[59] An election poster that showed the new prime minister (in the same pose as in Figure 6.7), with the slogan "Lend your strength to Koizumi's challenge. OK, let's reform" was a hot-selling item at LDP offices, with six hundred thousand copies sold.[60] Four years later, Koizumi called early elections for the House of Representatives, after some of his party's members refused to

Figure 6.7

support his bill to privatize the postal system. The election was almost a "referendum" on Koizumi's privatization plan and on his reformist slogan of "*Kaikaku.*" The prime minister would not allow the MPs who had not voted for postal privatization to run with the party designation, and seventeen of thirty-seven lost their seats. Koizumi won a huge victory, garnering 62 percent of the seats for his party and an additional 6 percent for the Clean Government Party, his coalition partner. The reformist Democratic Party of Japan (created in the previous decade by defectors from opposition parties) lost much support in the urban and suburban districts, and the number of seats it held fell from the 177 it had two years earlier to 113. After this debacle, Okada Katsuya, the party's leader, resigned.[61]

Having achieved a record that was somewhat less impressive than his almost mythologized image, with even his postal privatization measure not to be finalized for eleven more years in the future, Koizumi stepped down in 2006, designating Chief Cabinet Secretary Shinzo Abe, a conservative, as his successor. Koizumi was presented as a needed "breath of fresh air," after the scandals that preceded him. The power he acquired and sustained was testament to the importance of image management in modern politics, even in a country that had seen little of it. This was particularly evident at the beginning of his ascent, when teenage girls had lined up to purchase posters of him and "Lion King" mobile phone fobs, and when he had ensured that the television networks covered his visit with leprosy victims. Later, Koizumi became a sometimes tieless, charismatic, movie-star-like "man of the people," following in the footsteps of Tony Blair and Bill Clinton, and pushed for reform as an end, using image management and media manipulation as the means to stay in power. The image was not particularly subtle, since his posters referred to him as the "Friend of the Common People." The noble "Lion King" image can be seen in Figure 6.7, posted on a street in Tokyo during the 2005 election campaign. Some admired Koizumi's adroit public relations, reform bent, and political skills; others viewed him and the media strategists in the LDP as blatant propagandists who were guilty of grossly simplifying and repeating a message, with its "public reception ... carefully monitored and his topic and tone altered to best influence public perception," according to Kim Moogwi.[62]

Posters continued to be the primary election campaign medium. Ironically, as Bruce Wallace noted, "the Internet and digital technology ... are not allowed [in election campaigns] in one of the most technology-obsessed nations on Earth."[63] This prohibition was not technically legislated, but many viewed the Web (along with canvassing, large billboards, and unfolded fliers at campaign events) as an unacceptable intrusion of privacy and good taste. Generally, large advertising companies design television spots and printed material for the parties in Japan, and individual candidates hire smaller political consulting firms that design posters, computerize direct mail lists, and periodically use market research to tailor their clients' campaign speeches. The poster designs are rarely unconventional; a major departure from the norm is a sometimes larger-than-mandated size (but only if it is shown before the formal campaign period) or an occasional display of a candidate from the waist up.[64]

ର *Taiwan: The Rise and Fall of the Kuomintang Party (1949–2004).* The Kuomintang forces of Chiang Kai-shek, defeated in mainland China, came to Taiwan in 1949, and for half a century the main island (and several smaller ones) experienced what Jonathan Manthorpe called a "regime of reasonably benevolent despotism," but which Dennis Roy characterized as one of "repression" and "White Terror."[65] Chiang ruled as president until 1975, and his Kuomintang Party (KMT) continued its reign until 2000, when the main opposition party's candidate for president was elected. In 1986, this political party, the Democratic Progressive Party (DPP), was formed, but it was declared illegal by the government that year. The DPP's platform called for a plebiscite to decide Taiwan's status as a nation, direct election of the president, an expansion of civil liberties, termination of the state of martial law and compulsory military service, and more liberal benefits for the disadvantaged. Although it remained an illegal party during the 1986 elections, the DPP won a dozen of the seventy-three contested seats in the Legislative Yuan (the parliament), and the KMT won nearly all the others.[66] Martial law ended in 1987, and political parties other than the KMT became legal. In the election two years later for seats in the Legislative Yuan, the DPP won 29 percent of the vote (compared to the KMT's 59 percent).[67]

The government largely controlled the mass media. A non-Kuomintang television station did not broadcast until 1997, making it difficult for the opposition to convey its messages before then. In 1991, the regime did not even permit, by some accounts, the Democratic Progressives' election posters calling for the formation of a Taiwanese republic that would apply for admission to the United Nations. The KMT held to a "one-China" stance. The voters rejected the DPP position for independence in the election for the National Congress (the less important legislative body) that year, giving the party only 24 percent of the vote, and the KMT 71 percent.[68] During this period, the Kuomintang generated much more money than the opposition did for sound trucks, leaflets, and posters. Some also accused it of buying votes. Many considered the KMT to be "the richest political organization in the world"; the party managed over one hundred corporations and owned stocks worth about four billion dollars. The DPP, nevertheless, attracted support from voters; its share of the vote total was usually about 30 percent in several national elections. The opposition party used posters and other printed material extensively for most of the 1990s to communicate with the populace. Finally, the Democratic Progressives broke through when its candidate, the former mayor of Taipei, Chen Shui-bian, won the presidency in 2000. He gained 39 percent of the vote, beating independent candidate, former provincial governor James Soong (a defector from the KMT), who received 37 percent, and KMT candidate Vice President Lien Chan, who obtained only 23 percent. The party also won the Legislative Yuan elections of 2001, when it received 39 percent of the seats (over the KMT's 30 percent, the People First Party's [PFP] 20 percent, and the Taiwan Solidarity Union's 6 percent shares). The split in the KMT (with Soong having founded the People First Party) enabled Chen and the DPP to win both elections.[69]

The presidential election campaign of 2000 was contentious. The ruling party fought hard to retain power. Its posters reflected the scare tactics that it settled on as its dominant propaganda strategy. One KMT poster, for example, included soldiers with gas masks, marching off to war, with the slogan "Don't Let the Nightmare Become a Reality." This approach played upon the fears of many that the DPP's position in favor of Taiwanese independence would lead to a military attack by the Chinese People's Liberation Army. Consequently, Chen emphasized ending Kuomintang "corruption" and improving social services in the Democratic Progressives' propaganda campaign, rather than independence, as well as emphasizing youthfulness and dynamism (as opposed to the opposition's more stolid image) with the slogan "A young Taiwan, a new government with vitality." One poster featured Sun Yat-sen, the revered nationalist with an incorruptible image, wearing a DPP knitted hat to promote Chen. In addition, a full range of campaign merchandise—a mug, teapot, doll, key ring, notebook, towel, umbrella, flag, and T-shirts (as well as songs, such as a rap version of "Happily Looking to the Future")—was produced to promote the party. The campaign featured Chen on most items, as well as a Web site, which was used to raise money for the campaign. Of course, the KMT did likewise, producing such items as campaign jackets, scarves, neckties, socks, towels, and mobile phone covers, all emblazoned with a butterfly logo.[70]

The three candidates set up Web sites. Among them was one where Chen asked voters to e-mail cabinet recommendations. The most vicious election propaganda was conveyed via the poster medium, but despite the inflammatory distortions, Taiwan's first non-Kuomintang government took the reins of government peacefully after the election. For at least a decade, the KMT had used emotional images of violent chaotic societies and politics in posters and television ads, as well as invasion from the mainland, to try to scare the electorate into supporting its candidates, who preached maintaining order and stability. But such images failed to stir as many voters, who had seen them repeatedly over the years. By the 2000 election, this strategy, wrote Gary Rawnsley, "no longer resonate[d] with a large proportion of Taiwan's electorate," not even with many military veterans.[71]

In early 2001, public approval of Chen's performance had plummeted from almost 80 percent to between 25 and 35 percent (depending on the poll).[72] This decline could be attributed to a number of causes, including a recession, the KMT majority in the parliament, and a debate about halting construction of a nuclear power plant. Although economic matters dominated the 2001 parliamentary election campaign, with Soong's party and the KMT critical of government policies, the DPP countered by successfully pinning much of the blame for the recession on its opponents in the parliament. The Democratic Progressives managed to convey their message despite having less money to spend. Campaign expenditures for television advertisements were about ten times what they were for newspaper and magazine ads; the parties were able to exceed limits through loopholes in the law. The KMT outspent the DPP by margin of almost 2 to 1, much of its money going for negative TV spots. About half of the DPP's and PFP's television ads were negative; in addition, about half were image management. The Internet was *less* utilized than it had recently been. Posters, banners, and billboards appeared everywhere at election time, displaying smiling (sometimes waving) candidates for parliament against colorful backgrounds. DPP candidates did not usually wear ties in their posters; conversely, KMT candidates most often wore them in theirs. Following the election, the Taiwan Solidarity Union (which had been established by dissident Kuomintang members to help the Democratic Progressives gain a parliamentary majority), and several other legislators, joined with the DPP to form that majority in the Legislative Yuan.[73]

By the presidential election of 2004, Soong had moved enough toward the KMT positions to run for vice president with Kuomintang leader Lien Chan in the Pan-Blue Alliance. A Chinese missile buildup, aimed at Taiwan, was the main campaign issue: Chen's opponents blamed him for causing it; his proponents, however, stated that his nationalistic policy was even more justified, given China's threat. Standard Pan-Blue posters showed the main candidates with their arms around one another and waving, often standing before banners and flags. One striking poster featured two abstract riders in tandem on a bicycle. The Alliance's slogan summed up the key issues: "Work hard on economy, Work hard on peace, Save Taiwan." The campaign was at least as impassioned as the one in 2000, and was marked by the first televised debates between the presidential candidates and record rallies. On just one day, more than one million people reportedly took part in a DPP mobilization and three million participated around the country to support the Pan-Blue Alliance.[74]

A two-sided campaign poster, purportedly endorsed by the Taichung City Pan-Blue Alliance election campaign headquarters, compared Chen to Osama bin Laden and Saddam Hussein (Figs. 6.8 and 6.9), while a newspaper advertisement compared him to Hitler.[75] On one side of the poster, the al-Qaeda head is shown declaring, "I am the very skilled terrorist leader bin Laden, and the person I admire most is Taiwan's Ah-bian!" (with the burning World Trade Center buildings added, and text that said that Chen was guilty

Figure 6.8

Figure 6.9

of "starting fires and inciting chaos"); on the other side, the Iraqi leader is shown holding a rifle. A KMT spokesperson reportedly said to one American election observer, "these were fair comparisons because Chen Shui-bian was sowing divisiveness and division among the people of Taiwan."[76] Other KMT officials allegedly argued that the poster was "creative," with one (a former mayor) quoted as stating, "We want people to know that Chen is dangerous, that his actions are those of terrorism."[77] He was said to have added, "we chose to use the picture of Hussein because he unfairly controlled elections as the president of Iraq—just like Chen Shui-bian."[78] Approximately six hundred thousand copies of the poster were printed.[79] Chen's campaign was effective, however, and some were surprised by his narrow victory—with a 29,518-vote margin (or 0.24 percent) from over thirteen million cast.[80] As Gary Rawnsley stated, "Chen managed to increase his share of the vote by just over 10 percent since 2000, demystifying the idea that one plus one = two (i.e., that Lien and Soong were bound to win because their combined votes in 2000 were over

50 percent)."[81] One tactic was evident in DPP campaign material, which stressed the past differences that Lien and Soong had had dealing with the mainland Chinese.[82]

Heating the campaign even more was the first referendum ever presented to the country's voters, who were asked to vote on two options: to strengthen Taiwan's antimissile defense system and to talk with China.[83] Most people voted for both, but neither received the required majority.[84] The Pan-Blues opposed passage of the referenda (expressed in the heading of the Hussein poster, "Referenda are Precious and Sacred Objects of Democracies; They're Not Cheap Election Tools!"), whereas the Democratic Progressives supported them, printing posters that used the reliable "I Want You" approach pioneered during World War I, depicting an attractive young woman in combat fatigues pointing at the viewers, beneath the slogan "Taiwan Needs You!"

Europe

The initial elections in Europe, as in many areas of the world during the nineteenth century, were limited to voters of the propertied classes. The first political parties appeared on the continent when constitutional monarchies were formed, starting with Great Britain in the seventeenth century (as we have seen in the previous chapter). In the early nineteenth century, other countries such as Belgium followed the same path, with impassioned electioneering marked by broadsides and campaign songs.[85] A bit later in the century, additional constitutional monarchies were established in Hungary after the 1848 Revolution, Bulgaria in 1879, and still later in other countries such as Poland (which was part of Russia) in which democracy was forestalled.

With the demise of Communism in the Soviet bloc in the late 1980s, old parties were resurrected and new ones were founded. These events soon led to elections, and posters were used extensively. To help these parties run their campaigns in these new democracies, external political consultants were frequently imported. Sometimes support came from political parties in other countries, such as the West German Social Democratic Party (which aided the East German Socialists with strategy and money) and the United States Democratic Party (which sent Madeleine Albright to Hungary to advise campaign managers on planning and financing). Business consultants such as Fred Martin, who had managed the U.S. presidential primary campaign of Albert Gore in 1988, also provided assistance. Two years later, Martin (along with Chilean pollster Marta Lagos) advised the Alliance of Free Democrats (SZDSZ) in Hungary during that nation's first democratic election since 1945. In May 2007, World Audit categorized most European countries as fully democratic, alongside established democracies (Australia, New Zealand, Canada, the United States, and three in Asia and four in Latin America). Eight former Communist countries (Estonia, Slovenia, Hungary, Lithuania, the Czech Republic, Latvia, Slovakia, and Bulgaria) were now deemed "fully democratic." Eight others (Croatia, Serbia, Romania, Bosnia and Herzegovina, Macedonia, Albania, Ukraine, and Georgia) were rated as "qualified" democracies, but Russia was seen as "moving away from democracy" (descending to rank 124).[86]

Survey data on the European Parliament elections of 1989 revealed that reading an election poster was the second most prevalent form of direct party-voter communication two or three weeks before the voting. Although a mean of 22 percent was reported for reading a poster (compared to 38 percent for talking to friends, family, or workmates), the results varied by country, with a high of 35 percent in Germany, and a low of 11 percent in Greece and the United Kingdom. In this survey, the mean percentage for posters of the twelve European nations was higher than it was for newspaper advertisements and radio programming (both 16 percent), but lower than for newspaper reports (26 percent) and television programming (51 percent).[87] The Internet is becoming more of a factor, with parties displaying posters on their Web sites. Additionally, most candidates for parliamentary seats have sites; in 2003, for example, more than 80 percent of the candidates of the victorious Centre Party of Finland had their own Web pages.[88]

Unfortunately, racist appeals on posters—reminiscent of ones produced in Fascist countries in the 1930s and 1940s—have persisted. Some Russian, Polish, and Austrian election posters have been anti-Semitic, and anti-Moslem posters have emerged. A poster distributed by the Danish People's Party during the 2001 election showed a young blond girl with the statement, "When she retires, Denmark will be a majority-Muslim nation."[89] In the same campaign, *Venstre* (the Liberal Party) erected a billboard that showed three Asian men, who had been tried for group rape, leaving the court after having been acquitted, with the caption "this will not be tolerated once *Venstre* gets in."[90] In that election, *Venstre* won the most seats in the parliament (a gain of 34 percent) and the People's Party came in third in seats (a 70-percent increase).[91] The Swiss People's Party (SVP) achieved even more than its Danish counterpart, winning the most votes in the parliamentary elections of 1999, 2003, and 2007, possibly helped by posters that depicted foreigners as criminals shredding the nation's flag.[92] In the last elections, the SVP achieved its best result, despite (or because of) issuing a subsequently banned poster that depicted three white cartoon sheep kicking a black one off the Swiss flag, as well as the slogan "Creating security" (Fig. 6.10).[93] Anti-immigrant poster campaigns by political parties have also been conducted recently in other European countries, including Austria, Belgium, the Czech Republic, Germany, The Netherlands, and France, as well as in New Zealand.

Figure 6.10

The poster has been one of the most important communication vehicles in election campaigns in European nations. World War II saw the medium used extensively in blatant propaganda campaigns, and this continued in postwar period politics. In 1946, the Italian Socialist Party issued a poster that featured Jesus Christ in the fields, with factories appearing darkly in the background, and a call to voters to support the party to end the exploitation of the poor by the rich. At first, the Communist Party (as part of the Democratic Popular Front with the Socialists) generally produced innocuous posters calling for "honesty" and "peace, freedom, and work," but by the 1950s, it was caricaturing its opponents as stooges of capitalism. Much earlier, however, the Christian Democracy Party had attacked the Front in its posters, with one showing a hand "exposing" the leftist-coalition parties pretending to be patriotic nationalists (the coalition's logo had Giuseppe Garibaldi on a star), but instead being controlled by Stalin (Fig. 6.11). Political posters were ubiquitous during this period. In the early 1950s, the *New York Times* reported, "copies of election posters … [were] plastered over all available walls in cities, towns, villages and hamlets of Italy."[94] According to Luciano Cheles, "until the mid-1970s, posters were for the opposition parties the principal means of making their

views known to the general public," since most of the newspapers and broadcasting media in Italy "were biased in favour of the ruling coalition."[95] After a 1976 court ruling that led to the deregulation of broadcasting, a mixed system emerged, as private networks became vital political forces.[96] As in many other countries, by the 1980s, posters, rallies, and parties declined to a secondary status in Italy, as the significance of television, marketing,

Figure 6.11

and individual leaders' personalities grew.[97] As mentioned earlier, however, posters and billboards made a dramatic resurgence after the 2001 legislation prohibiting paid political television advertising.

Survey data and market research have influenced European political campaigns. A survey taken by a research and consulting institute before Austria's 2004 presidential election indicated that the voters desired a president who would well represent the country in foreign relations; act in a nonpartisan manner; possess political experience; pursue social justice; mediate in domestic conflicts; and deal with issues concerning the balance of political power.[98] The campaigns of the two major parties played to the strengths of its candidates and to the wishes of the electorate: Benita Ferrero-Waldner of the People's Party had been foreign minister; Heinz Fischer of the Social Democratic Party had been the nonpartisan president of the parliament, a practitioner of mediation, and connected with balance-of-power politics. Their billboard posters emphasized the qualities rated important in the survey. Figure 6.12 shows Ferrero-Waldner with clenched fists and the slogan "The first one, who fought for Austria like a lion" (an allusion to her stand opposing the European Union's sanctions against her country in 2000). Fischer's billboards and posters emphasized his actions for "peace and neutrality," and personal qualities of "honesty" and "fairness" (Fig. 6.13). Although he lacked his opponent's international experience, his campaign overcame that negative perception on the strength of other qualities valued by the voters, whereas Ferrero-Waldner's did not appear to counteract her weaknesses (primarily being blamed for social-service cutbacks). Fischer won the election by 4 percentage points.[99] In addition, Ferrero-Waldner's billboards and posters obviously targeted women, particularly those under forty-five, appealing to them to elect "the first one" (i.e., female president of Austria). Nevertheless, her 26-point advantage over her male opponent in December 2003 almost completely vanished by the April 2004 election.[100] This campaign failed because Ferrero-Waldner was too conservative for many in the targeted group, her record on women's issues was thought by some to be inadequate, and her opponent

Dr. Benita Ferrero-Waldner

www.benita.at

Die Erste, die wie eine Löwin für Österreich gekämpft hat.

Figure 6.12

Am 25. April
Heinz Fischer

Unser Land braucht wieder mehr Fairness.

Politik braucht ein Gewissen.
Dr. Heinz Fischer.

www.heinzfischer.at

Figure 6.13

received a great deal of support from prominent female politicians.[101] Propaganda has a better chance of succeeding when there is a strong basis in reality.

Germany from the Prussian Monarchy of the 1840s to Reunification in 1990. In Prussia in the 1840s, provisional Diet members lobbied King Frederick William IV for a "United Diet" (a national parliament), which he convened in 1847 in Berlin. Unfortunately, the monarch would not allow a constitution with a permanent parliamentary body, and the alienated nobles, bourgeois, and farmers were told to go home. The next year, the deposition of Louis Philippe in France led to mass demonstrations, demands for freedoms and a national parliamentary body, and elections in many German states. Elections for a national assembly were conducted, with 75 to 90 percent of adult males eligible to vote, depending on the laws of their state of residence. There were no political parties, and those elected were prominent local lawyers and other professionals, as well as aristocrats. Moderate liberals comprised the assembly's largest faction. The constitution drafted by the National Assembly abolished aristocratic titles and demanded parliamentary control of the police and judiciary, but this (and some violent protests) led to repression by Prussian troops. Prussia became "a police state"; "universal suffrage" was undermined by a system of categorizing voters based on the amount of taxes they paid, which allowed the wealthier citizens to elect the largest number of representatives to parliament.[102]

In the Prussian elections of 1861, the newly formed Progressive Party won most of the seats; the Old Liberals—whom the more leftist Progressives viewed as too passive—came in second; and the conservatives placed a distant third. A conflict between the parliament and king led to Otto von Bismarck becoming the dictator of Germany. Bismarck succeeded in unifying Germany (and the king of Prussia was made emperor), and orchestrated the enactment of universal male suffrage. However, as Jonathan Sperber noted, the deputies to the Reichstag (the lower house of the German parliament) had their powers "reduced to a bare minimum" in the imperial empire run by Bismarck. Despite the little power wielded by Reichstag members, the campaigns to secure seats in that body were fought fiercely, and lithographed broadsides were quite evident around election time. There were six main political parties in Bismarck's Germany; the Social Democratic Party (SPD), founded in

1875, is the only one remaining today. Although menaced by antisocialist and preemptive social-welfare legislation orchestrated by Bismarck, the SPD steadily increased its share of the vote from 3 percent in 1871 to 20 percent in 1890 (when Bismarck resigned), and to 35 percent in 1912 on the eve of World War I.[103]

According to Brett Fairbairn, "the SPD was the first modern, mass party in Germany," and the other parties copied its "permanent electoral organization, centralized campaigns, mass agitation and propaganda, and tight integration with particular social-economic groupings rather than appeals to the idealized patriotic 'citizens' of the liberal model."[104] The "professional politicians" of the Social Democratic Party introduced a "new politics" of demagoguery that put many of the "notables," who were unwilling to campaign and organize in this manner, at a great disadvantage at the turn of the century. The Center Party was a moderate conservative Catholic party, which Bismarck tried to undermine too. Eventually, it became the Christian Democratic People's Party in 1919, and then two modern parties, the Christian Democratic Union (CDU) and Christian Social Union (CSU). By the 1890s, the Center Party had become a key party in the Reichstag, which could block legislation the government desired. Other liberal and conservative parties abounded, along with regional ones such as the Lithuanian Party. Candidates for the Reichstag produced broadsides and delivered speeches at meetings, and the Socialist and anti-Semitic orations, by some accounts, created the most enthusiasm.[105]

Germany witnessed eight parliamentary elections between 1919 (when the so-called Weimar Republic was formed after World War I) and 1933 (when the National Socialist German Workers—or Nazi—Party effectively gained power in the Reichstag). Election campaigns in Germany, an anonymous correspondent for the *New York Times* noted in 1919, were "very much like those in the United States," with huge "street demonstrations … unheard of in the elections for the old Reichstag"—some numbering four hundred thousand people—and the myriad handbills were a "novelty." Special pillars were erected at every street corner to display red posters with government announcements on them, continued the reporter, with "gorgeous designs announcing political meetings or the opening of a new dance hall."[106] Another *Times* correspondent, George Renwick, differed with his colleague, however, and wrote that little electioneering had occurred—just "official announcements" and a "few placards."[107] Perhaps they were in different areas of the country. One thing is clear: Germans were accustomed to seeing in a public venue posters that advertised products, and talented graphic designers used visuals and text to capture attention. This was in accord with the business culture, and company managers were cognizant that the differences between product brands were generally a matter of visual appeal.[108]

The Social Democratic Party won the National Assembly elections of 1919, but failed to obtain a majority of the seats. Its 38 percent of the vote, however, was much greater than the second-place Center Party's share, which was only 20 percent, and that of the Democratic Party's (DDP) 19 percent.[109] The main socialist party would never again perform that well in the post-World War I period, as the German Communist Party (KPD), and then the Nazis picked up strength at the polls. A variety of factors led to this, including the Social Democratic Party's failure to socialize the economy and fight for the causes of workers and farmers (losing many of them to the KPD and parties to the right, respectively), and later having to deal with the Great Depression under weak, uninspiring leadership. The Social Democrats held on to power for much of the postwar period by joining in coalitions with middle-of-the-road, center-right, and liberal parties, particularly the Center Party, Democratic Party, and the People's Party (DVP). Finally, in 1930, this stay-in-power strategy failed. The Social Democratic Party would not regain power for almost four decades.[110] The posters of the SPD and its coalition partners, beginning in 1919, illustrated their middle-of-the-road strategy. A DDP poster from that year's election campaign, for instance, showed, literally, a *road* to prosperity, with a well-dressed man pointing the way—taking neither the path to Bolshevism nor reaction (Fig. 6.14). Other Democratic Party posters

Figure 6.14

focused on issues, often in dramatic ways. In the 1924 election campaign, for example, the DDP issued a striking lithographic poster that illustrated a torch (labeled "DDP comes to the rescue") burning piles of marks, with the smoke (labeled "Inflation") morphing into a ghoulish face.

The Center Party (which was called the Christian People's Party in 1919) did fairly well in most of the elections between the two world wars, and held cabinet positions in almost every government. *Zentrum* (as it was known) polled a consistent share of the vote

Figure 6.15

from 1920 to 1933, ranging from 11 to 14 percent.[111] *Zentrum*'s supporters were mainly Catholics, and the party shifted its positions to the right in the 1920s in an attempt to broaden its base. The liberal-republican Democratic Party lost the respect of many middle-class voters, with its weak response to a putsch in 1920, and the monarchist DVP benefited in the election that year (increasing its share of the vote from 4 percent to 14 percent).[112] Its anti-Communist slogan, "From red fetters will make you free, a vote cast for the DVP," undoubtedly resonated with many voters, and the party's posters particularly targeted farmers, who were worried about losing their property: one portrayed the red figure of Death as a man in the fields, along with the slogan "Who can help? The German People's Party" (Fig. 6.15). The Nazis probably copied this design, when they issued a similar election poster in 1932 (see Fig. 6.22). The conservative National People's Party (DNVP) and the breakaway socialist party, the Independent Social Democratic Party (USPD), also increased their percentages significantly, at the expense of the DDP and SPD.[113]

The breaking up of the USPD later in 1920 benefited the Communist Party greatly, leading to an increase in its share of the German vote from 2 percent in 1920 to 13 percent in 1924.[114] The Social Democratic Party was out of the ruling coalitions from the end of 1923 to the middle of 1928, when it achieved its highest percentage of the vote—30 percent—since the first Weimar election.[115] Following the Great Depression, however, the Social Democrats lost support at the polls, dropping to under 25 percent of the popular vote in 1930 and to 20 percent in 1932.[116] The economic hard times, on the other hand, helped the more dynamic, extreme parties: the Communists rose from less than 11 percent in 1928 to 17 percent in 1932 and the Nazis profited the most, climbing from under 3 percent to 33 percent.[117] The Nazi Party ran an exceptional coordinated propaganda campaign, which was especially effective in targeting segments of the population most affected by the depression, evident in the Nazi Party posters in the

1920s and 1930s. Its success was aided by the feebleness of the major political parties in the Weimar Republic in postwar Germany. Walter Rinderle and Bernard Norling summed up the situation succinctly: "None of the major political parties in the Weimar years inspired anyone."[118] The government led by Heinrich Brüning of the Center Party did little to help the unemployed workers during the Great Depression, and many in the working class— who rejected real and perceived atheism, Jewishness, internationalism, and the socialism and weakness of the Communists and Social Democrats—gravitated toward the Nazi Party.[119] The KPD did produce riveting poster designs. Figure 6.16 shows a typical Communist election poster in the 1920s (soliciting votes for party chairman, Ernst Thälmann), a gigantic red worker sweeping away failed policies, along with corrupt capitalists and

Figure 6.16   politicians. Other Communist posters added Nazis to the list of groups caricatured; they showed well-fed Russian babies, impoverished German laborers, skeletons with bombs (demonstrating the party's stand for disarmament), red flags, and depicted the Social Democrats as traitorous.

Social Democratic posters and broadsides targeted both the Nazi and Communist Parties as "enemies of democracy" and opposing "the bourgeois block" (most of which is evident in Figure 6.17). One poster included caricatures of Hitler and Thälmann. In addition, the party's posters were critical of military spending—one shows downcast youths holding empty bowls as other political parties wave at a destroyer, after having agreed to spend eighty million marks on weaponry rather than food (Fig. 6.18). The SPD also targeted women, who were enfranchised in 1918. It distributed broadsides stating that it had been the only party to favor female suffrage in the Weimar constitution. The Social Democratic Party *had* been a strong supporter of female suffrage in prewar Germany, and had organized a women's section, but liberals and the Center Party later favored enfranchising women. Ironically, German women voted more for conservative parties in Weimar elections than they did for the SPD. Many Social Democratic Party posters

Figure 6.17   *Figure 6.18*

depicted overburdened workers, the elderly, and the blind, as well as women, along with pleas for "justice, peace, and freedom." One later SPD poster featured a drawing of elderly people receiving reduced pensions from a Nazi bank teller. Some of the party's posters simply employed positive imagery, such as the rays of a bright red sun streaming through an open window—an image also used in the 1920s by the British Conservative Party (see Fig. 5.14, Chapter Five). Overall, as Corey Ross concluded, "the democratic parties, especially the SPD … emphasize[d] rational persuasion and education as opposed to more emotional propaganda … [in their] propaganda efforts."[120] The Social Democratic posters and other propaganda could not be as effective as that of the Nazis and Communists, since, as Ross noted, it was problematical for a "rational" democratic political party to design emotional appeals to combat such foes.[121]

For Adolf Hitler and his National Socialist German Workers Party, the poster was probably the primary weapon in their propaganda campaigns, culminating in the 1932 Reichstag election contest that led to Hitler becoming chancellor of Germany. According to David Pike, Hitler was influenced by the principles of American advertising, from which he "had learned that mass suggestion was the secret and that a Wagnerian *Gesamtkunstwerk* had to come into play."[122] The creation of this synthesis of all elements in a carefully controlled propaganda package was crucial in swaying and then poisoning the public. Hitler's study of advertising methods taught him that exaggeration, misleading statements, and lies were a common means to sell a product, or, as he asked in *Mein Kampf*, "What, for example, would we say about a poster that was supposed to advertise a new soap and that described other soaps as 'good'?"[123]

Hitler's principal election organizer and propagandist was Joseph Goebbels. Goebbels was influenced by a book, *The Crowd: A Study of the Popular Mind*, by psychologist Gustave Le Bon.[124] Le Bon had a great interest in how to capture the attention of and persuade a crowd, which he depicted as "a servile flock that is incapable of ever doing without a master."[125] He wrote in 1895 that crowds could even be incited to commit acts of violence by employing three principles: affirmation, repetition, and contagion.[126] The first two principles were useful to both politicians and business people advertising their products, according to Le Bon;[127] the Nazis employed all three principles to distort the truth, plant lies in the public mind, and work the masses into a frenzy of outrage and hatred. Just as advertisers helped sell candy bars and automobiles by exaggerating their attributes, repeating images, slogans, and contentions, and playing on the emotions of consumers, the Nazis sold their product and services similarly. In addition, Hitler had examined the use of symbols in other political movements, even Marxist ones.[128] The swastika, in fact, had been a symbol for thousands of years in many cultures, often denoting good luck, happiness, and peace.[129]

The perversion of this symbol by the Nazi Party, and its pushing advertising methods to their extreme, resulted in Goebbels' orchestration of falsehoods and hatred toward Jews in the 1932 elections. This helped boost support for the party among Germans disaffected by events following World War I, such as the occupation of the Ruhr by French soldiers, and, most particularly, the economic problems during the Great Depression. Hitler and Goebbels were influenced by American public relations and advertising men such as Bernays who sometimes advocated such deceptive campaigns. Bernays, in turn, was interested in the theories of Le Bon, and Bernays' uncle, Sigmund Freud.[130] A successful political leader, wrote Bernays, must "cater to the vote of the masses ... [via] the expert use of propaganda," playing to group "impulses and emotions" in a coordinated manner.[131] In fact, Bernays, in his 1928 book *Propaganda* (a copy of which was in Goebbels' library[132]), presented Nazi leaders (*already* in tune with mass psychology theories and promotional strategies that played with the facts) with a useful model of how to influence the public by "creating pictures" even if the imagery and attitudes were distorted and racist:

> When an Imperial Wizard [of the Ku Klux Klan], sensing what is perhaps hunger for an ideal, offers a picture of a nation all Nordic and nationalistic, the common man of the older American stock, feeling himself elbowed out of his rightful position and prosperity by the newer immigrant stocks grasps the picture which fits in so neatly with his prejudices, and makes it his own.[133]

Posters were seen as a key propaganda element of coordinated election campaigns by the Nazis, and were exploited extensively with leaflets, films, newspaper articles, newsreels, gramophone recordings, and radio programs. As early as 1926, the Nazi Party published a brochure outlining the tasks of its Propaganda Department, and identified "clever, concise, large and striking" posters as the best way to promote meetings and publicize the daily party newspaper, and a good method by which to promulgate ideas.[134] Even earlier, during the Reichstag election campaign of 1920, broadsides were used to announce meetings, calling on citizens to reject the established political parties in a Germany "corrupted" by Jews. These were printed on red paper—red was the preferred color of the Nazis— undoubtedly chosen for its emotional connotations and to elicit interest.[135] Most were text only, but occasionally one would feature illustrations, such as a 1924 broadside, aimed at workers, which included caricatures of labor leaders with grotesque noses. At least one election poster titled "Germany's Liberation" was produced that year. It contained an eagle, having broken its chains, and a red swastika. Pictorial posters were more plentiful in both the 1928 and 1930 election campaigns, and by 1932, the Nazi Party printed five hundred thousand posters and put them up throughout Germany during the election campaign period.[136] Many were large, colorful, and striking in design.

Hitler viewed the propaganda circulated by the Allied powers during World War I, as well as that generated by the "the Socialist-Marxist organizations," as masterful—contrary to his perception of the German propaganda during the conflict.[137] He believed that the simpler, more stereotyped messages of the arresting American and British posters had been more effective,[138] even though most of the "atrocities" depicted in them were fabricated.[139] The more complex German and Austrian posters that were issued featured the indirect symbolism of knights and eagles (rather than blatant atrocities), textual messages that were often ponderous, elaborate lettering, and artistic renderings that might lead viewers to admire their stylishness (rather than be outraged by their message). Nazi posters had eagles too, but they were not stylized and the message was almost always straightforward.

Hitler realized the importance of devising propaganda for "less educated masses" that would attract them and deliver the message clearly and emotionally, rather than (as he put it) being concerned "with drivel about aesthetics."[140] Thus, the Nazi Party's posters included visuals and slogans that were simple, eye-catching, and direct. The propaganda's message had to be pared down to "a very few points" and these had to be repeated incessantly.[141] It was not that Hitler—a former art student—did not care about design, but rather he believed that the "form and color" of the posters should be subordinate to the persuasive

Figure 6.19   *Figure 6.20*

purposes of messages that were in accord with principles of mass psychology.[142] The main themes in the Nazis' election posters were Germany's mistreatment by the Allies after World War I; the desire to restore pride in the fatherland and its people; the need for a powerful leader—Hitler; the need for jobs, land, and food; and the evil and/or corrupt

Jews, Bolsheviks, international capitalists, and political system and its parties. One Nazi Party election poster from 1932, for example, presented a charcoal drawing of rows of despondent workers, with the slogan "Our Last Hope: HITLER" (Fig. 6.19); another by the same artist, known as Mjölnir, portrayed a huge German man with a swastika belt breaking free of his shackles (Fig. 6.20).

Figure 6.21

Many of the posters distributed by the Nazi Party during the election campaign periods played on the fears and resentments of people. The Nazis took the stereotyping and fear approaches that had been used in designing the Allied posters during the Great War and ramped them up. Nazi Party posters depicted Jews (replacing the "Huns" present in Allied posters) as sneaky, grotesque figures (see Fig. 1.11, Chapter One) and as snakes charged with usury and corruption, as well as being responsible for Germany's defeat in World War I, the Versailles Treaty, war guilt, unemployment, inflation, prostitution, and civil war. A number of the election posters also featured drawings and photographs of Hitler in strong, dynamic poses—the leader who would save the German people (*Volk*). In addition, the symbols of the eagle and the swastika were used together, again—this time with a crowd of Germans with raised hands in support of the Nazi-voting list (Fig. 6.21).

Other Nazi posters targeted groups of voters, such as farmers and workers—and many were tailored for them during the 1932 election campaigns. One, for example, featured a gigantic three-dimensional swastika over some factories and a blond "Aryan," looking down on the capitalists and Communist Party organizers (with a Jew whispering in one's ear) who were attempting to convince laborers to support them; another showed a despondent farmer and his crying wife, with the figure of Death looming over their homes and the caption "Farmers in need. Who helps? Adolf Hitler!" (Fig. 6.22); and another poster highlighted drawings of women, urging them to vote for the Nazi Party's list. Until the agricultural sector fell into depression in 1928, the Nazi Party targeted industrial workers in its posters, largely ignoring the farmers.[143] This appeal did not achieve great gains until the 1930s, as most of these voters continued to support the Socialist and Communist Parties.[144] Thereafter, however, a change of tactics in Nazi propaganda occurred, and Hitler, Goebbels, and others

Figure 6.22

"attacked the parties in power and their rivals out of power for their real and alleged weakness, corruption, bureaucratic ineffectiveness, and indifference to the welfare of the farmers," according to Rinderle and Norling.[145]

Beginning in 1928, the Nazis began to stress the importance of the "*Volk* community" and the need to help it, and the campaign brought farmers into the party. The theme to restore pride in Germany also proved attractive to some Protestants in the Center Party (with its romanticization of the past, and its suspicions about the efficacy of democratic institutions), and they supported the Nazis at election time, drawn to some of the themes in Nazi propaganda, particularly the need "to restore German greatness."[146] The copious use of symbols such as eagles, bread, muscular farmers, and storm troopers in the Nazi Party posters conveyed the message that, under Hitler, the nation would prosper and be strong. Another Nazi propaganda tactic was to illustrate German soldiers from World War I in the party's posters, alongside captions such as "Two million dead. Did they die in vain? Never! Front soldiers! Adolf Hitler is showing you the way!" Also in the poster campaigns during these election periods were designs that featured brawny arms hoisting Nazi flags with slogans such as "The people rise!" In addition, a tall, modern building in the form of a swastika dominated one Nazi poster, titled "Hitler Builds." Clearly, the imagery and catchphrases were meant to communicate the dynamism of Hitler's party, in contrast to Germany's deplorable situation.

Goebbels certainly comprehended the importance of tailoring messages to segments of the population. He understood—just as advertising executives did—that a political party had to "adjust to those it wishes to reach[,] with … the propagandist's speeches or posters that are aimed at farmers … different than those aimed at employers," as he said in a speech, and with the message presented in extremely simplified, clear-cut terms.[147] This is manifest in a 1930 election poster produced by Goebbels' propaganda unit, which posed a number of extremes, including "Race or Bastard" and "National Socialism or Bolshevism." Goebbels' speakers were trained in special schools, and themes and techniques "were studied carefully and their effects on different audiences noted," according to Rinderle and Norling.[148] These speeches—like the posters—targeted audiences with clear, albeit distorted messages, while issues were presented in a "black versus white" manner and messages customized for war veterans, government workers, farmers, and many other groups.[149] By the March 1933 Reichstag election campaign, about six thousand trained speakers descended on towns and villages, convening meetings and providing "good entertainment" by parading marching SA soldiers with flags[150]—much like the mass political rallies in the United States in the nineteenth and twentieth centuries (see Chapters Two and Three).

In the 1930 Reichstag elections, the Nazi Party dramatically increased its share of the vote from less than 3 percent in 1928 to more than 18 percent.[151] The party's strategy was to posture itself as the only effective alternative to Bolshevism, portraying the other political parties as inept or corrupt.[152] One poster again featured a snake—this time labeled "Marxism" and "High Finance"—choked by a Nazi hand. Another poster urged voters to attend party meetings, with admission fees for the "war injured and the unemployed half price" and "Jews not admitted." Other posters presented images of the harsh economic conditions, contrasted with positive, future ones—such as bountiful wheat fields, shown with the swastika. By November 1930, millions were without a job: an estimated 20 percent of the working-age population was unemployed; the percentage rose to 38 percent in 1932.[153] The terrible conditions of the Great Depression seemed to be the primary motive for the dramatic increase in the vote totals for the Nazi Party, whose coordinated propaganda campaign helped get across its message to a desperate population. The Nazi Party had become the second most popular party—only six points behind the Social Democrats, who attracted 24.5 percent of the vote in the 1930 elections.[154] Soon afterward, the Nazis formed the Reich Propaganda Directorate, and regional leaders provided it with reports on popular opinion.[155]

Filled with lies and distortions designed to win over Catholic voters and other reluctant groups, Nazi newspapers proliferated by the 1932 Reichstag elections. Newspaper and poster propaganda, mass meetings and parades, and street violence characterized the campaign in early 1932. Radio was used in a clever way to launch the campaign of the venerable Field Marshal Paul von Hindenburg, who was Hitler's main opponent in the presidential election in March of that year. Chancellor Brüning made a speech in the Reichstag supporting Hindenburg, but under German law, such speeches could not be broadcast from the floor; instead, a *recording* of the speech was broadcast, which was not outlawed. In many rural areas, there were no newspapers, particularly for Hindenburg, so posters and pamphlets were the main media of propaganda. Hindenburg, supported by the Center, People's, Socialist, and other parties, barely missed a majority of the vote (Hitler trailed him by a margin of more than 19 percent), necessitating an April runoff. Hindenburg won 53 percent to Hitler's 37 percent, despite an unprecedented Nazi propaganda campaign, the party having distributed an estimated eight million leaflets and six million posters, and, having held three thousand meetings daily.[156] A biographic film of Hindenburg was screened in urban movie theaters, and his second-round campaign was helped by parties such as the Social Democrats, which produced a poster of Hitler wielding an axe against a group of workers being led to a guillotine via a ballot urn.[157] The Nazis were not the only party to use emotional visual imagery in the election posters of the period.

One Nazi poster design had two rows of photographs of Jews beneath the declaration "We are voting for Hindenburg!" and two rows of Nazi leaders below "We are voting for Hitler!" Another featured two citizens, with the caption "Workers of the mind and hand Vote for the soldier of the front Hitler!" One purpose here was to remind people that Hitler had earned his German citizenship by fighting in the country's army; this served to counter criticisms of the Nazi leader, who was born in Austria. Another poster showed lines of unemployed workers for Hitler. Hitler himself appears in another poster sans uniform, but instead wearing a business suit, to make him look "presidential." Broadsides continued to play a part in German election campaigns, including the ones in 1932. A two-sided broadside titled "Why Hitler?" specified the reasons to vote for the Nazi leader; its emphasis was on his leadership qualities, clear goals, commonality, and deriding the opposition candidates. Another broadside—targeted at conservatives who might have favored Hindenburg—stressed that Hitler was a veteran who had not accepted any benefits, even though he had been wounded twice.

In the Reichstag elections in July 1932, the Nazis achieved the highest percentage of the vote of any party (37 percent) doubling their share from two years earlier—with the Social Democratic Party second (22 percent).[158] Among some of the images the Nazi posters for this campaign displayed were those of uniformed party members marching toward the Reichstag building, a pile driver smashing both the Center Party and the Communists, and one dominated by a cross, with the text "Over 300 National-Socialists died for you—murdered by Marxist subhumanity [in street fights]!!! For work and food vote Adolf Hitler List 2." The Nazi propaganda machine used every possible symbol—even religious ones—to appeal to various groups. The Nazis' share of the vote fell slightly to 33 percent in the November Reichstag elections, but the percentage achieved by the runner-up Socialists declined as well (to 20 percent).[159] Numerous poster designs were issued, and previous themes were continued, but much more emphasis was placed on rebuilding a "New Germany." There were also Nazi billboards attacking President Hindenburg. Radio and film was not used much, but by January 1933, after Hitler had been appointed chancellor and new parliamentary elections were scheduled, the Nazis used radio extensively to spread propaganda about Hitler as an honest leader who would guide Germany out of the Depression. The March 1933 Reichstag elections resulted in an increase in the Nazi Party's share of the total vote to 44 percent (with a turnout of 89 percent).[160] Posters showed Hindenburg and Hitler shaking hands, helping to validate the party and its leader. Arrests of opponents soon followed, newspapers were shut down, and Germany became a totalitarian state, with billboards displaying the election decrees of the government.[161]

From the onset of their movement, Hitler and the Nazi leaders were cognizant of the importance of using a propaganda campaign, which had all elements coordinated to influence and then convince voters to support them. The campaigns implemented theories and principles of mass psychology, advertising, and persuasion, after primitive "market research" was conducted. One key component in the Nazi's media propaganda blitzkrieg was the poster. Hitler and Goebbels wrote extensively about their design and use. The party's posters typically had the following characteristics: large size to attract attention; memorable slogans, text, and graphic images, including a striking symbol (i.e., the swastika); the color red to emphasize important aspects, or, as previously noted, broadsides printed on red paper; large, bold type for key words; exclamation marks; and a few simple and repeated points that were usually exaggerated or false. Hitler had learned well the lessons of anti-German propaganda in World War I, and Nazi posters were in many ways like those of the Allies during the Great War: stereotypes of Jews, bankers, and Communists were used instead of "Huns" in simple, blatant, and clear designs, in which idealized "Aryans" dominated. Advertising's exaggeration of mothers, children, and racial groups was well known, and the Nazis presented not only idealized depictions of the "Aryan race," but negative images of Jews and other minorities.

It is ironic that many of the tactics in the election campaign developed for Harding in 1920 by Lasker, a Jewish-American advertising pioneer, would be similar to those that Hitler would employ in the next decades. One should not be astonished by this, given

Hitler's fascination with advertising methods. Of course, the image that Lasker fashioned for Harding was one that would work in the context of American politics—that of being a "down-to-earth man of the people" and an "inspiring" leader. The image created for Hitler was one that was perfect for the Germany of the times—that of a "heroic" and "visionary" leader. Neither image was accurate, but the 1920s was not the first decade in which image management would be an approach taken in politics. Of course, when posters and broadsides were designed for undecided voters, Hitler was sometimes depicted as a "man of the people" as well. Much of the Nazi electoral accomplishments in the early 1930s can be attributed to its application of advertising principles. This was noted in 1932 by advertising executive Ernst Growald, who stated, "Hitler's success rests in large part on excellent advertising, which is especially effective since his opponents cannot mount anything nearly as powerful against it. The advertising-fetish of the Nazis is the swastika, which is propagated better than any factory or firm symbol ever was."[162] Growald knew about advertising, posters, and graphic design. He had been sales manager of Berlin's biggest printer of advertising posters and was the agent for Lucian Bernhard—one of Germany's foremost poster and type designers, and the first professor of poster design at the Kunst Academy in Berlin.[163]

After World War II, the conservative Christian Democratic Union Party—essentially descended from the Center Party—was created, and Konrad Adenauer, formerly the mayor of Cologne, was its main leader. The party's posters were identified by its symbol—a cross and the acronym "CDUD" (*Christlich Demokratische Union Deutschlands*). The Social Democratic Party was reestablished and the liberal Free Democratic Party (FDP) was founded. East Germany became a Soviet-dominated authoritarian state. In free Germany, a parliamentary system of government was launched, and Bundestag elections were held in 1949. The free market CDU and the like-minded CSU, in Bavaria, won 31 percent of the popular vote combined, and the Bundestag (the new lower house of the parliament) elected Adenauer chancellor by a one-vote majority. Adenauer cast that vote. His government was a coalition of the two Christian parties, the FDP (which had a 12-percent share of the vote), and the nationalist German Party (DP, which received under 6 percent). The Social Democrats (with 29 percent) and Communists (with under 6 percent, which barely met the threshold to gain a seat in parliament) were excluded from the government.[164]

By the next elections, in 1953, the economic revival, orchestrated by the Christian parties, helped them greatly increase their share of the vote to 45 percent, while the Social Democrats remained at 29 percent, the Free Democrats' percentage fell to under 10 percent, and the Communists' 2 percent failed to earn it a seat.[165] During the campaign, Adenauer stated that if his coalition did not win the election, it would be "a victory for the Soviet Union."[166] His party's posters, however, were more temperate, averring that the chancellor had "restored Germany to a position of honor and prestige in the world." A Communist newspaper printed a poster showing Adenauer, but added a wig and mustache so that he looked like Hitler. The Social Democrats were critical of the United States for supporting the chancellor's party, and put up posters, headlined "Eisenhower—election help for Adenauer"; in them the American president was depicted helping the aged German leader onto a mechanical horse. These posters were placed on public notice boards. By 1956, the

Free Democrats were no longer in Adenauer's ruling coalition, which, in the following year, achieved its best percentage of the popular vote, slightly over 50 percent, owing to the continuing economic boom, indexed pensions, and staunch anticommunism (particularly after the 1956 Hungarian revolt). CDU posters featured a determined-looking Adenauer, and the slogan "No Experiments!" in bold letters above his name. The Social Democrats' main strategy was to demand more housing units, and the party improved three points in the popular vote (while the Christian parties picked up fourteen points).[167]

In 1958, elections in West Berlin occurred, and the Social Democratic Party and its leader, Willy Brandt, who became mayor, gained power there. Brandt and Adenauer were the two prominent leaders in postwar Germany, and the former, wrote Martin Kitchen, was "the outstanding example of the new type of Social Democrat," dismissing Marxism and favoring a free market economy and NATO.[168] In the 1961 election, Brandt was the SPD's candidate for chancellor, and although his party failed to unseat the Christian coalition, it did increase its share of the popular vote from 32 percent to 36 percent, after a campaign that was overshadowed by the building of the Berlin Wall.[169] Billboards were a significant element in the campaign. The two Christian parties spent 22 percent of their funds on them, which was more than was expended on newspaper ads (20 percent), publications (19 percent), radio, television, and film combined (16 percent), and meetings (10 percent).[170] Adenauer was forced to join again with the FDP (which increased its percentage of the popular vote four points to 13 percent) in an unsteady coalition, but it broke up in 1966 (replaced by "the Grand Coalition" of the CDU, CSU, and SPD).[171] By the election of 1969, Adenauer, who had resigned in 1963 at age eighty-seven, no longer led the CDU, and the two Christian parties achieved a margin of only about three points over the Social Democrats.[172] As a result, Brandt became chancellor, as head of an SPD-FDP coalition. The next election, three years later, centered on Brandt's policy of reaching out to Soviet-bloc countries, including the one in East Germany, and the Social Democrats edged the Christian parties for the first time, even though CSU leader Franz-Josef Strauss labeled Brandt the "partisan from Norway."[173]

The West German economy was hit by the general European recession in the early to mid-1970s, and the SPD-FDP government (led by former finance minister Helmut Schmidt as chancellor) lost some of its luster. Social Democratic posters issued before the election of 1976 highlighted its achievements, including land reform. One showed a man relaxing in a hammock while workers measured land, and the slogan "Thanks to SPD he got this land from bad speculators" (see Fig. 6.2). This strategy was largely negated by the economic downturn. The CDU campaign (with Helmut Kohl, the party's leader in the Bundestag, as its candidate for chancellor) produced the more effective propaganda: the slogan "Freedom instead of Socialism," and photographs of the Berlin Wall and locked-up factories were prominently displayed. Toward the end of the campaign, however, Social Democratic newspaper, poster, and billboard advertisements with attractive females, and children and grandmothers, along with a resolute Schmidt (who was perceived, in polls, to be more popular than his party), appeared to improve the SPD's image. The SPD-FDP coalition was able to retain power, but just barely, when the two parties polled slightly over a majority of the popular votes and the Christian parties obtained a bit less than 49 percent.[174]

The voters in 1980 kept the ruling coalition and Schmidt in power, even though the CSU attacked the chancellor in a film that implied he had been a supporter of Hitler's government, and despite a loss of some votes to the new pro-environment, antinuclear Green Party. The lion's share of the campaign budgets was for printed material in 1980: the Christian parties spent 35 percent on publications; 20 percent on billboards; 20 percent on newspaper advertisements; and only 3 percent on TV, radio, and film and 17 percent on meetings. The expenditures were similar for the Social Democrats: 34 percent was spent on publications, 29 percent on billboards, 26 percent on newspaper ads, 7 percent on meetings; and 4 percent on TV, radio, and film. The Free Democrats' spending was not much different, although more money went for newspaper ads.[175] Two years later, Schmidt's government fell when it lost a no-confidence vote, and a CDU-CSU-FDP coalition replaced it, with Kohl as chancellor.[176]

The 1983 election was a victory for the Christian parties, their combined share topping the Social Democrats 49 percent to 38 percent. Although the Free Democrats' share of the total vote decreased from over 10 percent to slightly less than 7 percent, it did well enough to remain in the coalition, even though the CSU attacked it as dominated by left-liberals.[177] A poster, anonymously released, featured only a caricature of FDP leader Hans-Dietrich Genscher as an elephant whose trunk was knotted and with a flower in its tail (Fig. 6.23). Some of the Social Democratic posters were creative, as well. One included a

Figure 6.23

drawing of SPD leader Hans-Jochen Vogel below a snowman melting in the sunshine of spring. Another depicted him telling a young man worried about the deployment of nuclear weapons in Germany that he would work hard to bring the superpowers to the negotiating table as chancellor (Fig. 6.24). The poster was clearly designed for both those on the left and the young. Many posters featured the parties' leaders, as they had for decades. A typical example can be seen in Figure 6.25, showing Kohl and

the German colors, and a textual message indicating that the chancellor created confidence, work, and peace, and could be trusted to ensure a prosperous future for all. Other posters produced for the main parties in the 1980s incorporated the German flag, workers, mothers and children, and photographs of Berlin.

By the 1980s, commercial television channels had proliferated, and the medium became a more important factor in West

Figure 6.24

BUNDESKANZLER
HELMUT KOHL

Dieser Kanzler schafft Vertrauen
Arbeit, Frieden, Zukunft
Miteinander
schaffen wir's CDU
sicher
sozial
und frei

Figure 6.25

German politics. The parties were assigned free time on governmental television and radio stations, the number of seats held in the Bundestag determining their allotment, but they were prohibited from buying air time for political broadcasts (although these were allowed on the private channels). Nevertheless, the increased use of television for political purposes led to an increased personalization of German election campaigns, the medium directing voters' attention to such nonverbal attributes as attractiveness, personality, clothing, and body language.[178] Of course, posters did this too, but not to the same extent, and without motion.

Although the two Christian parties lost some support in the 1987 election, Kohl's coalition was able to stay in power with the slogan "Carry on, Germany!" This happened as the Social Democrats also lost votes amid warnings about "Red-Green chaos" if the SPD and the anti-NATO Green Party took power in a new coalition (Fig. 6.26). The incumbents were helped by an improved economy, and a reduced budget deficit (although unemployment remained high). One controversial issue was the development of nuclear power stations, which Kohl strongly supported, but the Greens, and even some members of his own party, opposed. The nuclear accident at Chernobyl, which occurred the year before the German election, undoubtedly helped the Greens improve their proportion of the popular vote. The SPD lost support to the Greens (who increased their share by almost three points to over 8 percent) when the Social Democrats' stand on water pollution was perceived as weak, while chemical pollutants leaked

Versöhnen

statt spalten.

Figure 6.26

into the Rhine River.[179] Green Party's posters focused on its antinuclear position, showing yellow sunflowers, white doves, and green grass, nuclear plants looming in the background, adding slogans such as "Atomic energy is not safe—let us use nature's power!" Other Green posters decried toxic spills, and they were enhanced by depictions of animals, butterflies, and dead trees. The SPD's call for increased taxes on those with high earnings was countered by CDU's posters, which predicted that such an approach would result in "less for all" (Fig. 6.27).[180] Some Social Democratic posters of the period, featuring families, for example, seemed pallid in comparison.

Two years later, the East German dictatorship began to crumble. Gigantic demonstrations occurred late in the year—one of which, in Leipzig, drew about three hundred

Weniger für alle.

Figure 6.27

thousand. In November, the border between the two Germanys was opened, but there were groups in both sections that were against party reunification, including the Social Democrats and the Greens. Kohl proposed a confederation, with unification an option if the public desired it. Many in the Social Democratic Party then favored the chancellor's plan, but the Greens were still opposed (along with every major world leader except U.S. President George H. W. Bush). As other countries moved to support Kohl's ideas, his stature rose markedly. Although the new political groups of East Germany, the Green Party, and the "post-nationalist" wing of the SPD led by Saarland premier Oskar Lafontaine all opposed immediate reunification (if at all), public opinion in both states favored it.[181]

In East Germany's parliamentary election of March 1990, the CDU, and associated parties in the East, won a resounding victory. They gained almost a majority of the vote (while the runner-up, SPD, barely exceeded 20 percent).[182] Most of the posters and other printed material used in the campaign were produced in West Germany. In October, the Christian Democrats won a tremendous victory in the state legislative elections in the East, with Kohl's face—this time seen smiling—featured on most CDU posters, alongside the slogan "Helmut Kohl, Chancellor for Germany." Negotiations between the two German states had culminated in an agreement that unification would occur on December 2, 1990, when the West German Bundestag election was to take place, and every German was to be eligible to vote. The election campaign pitted the optimistic Kohl (with his slogan "Yes to Germany, Yes to the Future") against the Social Democratic Party's candidate for chancellor, Lafontaine, whose predictions about economic troubles, and continued calls for prohibiting nuclear power stations and enacting stricter environmental legislation, did not sway many voters. The result was a 10-point margin of victory for the Christian parties.[183] One CDU poster was headlined in English "Touch the Future!" and targeted young men to support *der union* (Fig. 6.28). An example of the Social Democrats' campaign approach, which emphasized

Figure 6.28

specific issues other than reunification, can be seen in Figure 6.29, showing a trash heap and the slogan "If we continue to unpack this way, we might as well pack it in."

The December 1990 election was also the first campaign in which paid TV spots were aired in significant numbers on the rapidly expanding private television stations (although mainly in the West), which probably led to more of an emphasis on image management. In fact, a study of party TV spots revealed that 58 percent of

Figure 6.29

them were image-oriented.[184] All Christian Democratic newspaper ads included at least a reference to Kohl, whereas six of ten Social Democratic press ads named and/or showed

Lafontaine.[185] The CDU was particularly well organized for the election campaign: the party committee had met more than a year earlier to begin preliminary strategic planning, forming a campaign committee charged to supervise public relations activities, along with a supervisory committee chaired by Kohl that would conduct surveys regularly. A coordinated campaign was devised, employing common symbols and colors on posters, leaflets, and other material at all levels; three thousand posters were distributed to each party district at no charge. A nationwide billboard campaign was carried out, also. In addition, CDU commercials—targeting mainly young voters—were screened in movie theaters and discos. The Social Democratic Party was well organized, too, but its qualitative survey data from East Germany was not representative. Nevertheless, the Social Democrats also had a common design for its posters, brochures, and leaflets, which they tested with randomly selected voters, as well as a national billboard campaign.[186]

The posters of Lafontaine smiling, with the Social Democratic slogan "The New Way," probably did little to improve the personality popularity ratings of the party's leader, who received a 1.1 (compared to Kohl's 2.1) on a scale of -5 to 5 that measured this attribute.[187] The Christian Democrats achieved the same percentage of the popular vote, even with an expanded electorate, whereas the Social Democrats lost three points. The western Green Party's opposition to reunification hurt them at the polls, as well, and it received only 4 percent of the vote (a staggering loss of four points), which was below the 5 percent threshold for representation in parliament.[188] The Greens did distribute posters with issues and designs calculated to attract attention and arouse passions. One of the posters for its Alliance 90 coalition, with several East German groups, featured rows of posterized police and text calling for the disarmament of the police and the dissolution of the constitution (see Fig. 1.17, Chapter One); another, which targeted female voters, had a woman's hands placing a "Groucho-Marx"-type nose, mustache, and glasses over the genitals of a classical male statue, accompanied by the slogan "Invasion of the male domain" (see Fig. 1.2, Chapter One). The FDP, its popular leader Genscher having played a key role in the unification process as foreign minister, won 11 percent of the vote (a 1-point improvement).[189] Its posters were creative as well: one depicted pregnant men, and the slogan "If men felt as we did, there would be enough playgrounds" (Fig. 6.30).

The ruling coalition, led by Kohl, had received a mandate to unite Germany. Research findings, overall, revealed that the election campaigns of the coalition parties were superior to those of their opponents: after June, among SDP and Green Party supporters, there was nearly a 21-point shift toward the CDU, CSU, and FRP, but there was only an 8-point move in the other direction.[190] Studies also indicated that, although "personalization" was a key strategy in the 1990 campaign, Germans (at least in a study of voters in the West) were more interested in the parties and issues, rather than in the individual leaders.[191]

Figure 6.30

ca *Poland and the Free Elections of 1990 and 1991.* At the end of the thirteenth century, Poland's dukes elected the country's kings. Beginning in 1573, the gentry (even those who were impoverished) elected the king after much debate, wining, and dining.[192] Members of the parliament also were elected. In 1831, however, Russia invaded Poland, defeated its army, and eliminated the constitution and the parliament. Poles elected representatives to the parliaments of Galicia in the 1860s, Prussia in the 1890s, and Russia at the beginning of the twentieth century, but they did not have their own governmental bodies for most of this period. Uprisings in 1848 in parts of Poland (inspired, as in Germany and other countries, by the toppling of Louis Philippe) motivated the Austrian emperor to co-opt the revolution by promising to abolish Polish serfdom and distribute land, followed by military action that defeated the Polish forces. After World War I, Poland became an independent republic (patterned after France's Third Republic), with its lower house of parliament (the *Sejm*) wielding the most power. However, proportional representation led to formation of thirty-one political parties and unstable coalitions in the body, and by the 1920s and 1930s, the constitution was suspended and military dictators ruled the country.[193] By 1935, elections were held, with little campaigning, to select a nonpartisan parliament from lists of mainly pro-regime candidates. After World War II, the Russian army occupied Poland; this led to the formation of a coalition government, which included the Peasant Alliance and the Socialists, but dominated by the Communists. The latter party won rigged elections in 1947. The Communist Party controlled the government and the society for another forty-two years, and all elections were one-party affairs, characterized by propaganda campaigns with an abundance of party slogans and posters, loud speakers on automobiles, and "educational" meetings.[194]

The end of Soviet Communist domination of Poland began in 1980. That summer, workers at the Gdansk shipyards established free unions and launched a strike, during which they occupied the yards, with a previously fired electrician, Lech Wałęsa, joining the strikers. The strike expanded to other cities, and Wałęsa headed a movement that extolled nationalism, Catholicism, and freedom. About two weeks after the Gdansk workers had commenced their action, the government agreed to their right to organize their own trade unions, which became known as Solidarity and soon had ten million members. The Solidarity posters produced in 1980 and 1981 were intended to publicize dates and places of actions, and the movement's logo incorporated the national flag and its red-and-white colors, and its "painterly looseness … [was] said to refer to a surging crowd," according to Danuta Boczar.[195] Unfortunately, Solidarity was declared illegal at the end of 1981, and the Polish army seized control, putting Wałęsa and other union leaders in internment camps while others went underground. The underground urged boycotts of the decade's elections, distributing "Don't vote" cards and leaflets.[196]

Solidarity was again declared legal in early 1989. Soviet ruler Mikhail Gorbachev had loosened his regime's hold on the satellite countries, but economic, social, and political conditions in Poland had deteriorated. A series of "Round Table Talks" ensued, and a plan for the establishment of democratic institutions and procedures was negotiated. The first elections that year were not completely free, and only 35 percent of the Sejm were elected democratically.[197] In spite of this, Solidarity ran a campaign that featured large posters (some of which were torn down by police, according to the party), banners, TV spots, radio programs, bumper stickers, buttons, leaflets, and newspapers (although printing companies sometimes refused to print them or censorship was imposed).[198] Each candidate on the party's list posed with Wałęsa, the dynamic freedom fighter, and these photographs were printed on posters with the Solidarity logo (Fig. 6.31). In a special Solidarity poster for this election campaign, Gary Cooper (as the American sheriff in the film *High Noon*) was shown with a ballot in one hand, instead of a pistol, along with the message "It's high noon, June 4, 1989." He was still a heroic symbol for the rule of law and the rights of the people over the oppressors, but now he had become an advocate for nonviolence as well (Fig. 6.32). Another poster showed sleeping children, with Solidarity's appeal to parents

Figure 6.31   Figure 6.32

to vote. In addition, a poster within a poster illustrated children putting up a "Vote for Solidarity" sign.

The new constitution stated that the president would be elected directly, and a runoff was mandated if, initially, no candidate gained a majority of the votes. The president was given the right to veto legislation, which could be overridden by a two-thirds vote of the Sejm. In addition to the Sejm, a senate was created, and members were elected directly (as were those sent to the lower house). In 1990, Wałęsa won the presidency in a free election. The presidential election campaign was intense, and the emphasis was on personality and an understandable distrust of parties. Posters and other political paraphernalia were widely distributed.[199] Undoubtedly, because of the Poles' legitimate suspicions about the mass media, this material played a larger role in Poland than in many other countries. In the first round, Wałęsa received over 39 percent of the vote, and Stanisław Tymiński, a businessman who had gone to Canada and Peru, came in second with almost 23 percent. In the runoff round, Wałęsa won by a 3-to-1 margin.[200]

In the 1991 parliamentary elections, there were almost one hundred parties listed on the ballots. "Occupation strikes" continued, as workers were laid off at bankrupt state factories, with orders no longer coming from the Soviet Union and Polish army, but with a rapidly growing private sector. Every party attacked the economic policies in the campaign, which often focused on making voters aware of one's party and getting them to remember its name. By this time, the Solidarity movement had split into several factions, with its center-left in the Democratic Union (UD), the unionists in the Self-Governing Solidarity Trade Union (NSZZ), and the center-right in the Center Alliance (POC). When the popular votes were tabulated, the UD was on top, but it had only slightly more than 12 percent of the total, with the Democratic Left Alliance (SLD) having gained a bit under 12 percent, and the Catholic Electoral Action, Center Alliance, and Polish Peasant Party all under 9 percent. The NSZZ represented many workers and was supported by 5 percent of the electorate. One of its posters featured a flower with the sun in its center, along with its famous logo, symbolizing a new beginning and oneness with everyone and everything (Fig. 6.33). Flowers had dominated several Solidarity posters in 1989 and one included a

Figure 6.33

sun, seen through a window. Interestingly, the Polish Beer-Lovers' Party received over 3 percent of the popular vote.[201] In general, the UD, which included many intellectuals, stood for pragmatic economic and political reform and the rule of law. It fell out of favor, however, after it refused to oppose abortion and combated the existing radical program designed to move the country's economy into the world of capitalism.[202]

The POC (which was in favor of privatization and membership in NATO) was asked to form a coalition government after the election, but it subsequently lost support because of a rift between its leader, Prime Minister Jan Olszewski, and President Wałęsa, and the continued economic distress. By the 1993 parliamentary elections, a new law was in effect that established thresholds, and thus limited the number of parties that could gain seats. Owing in large part to the anxieties during this period of economic dislocation, as capitalism was introduced, the SLD (the party of former communists) won the most popular votes and seats in the Sejm. Since then, there have been numerous crises and changes in government, but the overall economy has improved.[203] Poland is a young democracy, even though its democratic roots go deep into the past. In time, its constitution and political system should become more stable, particularly as the country becomes more westernized.

CR *Hungary's Fight for Democracy and the 1990 Election.* Soon after Poland achieved independence from the Soviet Union, Hungary (along with East Germany) came next in March 1990. Gorbachev began to withdraw troops from Hungarian soil in 1989 and 1990, and the Communist Party disbanded and reestablished itself as the Hungarian Socialist Party (MSZP). Sharing of power by the Communist and opposition parties did not occur in Hungary, as it had in Poland; rather, Communist reformers enacted a new constitution that created a multiparty democratic political system, and parliament selected a relatively weak president.[204]

Hungary had earlier experienced democracy. In 1848, when revolution hit France again, and the franchise was dramatically expanded in that country (as discussed in Chapter Four), a similar development occurred in Hungary. In a "peaceful revolution," led by Lajos Kossuth, Hungary broke free from the Austrian Habsburg Empire and a constitutional monarchy was created, which had a Diet, with a National Assembly (the equivalent of the British House of Commons), its members directly elected by the propertied classes, and another legislative body reserved for nobles and dignitaries (as was the case in Great Britain). The Diet ended most aspects of the feudal system, and ensured that many peasants would own land. The workers and landless peasants could not vote, but neither could the same groups in Great Britain after the Reform Act of 1832. An estimated 7 to 9 percent of the population was enfranchised—a great improvement from the less than 2 percent who had suffrage in the past.[205] Parliamentary elections soon took place, and most of those elected hailed from the nobility. The parliament formed a committee of national defense, and Hungarian armed forces initially defeated an invading army from Austria, although by 1849—with the help of the Russian army—the rebellion was crushed and Hungarian independence was finished.[206]

Eighteen years later, the Habsburg emperor allowed the Hungarians some independence, particularly internally. The parliament was firmly in the control of the landed classes, which held about 80 percent of its seats. Only 6 percent of the population was given the right to vote.[207] The election campaigns were similar to the British electioneering of the early eighteenth century, and local landlords and their political clubs managed them. Patronage, including wining and dining, was a major means by which to influence the small number of electors. In addition, the secret ballot did not exist. The only well-organized political organization was the Deák or Government Party, whose central committee routinely reviewed reports from local committees. By 1875, the two main parties of the left and center merged to become the Liberal Party, and the Conservative Party was established in opposition, followed soon by the Independence Party, which extolled the values of the exiled Kossuth.[208]

In the ensuing decades, other political parties were formed. But the liberals retained power until 1905, when a coalition, whose key force was the Independence Party (led by Kossuth's son, Ferenc), won the election. Opposition parties, including the Independent Socialist Peasant Party, and the National Independence or 48er Farmers' Party (with the latter in favor of universal suffrage), were organized. The elections of 1910, however, were won by the National Party of Work (with much support from well-to-do bourgeois and landowners who were members of the Liberal Party). With the exception of the short-lived liberal republic and its coalition government, headed by Count Mihály Károlyi's Independence Party after World War I, which did not last long enough for elections to be held, there were no real democratic politics again until 1989.[209]

Under the dictatorial Bála Kun, an equally brief Communist regime followed Károlyi's, and a "red terror" soon led to a "counter-revolutionary" one, with Vice Admiral Miklós Horthy becoming the authoritarian leader of Hungary. Parliament continued to meet, although political prisoners were abundant. Horthy served as president until the Soviet Army crossed into Hungary in 1944. Democratic parliamentary elections were held the next year, and the Communists' expectations of doing well were stoked by the land reform policies of the provisional government organized during the Soviet occupation. However, the Smallholders Party (which defended property rights, but also advocated moderate land reform) won every district; they garnered 57 percent of the votes of Hungarians, who cast secret ballots for the first time. The Communist Party obtained less than 17 percent, receiving a slightly lower percentage than did the Socialists.[210] The will of the people soon was thwarted when the Smallholders' leaders and their supporters were intimidated, exiled, and arrested, and Hungary fell behind Stalin's "Iron Curtain" (Churchill's characterization of the 1946 Communist takeover in Eastern Europe). Elections were rigged thereafter.[211] Ten years later, the Red Army savagely extinguished a brief revolt against Soviet domination, resulting in much loss of life and political repression.

After the "peaceful revolution" of 1989 had led to the new Republic of Hungary, the first democratic parliamentary elections took place in March 1990. One dozen parties campaigned with national lists for seats in the National Assembly, and proportional and direct representation were used to assign four-year terms to party members. Six of these parties exceeded the 4 percent minimum required for inclusion in a second round of voting, and the Magyar Democratic Forum (MDF) captured the highest proportion of the vote (41 percent, after receiving 25 percent in the first round). The MDF, which had been formed in the late 1980s, along with a number of other political parties, positioned itself as a moderate-conservative party (similar to the Christian Democratic party in Germany). Coming in second was the Alliance of Free Democrats (SZDSZ), with about 21 percent in the first round and 31 percent in the second. The conservative Independent Smallholders Party was third (with 12 percent and 10 percent in the two rounds). The reformist-Communists in the MSZP finished fourth in both rounds (with 11 percent and 6 percent, respectively), and their party's hardcore associates (under the Workers Party banner) failed to make it to the second round, being slightly under the threshold. Two minor parties that did qualify for the second round were the Federation of Young Democrats and the Christian Democratic People's Party. The former party's list attracted 9 percent in the first round and 2 percent in the second; the latter's list brought 6 percent and 4 percent, respectively.[212]

The MDF attracted many voters, particularly after the minor parties were eliminated in the first round, by promoting itself as the "Quiet Force" for a stable, moderate transition from Communism.[213] The posters of the MDF reveal some of its campaign themes. In Figure 6.34, for example, a trash bin is shown, along with symbols of the old regime (i.e., a statue of Stalin, Mao's and Kim Il Sung's writings, the Communist Party newspaper, a photograph of Lenin, and a secret-police pistol holder) to be swept up and discarded in a "nationwide spring cleaning." Another poster featured the parliament building and the colors of the national flag, with the party attempting to associate itself with political tradition and power. The MDF also aired photographs of the construction of the building in a five-minute television commercial during the campaign, as the narrator stated that the building faced westward.[214] In addition, the party featured

Figure 6.34

a Madonna-like pregnant woman, accompanied by the slogan "For a Magyar Future" in one of its posters.

The Christian Democrats also used religious imagery, but more blatantly (i.e., a cross smashing a red star) in an attempt to appeal to religious and anti-Communist voters (Fig. 6.35). In addition, many posters of its leader, historian and museum director József Antall, were displayed. The most compelling image, however, was presented in an MDF poster that illustrated the back of a bullnecked Soviet soldier, and pasted over his hat the message "Comrades, the End!" in Russian (Fig. 6.36). The MDF raised funds by selling

| *Figure 6.35* | *Figure 6.36* |

thousands of copies of this poster. Moreover, its imagery had such appeal that it resurfaced in 1991 in demonstrations in the Baltic countries. Several parties used past historical symbols. Examples of these are the crown of Saint Stephen (to appeal to monarchists and nationalists) in an MDF poster; a flower design (from a peasant motif, to appeal to rural voters) in an additional MDF poster; wheat in a Smallholders' design; and a red carnation (instead of a red star, to attract Communist voters) in an MSZP poster. Pictures of children and slogans extolling the family, God, and country were evident as well. Another image used in the campaign's election posters was a broken fork; one can be seen in Figure 6.37,

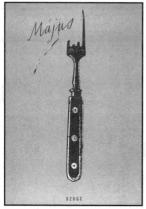

Figure 6.37

featured in an SZDSZ poster attacking May Day. The broken fork symbolized the failed economic and political policies of the Communist governments.[215]

Posters and banners appeared everywhere during the 1990 campaign, and it is apparent that much time, creativity, and money went into their design and distribution. The debate about poster design could become quite heated. One such discussion at SZDSZ headquarters led to a confrontation between the rabidly anti-Communist camp and the more moderate faction, and the phrase "against the Communists perpetuating their power" was finally rejected as too abrasive for a referendum campaign. Slogans that manifested on the party's posters included "Onward to a Free Future!" "A Free People Can Do Wonders," and "With a Clean Past for a Clear Future"—all of which were more positive. The SZDSZ also used TV spot ads, one of which went perhaps too far in its condemnation of the Communist "past" (symbolized as a sinking ship) and its bureaucracy (a film clip of a male clerk applying a rubber stamp to the exposed posterior of a female associate was screened). Some Hungarians criticized the ad as using "American tactics," even though Hungarians produced it.[216]

After the election, the MDF formed a center-right coalition government with the Christian Democrats and the Smallholders, which had 59 percent of the seats in parliament among them. The SZDSZ and another liberal party, the Federation of Young Democrats, along with the MSZP socialists, with 38 percent of the seats in the National Assembly among them, were the main legislative opponents. After its victory, the MDF stepped up its anti-Communist propaganda. But by the election of 1994, many voters (particularly urban workers) viewed the reformist-Communists and the Hungarian Socialist Party more favorably, since they had become disenchanted with the economic and land reform policies of the new government. Consequently, the MSZP won over half the seats in the parliament, with the MDF coming in a poor third (winning only about 10 percent of the seats).[217] Many Hungarian voters—in a new democratic republic—did not yet feel strong allegiance to any political party, and propaganda during election campaigns could move them to vote for parties different from what they had previously voted for.[218]

Hungary's main media of political campaign propaganda were television and printed material, particularly billboards, posters, and leaflets. Undoubtedly, there was some residual suspicion of television broadcasts, and opponents leveled accusations against the ruling Socialists about control of the medium. Reformers and protesters in the Communist world had favored the poster medium above all others to make their points, since television had been discredited. Researchers confirmed the perception of bias in public television broadcasts during the 1994 election campaign: the broadcasters devoted 64 percent of the political coverage to the ruling MDF that year, and it was all either positive or neutral; the MSZP, on the other hand, received only 11 percent of the coverage, and it was mainly negative.[219] Beginning with the 1998 election, most Hungarians had access to private television channels, which were not subject to influence by the ruling government, and

Internet advertisements became a factor, along with the continued employment of fliers, posters, billboards, banners, and newspaper ads, and increased use of direct mail and telephone calls.[220]

Latin America

In much of Latin America, "street poster art" is an influential political medium, with a "cadre system" established to quickly place posters in urban areas. Posters, according to Lyman Chaffee, are effective in delivering political messages to the general public in Latin America because it is easy to make the messages clear, emotional, and personally involving, and because the mass media will communicate the messages conveyed with posters (and banners) displayed in various events to the general public. The standard practice is to maximize the impact of a poster's message by pasting many copies of the same poster in rows or columns. This repetition attracts attention.[221]

Posters, broadsides, and billboards have been used extensively in election campaigns throughout the region. This is true even as the influences of television and the Internet have become greater than those of other media in some countries, and as the role of advertising personnel is more prominent than that of other advisors in the campaign process. Not only are outside political consultants brought in, but there also exists the Association of Latin American Political Consultants, with a large membership. Political marketing specialists have their own organizations in Argentina (as well as in Brazil), and it is clear from the Web site of the Argentine Association of Political Marketing that posters have been a key medium in the country's past and present elections. At the end of the nineteenth century and in the first decades of the twentieth century, the emerging political parties of Argentina distributed large numbers of posters and other smaller printed material for elections, which became increasingly fair. The Socialist Party displayed eight thousand posters and broadsides in Buenos Aires during the election of 1896, for example.[222] Posters that featured Juan Perón and his wife Eva were used in Argentina's 1940s and 1950s elections, although their regime was authoritarian after he was elected in 1946. Perón's cause was helped by an opposition poster that showed him holding the sweaty white shirt of a worker, with the slogan "The Sweaty One—the new fatherland colors," which Perón's campaign used in their campaign to target the *descamisados* ("shirtless ones").[223]

Democratic elections returned to Argentina for good in 1983, after more than three decades of chiefly military rule. The two major parties, the Radical Civic Union (UCR) and the Peronists, waged a poster war, depicting the Radical candidate, Raul Alfonsín, as a puppet of the United States and its companies. One Peronist poster presented Alfonsín holding a bottle of Coca-Cola®; an anonymous poster simply said, "Country Yes! Colony No!" UCR posters, however, presented their party's candidate as talking to the masses. Candidates have also appealed to nationalism in various ways. A poster for the victorious presidential candidate Néstor Kirchner, in 2003, for example, used the map of Argentina as the left side of the "K" of the candidate's name. While the majority of election posters have included portraits or waist-up photographs of the candidates, or only displayed their names, some have been sarcastic. A UCR poster in 1989, for instance, represented the Peronist presidential candidate, Carlos Menem, as a small figure next to the comparatively monumental leaders of the United States and the Soviet Union, George H. W. Bush and Mikhail Gorbachev. Sometimes cuteness has been displayed in posters, such as one issued by the *Frente de Todos* (Front for Everyone) Party during the 2005 National Congress election campaign, which showed a penguin and the statement "I prefer fresh air." In the past few decades, democracy has returned to many parts of Latin America, military dictatorships ending in Chile (ranked 20th by World Audit in May 2007), Uruguay (22nd), and Panama (38th), while Costa Rica (28th) continues as a stable democratic country. World Audit viewed most of the other nations in the region as "qualified" democracies, including El Salvador (46th), Brazil (52nd), Peru (53rd), Bolivia (55th), the Dominican Republic (59th), Mexico (61st), Nicaragua (63rd), Colombia (64th), Ecuador (65th), Argentina (67th), Honduras (71st), and Paraguay (74th).[224]

In many countries of Latin America, with dispersed populations, television is the ideal medium for political campaigns. In Brazil, for example, over 90 percent of urban households have access to television programming, as do 70 percent of rural homes, while the top four newspapers reach only one in ten voters.[225] Television employing celebrities, humor, and song is therefore the primary means of conveying messages in national campaigns. Nevertheless, the poster is still an important medium in Latin American elections, and huge versions have often been used in marches and other campaign events to draw attention to candidates. In Alejandro Toledo's successful 2001 race for the presidency of Peru, for instance, a giant poster, in which Toledo was depicted as an Inca ruler, dominated a rally, while marchers carried smaller posters with photographs of the candidate. The next year, in the Bolivian elections, the Movement Towards Socialism Party mounted a highly effective campaign with less than two hundred thousand dollars from the state. This took the party from 4 percent in the polls in March to 21 percent of the total vote in the June election, and its leader, Evo Morales, was only a few percentage points shy of winning the presidency. The key element of the campaign was a poster featuring a photograph of Morales and the statement "Bolivians: You Decide. Who's in Charge? Rocha [i.e., U.S. ambassador to Bolivia Manuel Rocha] or the Voice of the People."[226] Despite the rising importance of television in countries such as Chile, posters are ubiquitous, as one observer stated during the 2005 Chilean presidential election, when "one [couldn't] seem to leave the house without being subject to posters lined up on every street," according to one report.[227] That posters are essential in Latin America is not surprising, considering a recent survey found that almost 80 percent of the region's campaign managers believed the image of a candidate was the *most* important factor in a political campaign. Furthermore, 24 percent of these political professionals indicated that street posters were of "exceptional importance" in campaign advertising strategy, a percentage almost as high as for daily newspapers (29 percent) and private television (30 percent).[228]

⊂⊃ *Chile: Salvador Allende and the Suspension of Democracy (1970–1973).*

In September 1970, Senator Salvador Allende Gossens, a Marxist-socialist, was elected president of Chile, as head of *la Unidad Popular* (i.e., "Popular Unity" or UP)—a coalition of political parties of the left that advocated increased nationalism and land redistribution. The election campaign was a tumultuous one, with supporters of Allende excited and hopeful for change, and other voters fearful of what would happen in the country if he won. Some in Allende's Socialist Party called for seizing power, if he was not elected. Three years later, Allende was found dead, after a military takeover, the presidential palace bombed beyond repair, and General Augusto Pinochet Ugarte was declared the dictatorial leader of Chile. It was apparent that the Central Intelligence Agency (CIA) of the United States, under President Nixon, had worked to prevent Allende's election, and—after he had won—helped to destabilize the regime. One CIA memorandum stated: "The President asked the Agency to prevent Allende from coming to power or to unseat him."[229] In its destabilization efforts, the CIA assembled a propaganda campaign against Allende and his party, at a cost of over four hundred thousand dollars during the 1970 election, and spent much more later on, after he attained power. Additional funds came from American corporations. In particular, posters and wall paintings were used in a "scare campaign" in 1970, the former medium showing Cuban political prisoners about to be executed by a firing squad, and the warning that if Allende won the election, religious and family life would "end." An estimated eight million dollars was spent in anti-Allende actions in the three years before Allende's demise (the funds often exchanged at five times the official rate on the black market, meaning that the effort had tens of millions of dollars funneled into it in real-money terms). The CIA had mounted antileftist operations in Chile for years, including one that cost more than 2.6 million dollars in the 1964 presidential election, a majority of the funds being spent by the Christian Democratic Party having come from the United States.[230] The U.S. government had not prevented Allende's election and, when its covert activities became known, its image during the Vietnam War was further tarnished. It was not until 1989 that Chile was to conduct a democratic presidential election again.

That Chile had come to such a state was surprising. Before the coup, Chile was considered "one of the most stable and democratic countries" in Latin America, according to Arturo Valenzuela.[231] It had indirectly elected presidents for almost a century, beginning in 1830, although suffrage limitations existed (as they did elsewhere in the world). Its electoral system was similar to that still used in the United States, but direct election of Chilean presidents was mandated in 1925. There were only three "bumps in the road": in 1859, when a civil war broke out; in 1891, when Congress compelled a president to resign and more modern parties were formed; and in the 1920s and 1930s, when additional resignations of presidents were forced, after the military intervened. Allende was not even the first Marxist-socialist to run Chile: Marmaduke Grove Vallejo, who had been Commander of the Air, had filled that role in 1932, for at least twelve days, following a military rebellion.[232]

Allende had run for president previously, in 1964, but lost by a 17-point margin to the Christian Democrat, Eduardo Frei Montalva, in an election between only two major candidates.[233] The earlier 1958 election, on the other hand, was more typical of Chilean presidential contests, and an omen of what was to come in 1970. In that year, Allende was runner-up to Jorge Alessandri Rodriguez in a five-person race, losing by less than a 3-point margin, with Frei third—8 percentage points behind Allende.[234] The Socialist and most of his supporters accepted the results, but generally stable democratic institutions were not able to solve some fundamental problems in Chile, as Allende noted in 1970, when he stated, "although bourgeois democracy has reached a very high level here, no Government has solved the problems of housing, employment and education."[235] Finally, in the election of 1970, Allende won, when Alessandri and Radomiro Tomic Romero (Frei's successor in his party) split the moderate and conservative votes. The results were: Allende 36.2 percent, Alessandri 34.9 percent, and Tomic 27.8 percent.[236] Although he was the candidate of the ruling Christian Democratic Party, Tomic had been placed in a weak political position: he was forced to advocate for a continuation of the moderate program of nationalization and agrarian reform begun by the government, which had not satisfied many on either the left or the right.[237] A good indication of this loss of support was that the Christian Democrats' percentage of the vote in the 1969 congressional races had plunged to 31 percent, compared to 43 percent four years earlier.[238]

Allende's short-lived government used offset lithographic printing to boost enthusiasm for its programs, after it raised money during the election campaign by selling up to three thousand copies of each of thirty-six poster designs.[239] Unlike the posters of Fidel Castro's Cuba, those produced by Allende's regime were largely devoid of the concept of "revolutionary class struggle on an international scale," according to David Kunzle; rather they were concerned with the nationalization of the copper mines, voluntarism, and educational programs.[240] Generally, the UP's election posters had been conventional. One poster, for instance, showed a black-and-white photograph of an appealing young boy looking out at the audience, accompanied by the slogan "For you we shall overcome with Allende," and the blue-and-red UP logo. Another poster displayed a black-and-white photograph of a happy family of three vowing support for List Number 3 in the election (Fig. 6.38). A particularly colorful poster (displaying the red, white, and blue colors of Chile) featured a drawing of a mother and child holding the national flag and a slogan that advocated advancement for women as a patriotic act (Fig. 6.39). These epitomized many election posters from different countries in that they used imagery to try to influence voters to think of the future for their children and evoke an emotional response, a particularly popular propaganda theme during hard economic times (as Chile was then experiencing). Other posters simply showed an indomitable Allende with and without the slogan "*Venceremos*" (We Shall Overcome) (Fig. 6.40). On buildings, the conservative

Figure 6.38

Figure 6.39

Figure 6.40

coalition affixed gigantic portrait posters of its candidate, former president Alessandri, which simply said *"Alessandri Presidente."*

Television became a major factor in Chilean political campaigns in 1970. Alessandri's forces used scare tactics against Allende, warning of a "terror campaign" that would be unleashed if the moderate-sounding socialist was elected; Alessandri's image, on the other hand, was tarnished, since he lost much of his aura of nonpartisanship during the TV-spot operation. Adding to the emotional fervor of the election campaign was that the voting age had been lowered from twenty-one to eighteen, and many of the newly enfranchised voters were radical, if not revolutionary, in their views. The election was an extremely close one, and Allende emerged with a narrow plurality of less than forty thousand votes. However, a majority was necessary under the country's constitution, and the Congress had to choose between the two candidates with the most votes—in this case, Allende and Alessandri. Allende was selected in October, with many Christian Democrats supporting him, after he consented to several amendments to the constitution guaranteeing various rights.[241]

℞ *Honduras: The Constitutional Crisis and Presidential Election of 1985.* Honduras is a tiny nation, which had a population of only 4.4 million people in 1985 (compared to its neighbor, Mexico, which then had a population of about 78 million).[242] In that year, a bizarre election took place. The 1980s was a decade of great crisis for Honduras, as the world recession hit the country particularly hard and debt soared. Military repression also increased in the 1970s and 1980s, and the United States provided aid during the presidency of Roberto Suazo Córdova, while Contra forces set up camps in the country to combat the leftist Sandinistas in Nicaragua and the Honduran military used harsh tactics, including executions, to battle domestic insurgents supported by the Sandinistas.[243]

The two primary political parties of modern Honduras, the Liberal Party (PL) and the National Party (PN), contested the election of 1985. The anticlerical movement of the 1880s had led to the founding of the PL, and the party has had much support from landowners and peasants, as well as from urban and business voters. When the PL split up in the initial decades of the twentieth century, the more conservative PN was established, with strength in the countryside. Regardless, civil wars took the lives of an estimated thirteen thousand citizens between 1892 and 1924; elections until well after World War II were often marked by fraud and military force, frequently followed by presidential dictatorship and domination of Congress. Military coups occurred, in the postwar period, in 1956, 1963, 1972, 1975, and 1978. The derogatory name "The Banana Republic" was given to Honduras in the early twentieth century, after the United Fruit Company bought the country's banana company, and began to exercise undue influence. Honduras became the world's sole country whose primary export was bananas. In 1877, only 7 percent of the population could vote, and women were not enfranchised until 1955; by 1948, the extension of suffrage to more males had increased the percentage of eligible voters, but only to 18 percent.[244] In the early 1980s, the Liberal administration of Suazo (who had won the presidency in 1981 by a large margin) was supported by the armed forces; the military leadership, under General Gustavo Álvarez Martínez, controlled national security and foreign policy, while the government devised domestic policy.[245]

Before the presidential election of 1985, a political crisis erupted. Suazo, who was not permitted by the constitution to run for reelection, engineered the nomination of an elderly politician, Oscar Mejía Arellano, as the candidate of the conservative faction of his party. Three other PL factions nominated candidates, including José Azcona Hoyo, and three PN factions ran candidates, but Rafael Leonardo Callejas gathered the most support by far. Under the constitution, if no candidate received a majority, the Supreme Court of Justice decided the election. However, the constitution also allowed the Congress to remove justices, and that is what soon occurred, with five of nine removed. Suazo had the five new justices arrested and they were charged with treason, along with the congressional deputies who had voted them in. The legislature then censured the president and moved to limit his power, while establishing primary elections for each party. Suazo vetoed this latter measure. The crisis was "resolved" when military officials forced negotiations between the two branches of government, and the representatives of the legislative branch withdrew the demand for a primary system and abrogated the bill that dismissed the five justices.[246]

The agreement called for the leading candidate of the party whose candidates won the most votes to be elected president. The Liberal Party had helped itself by ruling that the constitution allowed more than one candidate from a political party to run. During the campaign, Liberal Azcona stated that he would drive the Contras back to Nicaragua twenty-four hours after he was inaugurated, while Callejas, of the National Party, was a bit more sympathetic toward them, stating that they existed because of oppression in Nicaragua. Neither candidate differed significantly on the Nicaragua threat, however, since both had taken anti-Sandinista stances. The campaign centered on personalities rather than issues. This was not surprising, since, as political scientist Mark Rosenberg concluded, the politicians of the nation focused on "competition and power, not national problem-solving."[247] Azcona gained support due to his criticism of Suazo's harsh tactics, whereas Mejía seemed to lose votes because of his close association with the outgoing president. These two main PL candidates attacked each other at least as much as they criticized Callejas.[248]

Most of the posters issued during the campaign were traditional in design and emphasized personality. Photographs of the various candidates dominated, but other elements, such as a hand casting a ballot or a party flag, were added. A poster for Mejía showed him in a rancher's hat and included a photograph of Modesto Rodas Alvarado (wearing a similar hat), whose name was attached to the faction backing Mejía, the *Movimiento Liberal Rodista* (Fig. 6.41). One for Callejas showed him in informal attire, above pledges to unify the country, respect the foundations of government, and not to

Figure 6.41

raise taxes (Fig. 6.42). A poster for Azcona showed him in a suit and tie, smiling and looking directly at the voters, with the PL flag behind him (Fig. 6.43). The same flag was

Figure 6.42   Figure 6.43

included in Mejía's posters.

The alteration of the political rules enabled the Liberal Party to retain the presidency, when the combined vote for its candidates was 54 percent, and its top vote getter, Azcona, took office the next year, even though he polled less than 30 percent of the total vote and Callejas received 44 percent.[249] After the election of Azcona, the United States insisted that Honduras agree to economic reforms, which have continued, along with the growth of civilian (rather than military) control of government. The PN won the presidency in 1989, after Callejas rebuilt the party, with funds from businesses, and pushed for a program of modernization and reform. Extreme economic difficulties, however, brought the Liberals' return to power in the next election, with the two main parties alternately in power thereafter. The military has not intervened in the politics of the country for more than two decades since.[250]

Mexico: The Rise and Fall of the National Revolutionary Party (1929–2000).

Mexico achieved independence from Spain in 1821. In the decades that followed, debates and armed struggles between the liberal federalists (influenced by the French and American Revolutions, as well as by developments in Spain) and conservatives (supported by the church, military, and large landowners) characterized the politics of the new nation. The infant country also had to fend off invasion forces from Spain, Great Britain, the United States, and France during this period. The presidents were most often elected by the state legislatures. Benito Juárez (a liberal-federalist lawyer) rose to prominence in the late 1840s, when as the elected governor of Oaxaca, he gained national attention when he reformed the state's school system and national guard, reduced debt, and accomplished a successful building program. In 1852, Juárez finished his term of office, and was jailed about a year later, along with other liberal-federalist leaders, by Mexico's dictator, Antonio Lopez de Santa Anna. Juárez was then exiled to the United States, from which the liberal-federalists worked to overthrow the dictatorship militarily and propagandistically. By

1855, the "Revolution of Ayutla" had succeeded, and Juárez became the minister of justice of a provisional government. The subsequent "Juárez laws" brought the military and ecclesiastical courts under the control of the federal administration. In 1857, a federalist Mexican constitution was published, providing for a single legislative body and the indirect election of a president (with an electoral college established), and abolishing slavery. Very few people actually voted in presidential elections: nine thousand to twelve thousand electors took part in the presidential balloting from 1857 to 1877, although there were between eight million and nine million people in Mexico at that time. While the Constitution of 1857 provided for universal male suffrage, in reality, few citizens voted in most election contests at any level. This reflected a lack of confidence in the process because of corruption, the belief that the results were preordained, and illiteracy.[251]

The liberal-federalist government survived a three-year civil war. During this time, Juárez, who had been elected chief justice of the Supreme Court by Congress, became president.[252] Soon afterward, Mexico was forced to combat an invasion by France, under Napoleon III. It was not until early 1867 that the Juárez government and its troops emerged victorious. In October, Juárez easily won the presidency in an election against General José de la Cruz Porfirio Díaz, a member of Juárez's divided Liberal Party. Juárez gained almost 72 percent of the 10,380 votes from the 180 (out of 208) electoral colleges that issued reports; Díaz received only 26 percent.[253] An election broadside for Juárez presented to voters a multitude of reasons to support him, including "destroying privileges," "saving the constitution," advancing the cause of secularization, and his honesty (Fig. 6.44). Despite several noteworthy reforms, including the establishment of a free, secular primary educational system, Juárez's prestige gradually lessened, and by the presidential election

Figure 6.44

of 1871, he was opposed for a fourth term by Díaz and Supreme Court Chief Justice Sebastián Lerdo de Tejeda, a moderate Liberal. Political clubs were formed to support the candidates, and newspapers propagandized for them. Although Juárez did not gain the 51 percent of the electoral votes needed to win the office outright (he gained about 48 percent of the 12,256 total),[254] Congress reelected him. However, Juárez had a heart attack, and died the next year. Lerdo de Tejeda assumed the presidency; he was elected, in his own right in 1873, and he served until 1876, when Porfirio Díaz and his forces seized Mexico City, and forced Lerdo into exile. Twelve years later, Lerdo de Tejeda died in New York City.[255]

Porfirio Díaz held power for more than three decades. Elections were rigged and

Congress was either loyal to the regime or harassed into submission. Large landowners could control their peons' votes. A contested presidential election was finally held in 1910, but Francisco Madero, who ran against Díaz, lost through fraud, was imprisoned, and then—after deposing Díaz militarily—was killed in 1913. In the early years of the twentieth century, portraits of Díaz and other leaders in "heroic" poses were widespread, and he appeared in the first Mexican films. Opponents of the Díaz regime disseminated pamphlets and newspapers, and artists, such as José Guadalupe Posada, printed broadsides that satirized the dictator and extolled those who challenged his rule. Under Díaz, literacy increased from 14 percent in 1895 to 20 percent in 1910, and the number of newspapers, magazines, and periodicals of a cultural nature increased almost 800 percent from 1884 to 1907. This trend, in some respects, helped the opposition.[256]

By 1917, military forces led by Venustiano Carranza defeated those under Pancho Villa and Emiliano Zapata. The Constitution of 1917 (which is still in force) was then passed. It was a liberal document, which included a bill of rights, reaffirmed a bicameral legislative system, an eight-hour workday, and other social and labor provisions. The next year, the new Congress enfranchised married, literate, eighteen-year-old males; and unmarried, literate, twenty-one-year-old males. The civil war continued until 1920. In the decade of conflict, "The Mexican Revolution" had ended with two hundred thousand to two hundred fifty thousand dead and the estimated loss of 37 percent in the Gross Domestic Product.[257] After the assassination of former president Alvaro Obregón during the election campaign of 1928, the *Partido Nacional Revolucionario* (later known as the *Partido Revolucionario Institucional* [PRI]) was established in 1929. The National Revolutionary Party's predominant position in Mexican politics was not to be dislodged for the rest of the century. For most of this time, it was "almost completely symbiotic with the Mexican state, … subsumed most labor and campesino (rural peasant) organizations, and … exercised enormous powers of patronage," according to Linda Hall.[258] In addition, mass media favored the PRI: reports generally favored its candidates, and election television broadcasts (instituted after 1977) for the PRI were placed in prime-time slots while opposition broadcasts were transmitted during low-viewing periods.[259]

Elections were one-sided affairs until the 1980s. For example, in 1920, Obregón won 96 percent of the votes cast for president; in 1946, PRI presidential candidate Miguel Alemán received 78 percent, and Ezquiel Padilla, the candidate of the *Partido Demócrata Mexicano* (PDM), obtained only 19 percent; in the 1958 presidential race (the first Mexican election in which women could vote), Adolfo López Mateos of the PRI won 90 percent, and his party's candidates garnered all but one of the seats in Congress; in 1964, Gustavo Díaz Ordaz achieved 89 percent; and in 1982, Miguel de la Madrid won the presidential race, gaining 72 percent of the votes cast.[260] In 1968, just before the Olympic Games were held in Mexico City, the Díaz regime forcefully suppressed the student rebellion there. The campaign poster for Díaz four years earlier was of traditional design, showing a smiling Díaz and the slogan "Continuity in the revolutionary effort." It was assumed that most voters would associate the PRI—and its candidate—with the Mexican Revolution, and its ostensible goal of social justice.[261]

The one-party state, however, resulted neither in creating a large middle class, nor in a narrowing of the income gap between the upper and lower classes, more than a half-century after the party's founding. Some strides had been taken to meet the revolutionary goals of the people, particularly during the rule of President Lázaro Cárdenas in the 1930s, when most of the oil companies were nationalized, land and educational reforms were enacted, and the lower class grew more active politically in several organizations. In particular, labor and peasant leaders joined forces with Cárdenas to form national federations for their groups, as well as an organization for the military. The result was a broadly based party. By 1939, the party had over four million members—90 percent of whom were peasants or other workers.[262] Opposition to the PRI occurred outside the political system, taking the form of railroad strikes in the 1950s, student protests in 1968, and guerrilla movements in the 1970s. In 1983, some cracks in the PRI machine became evident, when the forty-four-year-old opposition party, the *Partido de Acción Nacional* (National Action Party, or PAN), won eleven municipal presidential elections. The National Action Party, which had similarities to European Christian Democratic parties, was founded in opposition to the land confiscations and nationalization program that had taken place under Cárdenas, and was supported by the Catholic Church, businesspersons, and conservative elements. Since the mid-1980s, however, the PRI has advocated the same economic policies as the PAN, the former party aligning itself more with business interests and taking a free market stance. This change in the PRI positions led to a split in the party, and the departure of several populist-nationalist members (including Cuauhtémoc Cárdenas Solórzano, the son of the former president and, himself, a former governor of his father's home state of Michoacán).[263]

A key year was 1988. Carlos Salinas de Gortari, the PRI's presidential candidate, won barely a majority of the votes (50.48 percent), which was, by far, the worst performance in the party's history—a decrease of more than 20 percentage points from that received in the previous election.[264] Salinas, the minister of budget and planning, was an economist with a doctoral degree from Harvard. Unfortunately, he had to defend the economic situation under de la Madrid's government, marked by poor growth, devaluation of the peso, rampant inflation, and widespread wage and price controls. Cárdenas ran under the banner of the newly formed National Democratic Front (*Frente Democrático Nacional* [FDN]), which included PRI dissidents, Socialists, and Communists. Cárdenas, whose speeches were replete with "revolutionary" rhetoric, called for the cancellation of the foreign debt and for economic policies that might help the poor. The fact that Cárdenas was a *mestizo* might have been a factor (Salinas was lighter complected), with FDN posters featuring him. Some of these posters added crowds of supporters to his portrait, in black-and-white photomontages. Other poster propaganda supporting Cárdenas was more blatant: issued by the Popular Socialist Party, one depicted the United States as a lazy thug, in bed beneath the American flag, a dollar sign tattooed on his arm, connected intravenously to the skeletal figure of Mexico, with verbiage charging that the PRI was linked to U.S. banking interests. The PAN candidate, business executive Manuel Clouthier del Rincón, backed political reform, but his economic positions were similar to those of Salinas. One reporter, when describing his campaign posters, likened him to Santa Claus. But at least the PAN had a full-time staff at this time, which was not true in previous decades.[265]

After the balloting, and during the next decade, opposition parties alleged voting irregularities. Even a union leader, who had backed the PRI in the election, thought that the announced results in 1988 were fraudulent, stating, "The middle class and above voted for Clouthier and those below the middle class voted for Cárdenas"; when asked who voted for Salinas, he replied, "The computer."[266] There were massive protests, highlighted by banners and posters, with slogans such as "The People Voted and Cárdenas Won." After a week's delay, the PRI-dominated Federal Electoral Commission finally declared Salinas the victor, announcing that Cárdenas had received 31 percent and Clouthier 17 percent of the total vote. In addition, four FDN Senate candidates were certified as winners—the first time non-PRI senators would be seated. An opposition gubernatorial candidate was also permitted to take office, after a fair election in his state was conducted. Nevertheless, in the Chamber of Deputies elections, the PRI won only 49.9 percent of the seats (down from 74 percent in the previous legislative election in 1979), and the PAN gained 19 percent of them (up from under 11 percent); four other parties, mainly those in the FDN coalition, obtained the remainder.[267] The PRI had held on to power, but its aura of invincibility was damaged. Jorge Dominguez and James McCann conducted data analysis revealing that, despite the poor economic conditions, the only significant factors to explain why voters switched from the governing party to the opposition were institutional. This included union membership (with unionized workers continuing to support the PRI) and assessments of the PRI's strength and prospects, and a variable that concerned the personality of Salinas (particularly traits such as honesty, leadership, intelligence, charm, and concern for the people).[268] One could easily conclude that image management and perception, rather than issues, had influenced voters to defect.

In 1960, Philip Taylor, Jr., had ruled out the PAN "as a possible alternative to the PRI for discontented interests."[269] The party's presidential candidate, Luis Héctor Álvarez, had received only 9 percent of the vote two years earlier. In the next three decades, however, the PAN's candidates for president did progressively better, their percentages rising to 11 percent in 1964, 14 percent in 1970, 16 percent in 1982, and 17 percent in 1988.[270] A year after the controversial 1988 election, Cárdenas and other left-of-center leaders established the *Partido de la Revolución Democrática* (Democratic Revolutionary Party [PRD]). But when he ran as its candidate in 1994, he came in third, obtaining 17 percent of the vote, behind the PRI's Ernesto Zedillo Ponce de León (50.19 percent) and the PAN's Diego Fernández de Cevallos (27 percent).[271] Cárdenas' decline of 14 percentage points, from his share in 1988, was partially attributable to a loss of support to more leftist parties (some which supported him in his previous run). This was mainly because he was in favor of the North American Free Trade Agreement (NAFTA) and the privatization of several state-owned businesses. The PRI had again held on to power, sustained by the enactment of some electoral reforms; the revocation of restrictions on the church; a somewhat improved economy; and negotiations of the NAFTA agreement between the Salinas government and the United States and Canada. In addition, increases in funding for projects in health, education, transportation, and municipal and regional development helped recapture some working class votes. The Salinas regime also won support from voters concerned about a rebellion in the state of Chiapas, which the army repressed. The PAN's successes at the state and local levels in the 1980s, the party having gained governorships and legislative seats in half a dozen states and controlled more than one hundred municipalities, foreshadowed the dramatic increase in votes for its candidate in the 1994 presidential race. Together with effective organization and campaigns in cities and states, the party's themes of electoral and governmental honesty, encapsulated in its posters' slogan "for a Mexico without lies," worked well at the national level in that race. PAN supporters were negative about the state of the economy and its prospects, which undoubtedly boosted the party's vote totals. The election was deemed honest, by international observers, overall.[272]

Change finally arrived in 2000. Poet and former ambassador Homero Aridjis recognized the altered political climate during that year's presidential campaign: "Through the decades, the PRI created an atmosphere of eternal victory. But now the opposition has shown that defeat of the official party is possible. Mexico has changed."[273] In the 1980s, after the nationalization of the banks, business executives began to contribute funds to the PAN and offer themselves as candidates of the minority party. At this time, the PAN changed its image to broaden its appeal by having party propaganda emphasize "the threat to individual rights and personal liberty posed by state expansionism and the abuse of power by government authorities engaged in electoral fraud," according to Ann Craig and Wayne Cornelius.[274] Eventually, many workers (particularly in the manufacturing sector) and women (in various sectors) found this appeal compelling. One of the businesspersons who joined the PAN was Vicente Fox Quesada, who then won a congressional seat as a PAN candidate in 1988. He went on to run twice for governor of Guanajuato in the 1990s, succeeding in 1995. Three years earlier, Fox, without party sanction, began his campaign for president, which had not happened in previous campaigns. Fox was a multimillionaire, six feet six inches tall, who had been chief executive officer of Coca-Cola Mexico, where, as he stated himself, he "learned strategy, marketing, financial management, [and] optimization of resources."[275] Fox's strategy, he said, was to position himself as "an outsider, … an aggressive guy, a rough guy with boots and his sleeves rolled up, who wouldn't shrink from a fight for social justice."[276] Interestingly, he compared himself to both Lech Wałęsa and Nelson Mandela.[277]

Fox was promoted by a massive media campaign, which included a Web site, and television and radio spots, beginning in 1997. TV spots were then a recent phenomenon in Mexican politics. They were not aired until 1994, when the PRI initiated their use; the opposition parties were not allowed to buy airtime. Subsequently passed legislation, however, put the main parties on an equal footing, in terms of both the availability of television and radio time for purchase, and public funding for their campaigns. Although at least half of political television broadcasts were required to cover the principles, programs, and platforms of the parties, the content of the other half was left to the parties' discretion. The media-savvy and charismatic Fox also had the advantages of his monetary resources, and advice from media and advertising consultants (including U.S. Republican public relations advisor Rob Allyn). Communicated to many voters was the image of Fox as a tough, "down-to-earth" opponent of the one-party regime, and an effective state governor. By fall 1999, he had achieved name recognition of better than 80 percent,[278] after starting out as a known political commodity in only his home state and among the elite. In his final TV spot, Fox appealed directly to voters to reject the status quo: "This July 2, rain, thunder or lightning, you have a date with history. Don't let it go by." Images of Fox, along with Macromedia Flash video and animation effects, dominated the PAN Web site. In addition, it offered his biography and the goals set by the candidate and party. The PRI and PRD also had a presence on the Internet: the former party had "a fanciful, high-tech site boasting a techno soundtrack not found on the other political party sites," according to Ron Mader;[279] the latter party's site was relatively simple, providing platforms, election results, and a news portal.[280]

Fox's positions were designed to appeal to many voters: loans for small business operators; modernization of the agricultural sector; decentralization of the bureaucracy; encouragement of foreign investment; transformation of the educational system; allowance of free movement across the border with the United States; an end to the influence of drug lords on the government; and the termination of other forms of corruption, including electoral fraud. Economic and educational problems, including a huge gap between the wealthy and poor in both these areas (an average amount of schooling of seven years in the latter), continued to plague Mexico. Almost 40 percent of its population was classified as living in poverty.[281] Fox's campaign appeared to be gaining converts. The PRI advertising campaign ramped up after Fox's was already in high gear. PRI candidate Francisco Labastida Ochoa's TV spots alluded to the U.S. invasion of Mexico in 1847 and disparaged Fox (dressed in American cowboy attire) as a man tied to foreign interests. This was the first election in which the PRI needed to run negative advertisements. Fox retaliated by referring to his PRI opponent as "Shorty" and "Sissy," as well as pronouncing "Labastida" in such a way to make his name into the slang word for "transvestite." Cárdenas' coalition of five parties, the Alliance for Mexico (led by his PRD), tried to both prevent defections on the left to Fox by criticizing the PAN candidate's past position to privatize the Mexican oil company (later recanted), and associating Cárdenas with his father and Juárez.[282]

It was apparent from the many campaign posters put up by all the political parties in 2000 that the PRI was no longer the only political organization that could win a national election. Six years earlier, there had been few posters for the PAN or the PRD, according to Michael Barone. Posters for Cárdenas showed him smiling directly at the voters with party colors behind him and the slogan "con Mexico, a la Victoria." A Fox poster promised that he would create jobs with better wages, and showed him broadly grinning at the voters, who could be seen faintly in the background, along with the slogan "*Ya!*" (Enough Already), the "Y" changed to a hand making the "V" for "Victory" sign (Figure 6.45). Both the main message and the visuals addressed the voters directly: Fox made "eye contact" with them while his commitment was *contigo* (with you). A billboard reinforced the message by declaring, "Mexico needs all of us." Another poster featured Fox flourishing the "V" sign, with the logos of the PAN and *Verde Ecologista de México* (Mexican Green Party) behind him. This minor party also nominated Fox, and he ran under the coalition banner of the Alliance for Change. Labastida's posters and billboards showed him looking out at the audience seriously or smiling slightly, with slogans such as "Vote for the power that serves the people" and "Change with Purpose." Labastida was another economist, who had been in charge of three ministries in past governments, and had served as a

MI COMPROMISO CONTIGO ES UN EMPLEO MEJOR PAGADO.

VOTA

VA

EL CAMBIO QUE A TI TE CONVIENE   ALIANZA POR EL CAMBIO

Figure 6.45

governor and an ambassador. He proposed to narrow the gap between the rich and the poor, improve the educational system, and fight corruption.[283]

The election was expected to be close: the last poll published by the newspaper *Reforma* before the balloting revealed that potential voters preferred Labastida over Fox by 3 percentage points (which was also the margin of error). Cárdenas trailed badly, many of his supporters already having switched to Fox—the opposition candidate who could win.[284] The election results were: Fox 43 percent, Labastida 36 percent, and Cárdenas again with 17 percent.[285] Remarkably, forty years after Taylor had ruled out the PAN as an alternative to the PRI, the party had succeeded in toppling the PRI from power, following seventy-one years of authoritarian rule. On December 1, 2000, for the first time in Mexico, power was transferred peacefully from one party to another. While Fox was a dynamic figure, polling data indicated that about 67 percent of the ballots supporting him were from voters who favored changing the system, while 28 percent favored the candidate himself.[286] At the same time, his coalition won the legislative elections, gaining 45 percent of the seats in the Congress, whereas the PRI obtained 42 percent, and the Alliance for Mexico captured only 13 percent.[287]

After the defeat, the outlook did not appear favorable for the PRI: "Look at the demographics," said one political scientist. "They received votes from rural people, who are moving to the cities. They received votes from old people, who are dying. And they received votes from illiterate people, who are becoming more educated"; "with respect to the PRI's future," stated another political scientist, who had been a party official, "an optimist would have to be a badly informed pessimist."[288] The PAN won the presidency and the Congress again in 2006, in what were considered fair elections by observers, barely beating a coalition headed by the PRD. Former energy minister Felipe de Jesús Calderón Hinojosa, the PAN candidate whose slogans were "clean hands" and "so we can live better," won by a margin of less than 1 percent over the former mayor of Mexico City, Andrés Manuel López Obrador, the presidential candidate of the PRD-led coalition. The PRI presidential candidate (and party president), Roberto Madrazo Pintado, placed a weak third (even though there was an alliance with the Green Party).[289] TV spots dominated the PAN's advertising campaign, designed by Ogilvy & Mather Mexico, with advice from political consultant Dick Morris (discreet, because he was an American). The campaign compared López Obrador to Hugo Chavez, the leftist president of Venezuela, and called him "a danger to Mexico." A poster for López Obrador reinforced the "radical" imagery with its slogan "For the good of all, the poor first" and with a huge fist emerging from a group of workers. The attacks on López Obrador appeared to damage his standing in the polls. Fox's record had not been a perfect one, but there was more economic stability with a strong central bank. Job growth and wage increases, however, lagged when the economy slowed down. The lack of a majority in the legislature led to the blockage of some of Fox's economic reform bills, but the budget had been balanced, election legislation passed, and free health care and educational benefits extended to more families and their children. Most of all, a multiparty democracy had seemingly been established.[290]

Since 2000, posters for *all* parties have been plastered on the stucco walls, telephone poles, roofs, billboards, and car windows in every Mexican town and city. Often party logos accompany them. Bumper stickers appear on almost every car.[291] They seem to be an important element in the politics of the nation, even as television and Internet use intensifies. The campaigns are now more coordinated, under the direction of internal and external political consultants. These campaigns can transform a business executive, such as Fox, into a recognized leader in a relatively brief time, and alter the politics of a country.

◯R℩つ

While issues are still highlighted on election posters around the world, the personalities of leaders have become more important in many political propaganda campaigns. This has been manifest in the posters produced. Leaders such as Fox, Koizumi, Mandela, Wałęsa, and Kohl posing with candidates for the legislature have dominated these posters. Other personality images have been used on election posters, including, decades later, even that of an American sheriff in a Hollywood film, in Poland. Such imagery has also been used in negative campaigns: Lenin, Stalin, and a Soviet soldier have appeared on Polish and Hungarian election posters, and Osama bin Laden and Saddam Hussein were seen in Taiwanese posters, for example.

In addition, attack strategies have employed symbols or organizations, such as the dollar sign or Coca-Cola, to criticize the relationship of an opposition party or leader to a foreign power. Sometimes another nation's leader is shown dominating the opposition leader in a poster, such as when German Chancellor Adenauer was seen being helped onto a mechanical horse by U.S. President Eisenhower. Another negative propaganda tactic is to show immigrants on posters to provoke resentments against foreigners and government policies. Many campaign posters, of course, continue to feature a candidate and a slogan. These are now more likely to add a logo and display the person smiling and looking directly at the audience. Other conventions that can been seen in posters during election campaigns are families, children, and women (sometimes pregnant), as well as the association of present and past leaders, such as mainland China's Sun Yat-sen and Taiwan's Chen Shui-bian. Additional symbols often incorporated in election posters are flags, buildings, crowns, Jesus Christ, and other national and religious icons.

The increase in negative campaign strategies and personalization in election posters may well be due to the influence of political consultants, who have become more active in many countries since the 1970s. Decades earlier, advertising personnel were employed in election campaigns, and a wider variety of marketing techniques and artistic styles were more widely used in the political arena. The involvement of these consultants coincided, roughly, with the advent of mass media, particularly television, in the election campaigns in many countries. However, use of the poster medium was more vital in much of the world than it was in the United States. Several legislative factors spurred this, including stringent limits on campaign spending, restrictions on content in mass media political advertisements, and prohibitions against paid televised ads.

CHAPTER SEVEN

How Effective Have
Political Posters Been?

In the 1800s, and into the twentieth century, when posters and broadsides were the primary means of propagandizing in election campaigns, there were no researchers working to investigate their effects on voters. How effective were they back then? One indication of that can be found in the recruiting and fundraising figures that may have resulted, at least partially, from the mammoth poster campaigns conducted during World War I. While it is difficult to regard these propaganda posters as the main reason why men enlisted and war loans were purchased (since the medium was only one means by which the war was "sold"), they probably had a great effect. Maurice Doll termed them "the major weapon in the Victory Loan Campaign" in Canada, for example. It was reported that in 1918 this effort cost more than two hundred thousand dollars, of which about sixty thousand dollars was devoted to posters (the largest expense in the campaign). The result was that over eight hundred thousand people subscribed more than six hundred million dollars.[1] The five United States loan drives yielded in excess of twenty billion dollars, and the nation's posters (of which the most famous was Flagg's "I Want You for U.S. Army") were a large part of the fundraising campaigns.[2]

The large sums of money that political parties have spent on posters in many countries attest to the *belief* that they can have an affect on citizens' voting behaviors. This assumption is considered even more valid if imagery and slogans on posters are chosen carefully, based on market research, to strike a "responsive chord" with voters on a theme, as Tony Schwartz stated. Accordingly, posters are then thought to have a greater chance of "setting the tone" in an election campaign, being picked up and publicized by the mass media, and swaying wavering voters. Many in the electorate, however, would have already decided on the candidates and parties for whom they will vote. This is attributed to party allegiances, sentiments about specific candidates and issues, economic conditions, and many other factors. Media, including posters, can only reinforce the preferences of these voters. Many are indifferent to political marketing during a campaign. One Scottish market research firm, for example, found that 72 percent of the voting public was not interested in any election posters.[3] Of course, that still left 28 percent interested, and many of those people could have been "swing" or "floating" voters (those who have no firm allegiance to a party or candidate, or who change their stated party preferences during a campaign period).

The two major parties in Great Britain, on average, lost between 23 and 29 percent of their voters in consecutive elections held from 1966 to 1979.[4] In the March–June 1987 campaign period, 38 percent of the British electorate revealed in interviews that they had changed their party preferences.[5] According to L. Patrick Devlin, a substantial number of Americans are "disinterested, late deciding, or undecided," and advertisements are designed to persuade them to commit to a candidate or party, if undecided, or to switch allegiances.[6] An estimated 20 to 30 percent of voters have been undecided in U.S. national elections.[7] An analysis of survey data collected in December 1990 during Germany's Bundestag election campaign disclosed that almost 14 percent of the voters were "converts" (meaning that their votes went against their political predispositions and preferences), and that 66 percent of *this* group voted for the CDU-CSU-FDP coalition.[8] In the 1972 landslide U.S. presidential election, it was determined that approximately 3 percent of the electorate was influenced by televised political advertisements.[9]

In a close election, posters can make a difference. Some interesting research, conducted before the 1996 parliamentary elections in Great Britain, suggested that this could be so, and poster campaigns have persuaded swing voters, in particular, to change their political preferences. As we have seen, the role of posters was often prominent in British elections, and the 1996 campaign was a heated one, in terms of its marketing imagery (i.e., the Conservatives' release of the "Demon Eyes" posters of Blair). During that campaign, a research firm, Davies Riley-Smith Maclay, used focus groups to investigate the effects of several election posters on voters who lacked strong party allegiances. It was found that the posters moved the focus group members who were 25–34 years old away from both the Tories and Labour to some extent. As for specific poster designs, the investigators discovered that, although many participants did not take the Blair "Demon Eyes" poster seriously, another design in this series was effective: it employed the same slogan as the Blair poster "New Labour, New Danger," but displayed two eyes, instead of the Labour leader, peering out from behind a red curtain (which was similar to Figure 5.29 in Chapter Five). The imagery frightened the focus group members; they associated it with the iron curtain, the red flag, Reds hiding under a bed, and the curtain concealing other Labourites.[10]

Overall, there is some indication that campaign advertising does have some impact on voting behavior. Multiple-regression analyses by R. J. Johnston found that campaign expenditures for advertising (80 percent spent for printing, mainly posters and leaflets) in the British General Elections of 1974 had no significant[11] effects on voters in contested constituencies, except those by the Liberal Party.[12] However, a later study of the 1987 election data, by the same author (and C. J. Pattie), revealed a greater impact. In the latter investigation (in which there were data only for Labour Party's campaign expenditures), Labour's advertising spending significantly improved its performance in Conservative-held districts.[13] Data analysis for the 1992 British election showed that this effect was not significant for Labour spending in campaigns to win Conservative seats, but that advertising expenditures significantly improved the Conservatives' percentage of the vote when the situation was reversed, as they also proved to be for the Liberal Democrats in reducing support for Labour.[14] The authors concluded that campaign advertising in British elections was generally effective, particularly for out-of-power parties against incumbent ones.[15] Posters can be influential tools in promotional campaigns. For example, an inexpensively produced poster created at the University of Utah to promote a workshop about design careers for high school students produced record enrollment for the course.[16] Indications are that posters have efficiently promoted attractions, such as museums, parks, and resort areas. Posters displayed on Chicago's rail lines in the 1920s reportedly attracted commuters because the designs were striking in color, and they were simple, using much less lettering than other advertisements.[17] One of them, promoting the Field Museum (which had not advertised previously), apparently had much to do with tripling the museum's attendance within three weeks of its first display.[18]

Of course, posters and billboards are usually part of coordinated promotional packages. These may also consist of television and radio commercials, newspaper and magazine advertisements, Web pages, direct mail pieces, videos, bumper stickers, T-shirts, and other paraphernalia. Market researchers have generally found that such campaigns are often effective. For instance, a 1998 promotional campaign for a bank was shown to have increased name recognition and brand imagery.[19] In 2000, the Australian Associated Brewers used television commercials, newspaper advertisements, a Web site, bar mats, and posters (placed on beer trucks and distributed in pubs) in its fight against the government increasing the beer excise tax. Researchers found that the campaign elevated issue awareness among beer drinkers to 89 percent, and almost 20 percent of this group signed a petition objecting to the government's plan. As a result, the excise tax was repealed and tax revenues were rechanneled to alcohol education programs.[20]

Although there has been little research to determine the effectiveness of posters for a variety of purposes, there is some evidence to support the belief that they can be invaluable, given good design and planning. In social marketing, for example, Phillip Coffey found that 82 percent of a small sample of conservationists believed that a series of threatened wildlife posters were well designed and 76 percent believed they had made an impact.[21] Five months after seeing six propaganda posters, children age twelve to fifteen recalled basic ideas and content in these posters.[22] An early study exposed experimental participants to road safety posters for three minutes, and found significant differences (with a control group) on the amount of information that was applied to the interpretation of problematic traffic situations and on recall.[23] A later experimental study revealed that safety posters in an airport significantly decreased unsafe passenger behavior (i.e., not using stairway handrails) in general, and that when "high threat" content (e.g., a businessman unconscious on a stairway) was displayed, they were most successful.[24] Another study reported that large, specially designed, color safety posters resulted in significant improvements in steelworkers' performance in hooking up slings.[25]

An advertising agency, Reagan Outdoor Advertising, conducted a study in Austin, Texas, which was designed to measure the effectiveness of billboards whose messages had political overtones. The firm erected forty-eight 30-sheet posters that stated, "Calvin Coolidge was the 30th President."[26] A pretest/posttest comparison found that unaided recall of this fact went from under 1 percent to almost 34 percent in two months (a significant difference).[27] As Elizabeth Tucker pointed out, since "advertising effects," such as liking and brand salience, are often contingent on recognition, this finding has implications for all marketing personnel, including political consultants.[28] Some research studies suggest that political posters can affect election results. Posters advertising the position of the Valley Party in London, for example, appeared to help it gain a remarkable 11 percent in the 1990 local elections for Greenwich Borough Council, even though the party's only issue was a football club's return to the borough.[29]

In general research, there have been indications that negative print-advertising strategies can help achieve election campaign goals. Bruce Pinkleton, for example, found that negative-comparative print advertisements about U.S. candidates' positions in 1992 decreased evaluations (by undergraduate university students) of targeted candidates (without lowering those of sponsoring candidates).[30] Ten years earlier, a study by Sharyne Merritt also showed that negative advertising led to lower opinions of targeted politicians—this time by actual voters, but the ads at the same time appeared to generate negative sentiments about sponsors in a California state assembly race between Democrat Tom Hayden (using television commercials) and Republican Bill Hawkins (using billboards). Party identification came into play also: 52 percent of the Republicans who saw Hawkins' anti-Hayden billboards responded negatively toward his opponent, whereas only 27 percent of Democrats did so; 61 percent of Democrats indicated they were negative about Hawkins after being exposed to his billboards, but only 22 percent of Republicans felt that way. Data revealed that Hawkins' billboard campaign backfired: 56 percent of the district's voters who saw them had *favorable* evaluations of Hayden, while only 41 percent of those who did not see them felt positively about the Democrat (a significant difference).[31] Furthermore, Ronald Hill's study of the effects of negative-comparative and attack print advertisements during the 1988 U.S. presidential election campaign, with university students as his subjects, suggested that such ads could yield negative evaluations of ad sponsors, but had little impact on the evaluations of the targeted politicians.[32]

Other variables, with implications for election poster designers, have been shown to have an impact, as well, at least in experimental studies. The colors used in political posters can affect voter perceptions. In one study with college students, certain color combinations (such as white on green and white on blue) were found to be associated with positive personality ratings of political candidates displayed in campaign posters, whereas a favorite of some campaign consultants (i.e., orange on blue) was associated with ratings that are more negative.[33] The interpretation of colors can differ in various cultures. For example, as Wendy Winter discovered, red had a different symbolic meaning in Africa than in the West, and the use of the color in safety posters led Bantu industrial workers to misinterpret their meaning, since they equated red with "fire," not "danger."[34] Many people show preference for certain colors, and they associate them with emotions, concepts, and places.[35] In the late 1990s, the Roper/Pantone Consumer Color Preference Study found that, in the United States, 35 percent of persons 18 years old or more chose blue as their favorite color.[36] Studies elsewhere found that blue is the preferred color in several other cultures as well.[37]

The use of slogans is another variable that is believed to be effective in advertisements,[38] including those in the political arena.[39] Slogans on election posters such as "Labour Isn't

Working," "*La force tranquille*," "*Kaikaku*," "Tippecanoe and Tyler too," and "America First!" have been popular, and thought to be influential. A study of social movement slogans such as "Get Out of Vietnam" and "No more nukes," revealed that 43 percent of them communicated demands and solutions. The study's authors stated that the function of slogans is usually to simplify the complex and evoke emotions, implying that this increases the likelihood of persuasion, particularly when slogans are displayed on T-shirts, posters, and bumper stickers—giving rise to a sense of identification with a cause or candidate.[40] More investigation is needed on the effects of slogans, however. Yet another variable is the inclusion of celebrities in political advertising. A research investigation in Belgium determined that the presence of a well-known figure was the main factor in the recognition of election posters,[41] as noted in Chapter One.

Typically, an election poster presents a candidate in a most positive way: smiling, but firm, and looking directly at the voters. A candidate's attire is either casual (to show a relationship with average people) or businesslike (to indicate a "professional" attitude about serving in office). One U.S. study found that the appearance and style of fictitious Caucasian male candidates in photographs in campaign fliers affected voter perceptions of a candidate, and even voting behavior. The researchers, headed by Shawn Rosenberg, found that "nonverbally desirable candidates" won two of three mock elections in the study, regardless of party affiliations or position on the issues, by significant margins. The investigation's findings were similar for both undergraduate university students and for adults.[42] Another study by Rosenberg yielded comparable results for both these groups, whose subjects believed that the candidates in the photographs were actually running for congressional seats. It was also determined that different poses, such as looking straight at the camera, influenced perceptions about individuals and their competence, trustworthiness, likeableness, and fitness to hold public office.[43] A later study conducted by a Rosenberg-led team showed similar findings when photographs of Caucasian women were used.[44]

Another variable, uncovered in research studies of TV spot ads aired during the 1984 and 1988 U.S. presidential campaigns, is the use of emotions, including hopefulness, trust, reassurance, uncertainty, anger, and anxiety.[45] It was apparent that emotional appeals were heavily employed in these spots, as they have been in some election posters. Montague Kern's analysis of the 1984 spots (containing a human figure), for example, found that almost 98 percent presented an emotional appeal. Kern's content analysis also found that symbols, relating to childhood, youth, old age, labor, and business interests, were particularly evident in a substantial number of ads. There were also spots that featured blacks and women, which were designed to appeal to these groups, and attack ads that included leaders who many perceived negatively and symbols that would associate the opposition with "moneyed interests."[46]

Posters are much utilized in political elections in some European countries such as Belgium, where political parties are given limited time on public television and are not even allowed to purchase commercial broadcast time. Belgian parties in the 1991 election regularly employed slogans in their posters. Belgium's Liberal Party devised their slogans based on market research, after identifying "six opinions with which an average of about

70–80 percent of the electorate agreed. The party then proposed itself as the only one with a *real* and *realistic* answer to those problems or issues," according to Jan Van den Bulck.[47] This study, however, found that voters, at least in Belgium, who recognized the issues presented in campaign posters, did not always associate particular parties with solutions to problems. Van den Bulck's concluded that a party's posters could help its electoral chances the most when the issues highlighted were "automatically and positively associated" with it, rather than when an issue was associated with another party.[48] Furthermore, a study conducted during the 1972 U.S. presidential campaign indicated that some political television advertising increased issue salience.[49] Another study carried out during the same campaign found that political television commercials seemed to alter voter beliefs about both Nixon's and McGovern's positions.[50] An analysis of 1983 British election survey data revealed that in constituencies in which campaign spending (much of it for posters) was highest, voters had the lowest variance in their perceptions of Conservative party positions on three of four issues; the opposite was true where expenditures were lower. Again, posters appeared to effectively communicate the party's stands on issues. Furthermore, the data analysis revealed that the Conservatives' campaign spending was significantly related to statements by people that they had voted for the party, even with other factors (such as socioeconomic level and strength of party identification) controlled.[51]

The amount spent on election campaigns can affect the number of voters who are exposed to the posters printed. The results of a survey study conducted during the 2001 British election campaign indicated that exposure to posters was substantially less than had been the case four years earlier for all parties (50 percent of the electorate, compared to 70 percent in 1997), but similar decreases were found for leaflets (69 percent/89 percent) and television broadcasts (58 percent/73 percent).[52] One difference was that, because videos had become relatively inexpensive, Labour mailed many more of them to voters.[53] Still, exposure to these videos was low (1 percent), just as it was to a party Web site (2 percent).[54] Contact with election posters was relatively high in Great Britain, and other countries as well. More West German voters, for example, indicated that they had seen posters during the Bundestag election campaigns in 1965 (92 percent) and 1976 (96 percent) than any other communication medium.[55] Postelection surveys in Japan showed that between 54 percent and 69 percent of the electorate reported contact with campaign posters in national elections held between 1992 and 2000.[56] Exposure to posters—resulting in greater name recognition of candidates—has been found to predict votes received in a simulated university election. It was hypothesized that this effect was likely to be greatest in election campaigns with lesser-known candidates and without prominent issues.[57]

Research findings about other media, particularly television, have shown that political advertising can have significant effects. As early as the 1940 U.S. presidential election, a research team led by Paul Lazarsfeld found that treatment of issues in mass media propaganda could result in voters placing more importance on the issues depicted. These researchers also discerned that propaganda seemed to activate "the latent inclinations" of the voters, arousing interest, increasing their attention to election campaign messages, and affecting the voting behaviors of some citizens.[58] Research in the 1990s further indicated that political television advertisements, shown during national elections in France, Germany, and Poland, influenced the preferences of voters and the images they held of politicians.[59] The effects of manipulating candidate images was seen in the research reported by Rosenberg's teams; this was particularly true in their investigation that exposed subjects to women candidates' campaign fliers. Photographs were varied in terms of how the candidates were posed; the candidates' smiles, facial features, clothing, and photographic backgrounds also varied. In a mock U.S. congressional election in 1988, it was found that not only were the experimental participants' evaluations of the candidates influenced, but voting preferences were also affected significantly by the image manipulation.[60] The conclusion was that the quality of the image conveyed via printed material could, therefore, win or lose an election for a candidate. The poster is a medium that can build or reinforce an image or, for that matter, spotlight an issue or theme.

Survey data from the European Parliament elections of 1989 revealed that reading an election poster ranked second in popularity. Posters, however, were not listed as among the most *helpful* sources of information; television headed this list.[61] Since election campaign posters generally did not provide much, if any, information, these results are not surprising. More telling is how voters perceived the *influence* of the medium. A British study, for example, found that 2 percent of voters in 1979 and 3 percent in 1983 reported that poster and newspaper advertising had affected them. In the same years, 15 percent of voters surveyed reported that they had been influenced by PEBs in 1979 and 16 percent did so four years later. As Ian McAllister noted, the effect was mainly to reinforce, not to persuade: most of those reporting influence indicated that televised broadcasts of the party with which they identified had affected them; 11 percent of Conservatives, for instance, were influenced by a Conservative PEB, but only 3 percent noted such an effect due to a Labour PEB in 1979. The same pattern generally existed for printed political advertising, with the most dramatic effect seen for Social Democratic Party Liberal-Alliance voters in 1983: in that year, 5 percent of these voters reported being influenced by the posters and newspaper ads of the Alliance, but not at all by those of the two main parties. McAllister's study provided evidence that *printed* political advertising could influence voting behavior. His multiple-regression analysis estimated that there was a 0.4 percent gain in the Conservative vote in 1979, due to that party's posters and newspaper advertisements. In terms of percentages, the study reported that Conservative voters who had been influenced by a Conservative poster or newspaper ad were 19 percent more likely to vote for the party (a significant difference). It may be recalled that 1979 was the election year that witnessed that extraordinary advertising campaign designed by Saatchi & Saatchi, which featured the "Labour Isn't Working" posters. In 1983, however, McAllister found that 0 percent of the vote was gained by Conservative printed political advertising, and Labour gained an estimated 0.2 percent. This was due to a significant proportion of Labour voters who were influenced by a Labour poster or newspaper ad (10 percent of them found to be more likely to vote for the party). In the same years, the impact of PEBs was somewhat greater: the estimated vote gain for the Conservatives was 1.2 percent in 1979 and 0.9 percent in 1983; for Labour, it was 0.9 percent and 0.8 percent, respectively. In these years, the data revealed that canvassing had no significant effect on the voting outcomes in Great Britain.[62]

Almost two decades later, voters surveyed in the United Kingdom during the 2001 election campaign indicated that billboard advertisements had affected one in ten persons—2 percent reported that the ads had a "great deal" of influence on them and 8 percent indicated a "fair amount." In comparison, the percentages for televised broadcasts were 6 percent and 16 percent for the same response categories.[63] In addition, the survey data from 1992 to 2000 in Japan revealed generally similar findings about the influence of election posters in that country: when participants were asked if the medium assisted their voting decisions, the percentages ranged from 5 to 9 percent for posters (about the same as for newspaper advertisements).[64]

The display of posters often continues after the voting has occurred. This *might* reinforce citizens' identification with parties and help them in the next round of elections. Researchers *have* found that a "basking-in-reflected-glory" effect can occur for posters and homeowners' lawn signs. This phenomenon lasted for one week after the 1999 general elections in three urban areas of Flanders: a significant relationship was found to exist between the performance of the winning or losing party and the exhibition of those parties' printed material. Homeowners were more likely to display the posters and lawn signs that favored the victors and to remove those for the defeated parties.[65]

ଔଯ

Research has given some indication that the deployment of well-designed posters has resulted in desirable outcomes. Promoters whose goal was to increase attendance at various attractions seemed to have had their posters achieve such an effect. Poster campaigns to promote safety have been found to be successful. An informal "cost-benefit analysis" suggests that the loan-drive campaigns (dominated by posters) were successful during World War I in that they brought in thousands of dollars for each dollar spent. Great amounts are still expended on political posters and billboards, including those used in election campaigns. Researchers have found that campaign-advertising expenditures in Great Britain (where posters have played a greater political role than in many other countries) have helped communicate parties' issues more effectively and improved their share of the vote. Posters are usually one component of a package, with television broadcasts often the centerpiece. Though it is difficult to ascertain the impact of any one medium on the electorate, a number of research studies have done so.

Many voters are disinterested in all forms of election propaganda, including posters and billboards. Perhaps only three in ten are interested in these political media, but many of these persons may be swing or floating voters, who can decide a close election. One focus group study, in fact, showed that posters influenced young British swing voters during the 1996 election campaign. Political posters and billboards have also been found to increase recall—important in boosting brand salience. Exposure to election posters and their popularity have been high in several countries. The subsequent name recognition led to votes for candidates in one study.

Researchers have explored various political marketing approaches and their effects. These strategies have included positive and negative advertising, spotlighting issues, image formation, and emotional appeals. Other variables of interest to election poster designers have been poses, attire, photographic backgrounds, symbols, color, slogans, and the incorporation of well-known figures or members of targeted groups. Many studies have investigated effects of political television advertising on perceptions of issues, images and evaluations of candidates and parties, and voting behaviors, with significant effects reported. Five to ten percent of British and Japanese voters have noted that election posters and billboards influenced their voting decisions in studies conducted between 1992 and 2001. The percentage of British voters who reported that televised political broadcasts influenced them was about double of that. Although a small percentage of the electorate in modern times have indicated that their political opinions have been swayed by posters and billboards, as well as newspaper advertisements, researchers have found some vote gains that can be attributed to the use of these print media in election campaigns. Most of the gains were due to a reinforcing effect on voters who identified with a party. The impact of television PEBs was shown to be greater, but still hovered around a 1 percent gain. Apparently, all these media (at least in Great Britain) are most important in close elections. Reinforcement seems to continue (as suggested by the 1999 study in Flanders) when lawn signs of the victorious party are displayed more frequently than those of the vanquished.

CHAPTER EIGHT

Conclusions and Future Trends

Since the 1800s, posters, billboards, and, sometimes, banners and broadsides, have played a part in the election campaigns on every continent. In the nineteenth century, their political communication role was dominant; today, it is secondary in most nations, with these media typically components of coordinated political marketing packages. Nevertheless, they can make a difference (as research has suggested) in close elections, particularly by influencing swing or floating voters. While it is likely that Eisenhower and Johnson (and—later—Nixon, Carter, Reagan, and Clinton) would have won the U.S. presidency without the efforts of advertising and political marketing firms, the poster campaigns probably increased their margins. Such efforts, however, probably were instrumental in both the victories of George W. Bush. In addition, later political endeavors in several countries modeled their strategies on U.S. campaigns' marketing strategies, which could have helped determine electoral outcomes, and homegrown consultants, such as Séguéla and Bell, devised innovative and effective campaigns in which posters were critical elements, which could very well have ensured success at the polls for their clients.

Television is the chosen medium in many countries today because it can reach the most voters. Modern television broadcasts, often using a succession of images of citizens and catchy slogans, are designed to do what the broadsides, posters, and banners attempted to accomplish in the past: define the issues, build candidate or party images, show common cause with "the people," and often denigrate the opposition. During the 1988 campaign, Theodore White noted, "Television's role has grown in every campaign since 1948 … [and] politicians always do what the political environment prompts them to do. George Washington had a barrel of hard cider in his front yard when he ran for the House of Burgesses, so the voters could have a drink on the way to the polls. … George [H. W.] Bush has attack television commercials."[1] Bush's political marketing advisors also employed direct mail methods, reinforcing the TV spots with fliers, as part of a coordinated propaganda package designed to push all the "right" buttons to scare substantial numbers of white voters: a mug shot of a scowling black man, a murder and rape, and weekend passes letting dangerous prisoners out on the streets. Undoubtedly, most of those in the intended audience had no difficulty grasping the messages' words and images that communicated the fundamentals of "race," "violence," and "soft liberal." After all, they had decoded television commercials for years, and both commercial and political propaganda use strong iconography.[2] TV political spots and product commercials have much in common with election poster and lawn advertisements: their messages have almost always been reduced to a few, carefully selected, pretested words and images that encapsulate why people should vote for a candidate or party, as well as—after much repetition—building "brand familiarity." Since Lasker entered politics, advertising techniques have led to a paring down of the message and a greater attention to visuals.

While poster and billboard campaign designers around the world have used some American strategies, they have developed many of their own to communicate themes, set the campaign's tone, shape images, and interest the electorate, sometimes by attacking an opponent's personality and issues. The images and words presented on the positive posters are often meant to express "prosperity," "country," and "jobs." Negative messages employ slogans such as "Labour Isn't Working," along with the display of powerful visuals. The controversial posters frequently are conveyed to most voters via the mass media, which provide free publicity. The messages imparted by most election posters and billboards are propagandistic. Their purposes are not educational, nor are the messages factual. Information—both visual and verbal—is manipulated, even distorted, to help a candidate or party, and to damage those in opposition. The modern billboard and poster attacks on Heath, Blair, Hague, and Howard were a continuation of a tradition in British politics, begun over one hundred years ago with the negative printed advertisements against Disraeli, Gladstone, George, and Campbell-Bannerman. British leaders, however, have been shown far less often on posters than their counterparts in the United States and France (and other countries led by elected presidents), and issues have been emphasized more in British campaigns than in these other two nations' campaigns. Nevertheless, some "presidentialization" of British politics has occurred in Great Britain, along with intensified political marketing efforts, and more focus has been placed on party leaders, who have appeared more than before in all media, including election posters.

Early American political consultants, such as Kendall, Van Buren, Hanna, Creel, and Lasker were acutely aware of the importance of symbolism, slogans, and visuals. Misrepresented facts and mythologized imagery were routinely employed in the campaigns that they orchestrated. This is true for others, as well, such as Binns, who pioneered the attack ad, and the Nazis, whose techniques were derived from advertising, with anti-Semitism mixed in. American candidates were often portrayed in posters as "military heroes" or in touch with the "common man" (and sometimes both). British parties, such as George's Liberals, depicted themselves as advocates for the commoners and their interests versus those of the wealthy and titled. Later, British politicians were shown in pubs, at football games, or in the working-class neighborhood in which they had been reared to illustrate their accord with the commoners. Sometimes the "harmonious" relationship was communicated conspicuously, as when posters in Japan declared that Koizumi was the "Friend of the Common People."

Political consultants ensured that broadsides, banners, posters, fliers, and, subsequently, billboards, were developed with what were thought to be appropriate verbal and visual elements, and that key segments of the electorate were targeted. These media were part of coordinated propaganda campaigns that included such components as songs, marches, campaign newspapers, pamphlets, and buttons and other paraphernalia. Added later would be press releases, newsreels, radio and TV spots, and Web sites. Increasingly, consultants, particularly from advertising and marketing, refined these propaganda tactics, using easy-to-read type fonts and simple imagery, as well as celebrity endorsements. Visuals became increasingly important in political propaganda—both in posters and in more modern communication technologies. Of all the older media that used printed or auditory words, posters best adapted to the changed times, emphasizing pictorial elements and being easily transmitted electronically or aired in newscasts.

MTV advertising techniques, which have served the needs of the music industry, also affect election campaigns. Political TV spots around the world comprise short video segments, the images selected and edited to gain attention, and they make a point or relate the candidate to targeted voters. Background music and, sometimes, sound effects, are also used to effect certain emotions. Election posters and billboards have also, for decades, employed imagery and targeting to be quickly noticed and to transmit messages. In a faster, more impatient electronic age, with various media competing for the consumers' attention, these vehicles can be effective, particularly if they are stylish and easy to comprehend. Since not much time is available to viewers, poster designs must be simplified to a few basic elements; typically, they should convey a message using carefully devised slogans and visuals that educe affective responses that might influence voting behavior. This is exactly what nineteenth-century designers did (along with making outrageous charges against opponents on broadsides); the only major differences are that the message became streamlined over the years and color was used more extensively, often in the background.

Advertising and marketing consultants drastically changed politics, and their influence continues. These advisors design campaigns that are in accord with the concerns of the electorate. They use polls, surveys, and focus groups extensively to select strategies and distribution methods, such as database marketing, direct mail, and Internet advertising, from the business world, to reach targeted audiences. The market research in these cases helps identify one or two issues that are repeatedly delivered via the various media selected, the brand established with imagery, and the message expressed efficiently with a slogan. Sometimes the strategy in many countries dictated that the "common people" would be depicted in election posters; sometimes, it led to positive themes (e.g., "good times"), or attacks on corruption or poor economic conditions would be illustrated; and, in other instances, the focus was on a dynamic leader. Slogans such as "It's full employment. Keep it so!" added emphatic reinforcement. Many countries are now in a stage of political marketing that Avraham Shama called "market-oriented," with loyalties to parties having waned, and the number of independent, swing, and floating voters having increased greatly.[3] At this stage, posters and other printed material are designed to be most effective with targeted audiences: these can be evangelical Christians in the United States, younger women in Austria, environmentalists in Germany, or theatergoers in England. The *modern* broadside is the flier, handed out at street corners and meetings, folded and mailed, sent as an e-mail attachment, or posted on bulletin boards.

Exaggeration and distortion are propaganda tools routinely employed in poster campaigns. The marketing propaganda strategies used have been negative advertising and emotional appeals designed to instill fear in voters. These strategies sometimes work well, as appeared to be the case in the Horton advertisements and some of the British campaigns that warned the public not to vote for the opposition, which would "wreck" the economy; sometimes they do not, such as with the "Bliar! Bliar!" posters and the Kuomintang's posters with gas-masked soldiers to suggest that the opposition's policies would result in war with China. In many countries, negative strategies have manifested in "fear of the left," "fear of the right," and anti-immigrant and anti-foreign advertisements: posters displaying stereotypically "wild" radicals, conservatives "owned by big business," politicians as lapdogs of other countries, "warmongers" of various political bents, poverty and unemployment; TV spots implying that voting for the opposition might lead to atomic annihilation or terrorist attacks; and televised speeches pointing to the danger of homes and property being seized. Other images are calculated to play upon the hopes, fears, and resentments of the electorate. Good examples of these propaganda approaches can be seen in the imagery incorporated in Nazi election posters: plentiful harvests, humming factories, and gleaming buildings just constructed; the figure of Death hovering over property, unemployment lines, and "impure" and "money-grubbing" Jews. A multitude of parties in the United States, France, Germany, Great Britain, Italy, Japan, Poland, and Taiwan have used rising and setting suns to symbolize past achievements and future hopes under their leadership.

How are things different in the twenty-first century from those in the nineteenth? It might prove useful to compare the 1828 broadside campaign for Jackson in the United States and the 2004 poster-lawn sign campaign for Kerry. How were things similar in the two election campaigns that were 176 years apart? How were they different? In both campaigns, the records of military heroes who ran for president were attacked: in 1828, a broadside charged Jackson with committing atrocities during wartime in the previous decade; in 2004, TV spot ads and printed material mailed to targeted voters accused Kerry of lying about his experiences during the Vietnam War three decades earlier. The media and delivery methods chosen to make accusations to attack the characters of both candidates were appropriate for the times, and were difficult to answer. Furthermore, both the Swift Boat Veterans and Coffin Handbill denunciations used visuals (showing film footage and photographs from Vietnam, and rows of coffins) to increase the impact of the messages. Anti-Jackson newspapers launched other attacks, which were a large part of the 1828 campaign; in 2004, there were brochures and leaflets that functioned similarly to the nineteenth-century printed attacks, but TV spots and Internet sites seemed to inflict significantly more damage.

Positive advertising techniques were also part of both campaigns. Pro-Jackson broadsides, prints, and biographies, as well as pro-Kerry TV commercials, lionized the candidates' reported valor and leadership during wartime. Jackson's propaganda, however, successfully characterized him as a man who rose out of poverty and was in touch with "the common man"; Kerry's did not even attempt to communicate this image to the public. Even in his union-produced poster, many perceived Kerry as rather stiff and restrained—almost as "aristocratic" as the Jacksonian image devised of Adams. The image of Kerry's opponent, George W. Bush, on the other hand, was one of being a down-to-earth enemy of the power elite in Washington, academia, and cultural circles. While not apparent in his posters, this image was evident in the television advertisements showing him on his ranch. Although Bush never could communicate that he had the modest farm background of a Carter or the workingman image of a Lincoln, his image *did* seem almost like that of Reagan, the "rugged, no-nonsense, God-fearing rancher." This was remarkable, as Nicholas Lemann noted, since Bush had been born into a prominent, wealthy family whose background of Episcopalianism, Yale University, and business connections was hardly "humble."[4] Like so many politicians before him, however, Bush inculcated the image of himself as a rural "outsider" with fundamental values (in his case, those of religious fundamentalism) in the public mind.

Posters—often the vehicles of positive image manipulation in the United States—issued by the Democrats in 2004, continued to present Kerry as either a smiling campaigner or implied that he would be tougher than his opponent against America's enemies, using the slogan "A Stronger America." In Jackson's time, there were no advertising slogans; rather, there were nicknames (such as Jackson's "Old Hickory") that embodied the character of the candidate. Those posters that included photographs of Bush showed him with a serious expression, gazing into the distance—a man who seemed preoccupied with the fight against terrorism. The main poster of Kerry's campaign was similar in design to that of Bush's campaign, and stylized flags were the sole symbol. In 1828, flags as well as hickory trees and brooms graced Jackson tickets. The party was not designated on most of the broadsides, posters, and tickets distributed in either the nineteenth- or twenty-first-century campaigns. Party loyalty was not a big factor in the early days of political-party formation nor was it in the Kerry versus Bush race, when people voted more independently and the focus was on the persons running (as it was in the Jackson versus Adams contest).

Many more lawn signs and bumper stickers were circulated than were posters in 2004. They appeared in yards and on automobiles to promote Kerry and Bush. In Jackson's campaigns, parades with banners helped gain him attention in American towns. Today, broadsides are not used nearly as much as in the nineteenth century, although fold-out brochures and other print material are still employed to praise or attack the candidates' records, personalities, and their stands on issues. These—like the Coffin Handbill that was released in Philadelphia—have usually been distributed locally, but can also have a nationwide audience. From their inception, U.S. election posters have typically imparted positive images of candidates, with the focus on character; printed matter, however, often mailed to demographically selected groups, has often continued the political advertising tradition begun long ago with broadsides (as have television and radio), with many negative messages dispersed along with the positive ones.

Both of the campaigns of 1828 and 2004 followed the fundamental principles of political persuasion in American elections, as outlined by Phillips at the beginning of Chapter Two: the campaigns' propaganda focused on candidates' (1) *character,* with proponents trying to convince voters that their men were wise and courageous, and that their opponents were imprudent and even reckless; (2) *honesty,* with the opposition questioning all four candidates' accounts of past actions, while supporters praised their nominee's truthfulness; and (3) *concern about the voters*, and the issues that seemed to matter to them. Many of the posters or broadsides in both election campaigns were good at manipulating the character images of Jackson and Bush particularly, with the former candidate portrayed as a war hero, and the latter one, a dogged fighter against "Islamic terrorism," and both men depicted as "being in touch" with "the common person" (in contrast to their opponents). Other media of the times were exploited, maligning all four of the candidates. These included broadsides, newspaper articles and supplements, handbills, fliers, and brochures, songs, and radio and television advertisements.

Conclusions

❦ *Political poster propaganda is designed to elicit emotional reactions.* One strategy has been negative advertising, sometimes with the application of scare tactics. Attempts to increase fears and prejudice in the electorate, via broadsides, fliers, or posters, have occurred for well over a century. In the United States, examples abound. Among them are the 1864 anti-Lincoln, pro-McClellan broadside; 1880 anti-black, pro-Hancock broadside; 1928 anti-Catholic, anti-Smith broadside; 1948 pro-Thurmond broadside; and 1988 Willie Horton broadside/flier. Such printed condemnations have often been anonymously authored, or released by "committees." Elsewhere, posters issued by the Nazi Party in Germany, the Bharatiya Janata Party in India, and the Peronists in Argentina, to name a few, focused on issues and events that inflamed the passions of many in the electorate. Broadside and poster attacks on opponents charging them with corruption, featuring slogans and symbols to add emphasis, have been issued since the first elections. Positive emotions, however, have been injected too, by including family scenes and other managed images. Slogans promising "a better life" have been used in posters displayed in several continents. Pushing the emotional buttons of the electorate has been accomplished by the political advertising of various parties in different countries: in a study of the effects of televised spots and party broadcasts during national election campaigns in France, Germany, Italy, and the United States, it was found that the advertising that resulted in feelings of patriotism, optimism, confidence, excitement, and security generally increased candidates' positive image ratings.[5]

Fewer symbols were included in U.S. election posters during most of the twentieth century than before, although the nation's flag still is frequently incorporated (or at least its colors are). The flag—stylized in modern U.S. campaign posters—is the one symbol that is usually thought of as an essential element, with designs simplified so that the message can be interpreted quickly. Simplification of symbols has been evident in other countries' campaigns as well; the remaining ones include national flags and buildings, the socialist red rose, the "V" for "victory" or "peace," and crosses, crescents, and other religious symbols. Political marketing consultants have advised parties to change their logos, even if the colors were retained. The British Labour Party, for instance, jettisoned the red flag it had displayed for a red rose—the symbol of the Socialists in France, Japan, and several other countries—which was much less associated with the class struggle and the Soviet Union in the public's mind.[6]

Bright colors have also functioned in posters to attract attention and to help stir the electorate. This was particularly important in post-World War II Italy, in which the competition for wall space for posters was fierce, given that there were many, often poorly funded, political parties.[7] Certain colors have been used because of their popularity, or emotional and symbolic connotations. Although most U.S. campaign posters have red, white, and blue colors, those in much of Carter's 1976 material featured green as the dominant color to imply the "freshness" of his ideas, the "rebirth" of idealism,[8] and perhaps environmentalism. In many countries red connotes "danger," a fact that did not escape a Conservative Party designer in Great Britain, who planned a dominantly red poster that stated "!Warning! Blair's stealth tax rises ahead."

ℭℜ *Image management is important in election posters.* Political poster designers have employed many of the techniques that seem to have worked in the advertising world to draw attention to and sell products: the use of slogans, symbols, color, "eye contact," perspective, simplicity, graphic image manipulation, and both positive and negative visual imagery. Posters have been one component in propaganda or mass persuasion campaigns at election time; propaganda has been a means to influence public opinion about candidates and parties, and effect desired voter actions. Election campaigns have often been little different from advertising campaigns; new candidates have been packaged to introduce them to "consumers" in appealing ways, with old ones repackaged and promoted, and comparisons made with other "products." Even before advertising personnel were recruited to design American election campaigns in the twentieth century, this "packaging" process occurred, most notably with Harrison in the 1840 "Log Cabin" campaign and Lincoln in the 1860 "Rail Splitter" campaign. In nineteenth-century France, portraits of both Louis Napoleon Bonaparte and his mythologized uncle were distributed during election campaigns; in the same period, portraits of Disraeli and Gladstone were circulated in Great Britain. Twentieth-century examples in the United States include the marketing of Harding, in 1920, as a man who *looked* "presidential"; Eisenhower, as the "likeable military leader" who would end the Korean conflict after the 1952 campaign; Kennedy, as a "vigorous" new leader in 1960; the "New Nixon" in 1968; Carter, as a "populist" in 1976; and Reagan and George W. Bush, as the "cowboy outsiders" in the 1980s and 2000s. In other countries, Thatcher was marketed as "The Iron Lady"; Blair's party as "New Labour"; Mitterrand as "La force tranquille"; Wałęsa as a "freedom fighter"; Kohl as the "unifier" of both Germanys; Mandela as the benign "healer" of his racially torn nation; Koizumi as "Lionheart"; Fox as the determined "down-to-earth" opponent of a one-party regime; and, earlier, Hitler as "Our Last Hope" and Churchill as "the resolute war leader." Most of these concepts manifested in the election campaign posters.

These political messages have been communicated both visually and verbally, but the former channel has been the most important in the marketing process. The textual message has been central in most broadsides, but visuals have been used in other media to win the audience's attention and to deliver vital aspects of the message. A 1996 TV spot titled "Wrong in the Past," promoting Bill Clinton for U.S. president, for example, disparaged Dole's record on various issues over his three decades in the U.S. Congress, while viewers saw pictures of the Republican candidate during that time that made him appear to have aged thirty years in thirty seconds.[9] The commercial depicted Dole as "both old and a Washington insider," Eleanor Randolph noted at the time.[10] The visual images of the rows of coffins in John Binns' broadsides; the 1860 campaign portraits of the relatively unknown Lincoln; and General Harrison on horseback, Grant and Shoemaker in work aprons, Hancock as a rooster, McKinley standing on a gold coin, and Harding in front of a giant American flag in election posters and prints must have had a great impression on the voters before radio, television, and the Internet made printed matter a less valuable campaign tool. Before the advent of electronic mass media, voters in the United Kingdom observed on election posters an apron-clad Campbell-Bannerman in a kitchen, Asquith on a horse branded "British Constitution," and a monstrous cat holding a suffragette in its teeth, as well as such scenes as workers ramming the House of Lords. Other countries' posters before World War II cast their leaders in similar roles. Dutch Prime Minister Colijn, for example, was depicted as the captain of "the ship of state" in 1925, and opponents of Hitler and Thälmann caricatured them in German election posters.

The images and slogans can be memorable. In the age of television, words were secondary in impact to the imagery of Willie Horton's face and of John Kerry windsurfing. For those who doubt the predominance of visuals in American politics since television became the medium of choice, we have only to recall the survey results after the Nixon-Kennedy debates, which indicated that radio listeners thought there was no winner, although television viewers thought Kennedy had won. Television also has amplified the "character" portion of a candidate's image, with words such as *personality*, *likeability*, and *charisma* (unlike in the days when a candidate stayed at home and had less contact with the voters). In the last century, posters gradually became more simplified. Today, they can communicate their message more efficiently when viewed in large numbers in the background on television or in newspaper photographs (as can the many lawn signs), and they continue to add some excitement to a candidate's campaign.

Just as new products are coupled with highly regarded images in advertisements, images are combined in political posters to associate a candidate or party with something positive. U.S. election posters have included portraits of admired past presidents, such as Washington, Jefferson, and Lincoln, and have incorporated a multitude of symbolic images, such as cornucopia, eagles, and flags, into the designs. Portraits of the candidates—often on window cards—also played a role in building a positive image of the candidates and trumpeting support for their campaigns in neighborhoods in past American campaigns. Symbolic images continue to be presented, as Jamieson noted, to "associat[e] the favored candidate with pictures of well-fed cattle, happy families, large bundles of grain, and bulging factories … " (with reverse scenery often depicted to indicate the consequences of the opposition gaining or retaining power).[11] Other conventions seen in election posters are children and women (sometimes pregnant), as well as relating past with present leadership: Sun Yat-sen has been used in Taiwan, Garibaldi in Italy, Juárez in Mexico, and both the retired Mandela and Mahatma Gandhi in South Africa—on a campaign poster in 2004 for the ANC. In some instances, political organizations, such as the PRI in Mexico and Solidarity in Poland, have been connected in their posters to revolutions.

In posters, attempts are sometimes made to associate opponents with oppressive leaders; examples have included both Adenauer and de Gaulle with Hitler, and Chen Shui-bian with bin Laden and Saddam Hussein. There also are occasions when opponents are paired with foreign leaders, to whom they are allegedly subservient, such as Adenauer to Eisenhower, and Blair to Kohl. In Latin America, in particular, candidates are often depicted as lackeys of the United States and its presidents and corporations, or socialists such as Allende are linked to Castro's Cuba, presented with images of repression. At times, visuals are planned to appeal particularly to members of target groups (such as college students, women, and senior citizens). Successful brand management for a candidate or a political party, as manifested in posters and other media, is characterized by simple visual imagery that is both powerful and appealing along with clear slogans and logos that resonate with the voters and their emotions. The most effective posters go beyond just helping boost acceptance for candidates and parties, but target voters using image manipulation and emphasizing key issues.

Image management is multifaceted. Most of the candidates shown on American election posters appear in head-and-shoulder views—not too close, but not too far away either—in other words, at a "safe" vantage point for voters to view their leaders. Military heroes who ran for president of the United States were usually shown uniformed and on horseback in the first half of the nineteenth century, but after the 1872 Grant campaign, they were generally dressed in civilian clothing. It was deemed unnecessary to show Eisenhower in his general's uniform, Kennedy in a PT boat, or Kerry on the Mekong River in their posters, although it did occur at least three times in the twentieth century (with Truman in his captain's uniform, in a Carter poster montage, and in a small George H. W. Bush poster). Even the choice of civilian clothing for a candidate can be important: Kennedy, for example, was told to wear more conservative attire to increase the likelihood that voters would view him as mature enough to be president; Carter and Reagan, on the other hand, wore work shirts in some of their posters in their initial presidential campaigns, to reinforce their images as "men in touch with the land and its people." Kuomintang candidates typically wore ties in their posters, but their Taiwanese opponents generally did not. To enhance his image, it was sometimes considered advantageous to have the candidate wear his eyeglasses (Truman, for example); more often, they were not seen wearing them (Eisenhower, Kennedy, Nixon, and Reagan, for instance), since most political consultants did not want to "hide" the candidates' eyes.[12] It became common, beginning with the 1952 election, to have U.S. presidential candidates smile and look directly toward the audience for the posters (as well as for the television commercials that were developed). Occasionally, a photographic "trick" is employed to enhance a leader's "majestic" quality, as when a poster of President Ford for his 1976 U.S. reelection campaign included a photograph shot from below. Researchers have found that image manipulation can affect evaluations of and preferences for candidates. Moreover, candidates who were perceived to have the most positive images were the likeliest to be elected.[13]

CR ***Themes are emphasized in election posters.*** This usually takes the form of innovative slogans. The most effective posters are "a cut above" the standard sales job, which most often includes a photograph of the candidate and a slogan. While negative poster campaigns may appeal to party loyalists and depress voter turnout, posters that "hit" on issues, such as high unemployment, which are meaningful for the general public or to targeted groups, are believed to be as helpful as are those that convey appealing aspects of a candidate's personality or character. Examples of slogans that were used effectively on posters include "He Kept us Out of War," "16 to 1," "Tippecanoe and Tyler too," and "I Like Ike" in the United States, and "We Shall Overcome," "A better life for all," "Life's Better with the Conservatives. Don't Let Labour Ruin It," and "No Experiments!" and "Enough Already!" in other countries. Of course, there have been several instances when highly negative campaigns seemed to work well. One could point to the Horton and Swift Boat Veterans TV spot ads and fliers as examples of attacks that employed negative campaign themes successfully. In the past, independent groups unleashed many negative attacks; among them were the 1828 broadsides against Jackson, although there is some evidence that national political strategists orchestrated these campaigns on occasion. Political parties and interest groups—most notably labor unions—have also printed posters and broadsides that have targeted their members to support candidates on the issues. In 1900, for example, the posters designed for the McKinley and Bryan U.S. presidential election campaigns attempted to show that the policies of their candidates would benefit workers. Another instance was in 1932, when both the Hoover and Roosevelt campaigns distributed broadsides: one was an attempt to portray the former candidate as "labor's friend," while another debunked the record of that "friend."

ꙮ *Legislation affects the use of posters, billboards, and banners in election campaigns.* Unlike in other countries, among them Chile, Great Britain, Italy, and Japan, in which laws led to the increased use of posters in elections (when television time for candidates was limited or even prohibited), laws in the United States had the opposite effect for posters and billboards there. Attack advertising can be employed with election posters and billboards, but not with broadcast media in some countries' election campaigns. One case in point is in France, where there has been a multitude of negative election posters. Since the 1950s, antilitter legislation (and other abovementioned factors) in the United States led to the heavy use of election campaign lawn signs, while limiting the display of posters and billboards in public places. Earlier, flag "desecration" laws at the turn of the twentieth century, which, among other things, forbid the use of the American flag for advertising purposes[14] ended the practice of printing candidate names, symbols, and slogans on flag banners. Of course, flags still appear on election posters and other campaign propaganda. Despite the laws restricting their use, campaign posters, especially when placed on billboards or lawns, have proven to be beneficial in political campaigns, since they cannot be turned off (like televised shows that involve a candidate) or discarded (like printed matter).[15] In all countries, as the vote was extended to more of the population, printed media such as broadsides and posters were designed to target them. In addition, as various groups, including immigrants, former slaves, farmers, workers, and women, obtained voting rights, their representation in election posters became more common. Other liberal legislation was sometimes passed that stimulated increases in the number of posters employed in political campaigns: for instance, the French Parliament's passage of laws that helped smaller businesses such as print shops, and its repeal of censorship laws.

CR *Election campaign posters are much utilized in countries where literacy is relatively low.* This was the case in the past. Even in this new century, one in five of the world's adults are illiterate. Posters and billboards are the primary political medium in many of these countries, particularly in rural areas. Heavily pictorial posters, for example, have dominated election campaigns in Afghanistan, Ghana, Honduras, India, Kenya, Mali, Nicaragua, Iraq, and Papua New Guinea. Often, logos are prominently displayed on these posters to communicate to illiterate voters which party to mark on their ballots.

CR *Technological developments and artistic trends influence election posters and their use.* The development of improved lithographic techniques made possible more attractive election campaign posters; further technological developments allowed for superior color lithographs, and then photographic images, to be deployed by political operatives. By the first quarter of the twentieth century, millions of campaign lithographs could be run off in the United States for less than five cents. The more recent media technologies of radio and television, in many countries, gradually relegated posters to a secondary status in election campaigns, in terms of the medium's share of expenditures. However, oftentimes actually more election posters were printed because of the development of less costly paper stock and printing methods. Themes that were delivered on radio and television were reinforced on posters. In countries where fewer people had access to radio and television sets and to the Internet, posters were more highly valued as political propaganda tools, and they were used much more frequently.

Prominent artists and illustrators—Nast, Christy, Flagg, Shahn, Pryse, Hahn, Kray, Mjölnir, Batellier, and Orosz—designed election posters and broadsides that were displayed in their countries. The graphic design styles in vogue permeated election posters, but the general trend was toward simplification and stylization. In the nineteenth century, Currier & Ives generated election posters that followed a standard formula in the United States, but as advertising and business executives replaced printers in determining political poster designs, these became more distinctive. Under Hanna, the Republican posters became much more individualized to match the personality of the candidate and the issues of the day. Thereafter, there were more unique designs, although many were still similar, the customary formula applied regardless of party. By the late 1960s, stylized fonts and key letters more frequently became "characters" in posters: in 1968, a large, stylized "N" and an "h" dominated Nixon and Humphrey posters. In the same decade that artists such as John Van Hamersveld, Malcolm English, and Wes Wilson were designing Pop and Op Art posters to promote rock performers, the Republican parties of both Italy and the United States were producing election posters using the same artistic styles. Fewer "arty" election posters have been produced in the United States, particularly when compared to other countries, as American party professionals usually opted for the safe, traditional approach. In other countries' political posters, past and present artistic styles have been employed, particularly in Europe, where Expressionism, Primitivism, Art Nouveau, Futurism, *De Stijl*, Op Art, and computer-generated graphic approaches have been more commonly seen.

Most modern election posters, however, have followed this simple format: a photograph of a smiling candidate, a slogan, and a party's logo. Posters that deviate from this plan may be very effective, since they can attract attention because they are different from what is expected, especially if they focus on issues of concern to voters or if they include other elements, such as people shown with a candidate.

ℭↄ **Mass produced, high quality, pictorial posters are often part of election campaign packages.** This is particularly true of the last century. These packages—sometimes in a folder or kit, and sometimes in the form of a detailed plan—have included a multitude of items, from buttons to Internet spots. By 1918, promotional packages were being devised by advertising personnel in the United States. Advertising firms were heavily involved in American election campaigns in the decades that followed, and various approaches were developed to appeal to targeted groups. Targeting around the world became more refined—as market research was brought to bear on the material designed—than in the previous century. It is true that a greater proportion of an American party's campaign budget has shifted from posters to television. Transformed posters, however, have emerged in the form of lawn signs (along with bumper stickers and T-shirts)—statements by many citizens that they are involved in the American political process, not just viewing TV spot ads while sitting idly inside their homes. Similarly, the display of window cards has continued in the United States, with these small posters placed in twenty-first-century store windows and home windows, although this practice has diminished somewhat as lawn signs became widespread.

Campaign packages, in which posters are key components, have been created in many other countries as well. For example, in the Ukraine, a Tymoshenko poster was the centerpiece of a kit that contained decals, a national flag, and a headband; in Poland, Solidarity's election package included large posters, bumper stickers, buttons, and newspapers; in Taiwan, the packages merchandising both parties featured posters, along with such items as a knitted hat, a mug, a teapot, a doll, T-shirts, and scarves; in Japan, "Lion King" mobile-phone fobs were created to accompany Koizumi posters. Sometimes a poster proved so popular that its sale became a source of revenue for a party, as was the case with the Labour Party's "Yesterday's Men" poster in Great Britain, the Magyar Democratic Forum's "Comrades, The End!" in Hungary, and Koizumi's "*Kaikaku*" poster in Japan. Increasingly, Web sites are now an integral element of campaign packages, alongside newspaper and magazine ads, press releases, direct mail, rallies, and radio and television spots.

In general, the posters, lawn signs, and billboards appear before the TV spots to "establish name identification, motivate volunteers, and give the impression of momentum, … [and to] prepare voters for the television advertising to come by familiarizing them with graphics, designs, and slogans," according to Sabato.[16] A much larger proportion of campaign budgets are devoted to posters and billboards in many other countries than in the United States, but the purposes are similar.[17] It is understood that these media are not persuasive in themselves, except in extraordinary cases.[18] Obviously, in national campaigns, a venue in which the candidates are well known, billboards are less frequently used to establish recognition, since, compared to posters and lawn signs, they are relatively expensive and unnecessary for this purpose.[19] When issues are deemed imperative, however, billboards are likely to be used more.

CRSO

Both British and French election campaigns have usually been a mix of positive and negative advertising themes—similar to the campaigns in many other countries. Polling data give political marketing consultants, in both countries, a good idea of voter beliefs, and the posters and other media are then designed to strengthen opinions and influence less-than-committed voters. One belief in 1992, for many British voters, was that Labour policies on taxation were unlikely to get the country out of a recession, even if it had occurred on the Conservative watch. The visual and verbal messages on the posters buttressed this belief. As one Labour shadow minister said, "At the time I did not accept it but I can now see that the poster 'You can't trust Labour,' got it exactly right."[20] The campaign designed for Mitterrand in 1981 branded his image and message as "La force tranquille" to best appeal to French voters, and negative posters depicted his opponent as insensitive and associated him with high unemployment. Mitterand's propaganda package gave voters a clear and emotionally loaded idea of the man (namely his personality) and the benefits to be gained in supporting him, in marked contrast to backing his opponents.

Another trend in France and Great Britain is to highlight party leaders in posters: de Gaulle's name was seen in his political posters more than was his face, but later French politicians, such as Mitterrand, Giscard d'Estaing, and Chirac, and their British counterparts, including Major, Kinnock, and Blair, appeared in photographs in election posters. The French and the British electorate have been increasingly manipulated into focusing more on personality than on issues and even parties. One reason for this is that consultants assemble campaign packages that use posters and billboards, with clever imagery and slogans (sometimes borrowed from each other's country), to market the parties' leadership. Legislation in both countries made these display media more important than in the United States, with its heavy emphasis on negative TV spots.

The three oldest large democracies in modern times have much in common, but there are differences too. One important distinction is that as early as the mid-nineteenth century in the United States, posters became more standardized than in the other two nations, regularly using the same designs for candidates—even those of different parties. In recent American elections, all parties have usually employed stylized designs that are often little more than giant corporate-type logos, devoid of photographic portraits and issues. In France and Great Britain, however, design similarities have been less apparent. British election campaign posters, particularly after advertising firms exerted more influence in and after 1959, were more frequently unique in design and message, and more pointedly negative and issue-oriented than most American posters of the period. The best British ideas were recycled, sometimes with refreshed variations. Designs in France were generally not as inventive, but in the early 1980s, parties, particularly the Young Socialists, often resorted to exaggeration. Later French election posters have generally followed a formula: candidates in conservative attire are presented, displaying warm, but not broad smiles, and looking directly at the voters. While several American posters satirized presidential candidates, including Carter, Mondale, and Clinton, *independent* groups produced these prints. In other countries, the mainstream parties have shown less reluctance to lampoon the opposition. Modern British parties have issued posters showing male candidates for prime minister pregnant or coifed with a female hairdo.

Future Trends

✌ What does the future hold for posters in politics? Recently, only a small portion of total advertising expenditures has been devoted to posters and outdoor advertising—by 1993, only 4 percent in the United Kingdom on posters and billboards[21] and in the mid-1990s, 1 percent in the United States on posters[22]—still substantial sums. However, even though advertisers spend proportionately less on the medium, "the globalization of electronic communication has provided new opportunities for posters," as Charles Flowers pointed out, since "the proliferation of television programming has fragmented the viewing audience. … But the poster can cheaply, effectively aim its message about a monstrous SUV to the railway platforms of bedroom communities; images of the athletic shoe designed to loft teenagers toward the basket will be pasted up near the playgrounds. … "[23] The same trend leads to the conclusion that there will be more opportunities to employ targeted election posters and broadsides/fliers.

We have seen how posters and broadsides/fliers were used to inform voters via direct mail in past campaigns. Lately, computer programs have been able to cross-reference lists of voters with multiple e-mail address lists. Political marketing specialists have then been able to "e-blast" millions of voters thought likely to be receptive to campaign messages, based on a number of factors: magazine subscriptions and merchandise catalogs mailed; online polls completed; demographic characteristics such as age, sex, ethnicity, and place of residence; voting frequency; and affiliations.[24] As early as 2005, it was estimated that U.S. voters had received over one billion unsolicited political e-mail messages at a fraction of the cost of regular mail or TV spots.[25] Today's political parties, "committees," unions, businesses, and religious and other advocacy groups can deluge voters quickly and inexpensively with electronic broadsides. In the future, more posters and other campaign messages will be sent electronically to targeted persons. The Campaign Network, for example, sent out a poster of Martin Luther King, Jr., as a PDF (portable document format) file, a delivery vehicle that was inexpensive and easy for recipients to print.[26] Todd Olsen, a partner in Olsen & Shuvalov, a Republican direct marketing consulting firm in the United States, added that political ads are created for both e-mail transmissions and direct mailings, now with more emphasis on "microtargeting."[27] Companies commonly use microtargeting to identify and target specific individuals, and send them e-mails that will be much more effective than more general, bulk e-blasts. Political consultants use microtargeting by "overlaying consumer data on what you buy and what you read with traditional election information," according to David Moceri.[28] For example, U.S. voters who drive Chevrolets and drink bourbon are more likely to be Republicans than they are to be Democrats.[29]

Political billboards have also been placed strategically to target segments of the population. Furthermore, spending on such billboards has increased dramatically in some countries, including the United States, where, in 2004, there was a 20 percent increase for outdoor political advertising.[30] In 2005 and 2006, overall spending on outdoor displays in the United States rose 8 percent.[31] We can anticipate that this will continue. Digital billboards, presenting different static messages every six to eight seconds, have begun to appear, and the political implications are obvious. Since all billboard messages must be perceived and comprehended in a very few seconds by highway drivers, they must be even simpler and easier to read than posters. Another compelling innovation is the rudimentary "talking poster," that can already sense when people are present and can deliver messages (including political ones). Versions are being perfected to be animated, to interact with voters, to have background music, and to match their data about individual voters to different messages for instant viewing.[32] Another development is the segmented billboard, which can be used by a political party to present its candidates for several different offices simultaneously. There are now, also, holographic posters that can be used to display candidates and issues dramatically.

With the rise of the Internet and increased globalization, politicians, graphic designers, and media and political consultants have become more aware of developments in other parts of the world. Whereas Van Buren, Binns, and Lasker toiled in relative isolation, consultants for Blair, Mandela, Fox, and Schröder did not. Modern poster designers are aware of the latest fonts and design ideas from other countries. This was true in the past, but today the transmission of ideas is faster and more extensive to all parts of the world. In the latter part of the 1800s, Gladstone borrowed some of the techniques used in American politics for his new Liberal Party. In the 1930s, Nazi and Communist Party poster designers took visual and verbal elements from the "social realist" posters of the Soviet Union. Hitler, Goebbels, and others studied the propaganda principles and techniques of advertising and psychologists, but today this process has accelerated.

Although television is now the key medium for political marketers, we can expect that the Internet will gradually cut into its share of election campaign advertising. In fact, television viewing has already begun to diminish in some countries. In the United Kingdom, for instance, from 2003 to 2005, average weekly television viewing (almost twenty-six hours per week) decreased by almost one hour per week, perhaps because the British were on their computers an average of ten hours per week and were playing video games an additional eleven hours per week.[33] Unlike other electronic technologies developed in the twentieth century, the Internet could enhance election posters. In the future, typical vehicles for viewing political posters will be e-mail and YouTube. All candidates and parties will use Web sites, as well, to stream TV spots and display other conventional media, such as press releases and posters. Political Web banners—the electronic posters and newspaper advertisements of the future—will be pervasive. The Internet is truly the *World Wide* Web: political parties in all parts of the world, even in countries in which computers are hard to find, are utilizing it. One trend that will strengthen the Internet as a political conduit is the advancement, by several organizations, of low-cost computers for the developing world.

In many countries, election poster designs in the coming years could have fewer photographs of candidates. This may be due to the growing drift toward print-your-own

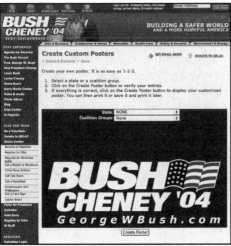

Figure 8.1

posters on parties' Internet sites, which began in 1996 with Dole's Web site. Since the images available on these sites have low resolution, their printing quality is poor. By 2004, the U.S. Republican Party allowed supporters to choose from a selection of coalition groups and states to create and print their own somewhat personalized poster (Fig. 8.1). This practice should persist with more creativity and safeguards (to prevent antagonistic posters) in the years to come. Another innovation came in 2006, when the British Labour Party conducted a contest to "Vote for your favourite campaign poster" on its Web site. The winner, "2+2 = 5" (referring to the Conservatives' "mistaken" economic notions), was then tested. The party also produced a series of posters on which visitors to its site voted. Testing of poster designs and slogans, and interactive voting on them, will probably occur more, just as virtual, interactive focus groups will be formed to discuss and obtain feedback on poster ideas. In addition, sensors will be placed on voters to determine their involuntary responses to different poster designs. The result should be posters that more effectively target segments of the electorate, as well as designs that have better general appeal. The Internet is becoming more of a factor worldwide, with parties' posters exhibited on their Web sites. Many more candidates, individually, will have Web pages on which their campaign posters will be displayed too.

There is some research evidence that posters do make a difference in election campaigns. They seem to function primarily to keep voters from defecting by reinforcing their party identification. In terms of actual votes, printed political advertising (including posters) can lead to some gains (although not as much as television broadcasts). The research suggests that well-designed posters, which capture the attention of voters during election campaigns, can help a party in a close election, particularly to sway wavering voters.

Some verification exists that promotional and political posters have been valuable. The creations of poster designers, whose goal was to increase attendance at various attractions, seemed to achieve this effect in some instances. Posters, banners, lawn signs, and billboards appear to have the unique ability to appeal to viewers on the move, by foot or in cars, buses, and trains, and communicate to onlookers enough visual and verbal information to have some impact. Posters are advertisements—with visuals and slogans designed to improve or degrade candidate images and convey themes; and advertising is a form of propaganda. Lasker and Goebbels were both cognizant of these realities. Posters have been, and will continue to be, part of the political environment to interest, increase acceptance, reinforce, and—for some voters—persuade and influence behavior.

Chapter One

1. Franklyn S. Haiman, "A Tale of Two Countries: Media and Messages of the 1988 French and American Presidential Campaigns," in *Mediated Politics in Two Cultures: Presidential Campaigning in the United States and France*, ed. Lynda Lee Kaid, Jacques Gerstlé, and Keith R. Sanders (New York: Praeger, 1991), 29.

2. Gary Yanker, *Prop Art: Over 1000 Contemporary Political Posters* (New York: Darien House, 1972), 16.

3. Josef Müller-Brockmann and Shizuko Müller-Brockmann, *History of the Poster* (New York: Phaidon Press, 2004), 25; and Howard Risatti, "The Contemporary Political Poster in Italy," *Art Journal* 44 (1984): 11.

4. See J. Müller-Brockmann and S. Müller-Brockmann, *History of the Poster*, 25, 27.

5. Ibid., 25.

6. See Robert Philippe, *Political Graphics: Art as a Weapon* (New York: Abbeville Press, 1980), 51.

7. J. Müller-Brockmann and S. Müller-Brockmann, *History of the Poster*, 26; and Réjane Bargiel, "Histoire de l'affiche Française … Des origines à la 2nde Guerre mondiale," *Musée de la Publicité*, http://www.museedelapub.org/pubgb/virt/histoire.

8. Philippe, *Political Graphics*, 40–41.

9. The first documented use of the word was in 1622, when the *Sacra Congregatio de Propaganda* was founded by the Pope Gregory XV. Anthony R. Pratkanis and Elliot Aronson, *Age of Propaganda: The Everyday Use and Abuse of Persuasion*, rev. ed. (New York: W. H. Freeman, 2001), 11; *Encarta World English Dictionary*, s.v. "Propaganda," http://encarta .msn.com; and U. Benigni, "Sacred Congregation of Propaganda," *Catholic Encyclopedia*, vol. 12 (New York: Robert Appleton Company, 1911), http://www.newadvent.org.

10. Philip B. Meggs, *A History of Graphic Design*, 3rd ed. (New York: John Wiley & Sons, 1998), 83.

11. Reformiert Online, "John Calvin, the Reformation in Geneva and the Beginnings of the Reformation in France," *Reformiert Online*, http://www.reformiert-online.net:8080/t/eng/bil dung/grundkurs/gesch/lek3/index3.jsp.

12. *Broadsides & Posters from the National Archives* (Washington, D.C.: National Archives and Records Administration, 1986), 7.

13. See Ingeborg Lehmann-Haupt, "German Woodcut Broadsides in the Seventeenth Century," in *An Introduction to the Woodcut of the Seventeenth Century*, ed. Hellmut Lehmann-Haupt (New York: Abaris Books, 1977), 230–233.

14. Meggs, *History of Graphic Design*, 81.

15. I. Lehmann-Haupt, "German Woodcut Broadsides," 230.

16. John Barnicoat, *Posters: A Concise History* (1972; repr., New York: Thames and Hudson, 1985), 7.

17. Bernard F. Reilly, Jr., *American Political Prints: 1766–1876* (Boston: G. K. Hall, 1991), xiv.

18. Ibid., 7–8, 20; and Bargiel, "Histoire de l'affiche Francaise."

19. See James Playsted Wood, *The Story of Advertising* (New York: Ronald Press, 1959), 150–152, 347.

20. Ibid., 347.

21. Nigel Potter, quoted in Outdoor Advertising Association of Great Britain, "Bacardi-Outdoor: Long-Term Brand-Building," http://www.oaa.org.uk.

22. Ibid.

23. Harold D. Lasswell, *Propaganda Technique in World War I* (Cambridge, Mass.: MIT Press, 1971; reprint of book under title *Propaganda Technique in the World War*, London: Kegan, Paul, Trench, Trubner & Company, 1927), 3; an article with the title "Praiseworthy Propaganda," printed in the *New York Times*, on April 23, 1923, http://proquest.com, stated that "'propaganda' has come to be a word of ill repute. ..."

24. Lasswell, *Propaganda Technique*, 206.

25. *Encarta World English Dictionary*, s.v. "Propaganda"; and *Roget's New Millennium Thesaurus*, s.v. "Propaganda," http://thesaurus.reference.com/browse/propaganda.

26. Harold D. Lasswell, "Propaganda," in *Propaganda*, ed. Robert Jackall (New York: New York University Press, 1995; reprint from *Encyclopedia of the Social Sciences*, vol. 12, ed. Edwin R. A. Seligman (London: Macmillan, 1934), 21; an article in the *Wall Street Journal*, in fact, referred to a "coffee propaganda" campaign in the first decade of the twentieth century, which was designed to promote the drinking of the brew in the United States of America. *Wall Street Journal*, "Food and Drink Propaganda," April 22, 1908, http://proquest.com.

27. David Welch, "Definitions of Propaganda," in *Propaganda and Mass Persuasion: A Historical Encyclopedia, 1500 to the Present*, ed. Nicholas J. Cull, David Culbert, and David Welch (Santa Barbara, Calif.: ABC-CLIO, 2003), 319.

28. Karen S. Johnson-Cartee and Gary A. Copeland, *Strategic Political Communication: Rethinking Social Influence, Persuasion, and Propaganda* (Lanham, Md.: Rowman & Littlefield, 2004), 155.

29. Garth S. Jowett and Victoria O'Donnell, *Propaganda and Persuasion*, 3rd ed. (Thousand Oaks, Calif.: Sage, 1999), 3.

30. Oliver Thomson, *Mass Persuasion in History: An Historical Analysis of the Development of Propaganda Techniques* (New York: Crane, Russak & Company, 1977), 7.

31. *Encarta World English Dictionary*, s.v. "Propaganda."

32. See Nathan Shedroff, "A History of Communications 35,000 BC–1998 AD," http://www.nathan.com/projects/current/comtimeline.html; Zentral und Landesbibliothek Berlin, "High-Speed Printing Machines, Handbills and Street Corners: The Citizens of Berlin Revolution Public," http://www.zlb.de/projeckte/1848; and Meggs, *History of Graphic Design*, 61–62, 133.

33. See Meggs, *History of Graphic Design*, 146–147; Steve Bartrick, "Information-Printing Methods: Line Engraving," http://www.antiqueprints.com; and Janet Gleeson, *Miller's Collecting Prints & Posters* (London: Miller's, 1997), 15, on printing processes in the nineteenth century.

34. See Barnicoat, *Posters,* 7.

35. See Harry T. Peters, *Currier & Ives: Printmakers to the American People* (Garden City, N.Y.: Doubleday, Doran & Company, 1942), 4, 14; David Lance Goines, "A Brief History of Pre-Electronic Printing," http://www.goines.net/Writing/hist_pre_electr_printing.html; Harry T. Peters, *America on Stone* (Garden City, N.Y.: Doubleday, Doran and Company, 1931; repr., New York: Arno Press, 1976), 21–22; J. Müller-Brockmann and S. Müller-Brockmann, *History of the Poster*, 45; Alan Livingston and Isabella Livingston, *The Thames & Hudson Dictionary of Graphic Design and Designers*, rev. ed. (New York: Thames & Hudson, 2003), 49; and Meggs, *History of Graphic Design*, 131–132, 147, on developments in lithography.

36. See Michel Frizot, "Light Machines: On the Threshold of Invention" in *A New History of Photography*, ed. Michel Frizot (Köln, Ger.: Könemann, 1998), 19–20; Goines, "Brief History"; and Kenneth Zerbe and Steven Kern, "The Photogravure Printing Process," *The*

Curtis Collection, http://www.curtis-collection.com/process.html, on early photography.

37. See Anne Cartier-Bresson, "Methods of Producing Photographic Prints," 756; Estelle Jussim, *Visual Communication and the Graphic Arts: Photographic Technologies in the Nineteenth Century* (New York: R. R. Bowker Company, 1974), 289–294; Walton Rawls, *Wake Up, America! World War I and the American Poster* (New York: Abbeville Press, 1988), 14; A. Livingston and I. Livingston, *Thames & Hudson Dictionary*, 86; Shedroff, "History of Communications"; Roberta L. Hursey, "The Lithographic Process," in *The Poster War: Allied Propaganda Art of the First World War*, ed. Maurice F. V. Doll (Edmonton, Alberta, Can.: Alberta Community Development, 1993), 21; Richard Hollis, *Graphic Design: A Concise History*, rev. ed. (New York: Thames & Hudson, 2001), 40; Estelle Jussim, "Changing Technology Changes Design," in *Graphic Design in America: A Visual Language History*, ed. Mildred Friedman and Phil Freshman (New York: Harry N. Abrams, 1989), 106; and Steven Heller and Seymour Chwast, *Graphic Style: From Victorian to Digital*, rev. ed. (New York: Harry N. Abrams, 2000), 213, on later developments in photography and printing, and their impact on poster design and use.

38. Susan Sontag, "Posters: Advertisement, Art, Political Artifact, Commodity," in *Looking Closer 3: Classic Writings on Graphic Design*, ed. Michael Berut, Jessica Helfand, Steven Heller and Rick Poynor (New York: Allworth Press, 1999; reprint of article published in Dugald Stermer, *The Art of Revolution: 96 Posters from Cuba* [New York: McGraw-Hill, 1970]), 196.

39. See Frank Ogden, "Volume VI: Lessons from the Future—Talking Posters," *Dr. Tomorrow*, http://www.drtomorrow.com/lessons/lessons6/28.html.

40. David Butler and Dennis Kavanagh, *The British General Election of 2001* (New York: Palgrave, 2002), 215.

41. David Butler and Dennis Kavanagh, *The British General Election of 2005* (New York: Palgrave, 2005), 69.

42. David Crowley, "The Propaganda Poster," in *The Power of the Poster*, ed. Margaret Timmers (London: V&A Publications, 1998), 103.

43. See Anne Classen Knutson, "Breasts, Brawn, and Selling a War: American World War I Propaganda Posters 1917–1918" (PhD diss., University of Pittsburgh, 1997), 215.

44. Meggs, *History of Graphic Design*, 71.

45. See *New York Times*, "Democracy and Literacy," February 22, 1928, http://proquest.com.

46. See Luciano Cheles, "Picture Battles in the Piazza: The Political Poster," in *The Art of Persuasion: Political Communication in Italy from 1945 to the 1990s*, ed. Luciano Cheles and Lucio Sponza (Manchester, UK: Manchester University Press, 2001), 126.

47. Laura Winter, "In Rugged Afghanistan, Posters Convey Campaign Message," *Radio Free Afghanistan*, October 7, 2004, http://www.azadiradio.org.

48. See United Nations, "United Nations Literacy Decade, 2003–2012," http://portal.unesco .org/education; and UNESCO, *EFA Global Monitoring Report: Education for All/Is the World on Track?* http://portal.unesco.org/education.

49. Shyamsunder Tekwani, "Visual Culture in Indian Politics: The Gaudy Billboard as Political Communication" (paper, International Communication Association annual conference, New York, May 29, 2005), http://www.allacademic.com.

50. See UNESCO Institute for Education, "Literacy Exchange: World Resources on Literacy: India," *Universität Hamburg*, http://www1.uni-hamburg.de.

51. Crowley, "Propaganda Poster," 144.

52. Jan Van den Bulck, "Estimating the Success of Political Communication Strategies: The Case of Political Poster Impact in a Belgian Election," *European Journal of Communication* 8 (1993): 471; and Canadian Foundation for the Americas, "Governance and Democracy: Mapping the Media in the Americas," http://www.focal.ca/home_e.asp.

53. Stuart Weir and David Beetham, *Political Power and Democratic Control in Britain* (London: Routledge, 1999), 86, 89; and Eric Pfanner, "On Advertising: Marketing to Voters in Britain," *International Herald Tribune*, April 18, 2005, http://www.proquest.com.

54.   See Christina Holtz-Bacha and Lynda Lee Kaid, "A Comparative Perspective on Political Advertising: Media and Political System Characteristics," in *Political Advertising in Western Democracies*, ed. Lynda Lee Kaid and Christina Holtz-Bacha (Thousand Oaks, Calif.: Sage, 1995), 16; Shaun Bowler and David M. Farrell, "The Internationalization of Campaign Consultancy," in *Campaign Warriors: The Role of Political Consultants in Elections*, ed. James A. Thurber and Candice J. Nelson (Washington, D.C.: Brookings Institution Press, 2000), 160–161; Van den Bulck, "Estimating the Success," 471; Pippa Norris, "Campaign Communications," in *Comparing Democracies 2: New Challenges in the Study of Elections and Voting*, ed. Lawrence LeDuc, Richard G. Niemi, and Pippa Norris (Thousand Oaks, Calif.: Sage, 2002), 144; *New York Times*, "Regulating Campaigns: How Some Other Countries Do It," November 13, 1988, http://proquest.com; and Fritz Plasser, *Global Political Campaigning: A Worldwide Analysis of Campaign Professionals and Their Practices* (Westport, Conn.: Praeger, 2002), 221.

55.   Anne Johnston and Jacques Gerstlé, "The Role of Television Broadcasts in Promoting French Television Candidates," in Kaid and Holtz-Bacha, *Political Advertising*, 48.

56.   Haiman, "Tale of Two Countries," 31.

57.   See Johnston and Gerstlé, "Role of Television Broadcasts," 49.

58.   Weir and Beetham, *Political Power and Democratic Control*, 24.

59.   American National Business Hall of Fame, "Albert Lasker," http://www.anbhf.org/laureates/lasker.html.

60.   James B. Twitchell, *AdCult USA: The Triumph of Advertising in American Culture* (New York: Columbia University Press, 1996), 121.

61.   Daniel M. Shea and Michael John Burton, *Campaign Craft: The Strategies, Tactics, and Art of Political Campaign Management* (Westport, Conn.: Praeger, 2001), 127.

62.   Ibid., 52.

63.   Edward L. Bernays, "Manipulating Public Opinion: The Why and The How," *The American Journal of Sociology* 33 (1928): 961.

64.   See Dominic Wring, *The Politics of Marketing the Labour Party* (New York: Palgrave Macmillan, 2005), 5, 38–42.

65.   Ibid., x.

66.   See Patrick Butler and Neil Collins, "Political Marketing: Structure and Process," *European Journal of Marketing*, 28 (1994): 19–20.

67.   Nicholas J. O'Shaughnessy, "The Marketing of Political Marketing," in *The Idea of Political Marketing*, ed. Nicholas J. O'Shaughnessy and Stephen C. M. Henneberg (Westport, Conn.: Praeger, 2002), 211.

68.   See Adrian I. Sackman, "The Learning Curve Towards New Labour: Neil Kinnock's Corporate Party 1983–92," *European Journal of Marketing* 30 (1996): 148–149.

69.   See James A. Thurber, "Introduction to the Study of Campaign Consultants," in Thurber and Nelson, *Campaign Warriors*, 3.

70.   Dennis W. Johnson, "The Business of Political Consulting," in Thurber and Nelson, *Campaign Warriors*, 39.

71.   Larry R. Sabato, *The Rise of Political Consultants: New Ways of Winning Elections* (New York: Basic Books, 1981), 57–58; Greenberg Quinlin Rosner Research, "International Campaigns," http://www.gqrr.com/index.php?ID=353; and Bowler and Farrell, "Internationalization of Campaign Consultancy," 164.

72.   Sidney Blumenthal, *The Permanent Campaign: Inside the World of Elite Political Operatives* (Boston: Beacon Press, 1980), 132–133.

73.   David Mark, "Baltimore Politics Goes to West Africa," *Campaigns & Elections*, February 2006, 44–45.

74.   Bowler and Farrell, "Internationalization of Campaign Consultancy," 164.

75.   Frank Esser, Carsten Reinemann, and David Fan, "Spin Doctoring in British and German

Election Campaigns: How the Press is Being Confronted with a New Quality of Political PR," *European Journal of Communication* 15 (2000): 210–211, 222.

76. Saatchi & Saatchi, "Who We Are," http://www.saatchi.com/worldwide/Who_We_Are.asp.

77. Fritz Plasser, "American Campaign Techniques Worldwide," *Harvard International Journal of Press/Politics* 5, no. 4 (2000): 49.

78. I&S creative director, quoted in James Sterngold, "Adverting," *New York Times*, February 6, 1990, http://proquest.com.

79. Esser, Reinemann, and Fan, "Spin Doctoring," 223.

80. Stanley Kelley, Jr., *Professional Public Relations and Political Power* (Baltimore, Md.: Johns Hopkins Press, 1956), 221.

81. Meggs, *History of Graphic Design*, 131.

82. See "Currier & Ives—The History of the Firm," http://www.geocities.com/scurrier/history.html; and Peters, *Currier & Ives*, 12–15, on the Currier & Ives company.

83. See Meggs, *History of Graphic Design*, 131, 156; Barnicoat, *Posters*, 16–17; and Catherine Haill, "Posters for Performance," in Timmers, *Power of the Poster*, 35, on poster houses and their operations, and on designs, symbols, and influences of lithographs and woodcuts.

84. Max Gallo, *The Poster in History* (New York: W. W. Norton, 2001), 167.

85. Rune Pettersson, "Information Graphics at the Turn of Two Centuries," *Journal of Visual Literacy* 17 (1997): 66.

86. Gallo, *Poster in History*, 193.

87. Stephan Donche, "Graphics and Politics, The Role of Graphic Design in Twentieth Century Political Propaganda" (master's thesis, California State University Dominguez Hills, 1995), 25.

88. Meggs, *History of Graphic Design*, 252.

89. Pratkanis and Aronson, *Age of Propaganda*, 319, 321.

90. John Hegarty, "Selling the Product," in Timmers, *Power of the Poster*, 223.

91. George F. Horn, *Contemporary Posters: Design and Techniques* (Worcester, Mass.: Davis Publications, 1976), 9.

92. Tom Purvis (speech, Bradford Publicity Club, February 2, 1929), quoted in Beverly Cole and Richard Durack, *Railway Posters 1923–1947* (London: Laurence King Publishing, 1972), 20.

93. Cole and Durack, *Railway Posters*, 135.

94. See Daina Stukuls, "Imagining the Nation: Campaign Posters of the First Postcommunist Elections in Latvia," *East European Politics and Societies* 11 (1997): 137.

95. Mike Salisbury, *Art Director Confesses: "I Sold Sex! Drugs & Rock 'n' Roll"* (Crans-Prè-Céligny, Switz.: RotoVision, 2000), 46.

96. Bjorn Sunde, "Politics the World Over: Propaganda, Posters and Campaign Images at New Hoover Exhibit," http://www.paloaltoonline.com.

97. British Broadcasting Corporation, "Can Adverts Win Elections?" *BBC News*, January 19, 2001, http://news.bbc.co.uk/1/hi/uk/1123777.stm.

98. British Helsinki Human Rights Group, "Serbian Presidential Elections," *BHHRG Online*, September/October, 2002, http://www.bhhrg.org/CountryReport.asp?ReportID=187&CountryID=20.

99. Van den Bulck, "Estimating the Success," 484.

100. Stephen Gundle, "Italy," in *Electioneering: A Comparative Study of Continuity and Change*, ed. David Butler and Austin Ranney (Oxford, UK: Clarendon Press, 1992), 181.

101. Kevin McElderry, "Politics as Sex: German Election Campaign Spices Up," *Daily Times* (Pakistan), September 2, 2002, http://www.dailytimes.com.pk.

102. Gail Deibler Finke, *Fresh Ideas in Invitations, Posters & Announcements* (Cincinnati, Ohio: North Light Books, 1998), 6.

Chapter Two

1. Cabell Phillips, "Torchlight, Train, Television," *New York Times*, September 18, 1960, http://proquest.com.

2. Judith S. Trent and Robert V. Friedenberg, *Political Campaign Communication: Principles and Practices*, 4th ed. (New York: Praeger, 2000), 14.

3. Joseph J. Ellis, *His Excellency George Washington* (New York: Alfred A. Knopf, 2004), 139.

4. Ibid., 216.

5. See *Presidential Elections Since 1789*, 5th ed. (Washington, D.C.: Congressional Quarterly, 1991), 154–155, on the Electoral College and early U.S. elections.

6. Ibid., 96.

7. A small anti-Jackson woodcut-with-letterpress broadside (which measured approximately ten by twelve inches), titled "Our Country ... Home Industry," addressed to "manufacturers and mechanics," was printed in 1824. It was critical of Jackson's position against tariffs and accused him of bias toward Great Britain, and described Henry Clay as "your hearty supporter." It is housed in the Library of Congress.

8. Reilly, Jr., *American Political Prints*, xiii, 32–33; and John Binns, *Recollections of the Life of John Binns: Twenty-Nine Years in Europe and Fifty-Three in the United States* (Philadelphia: John Binns/Parry and M'Millan, 1854), 246.

9. William C. Cook, "The Coffin Handbills—America's First Smear Campaign," *Imprint* 27 (2002): 26.

10. Binns, *Recollections*, 246.

11. Ibid., 245. Jackson biographer Robert V. Remini concluded that these six militiamen, who were executed during the Creek War in 1813, were guilty of the crimes for which they were executed. Robert V. Remini, "Election of 1828," in *History of American Presidential Elections 1789–2001*, vol. 2, ed. Arthur M. Schlesinger, Jr., and Fred L. Israel (Philadelphia: Chelsea House, 2002), 427; apparently Jackson merely approved the sentence of the court martial "by letting stand the decision of the court" (which, according to William C. Cook, was in accordance with the sentences of the day). Cook, "Coffin Handbills," 24.

12. Binns, *Recollections*, 246.

13. Binns recounts the entire incident of the night of the 1824 election in his autobiography. Ibid., 255–256.

14. Reilly, Jr., *American Political Prints*, 33.

15. Robert V. Remini, *Andrew Jackson: The Course of American Freedom, 1822–1832*, vol. 2 (Baltimore, Md.: Johns Hopkins University Press, 1981), 108–109, 122–123.

16. Cook, "Coffin Handbills," 25.

17. *Our Country* (Hagers-Town, Md.), "The Coffin Handbill," October 18, 1828, http://hdl.loc.gov/loc.rbc/rbpe.02903100.

18. Reilly, Jr., *American Political Prints*, 33–34.

19. See Norma Basch, "Marriage, Morals, and Politics in the Election of 1828," *Journal of American History* 80 (1993): 896; Roger A. Fischer, *Tippecanoe and Trinkets Too: The Material Culture of American Presidential Campaigns 1828–1984* (Urbana, Ill.: University of Illinois Press, 1988), 18, 27–28; and Allen Walker Read, "Could Andrew Jackson Spell?" *American Speech* 38 (1963): 189.

20. See Fischer, *Tippecanoe and Trinkets Too*, 17.

21. See *Presidential Elections Since 1789*, 100–101, 174.

22. David McCullough, *John Adams* (New York: Simon & Schuster, 2001), 545. By 1800, many states had dropped their property requirements for white male voters. Between 1812 and 1821, six newly admitted Western states allowed all males over the age of twenty-one to vote, and four older states gave up their property requirements. Sandra Browne, "Making Democracy

Work," http://www.lwvabe.org/history.html.

23. McCullough, *John Adams*, 544–545.

24. Jackson owned about 150 slaves at one time. Robert V. Remini, *Andrew Jackson* (1966; repr., New York: Harper Perennial, 1999), 41.

25. See William A. DeGregorio, *The Complete Book of U.S. Presidents,* 5th ed. (New York: Wings Books, 1997), 111.

26. Remini, "Election of 1828," 420.

27. John Patrick Diggins, "John Quincy Adams," in *'To the Best of My Ability': The American Presidents*, ed. James M. McPherson (London: Dorling Kindersley, 2000), 54.

28. Paul F. Boller, Jr., *Presidential Campaigns: From George Washington to George W. Bush,* 2nd rev. ed. (New York: Oxford University Press, 2004), 44; and DeGregorio, *Complete Book*, 111.

29. Amos Kendall, *Autobiography of Amos Kendall,* ed. William Stickney (1872; repr., New York: Peter Smith, 1949), 639.

30. Ibid.

31. Ibid., 308.

32. Melvyn H. Bloom, *Public Relations and Presidential Campaigns: A Crisis in Democracy* (New York: Thomas Y. Crowell, 1973), 10.

33. Ibid., 10–11; and Remini, "Election of 1828," 435–436; Kendall served for most of the 1832 election campaign as the Democratic Party's national chairman. In this capacity, he maintained a constant supply of propaganda to party personnel in the states, as well as urging the establishment of more party newspapers. Remini, *Andrew Jackson*, vol. 2, 375.

34. Bloom, *Public Relations*, 11.

35. Reilly, Jr., *American Political Prints*, 38.

36. See Joel H. Silbey, *Martin Van Buren and the Emergence of American Popular Politics* (Lanham, Md.: Rowman & Littlefield, 2002), 50–51; and Robert V. Remini, *Martin Van Buren and the Making of the Democratic Party* (New York: Columbia University Press, 1959), 123–146.

37. Remini, *Martin Van Buren*, 193.

38. Keith Melder, *Hail to the Candidate: Presidential Campaigns from Banners to Broadcasts* (Washington, D.C.: Smithsonian Institution, 1992), 39; and Silbey, *Martin Van Buren*, 52.

39. Wilson Sullivan (revised by Robert A. Rutland), "Martin Van Buren: The Red Fox," in *American Heritage Illustrated History of the Presidents*, ed. Michael Beschloss (New York: Crown, 2000), 116–117, 119.

40. See Democratic tickets, figures 1836–16 and 1836–17 in Reilly, Jr., *American Political Prints*, 89–90.

41. DeGregorio, *Complete Book*, 142; and Boller, Jr., *Presidential Campaigns*, 63–64.

42. DeGregorio, *Complete Book*, 128.

43. See Joel H. Silbey, "Election of 1836," in Schlesinger, Jr., and Israel, *History of American Presidential Elections*, vol. 2, 587.

44. Ibid., 582.

45. See *Presidential Elections Since 1789*, 101–103.

46. The Whig strategy was to run several regional candidates, and prevent Van Buren from gaining a majority of the votes in the Electoral College. In addition, an independent Democrat won the eleven electoral votes of South Carolina. Ibid., 155–156, 176.

47. See Richard M. Pious, "Martin Van Buren," in McPherson, *'To the Best of My Ability,'* 67–68.

48. W. Sullivan, "Martin Van Buren," 122.

49. See ibid., 69.

50. The Jackson forces in New York had used the same rhyme during the 1828 election in a broadside that ridiculed John Quincy Adams and his administration. The broadside is in the Bettmann/CORBIS Archives.

51. Ironically, Harrison's physical health at sixty-eight years of age might not have been that good, since he died of pneumonia about a month after he took office. Boller, Jr., *Presidential*

Campaigns, 66, 72.

52.   Such flag banners were used in U.S. election campaigns until the early decades of the twentieth century, by which time many state legislatures had passed laws that prohibited defacing the American flag. Robert Justin Goldstein, *Flag Burning & Free Speech: The Case of Texas v. Johnson* (Lawrence, Kans.: University Press of Kansas, 2000), 13; and Edmund B. Sullivan, *Collecting Political Americana* (New York: Crown, 1980), 129.

53.   Boller, Jr., *Presidential Campaigns*, 69–70.

54.   See Peter F. Nardulli, Jon K. Dalager, and Donald E. Greco, "Voter Turnout in U.S. Presidential Elections: An Historical View and Some Speculation," *PS: Political Science and Politics* 29 (1996): 482; and *Presidential Elections Since 1789*, 104, 177.

55.   The election-year print of General William Henry Harrison on horseback, designed in 1840, is similar to one of General Andrew Jackson, created by Nathaniel Currier, which was printed no earlier than 1835. In fact, the horses in both prints strike the same pose, except for the tail being different. The Jackson print is housed in the Library of Congress.

56.   Melder, *Hail to the Candidate*, 75–89, 91; and Robert Gray Gunderson, *The Log-Cabin Campaign* (Lexington, Ky.: University of Kentucky Press, 1957), 128.

57.   Gunderson, *Log-Cabin Campaign*, 4.

58.   Ibid., 156–157.

59.   DeGregorio, *Complete Book*, 192, 201–202.

60.   See Republican Party, "The Republican Party Platform, 1860," http://www.harpers.org/Re publicanNationalConvention.html; and DeGregorio, *Complete Book*, 217.

61.   *New York Times*, "The Presidential Campaign," September 13, 1860, http://proquest.com.

62.   Ibid.

63.   R. J. Brown, "Abe Lincoln's Campaign Newspaper," http://www.historybuff.com/library/re frailsplit.html.

64.   Ibid.

65.   Kathleen Hall Jamieson, *Packaging the Presidency: A History and Criticism of Presidential Campaign Advertising*, 3rd ed. (New York: Oxford University Press, 1996), 15.

66.   Melder, *Hail to the Candidate*, 108.

67.   James M. McPherson, *Battle Cry of Freedom: The Civil War Era* (New York: Ballantine Books, 1988), 222–224, 232; and DeGregorio, *Complete Book*, 234.

68.   McPherson, *Battle Cry of Freedom*, 232; and *Presidential Elections Since 1789*, 109, 182.

69.   James M. McPherson, "Abraham Lincoln," in McPherson, *'To the Best of My Ability,'* 120.

70.   Melder, *Hail to the Candidate*, 12.

71.   Arthur M. Schlesinger, Jr., *Running for President: The Candidates and Their Images, 1789–1896*, vol. 1 (New York: Simon & Schuster, 1994), 279.

72.   See *Presidential Elections Since 1789*, 110, 183.

73.   See David Herbert Donald, *Lincoln* (New York: Touchstone, 1995), 553; and McPherson, *Battle Cry of Freedom*, 716, on the 1864 U.S. presidential election campaign.

74.   See Nardulli, Dalager, and Greco, "Voter Turnout," 482; and Melder, *Hail to the Candidate*, 113.

75.   As Bernard F. Reilly, Jr., pointed out, this is a pun, with "See More" standing for Seymour, "Rads" for the Radical Republicans, and "bottled up" possibly for Grant's alcoholism. Reilly, Jr., *American Political Prints*, 582.

76.   James Grant Wilson and John Fiske, eds., "Horatio Seymour," in *Appleton's Cyclopedia of American Biography*, http://famousamericans.net/horatioseymour; Donald, *Lincoln*, 449–450; and McPherson, *Battle Cry of Freedom*, 609.

77.   DeGregorio, *Complete Book*, 322–323, 325–326; and U.S. Library of Congress, "Campaign of 1884. Tract No. 3. Why! Why!! Oh, Why!!!" http://hdl.loc.gov/loc.rbc/rbpe.2380370.

78.   *New York Times*, "Guarding Their Posters," November 2, 1888, http://proquest.com.

79.   H. K. Thurber, "A Fable," http://hdl.loc.gov/loc.rbc/rbpe.23804900.

80. Melder, *Hail to the Candidate*, 116.
81. See People's Party, "Populist Party Platform (1892)," http://www2.wwnorton.com/area4/search .htm; and *Presidential Elections Since 1789*, 117, 190.
82. People's Party, "Populist Party Platform (1892)."
83. Democratic Party, "The Democratic Platform" (1896)," http://www.iath.Virginia.edu/semi nar/unit8/demplat.htm.
84. William Jennings Bryan, "'Cross of Gold' Speech July 9, 1896, at the Democratic National Convention, Chicago," http://www.usconstitution.com/CrossofGold.htm.
85. Louis W. Koenig, "Grover Cleveland: The Law Man," in Beschloss, *American Heritage Illustrated History*, 285–288.
86. Ibid., 288–291.
87. Bryan, "'Cross of Gold' Speech."
88. Donald Young (revised by John Milton Cooper, Jr.), "William McKinley: Bridge to a New Century," in Beschloss, *American Heritage Illustrated History*, 305–308; DeGregorio, *Complete Book*, 361; and Morton Keller, "William McKinley," in McPherson, *'To the Best of My Ability,'* 174, 176. John D. Rockefeller's Standard Oil Company, *alone*, gave the McKinley campaign $250,000. Gilbert C. Fite, "Election of 1896," in Schlesinger, Jr., and Israel, *History of American Presidential Elections*, vol. 5, 1817. Hanna and the Republican Party distributed about 200 million pieces of campaign material to a nation of 15 million voters; Robert B. Westbrook, "Politics as Consumption: Managing the Modern American Election," in *The Culture of Consumption: Critical Essays in American History, 1880–1980*, ed. Richard Wightman Fox and T. J. Jackson Lears (New York: Pantheon Books, 1983), 153.
89. Michael E. McGerr, *The Decline of Popular Politics: The American North, 1865–1928* (New York: Oxford University Press, 1986), 145.
90. David Welch, "Advertising," in Cull, Culbert, and Welch, *Propaganda and Mass Persuasion*, 6.
91. Thomas Beer, *Hanna* (New York: Alfred A. Knopf, 1929), 165.
92. Ibid., 165–166.
93. H. Wayne Morgan, *William McKinley and His America* (Syracuse, N.Y.: Syracuse University Press, 1963), 229.
94. Melder, *Hail to the Candidate*, 122. On the Sunday before the 1896 election, Hanna had the McKinley campaign sponsor a flag day. Huge parades were held in the presence of prominent union veterans. Patrick J. Kelley, "The Election of 1896 and the Restructuring of Civil War Memory," *Civil War History* 49 (2003): 278–279; and U.S. Flag Depot, "The History of Flag Day," http://www.usflag.org/history/flagday.html.
95. Young, "William McKinley," 307; Jamieson, *Packaging the Presidency*, 16–17; and Boller, Jr., *Presidential Campaigns*, 101–102.
96. Jamieson, *Packaging the Presidency*, 17.
97. William J. Bryan, *The First Battle: A Story of the Campaign of 1896* (Chicago: W. B. Conkey, 1896), 618.
98. Boller, Jr., *Presidential Campaigns*, 170; and Jamieson, *Packaging the Presidency*, 17.
99. Therese Thau Heyman, *Posters American Style* (Washington, D.C.: National Museum of American Art, Smithsonian Institution, 1998), 70, 85; and Barnicoat, *Posters*, 42.
100. *New York Times*, "A Campaign of Education," July 26, 1896, http://proquest.com.
101. Bloom, *Public Relations*, 11; Boller, Jr., *Presidential Campaigns*, 171; and Fite, "Election of 1896," 1816.
102. Bloom, *Public Relations*, 11; and Ohio Historical Society, "National Presidential Election Results," http://www.ohiokids.org/oe/bbb/21.html.
103. See Nardulli, Dalager, and Greco, "Voter Turnout," 482.
104. See *Presidential Elections Since 1789*, 118, 191.
105. Untitled report, quoted in Melder, *Hail to the Candidate*, 133.
106. E. B. Sullivan, *Collecting Political Americana*, 126.

107. See advertisement in ibid., 144.
108. McGerr, *Decline of Popular Politics*, 162.
109. See *Presidential Elections Since 1789*, 119.
110. See ibid., 121.
111. Paolo E. Coletta, "Election of 1908," in Schlesinger, Jr., and Israel, *History of American Presidential Elections*, vol. 5, 2070–2071, 2080; and Boller, Jr., *Presidential Campaigns*, 188.
112. See *Presidential Elections Since 1789*, 120.
113. William H. Harbaugh, "Election of 1904," in Schlesinger, Jr., and Israel, *History of American Presidential Elections*, vol. 5, 1965, 1975–1976, 1987.
114. DeGregorio, *Complete Book*, 416–417; and *New York Times*, "Taft the Target of Wilson's Shafts," October 18, 1912, http://proquest.com.
115. *New York Times*, "Taft the Target."
116. Ibid.
117. See *Presidential Elections Since 1789*, 122, 195.
118. Arthur S. Link and William M. Leary, Jr., "Election of 1916," in Schlesinger, Jr., and Israel, *History of American Presidential Elections 1789–2001*, vol. 6, 2255.
119. See ibid., 2246–2248, 2255, 2257–2258, 2260–2262, 2264–2265.
120. Frank I. Luntz, *Candidates, Consultants, and Campaigns: The Style and Substance of American Electioneering* (New York: Basil Blackwell, 1988), 146–147.
121. Michael Beschloss, "A Campaign Portfolio," in Beschloss, *American Heritage Illustrated History*, 251.
122. McGerr, *Decline of Popular Politics*, 166.
123. Charles Evens Hughes, quoted in ibid., 167–168.
124. See *Presidential Elections Since 1789*, 122–123, 196.
125. Milton Esberg, chairman of the California Republican Committee, denied these charges, and indicated that over ten thousand dollars had been spent on posters that promoted Hughes. *New York Times*, "Johnson Blames Old Guard Leaders," November 12, 1916, http://proquest.com; and Link and Leary, "Election of 1916," 2257.
126. Link and Leary, "Election of 1916," 2269.
127. Donald R. McCoy, "Election of 1920," in Schlesinger, Jr., and Israel, *History of American Presidential Elections*, vol. 6, 2371, 2373; David Burner, "Election of 1924," in Schlesinger, Jr., and Israel, *History of American Presidential Elections*, vol. 6, 2486; Lawrence H. Fuchs, "Election of 1928," in *History of American Presidential Elections 1789–2001*, vol. 7, eds. Schlesinger, Jr., and Israel, 2605; and DeGregorio, *Complete Book*, 454, on the 1924 campaign; also see Donald MacGregor, "Ten Million To Be Spent in Presidential Quest," *New York Times*, September 7, 1924, http://proquest.com, on campaign spending from 1916 to 1924.
128. Clara Savage, "Money Bags in Campaign," *New York Times*, October 3, 1920, http://proquest.com.
129. *New York Times*, "Harding at Raritan for Week-end Rest," July 27, 1920, http://proquest.com.
130. MacGregor, "Ten Million."
131. John A. Morello, *Selling the President, 1920: Albert D. Lasker, Advertising, and the Election of Warren G. Harding* (Westport, Conn.: Praeger, 2001), 15.
132. See ibid, 65–66; and MacGregor, "Ten Million."
133. Morello, *Selling the President, 1920*, 66.
134. In 1980, George H. W. Bush (a candidate for the U.S. vice presidency) criticized the incumbent president, President Jimmy Carter, for his "flip flop[s]" on United Nations resolutions. A. O. Sulzberger, Jr., "Bush Begins a Series of Televised Campaign Programs," *New York Times*, October 18, 1980, http://proquest.com; in 1988, he attacked his Democratic opponent, Michael Dukakis, for his "flip flop[s]" on foreign investment in U.S. companies. Gerald M. Boyd, "Bush Says Rival Wants to Exploit U.S. Fears," *New York Times*, October 12,

1988, http://proquest.com; in 2004, Bush's son, George W., repeatedly called the Democratic candidate, John Kerry, a "flip-flopper" on foreign policy. Timothy Garton Ash, "Comment & Analysis: Great Vote, Grisly Result," *Guardian* (Manchester, UK), November 4, 2004, http://proquest.com.

135. John Zogby, quoted in Damien Cave, "Flip-Flopper," *New York Times*, December 26, 2004, http://proquest.com.

136. Richard Joseph Cinclair, "Will H. Hays: Republican Politician" (PhD diss., Ball State University, 1969), 127; *New York Times*, "Harding at Raritan"; Morello, *Selling the President, 1920*, 6, 27, 50, 53, 56; and *New York Times*, "Will Boom Harding."

137. Cinclair, *Will H. Hays*, 127.

138. *New York Times*, "15,000 Spellbinders Gathered for Harding," July 27, 1920, http://proquest.com.

139. Richard V. Oulahan, "Smith Visit Spurs the Oklahomans," *New York Times*, October 2, 1928, http://proquest.com.

140. MacGregor, "Ten Million."

141. Ibid.

142. Melder, *Hail to the Candidate*, 12.

143. Boller, Jr., *Presidential Campaigns*, 213–214; DeGregorio, *Complete Book*, 454, 470; and Richard M. Pious, "The Campaigns and Inaugural Addresses," in McPherson, *'To the Best of My Ability,'* 412.

144. Edwin Diamond and Stephen Bates, *The Spot: The Rise of Political Advertising on Television*, 3rd ed. (Cambridge, Mass.: MIT Press, 1992), 36.

145. Fuchs, "Election of 1928," 2607.

146. See *Presidential Elections Since 1789*, 124–126.

147. Burner, "Election of 1924," 2480, 2486.

148. See Boller, Jr., *Presidential Campaigns*, 214; and Nardulli, Dalager, and Greco, "Voter Turnout," 482.

149. Morello, *Selling the President, 1920*, 64–65.

150. Richard V. Oulahan, "New Hoover Group Seeks Kitchen Vote," *New York Times*, August 17, 1928, http://proquest.com.

151. Ibid.

152. *New York Times*, "Sees Women in State Rallying for Smith," September 23, 1928, http://proquest.com.

Chapter Three

1. Jamieson, *Packaging the Presidency*, 20–21.

2. *New York Times*, "National Campaigns May Cost $15,000,000," July 28, 1924, http://proquest.com.

3. Al Smith (radio address, 1928), in Al Smith, *Campaign Addresses* (Washington, D.C.: Democratic National Committee, 1929), 310, quoted in Jamieson, *Packaging the Presidency*, 21.

4. Crowley, "The Propaganda Poster," 109.

5. See Fischer, *Tippecanoe and Trinkets Too*, 191, on paper and printing changes.

6. Boller, Jr., *Presidential Campaigns*, 224.

7. Jamieson, *Packaging the Presidency*, 20–21.

8. See Fuchs, "Election of 1928," 2605, on Hoover's campaign strategy; see Boller, Jr., *Presidential Campaigns*, 224, on Hoover and Smith on the radio and in person.

9. Boller, Jr., *Presidential Campaigns*, 224.

10. Saul Braun (Revised by Lewis L. Gould), "Herbert Clark Hoover," in Beschloss, *American*

Heritage Illustrated History, 373–374; and DeGregorio, *Complete Book,* 488.

11.   Arthur Krock, "The Campaign Gets Under Way," *New York Times,* September 19, 1932, http:// proquest.com.

12.   FDR's percentages of the popular vote were 18 percent in 1932, 24 percent in 1936, 10 percent in 1940, and 7.5 percent in 1944. *Presidential Elections Since 1789,* 127–130, 200–203.

13.   See ibid., 127.

14.   *New York Times,* "Major Parties Unfit, Says Norman Thomas," October 13, 1932, http:// proquest.com.

15.   Ibid.

16.   Bloom, *Public Relations,* 13–14; and Westbrook, "Politics as Consumption," 153.

17.   Bloom, *Public Relations,* 14.

18.   Roy V. Peel and Thomas C. Donnelly, *The 1932 Campaign: An Analysis* (1935; repr., New York: Da Capo Press, 1973), 54–55.

19.   *New York Times,* "Party 'Mills' Ready for 1932 Publicity," February 21, 1932, http://pro quest.com; and Bloom, *Public Relations,* 14.

20.   Jamieson, *Packaging the Presidency,* 21.

21.   Orrin E. Dunlap, Jr., "Hoover, Roosevelt and Radio," *New York Times,* July 10, 1932, http:// proquest.com; Jamieson, *Packaging the Presidency,* 19; and Marvin R. Bensman, "The History of Broadcasting, 1920–1960," http://www.people.memphis.edu/~mbensman.

22.   Dunlap, "Hoover, Roosevelt and Radio."

23.   "Acceptance Speech by Governor Franklin D. Roosevelt, Chicago, July 2, 1932," in Schlesinger, Jr., and Israel, *History of American Presidential Elections,* vol. 7, 2791.

24.   John Carlile, quoted in Dunlap, "Hoover, Roosevelt and Radio."

25.   Ibid.

26.   *New York Times,* "Hoover Attack Sweeping," November 1, 1932, http://proquest.com.

27.   Ibid.

28.   Frank Freidel, "Election of 1932," in Schlesinger, Jr., and Israel, *History of American Presidential Elections,* vol. 7, 2733.

29.   Ibid., 2733.

30.   Turner Catledge, "Republicans to Launch a New Kind of Campaign," *New York Times,* August 16, 1936, http://proquest.com.

31.   Ibid.

32.   William E. Leuchtenburg, "Election of 1936," in Schlesinger, Jr., and Israel, *History of American Presidential Elections,* vol. 7, 2817.

33.   Ibid., 2820.

34.   Legacy Historical Antiques, e-mail message to author, January 27, 2005.

35.   DeGregorio, *Complete Book,* 491.

36.   See Fischer, *Tippecanoe and Trinkets Too,* 216–217, 220.

37.   See Ted Hake, *Hake's Guide to Presidential Campaign Collectibles: An Illustrated Price Guide to Artifacts from 1789–1988* (Radnor, Pa.: Wallace-Homestead, 1992), 138–140.

38.   See Fischer, *Tippecanoe and Trinkets Too,* 493; Leon Friedman, "Election of 1944," in Schlesinger, Jr., and Israel, *History of American Presidential Elections,* vol. 8, 3029–3031; and Jamieson, *Packaging the Presidency,* 26, on issues and radio broadcasts during the 1944 U.S. presidential election campaign.

39.   "Text of Statement on the PAC by Sidney Hillman to the House Campaign Committee," *New York Times,* August 29, 1944, http://proquest.com.

40.   The CIO-PAC had 31,250 copies of "Our Friend" printed, and there were 1,000 billboards of the design. Kenneth W. Prescott, *The Complete Graphic Works of Ben Shahn* (New York: Quadrangle/*New York Times,* 1973), 124–129.

41.   *New York Times,* "Farm Group Set Up to Fight 4th Term," September 23, 1944, http:// proquest.com.

42. *New York Times*, "The First Lady Receives Democratic Campaign Poster," September 9, 1944, http://proquest.com.

43. Frances Tumulty Van Riper, "Democratic Poster Shocks," *New York Times*, September 13, 1944, http://proquest.com.

44. Bensman, "History of Broadcasting, 1920–1960."

45. Fischer, *Tippecanoe and Trinkets Too*, 226.

46. Ibid.

47. See Richard S. Kirkendall, "Election of 1948," in Schlesinger, Jr., and Israel, *History of American Presidential Elections*, vol. 8, 3100–3103, for more on these two minor parties in this election.

48. Jamieson, *Packaging the Presidency*, 33–34.

49. Kirkendall, "Election of 1948," 3125–3126, 3129–3130.

50. See ibid., 3122–3126, on the campaigns of Truman, Dewey, and Wallace in 1948.

51. See *Presidential Elections Since 1789*, 130–131, 204.

52. Melder, *Hail to the Candidate*, 148.

53. Ibid., 148, 162; and Jamieson, *Packaging the Presidency*, 44.

54. Barton J. Bernstein, "Election of 1952," in Schlesinger, Jr., and Israel, *History of American Presidential Elections*, vol. 8, 3225; and W. H. Lawrence, "Eisenhower Urged to Use 'Amateurs,'" *New York Times*, August 1, 1952, http://proquest.com.

55. Lawrence, "Eisenhower Urged to Use 'Amateurs.'"

56. See Fischer, *Tippecanoe and Trinkets Too*, 242.

57. "Party Platforms of 1952: Republican Platform," in Schlesinger, Jr., and Israel, *History of American Presidential Elections*, vol. 8, 3281.

58. DeGregorio, *Complete Book*, 534.

59. S. Kelley, Jr., *Professional Public Relations*, 156.

60. Kevin Goldman, *Conflicting Accounts: The Creation and Crash of the Saatchi & Saatchi Advertising Empire* (New York: Simon & Schuster, 1997), 59.

61. Ibid.

62. "Party Platforms of 1952: Democratic Platform," in Schlesinger, Jr., and Israel, *History of American Presidential Elections*, vol. 8, 3268.

63. *New York Times*, "The Campaign," November 2, 1952, http://proquest.com.

64. Sabato, *Rise of Political Consultants*, 114.

65. Clayton Knowles, "Truman Is Defiant of 'Big-Money Boys,'" *New York Times*, October 28, 1952, http://proquest.com.

66. C. P. Trussell, "$2,214,087 Is Spent in G.O.P. Campaign," *New York Times*, November 1, 1952, http://proquest.com; Jamieson, *Packaging the Presidency*, 94; and Anthony Leviero, "Truman Calls U.S. to Guard Its Gains," *New York Times*, October 29, 1952, http://proquest.com.

67. See Jamieson, *Packaging the Presidency*, 57.

68. "Party Platforms of 1952: Democratic Platform," 3268.

69. Ibid., 3283.

70. Bernstein, "Election of 1952," 3248.

71. Ibid., 3249–3250, 3260.

72. *Presidential Elections Since 1789*, 132, 205; and Bloom, *Public Relations*, 72.

73. *Presidential Elections Since 1789*, 133, 206; and Jamieson, *Packaging the Presidency*, 94.

74. *New York Times*, "Campaign."

75. Bernstein, "Election of 1952," 3258.

76. Ibid.

77. Herbert R. Craig, "Distinctive Features of Radio-TV in the 1952 Presidential Campaign" (master's thesis, University of Iowa, 1954), 104.

78. Robert Bendiner, "How Much Has TV Changed Campaigning?" *New York Times*, November

8, 1952, http://proquest.com.

79. Ibid.; and Jamieson, *Packaging the Presidency*, 41, 46.

80. Bendiner, "How Much Has TV Changed Campaigning?"; Bloom, *Public Relations*, 53–54; and Jamieson, *Packaging the Presidency*, 86.

81. Melder, *Hail to the Candidate*, 171.

82. See Young & Rubicam, Inc., *Records of "Citizens for Eisenhower," 1952–1961*, http://www.eisenhower.archives.gov/listofholdingshtml/listofholdingsy/youngrebicamincrecords of195261.pdf."

83. Jamieson, *Packaging the Presidency*, 110.

84. Gladwin Hill, "California Leans Strongly to G.O.P.," *New York Times*, October 21, 1956, http://proquest.com.

85. Fischer, *Tippecanoe and Trinkets Too*, 236.

86. Ibid.

87. See Jay Bryant, "Paid Media Advertising," in *Campaigns and Elections American Style*, ed. James A. Thurber and Candice J. Nelson (Boulder, Colo.: Westview Press, 1995), 90, on billboards and name recognition (or identification) of U.S. candidates.

88. Theodore H. White, *The Making of the President 1960* (New York: Atheneum, 1961), 279.

89. *New York Times*, "Both Candidates Retain Backers," September 28, 1960, http://proquest .com.

90. *New York Times*, "Excerpts from Editorials on TV Debate," September 28, 1960, http:// proquest.com.

91. *New York Times*, "Blue and Gray Clothes Chosen by Candidates," September 27, 1960, http:// proquest.com; and White, *Making of the President 1960*, 286.

92. White, *Making of the President 1960*, 286, 289.

93. Richard F. Shepard, "73,500,000 Viewers Estimated To Have Seen Television Debate," *New York Times*, September 28, 1960, http://proquest.com; and "The Votes in the 1960 Election," in ed. Schlesinger, Jr., and Israel, *History of American Presidential Elections*, vol. 9, 3562.

94. White, *Making of the President 1960*, 290.

95. Ibid., 294.

96. See Bernstein, "Election of 1952," 3243–3244; and Malcolm Moos, "Election of 1956," in Schlesinger, Jr., and Israel, *History of American Presidential Elections*, vol. 8, 3346–3348.

97. See Bloom, *Public Relations*, 77, and Jamieson, *Packaging the Presidency,* 139.

98. *New York Times*, "G.O.P. Women Meet to Map Strategy," September 14, 1960, http:// proquest.com.

99. Alan L. Otten, "Nixon Clubs Spread Throughout U.S. with Washington Prodding," *New York Times*, June 9, 1960, http://proquest.com.

100. Richard Nixon (speech, Chicago, Ill. area, October 29, 1960), quoted in Harrison E. Salisbury, "Nixon's Attacks Become Harsher," *New York Times*, October 30, 1960, http:// proquest.com.

101. Ibid.

102. See *Presidential Elections Since 1789*, 134, 207.

103. Theodore S. Sorensen, "Election of 1960," in Schlesinger, Jr., and Israel, *History of American Presidential Elections*, vol. 9, 3466–3468.

104. See John Barlow Martin, "Election of 1964," in Schlesinger, Jr., and Israel, *History of American Presidential Elections*, vol. 9, 3586; and DeGregorio, *Complete Book*, 574–575.

105. DeGregorio, *Complete Book*, 570.

106. Charles Mohr, "Johnson, in South, Decries 'Radical' Goldwater Ideas," *New York Times*, October 27, 1964, http://proquest.com.

107. "Acceptance Speech by Senator Barry Goldwater, San Francisco, July 17, 1964," in Schlesinger, Jr., and Israel, *History of American Presidential Elections*, vol. 9, 3669.

108. Bensman, "History of Broadcasting, 1920–1960."

109. Charles Mohr, "Initial Campaign Buoys Goldwater," *New York Times*, September 13, 1964, http://proquest.com.

110. Pete Hamill, "When the Client Is a Candidate," *New York Times*, October 25, 1964, http://proquest.com; and Bloom, *Public Relations*, 163.

111. Hamill, "When the Client Is a Candidate"; and Nan Robertson, "Johnson and Goldwater Open Television Campaigns, with Both Planning Big Outlays," *New York Times*, September 15, 1964, http://proquest.com.

112. Hamill, "When the Client Is a Candidate"; and Robertson, "Johnson and Goldwater."

113. Such specific appeals in television spots during election campaigns are rare, with one study suggesting that only about one in twenty political TV election spots are in this category. Richard Joslyn, "Political Advertising and the Meaning of Elections," in *New Perspectives on Political Advertising*, ed. Lynda Lee Kaid, Dan Nimmo, and Keith R. Sanders (Carbondale, Ill.: Southern Illinois University Press, 1986), 146.

114. See *Presidential Elections Since 1789*, 135.

115. See Leonard Sloane, "Advertising: Democrats, G.O.P. Woo Voters," *New York Times*, September 27, 1964, http://proquest.com.

116. Sabato, *Rise of Political Consultants*, 115.

117. Diamond and Bates, *Spot*, 124.

118. Ibid., 112–114.

119. The term, "responsive chord," is reflected in the title of one of his books. See Tony Schwartz, *The Responsive Chord* (Garden City, N.Y.: Anchor Press, 1973).

120. See Diamond and Bates, *Spot*, 124, 126–127.

121. Robertson, "Johnson and Goldwater."

122. Diamond and Bates, *Spot*, 125.

123. Jamieson, *Packaging the Presidency*, 203–204.

124. Melder, *Hail to the Candidate*, 173–174.

125. Diamond and Bates, *Spot*, 131–132.

126. See Theodore H. White, *The Making of the President 1968* (New York: Atheneum, 1969), 188–223.

127. See Victor Davis Hanson, *Carnage and Culture: Landmark Battles in the Rise of Western Power* (New York: Anchor Books, 2001), 389–439.

128. Ibid., 393, 402–405.

129. White, *Making of the President 1968*, 279.

130. Richard Nixon (press conference, November 1962), quoted in DeGregorio, *Complete Book*, 587.

131. White, *Making of the President 1968*, 143.

132. David S. Broder, "Election of 1968," in Schlesinger, Jr., and Israel, *History of American Presidential Elections*, vol. 9, 3739–3740.

133. Harrison E. Salisbury, "Nixon: Then and Now," *New York Times*, September 16, 1968, http://proquest.com; and Jamieson, *Packaging the Presidency*, 241.

134. Joe McGinniss, *The Selling of the President: The Classic Account of the Packaging of a Candidate* (New York: Penguin Books, 1969), 36, 47.

135. Sabato, *Rise of Political Consultants*, 115.

136. James Fraser, *The American Billboard 100 Years* (New York: Harry N. Abrams, 1997), 140–141.

137. See *Presidential Elections Since 1789*, 209.

138. See ibid., 136; and White, *Making of the President 1968*, 353.

139. See *Presidential Elections Since 1789*, 136, 209; and White, *Making of the President 1968*, 353–354.

140. White, *Making of the President 1968*, 354–359.

141. Ibid., 365–366.

142.   Salisbury, "Nixon: Then and Now."

143.   See *Presidential Elections Since 1789*, 137, 210.

144.   See Jamieson, *Packaging the Presidency*, 278–282, 285; and DeGregorio, *Complete Book*, 598– 599, on the Nixon campaign's "dirty tricks" and Watergate crisis.

145.   Bloom, *Public Relations*, 289.

146.   See ibid., 278–281; Jamieson, *Packaging the Presidency*, 287–289, 314–318; Richard C. Wade, "Election of 1972," in Schlesinger, Jr., and Israel, *History of American Presidential Elections*, vol. 10, 3884–3885; and DeGregorio, *Complete Book*, 589, 595–596, on the 1972 U.S. presidential campaign, polling, the Vietnam War issue, and final election results that year.

147.   See DeGregorio, *Complete Book*, 585, 590, on the military records of Nixon and McGovern.

148.   Jamieson, *Packaging the Presidency*, 297–299.

149.   Linda Charlton, "G.O.P. Tries Cheers and Chats on Youth," *New York Times*, October 21, 1972, http://proquest.com.

150.   Ibid.

151.   Broadsides also were designed to motivate students to volunteer. For example, one black-and-white broadside had a photograph of McGovern on it, and the headline, "The whole country has heard that STUDENTS WANT McGOVERN," followed by "PROVE IT! Take a walk! He was there when we needed him. NOW HE NEEDS US! Go to the McGovern for President headquarters."

152.   See *Presidential Elections Since 1789*, 138, 211.

153.   Jamieson, *Packaging the Presidency*, 343, 350.

154.   Betty Glad, "Election of 1976," in Schlesinger, Jr., and Israel, *History of American Presidential Elections*, vol. 10, 3956; and Jamieson, *Packaging the Presidency*, 349–350, 366.

155.   Jamieson, *Packaging the Presidency*, 346.

156.   Les Brown, "Ford and Carter Ad Consultants Call Short TV Commercials Best," *New York Times*, November 1, 1976, http://proquest.com.

157.   John Deardourff and Daniel Yankelovich, quoted in ibid.

158.   Glad, "Election of 1976," 3972.

159.   Ibid., 3966, 3969–3970; and Jamieson, *Packaging the Presidency*, 364–366.

160.   Jamieson, *Packaging the Presidency*, 376–377.

161.   Joseph Lelyveld, "President's Latest TV Commercials Portray Him as Father Figure Who Inspires Quiet Confidence," *New York Times*, September 29, 1976, http://proquest.com.

162.   Ibid.

163.   See Eric Pace, "Reagan Declares Canal Treaties Should Be Rejected by the Senate," *New York Times*, August 26, 1977, http://proquest.com; and Joseph B. Treaster, "Reagan Is Critical of Carter on Rights," *New York Times*, June 10, 1977, http://proquest.com; and Adam Clymer, "Reagan Rallies Foes of Canal Pact," *New York Times*, March 18, 1978, http://proquest.com, on the controversy over the Panama Canal treaties and on "human rights."

164.   See Jules Witcover, "Election of 1980," in Schlesinger, Jr., and Israel, *History of American Presidential Elections*, vol. 10, 4069.

165.   "Presidential Debate, Cleveland, October 28, 1980," in Schlesinger, Jr., and Israel, *History of American Presidential Elections*, vol. 10, 4134.

166.   See *Presidential Elections Since 1789*, 139.

167.   See ibid., 140.

168.   See ibid.,139–140, 212–213.

169.   Jamieson, *Packaging the Presidency*, 430.

170.   William V. Shannon, "Election of 1984," in Schlesinger, Jr., and Israel, *History of American Presidential Elections*, vol. 10, 4139–4141.

171.   Ibid., 4166–4167, 4170–4171.

172.   *Los Angeles Times* poll data reported in Gerald M. Pomper, Ross K. Baker, Charles E. Jacob, Scott Keeter, Wilson Carey McWilliams, and Henry A. Plotkin, *The Election of 1984: Reports*

and Interpretations (Chatham, N.J.: Chatham House, 1985), 96.

173. Jamieson, *Packaging the Presidency*, 451.

174. See *Presidential Elections Since 1789*, 141, 214.

175. "Second Presidential Debate, Los Angeles, California, October 13, 1988," in Schlesinger, Jr., and Israel, *History of American Presidential Elections*, vol. 10, 4275–4276.

176. Andrew Rosenthal, "More Mud Than Ever Slung Through the Mail," *New York Times*, November 5, 1988, http://proquest.com.

177. *New York Times*, "Bush Flier Features Convict," October 24, 1988, http://proquest.com.

178. Rosenthal, "More Mud Than Ever"; and Jamieson, *Packaging the Presidency*, 484.

179. Diamond and Bates, *Spot*, 281.

180. Herbert S. Parmet, "Election of 1988," in Schlesinger, Jr., and Israel, *History of American Presidential Elections*, vol. 11, 4242.

181. Gordon Reece, quoted in R. W. Apple, "The G.O.P. Advantage," *New York Times*, November 9, 1988, http://proquest.com.

182. The AFL-CIO issued a similar poster for Bill Clinton, the Democratic presidential candidate four years later, but in the latter poster, Clinton was smiling and looking directly at the viewers (and there was no American flag behind him). Both the 1988 and 1992 posters had a box, labeled "Yes" with a check mark in it. The Clinton poster is shown in Figure 3.29.

183. Paul R. Abramson, John H. Aldrich, and David W. Rhode, *Change and Continuity in the 1988 Election* (Washington, D.C.: Congressional Quarterly Press), 52.

184. *National Election Studies* survey data reported in ibid., 157.

185. Haiman, "Tale of Two Countries," 28.

186. Ronald Reagan (speeches, Springfield, Mo., and Little Rock, Ark., October 27, 1988), quoted in Julie Johnson, "Reagan Calls Vote Against Democrats Good Negative Campaigning," *New York Times*, October 28, 1988, http://proquest.com.

187. See Apple, Jr., "G.O.P. Advantage."

188. George H. Bush, "Before the Republican Convention Accepting Its Nomination for President, New Orleans, August 18, 1988," http://www.geocities.com/presidentialspeeches/nomahbbush88.htm.

189. Bush's broken promise was featured in Clinton television commercials, which incorporated videotape of Bush's pledge, made four years earlier. Stuart Elliot, "Candidates' Spots Are Not Created Equal," *New York Times*, November 3, 1992, http://proquest.com.

190. See Robin Toner, "G.O.P. Looks at Clinton Draft Record and Spies Willie Horton," *New York Times*, September 10, 1992, http://proquest.com; B. Drummond Ayres, Jr., "Clinton Confronts Draft Record In a Frank Address to Veterans," *New York Times*, August 26, 1992, http://proquest.com; and Thomas C. Palmer, Jr., "Campaigning Symbols Can Mean Everything," *Boston Globe*, August 30, 1992, http://proquest.com.

191. See Michael Wines, "How the President Lost: a Campaign of Disorganization and Disappointment," *New York Times*, November 29, 1992, http://proquest.com; and DeGregorio, *Complete Book*, 655, on the Iran-Contra controversy and its impact on the 1992 U.S. presidential election campaign.

192. Elizabeth Kolbert, "For the Most Negative Ads, Turn On the Nearest Radio," *New York Times*, October 30, 1992, http://proquest.com.

193. See L. Patrick Devlin, "Political Commercials in American Presidential Elections," in Kaid and Holtz-Bacha, *Political Advertising in Western Democracies,* 189.

194. See Robert Reinhold, "Brochures, Fliers, Polls, Ads: Politics as a Business Slumps," *New York Times*, October 20, 1992, http://proquest.com., on political advertising, computer technology, and printed paraphernalia in the 1988 and 1992 election campaigns.

195. See Rachel L. Holloway, "A Time for Change in American Politics: The Issue of the 1992 Presidential Election," in *The 1992 Presidential Campaign: A Communication Perspective*, ed. Robert E. Denton, Jr. (Westport, Conn.: Praeger, 1994), 143–144.

196.   Ohio Historical Society, "National Presidential Election Results."

197.   Michael Kelly, "'Did Not!' and 'Did So!' Frame the Tax Debate," *New York Times*, September 1, 1992, http://proquest.com.

198.   Lynda Lee Kaid, "Political Advertising in the 1992 Campaign," in Denton, Jr., *1992 Presidential Campaign*, 119.

199.   See Ohio Historical Society, "National Presidential Election Results"; "The Votes in the 1992 Election," in Schlesinger, Jr., and Israel, *History of American Presidential Elections*, vol. 11, 4466; and *Presidential Elections Since 1789*, 211–214.

200.   See Ohio Historical Society, "National Presidential Election Results."

201.   Alex Castellanos, quoted in James Bennet, "Liberal Use of 'Extremist' Is the Winning Strategy," *New York Times*, November 7, 1996, http://proquest.com.

202.   Gerald F. Seib and John Harwood, "Clinton's Support Drops Below 50%, and GOP's Chances in Congress Improve," *Wall Street Journal*, November 4, 1996, http://proquest.com.

203.   Ann Oldenburg, "Election '96 A Battle of 'Family Values,'" *USA Today*, August 7, 1996, http://proquest.com.

204.   James Bennet, "Another Tally In '96 Race: Two Months of TV Ads," *New York Times*, November 13, 1996, http://proquest.com.

205.   See Rita Kirk Whillock, "Digital Democracy: The '96 Presidential Campaign On-line," in *The 1996 Presidential Campaign: A Communication Perspective*, ed. Robert E. Denton, Jr. (Westport, Conn.: Praeger, 1998), 180; and *The Freedom Forum*, "Poll: A tenth of voters getting candidate info online," http://www.mediastudies.org/templates/document.asp?documentID=11448.

206.   *The Freedom Forum*, "Poll."

207.   Jason Fry, "The Age of Internet Politics," *Wall Street Journal*, November 6, 1996, http://proquest.com.

208.   Paul Ekman, quoted in Leah Garchik, "A Picture Is Worth a Thousand Votes," *San Francisco Chronicle*, October 13, 1996, http://proquest.com.

209.   Kevin Sack, "In Strategy Shift, Gore Ads Question Bush's Capability," *New York Times*, November 3, 2000, http://proquest.com.

210.   Ibid.; Bennett Roth, "Campaign 2000: Gore Seeks to Nail Down Support in Crucial States; TV Spots Question Bush's Ability to Lead," *Houston Chronicle*, November 3, 2000, http://proquest.com; Michael Kranish and Yvonne Abraham, "Campaigns Unleashing Ad Barrage," *Boston Globe*, November 2, 2000, http://proquest.com; and Lynda Lee Kaid, "Videostyle and Political Advertising Effects in the 2000 Presidential Campaign," in *The 2000 Presidential Campaign: A Communication Perspective*, ed. Robert E. Denton, Jr. (Westport, Conn.: Praeger, 2002), 186, 188–189.

211.   Sack, "In Strategy Shift"; Peter Marks, "The Advertising Campaign: Democrats Hammer at Bush's Texas Record," *New York Times*, October 24, 2000, http://proquest.com; Judy Keen, "Bush, Cheney Hit Trail with New Approach Ads; Put Emphasis on Education, Tough Choices," *USA Today*, August 21, 2000, http://proquest.com; and Kaid, "Videostyle and Political Advertising," 188.

212.   Kaid, "Videostyle and Political Advertising," 187.

213.   Tobe Berkovitz, quoted in Alexandra Marks, "In This Campaign, Image Really Is Everything," *Christian Science Monitor*, April 11, 2000, http://proquest.com; and Michael Finnegan, "Bush Calls Attack Ads 'Tongue-in-Cheek,'" *Los Angeles Times*, September 2, 2000, http://proquest.com.

214.   The campaigns of both candidates produced more issue spot ads for television (84 percent for Gore; 63 percent for Bush). Kaid, "Videostyle and Political Advertising," 187.

215.   Ibid.

216.   Ibid., 186.

217.   See Rita Kirk Whillock and David E. Whillock, "Digital Democracy 2000," in Denton, Jr.,

2000 Presidential Campaign, 168.

218. See ibid., 174; Andrew J. Glass, "Bush, Gore Battle with Divergent Online Strategies," *Atlanta Journal-Constitution*, September 5, 2000, http://proquest.com; and Michelle Johnson, "Ask What the Web Can Do for You," *Boston Globe*, October 18, 2000, http://proquest.com, on Internet developments during the 2000 U.S. presidential election campaign.

219. Roth, "Campaign 2000."

220. Kenneth M. Goldstein, "The 2000 Vote for President," *Wisconsin Interest* 10 (2001): 26–27, http://www.wpri.org/WIInterest/vol10no1/Goldstein10.1.pdf.

221. Linda Greenhouse, "Bush Prevails," *New York Times*, December 13, 2000, http://proquest .com.

222. Had a large portion of Nader's 22,188 votes in New Hampshire gone to Gore, that state's 4 electoral votes also would have given him the presidency, since the margin for Bush there was only about 7,000 votes. Nader received 2.7 percent of the popular vote nationally, and Buchanan obtained only 0.04 percent. "The Votes in the 2000 Election," in Schlesinger, Jr., and Israel, *History of American Presidential Elections*, vol. 11, 4784.

223. See ibid.; and *Presidential Elections Since 1789*, 113–141.

224. See *Presidential Elections Since 1789*, 134.

225. Bush-Cheney '04, "In Acceptance Speech, President Bush Shares His Plan for a Safer World & More Hopeful America," Republican National Convention, New York, September 2, 2004, http://www.4president.org/speeches/georgewbush2004convention.htm.

226. Ibid.

227. John Kerry, "Text of John Kerry's Acceptance Speech at the Democratic National Convention," July 29, 2004, http://www.washingtonpost.com/wp-dyn/articles/A25678-2004Jul29.html.

228. Ibid.

229. CNN.com, "Election Results," http://www.cnn.com/ELECTION/2004/pages/results/president.

230. For the actual 2004 TV spot ads, see Michigan State University, "Ease History Campaign Ads," http://msu.edu/Easetrial/castream.asp; also see *Chicago Tribune*, "Scare Tactics: Candidates Run a Campaign on Fear as Final Days Approach," October 20, 2004, http://proquest.com, and Kerry, "Text of John Kerry's Acceptance Speech."

231. *Chicago Tribune*, "Scare Tactics."

232. John F. Harris, "Kerry as a Rich Target," *Washington Post*, April 24, 2004, http://proquest .com.

233. Minnesota Public Radio, "Ad Spending in Presidential Race Triples That of 2000," http://news.minnesota.publicradio.org/features/2004/11/01_ap_adspending.

234. See Glen Justice, "In Final Days, Attacks are in the Mail and Below the Radar," *New York Times*, October 31, 2004, http://proquest.com; and Jeff Zeleny, "Bitter Duel Is Dead Even," *Chicago Tribune*, October 31, 2004, http://proquest.com, on the use of direct mail and other print campaigns in the 2004 election.

235. Scott Dadich, "What You See Is What You Get," *New York Times*, October 9, 2004, A19.

236. Ibid.

237. Ibid.

238. Ibid.

239. James A. Chappell, "Make Your Own Bush/Cheney Poster," http://rlrr.drum-corps.net/politics/112.

240. See David Lieberman, "Cable, Satellite, Net Grab Chunk of Election Ad Bucks," *USA Today*, August 18, 2004, http://proquest.com.

241. Ibid.

Chapter Four

1.   Jean Charlot and Monica Charlot, "France," in Butler and Ranney, *Electioneering*, 148–149; and Tim King, "Once Chirac's protégé, he is now his bitter rival. But could this wily, dynamic upstart who admires America, Tony Blair and successful businesses ever win the French presidency?" *Prospect*, July 2004, http://www.prospectmagazine.co.uk/article_details.php?id =6225.

2.   George Burton Adams, *Civilization during the Middle Ages, Especially in Relation to Modern Civilization* (New York: Charles Scribner's Sons, 1901), 307; and Maurice Keen, *The Pelican History of Medieval Europe* (Middlesex, UK: Penguin Books, 1968), 202, 250.

3.   See Augustin Thierry, *The Formation and Progress of the Tiers État, or Third Estate in France*, vol. 1, trans. Frances B. Wells (London: Thomas Bosworth, 1855), 212–213, 345; Malcolm Crook, *Elections in the French Revolution: An Apprenticeship in Democracy, 1789–1799* (Cambridge, UK: Cambridge University Press, 1996), 8; and Alistair Cole and Peter Campbell, *French Electoral Systems and Elections since 1789* (Aldershot, UK: Gower, 1989), 35, on the selection of delegates to the Estates-General, and on its reconvening in 1789.

4.   See Crook, *Elections in the French Revolution*, 83, 106.

5.   Ibid., 106.

6.   See ibid., 54, 89; and Richard Hooker, "Revolution and After: Tragedies & Farces—The First Revolution," *Washington State University*, http://www.wsu.edu:8080/~dee/REV/FIRST .HTM; and Richard Hooker, "Revolution and After: Tragedies & Farces—Radical Revolution," *Washington State University*, http://www.wsu.edu:8000/%7Edee/REV/RADI CAL.HTM, on the 1791–1793 period.

7.   Crook, *Elections in the French Revolution*, 118.

8.   Ibid., 120–121.

9.   See ibid., 141–142, 144–145, 147–156; and Hooker, "Radical Revolution," on the events from 1797 to 1799.

10.   Roger Price, *A Concise History of France* (New York: Cambridge University Press, 1993), 166.

11.   Miriam R. Levin, "Democratic Vistas—Democratic Media: Defining a Role for Printed Images in Industrializing France," *French Historical Studies* 18 (1993): 93.

12.   Ibid., 95; and David G. Wilkins, Bernard Schultz, and Katheryn M. Linduff, *Art Past Art Present*, 5th ed. (Upper Saddle River, N.J.: Pearson Prentice Hall, 2005), 424.

13.   Price, *Concise History of France*, 168–170.

14.   Priscilla Robertson, *Revolutions of 1848: A Social History* (1954; repr., Princeton, N.J.: Princeton University Press, 1967), 75.

15.   See Roger Price, *People and Politics in France, 1848–1870* (Cambridge, UK: Cambridge University Press, 2004), 1.

16.   See ibid., 1; Price, *Concise History of France*, 171–173, 176; Robertson, *Revolutions of 1848*, 55–56, 75–76, 78; Maurice Agulhon, "La Première Élection Présidentielle (1848)," *L'histoire*, February 1981, 50; and Jeremy D. Popkin, *A History of Modern France*, 2nd ed. (Upper Saddle River, N.J.: Prentice Hall, 2001), 111, on the 1848 Revolution in France, and its aftermath politically, through the April elections.

17.   See Price, *Concise History of France*, 174.

18.   See *Price, People and Politics in France*, 2, 255–256; and Popkin, *History of Modern France*, 114.

19.   See Price, *Concise History of France*, 180.

20.   See ibid., 174, 181; James Chastain, "Louis Napolean Bonaparte," *Encyclopedia of 1848 Revolutions*, http://www.cats.ohiou.edu/~chastain/ip/louisnap.htm; Robertson, *Revolutions of 1848*, 76, 83; and Price, *People and Politics in France*, 113–114, 241, 379, 399, on the rise of Louis Napoleon Bonaparte and political developments in France from the summer of 1848

through 1857.

21. Price, *People and Politics in France*, 65–66.
22. L. Girard (ed.), *Les élections de 1869*, v–vi, quoted in ibid., 66.
23. See Price, *People and Politics in France*, 66, 250, 254–255, 263, 386, 405, on political events in the 1860s.
24. See Price, *Concise History of France*, 185.
25. See Popkin, *History of Modern France*, 129.
26. See ibid., 129–130; Price, *People and Politics in France*, 109–110, 383; and Price, *Concise History of France*, 185–186, 190, on image management and balloting in 1869 and 1870, and the fall of the Second Empire.
27. See Popkin, *History of Modern France*, 133–136; Gallo, *Poster in History*, 64; and Price, *Concise History of France*, 192–193, on the 1871 election campaign, subsequent events, and Victor Hugo.
28. Otto van Bismarck initiated universal male suffrage in Germany, but the elected legislators did not have any real power (which resided with the army, emperor, and the ministers). Popkin, *History of Modern France*, 138–139.
29. Price, *Concise History of France*, 196–197; and James F. McMillan, *Twentieth-Century France: Politics and Society 1898–1991* (1992; repr., London: Arnold, 2004), 3.
30. Cole and Campbell, *French Electoral Systems*, 50.
31. *New York Times*, "France," March 5, 1876, http://proquest.com.
32. Ibid.
33. Ibid.
34. Levin, "Democratic Vistas," 90–91.
35. Popkin, *History of Modern France*, 140.
36. Ibid.
37. See ibid., 156–158; and Price, *Concise History of France*, 199, on political events in France in 1885 and 1893.
38. See Levin, "Democratic Vistas," 83; Haill, "Posters for Performance," 35–37; and Gallo, *Poster in History*, 71–180, on lithographic posters in late nineteenth-century France.
39. Price, *Concise History of France*, 201.
40. See ibid., 205–206.
41. See ibid., 201, 204–206, 225; Popkin, *History of Modern France*, 159, 179; and Rose Strunsky, "Singer of Socialist Songs Sets Paris Aflame," *New York Times*, June 30, 1912, http://proquest.com, on political events and propaganda in France at the end of the nineteenth century until the start of World War I.
42. See Price, *Concise History of France*, 225.
43. See ibid.; and Popkin, *History of Modern France*, 203, on the election of 1919.
44. See Albert Halter, "Paul Dermée and the Poster in France in the 1920s and Jean d'Ylen as 'Maître de l'Affiche Moderne,'" *Journal of Design History* 5 (1992): 41–43.
45. See McMillan, *Twentieth-Century France*, 94; and Cole and Campbell, *French Electoral Systems*, 66–67.
46. See Popkin, *History of Modern France*, 209–210, 216; Price, *Concise History of France*, 229; and McMillan, *Twentieth-Century France*, 96.
47. P. J. Philip, "New Life and Spirit Animate France," *New York Times*, March 11, 1928, http://proquest.com.
48. See ibid.; Price, *Concise History of France*, 223–224, 228; Popkin, *History of Modern France*, 205, 208–209, 216; and Emil Lengyel, "French Leaders Unite to Save the Franc," *New York Times*, August 1, 1926, http://proquest.com, on political events in France during the post-World War I period until the start of the Great Depression in 1931; see John Calvin Brown, "Broadcasting Is Called a Vital Campaign Vehicle," *New York Times*, November 4, 1928, http://proquest.com, on the use of posters in this period.

49.   See Price, *Concise History of France*, 234.
50.   See ibid., 234, 239–241. Popkin, *History of Modern France*, 216–217; and Percy J. Philipparis, "France Votes to Keep the Right to Vote," *New York Times*, April 26, 1936, http://proquest.com, on post-Depression French politics to mid-1935.
51.   See Price, *Concise History of France*, 239; Popkin, *History of Modern France*, 221; and Philipparis, "France Votes," on political media during the 1936 French election, and the results.
52.   See P. J. Philip, "Blum Grapples with 'The 200 Families,'" *New York Times*, June 14, 1936, http://proquest.com; Popkin, *History of Modern France*, 221–225, 227, 247; and Price, *Concise History of France*, 246, on the aftermath of the 1936 elections, the Popular Front government, and the French Communist Party.
53.   Popkin, *History of Modern France*, 230–232.
54.   Ibid., 235.
55.   Ira Wolfert, "Free French Win," *New York Times*, December 26, 1941, http://proquest.com.
56.   See Popkin, *History of Modern France*, 229, 240–241, on de Gaulle's criticism of France's military strategy in the 1930s, and on the liberation of the country in 1944.
57.   See ibid., 247.
58.   See Price, *Concise History of France*, 303.
59.   See ibid., 302–303; and Popkin, *History of Modern France*, 249, on the political developments in France from October 1945 to May 1946.
60.   Popkin, *History of Modern France*, 249; and Price, *Concise History of France*, 303.
61.   Price, *Concise History of France*, 303.
62.   See Popkin, *History of Modern France*, 250–251; McMillan, *Twentieth-Century France*, 157; Joseph A. Barry, "A Battle for the Mind of France's Worker," *New York Times*, December 11, 1949, http://proquest.com; and Lansing Warren, "100 Injured in Paris Fights as Workers and Police Clash," *New York Times*, September 16, 1948, http://proquest.com, on postwar political events and governmental policies, and on the RPF and posters.
63.   Barry, "Battle for the Mind."
64.   Ibid.
65.   Ibid.
66.   *Princeton University Library, Department of Rare Books and Special Collections*, "Paix et Liberté Collection," http://infoshare1.princeton.edu/libraries/firestone/rbsc/finding_aids/paixliberte/index.html.
67.   See ibid.; and René Sommer, "Paix et Liberté: la Quatrième République contre le PC," *L'histoire*, December 1981, 26, on the *Paix et Liberté* organization and its posters; see Barry, "Battle for the Mind," on the propaganda campaigns of the RPF, and other anti-Communist groups, around 1950.
68.   See McMillan, *Twentieth-Century France*, 157–158; and Price, *Concise History of France*, 309, on the election of 1951.
69.   See A. E. Jeffcoat, "Election in France," *New York Times*, June 14, 1951, http://proquest.com; Price, *Concise History of France*, 310–311, 313–315; and Popkin, *History of Modern France*, 257–258, 260, on political events in France from 1951 to 1956; see Philip M. Williams, *French Politicians and Elections 1951–1969* (New York: Cambridge University Press, 1970), 41–42, on posters and handbills during the election of 1956.
70.   See Popkin, *History of Modern France*, 260; McMillan, *Twentieth-Century France*, 162; and Price, *Concise History of France*, 317.
71.   See Price, *Concise History of France*, 320.
72.   See ibid., 317, 319–320; Martin Alexander, "Duty, Discipline and Authority: The French Officer Elites between Professionalism and Politics, 1900–1962," in *The Right in France: From Revolution to Le Pen*, ed. Nicholas Atkin and Frank Tallett (New York: I. B. Tauris, 2003), 145; Popkin, *History of Modern France*, 261; and McMillan, *Twentieth-Century France*, 164, on political developments in France in 1958; see Williams, *French Politicians and Elections*, 97–98,

on political posters and pamphlets that year.

73. See Price, *Concise History of France*, 320–321.

74. Ibid., 320.

75. See ibid., 320–321; *Wall Street Journal*, "Key Issue in French Vote: Which Candidate Likes De Gaulle Most?" November 13, 1958, http://proquest.com; Popkin, *History of Modern France*, 261; and Harry G. Simmons, *The French National Front: The Extremist Challenge to Democracy* (Boulder, Colo.: Westview Press, 2001), 45, on political events in France from 1958 through 1962.

76. See Henry Giniger, "French Voters Get Baffling Advice on How to Vote on Algerian Question," *New York Times*, April 3, 1962, http://proquest.com; and Williams, *French Politicians and Elections*, 43–44, on the use of posters and broadsides during the 1962 referendum campaign, and afterward.

77. See John Frears, *Parties and Voters in France* (New York: St. Martin's Press, 1996), 145; Susan Emmanuel, "France," *The Museum of Broadcast Communications*, http://www.museum.tv; and Charlot and Charlot, "France," 144, on the growing importance of television.

78. See Jonathan Watson, "The Internal Dynamics of Gaullism, 1958–69," in Atkin and Tallett, *Right in France*, 246; Price, *Concise History of France*, 247–248, 320; Charles Hauss, "You *Can* Pour New Wine into Old Bottles: The French Right since 1958," in Atkin and Tallett, *Right in France*, 281–282; and Frears, *Parties and Voters in France*, 75, 145–147, on political developments in France during the late 1950s and early 1960s, and the election of 1965.

79. Frears, *Parties and Voters in France*, 144; and Open Society Institute, *Television across Europe: Regulation, Policy and Independence*, vol. 2, October 11, 2005, 677–678, http://www.soros .org/initiatives/media/articles_publications/publications/eurotv_20051011.

80. Popkin, *History of Modern France*, 272.

81. Henry Tanner, "TV Transforming French Campaign," *New York Times*, November 26, 1965, http://proquest.com.

82. Ibid.

83. Williams, *French Politicians and Elections*, 211.

84. By 1988, only 4 percent of voters polled found posters to be among the most useful sources of information, whereas the press received 37 percent, radio 30 percent, private conversations 20 percent, opinion polls 12 percent, campaign-trail speeches 6 percent, and leaflets 4 percent. See Charlot and Charlot, "France," 145.

85. Ibid., 151.

86. See Tanner, "TV Transforming French Campaign"; and Frears, *Parties and Voters in France*, 146–147.

87. See Williams, *French Politicians and Elections*, 190; Charlot and Charlot, "France," 148; and Joe Napolitan, "AAPC and IAPC: Looking at the Differences—American Association of Political Consultants; International Association of Political Consultants," *Campaigns & Elections*, August 1995, 67, on the role of consultants in French politics.

88. See Simmons, *French National Front*, 58; and Frears, *Parties and Voters in France*, 173–174, 227.

89. See Simmons, *French National Front*, 58; Frears, *Parties and Voters in France*, 148; and John L. Hess, "Poster-Makers at the Beaux Arts Keep the Revolt Alive," *New York Times*, June 4, 1968, http://proquest.com, on the French election of 1968, the protests and posters that year, and the resignation of de Gaulle.

90. See Frears, *Parties and Voters in France*, 149, 151.

91. See ibid., 175–176.

92. See ibid., 148, 176–177, on the French elections of 1969 and 1973, and televised political appeals in this period.

93. Hauss, "You *Can* Pour New Wine," 282.

94. Ibid., 287.

95. See Frears, *Parties and Voters in France*, 151, 154, 157.

96. See ibid., 151, 155–157; and Price, *Concise History of France*, 342.

97. Price, *Concise History of France*, 342.

98. Manuel Álvarez-Rivera, "Election Resources on the Internet: Presidential Elections in France," http://www.electionresources.org/fr/president.php?election=1981.

99. Simmons, *French National Front*, 71.

100. See Frears, *Parties and Voters in France*, 180–181.

101. See ibid., 181; Richard Eder, "Communists Are Hoping to Pick Fruits of Mitterrand's Triumph," *New York Times*, June 12, 1981, http://proquest.com; and Simmons, *French National Front*, 71.

102. See Popkin, *History of Modern France*, 283.

103. See Roger Price, *A Concise History of France*, 2nd ed. (Cambridge, UK: Cambridge University Press, 2005), 429, 433, 442, 450.

104. See Frears, *Parties and Voters in France*, 169; Hauss, "You *Can* Pour New Wine," 283–284; and Simmons, *French National Front*, 41–45.

105. See Simmons, *French National Front*, 2–5, 62, 64, 72–73, 267; Jim Wolfreys, "Neither Right Nor Left? Towards an Integrated Analysis of the Front National," in Atkin and Tallett, *Right in France*, 265; and Price, *Concise History of France*, 361, on the impact of immigration on French politics, and Le Pen and his political party.

106. See Simmons, *French National Front*, 77, 79, 297; Frears, *Parties and Voters in France*, 185; and Price, *Concise History of France*, 2nd ed., 442, on Le Pen's use of media, particularly television, and on FN vote percentages, 1981–1997.

107. Popkin, *History of Modern France*, 284–285; and Frears, *Parties and Voters in France*, 76.

108. The *Union pour la Démocratie Française* was a coalition of smaller parties that had supported Giscard d'Estaing for president. See Frears, *Parties and Voters in France*, 41, 185; and Price, *Concise History of France*, 353 on the UDF and the 1986 elections and their aftermath.

109. Price, *Concise History of France*, 353.

110. Ibid., 352–353.

111. Richard Bernstein, "Split on Right Is an Asset to French Socialists," *New York Times*, February 9, 1986, http://proquest.com.

112. See Popkin, *History of Modern France*, 286; and Frears, *Parties and Voters in France*, 163.

113. See Price, *Concise History of France*, 356.

114. James M. Markham, "Mitterrand, Dispelling Doubts, Stands for Re-election," *New York Times*, March 23, 1988, http://proquest.com.

115. See Popkin, *History of Modern France*, 287; Frears, *Parties and Voters in France*, 160, 163; William Safire, "Staying the Same," *New York Times*, April 11, 1988, http://proquest.com; Haiman, "Tale of Two Countries," 35; Markham, "Mitterrand, Dispelling Doubts"; and James M. Markham, "Waiting for Raymond (What's the Rush?) Barre," *New York Times*, January 28, 1988, http://proquest.com, on the 1988 French presidential election.

116. See table of results of IFRES poll in Charlot and Charlot, "France," 142.

117. Ibid.

118. Jacques Séguéla, "Advertising: The Best Technique Invented for Communicating," *Media Mente*, March 4, 1998, http://www.mediamente.rai.it/mmold/english/bibliote/intervis/s/seguela.htm#link006.

119. Katherine Hale, "The Spinning of the Tale: Candidate and Media Orchestrations in the French and U.S. Presidential Elections," in Kaid, Gerstlé, and Sanders, *Mediated Politics in Two Cultures*, 202.

120. Kay Lawson and Colette Ysmal, "France: The 1988 Presidential Campaign," in *Electoral Strategies and Political Marketing*, ed. Shaun Bowler and David M. Farrell (New York: St. Martin's Press, 1992), 117.

121. Ibid., 104; Frears, *Parties and Voters in France*, 144; and Charlot and Charlot, "France," 152.

122. Alan Riding, "French Campaign Deepens Voters' Suspicions," *New York Times*, March 14, 1993, http://proquest.com.

123. See ibid.; *New York Times*, "Regulating Campaigns"; and Lawson and Ysmal, "France," 103–104, on the regulations controlling election billboards and posters.

124. Gail Russell Chaddock, "Power of the Poster Persists in Paris," *Christian Science Monitor*, April 18, 1995, http://proquest.com.

125. Instead of U.S.-style political advertisements, candidates in France typically use their free airtime to broadcast speeches and question-and-answer shows. Laurence Pantin, "Fifty Years of Political Ads," *Media Channel*, http://www.mediachannel.org/arts/perspectives/pol_ads/index.shtml; Haiman, "Tale of Two Countries," 31; and Johnston and Gerstlé, "Role of Television Broadcasts," 48.

126. Lawson and Ysmal, "France," 117.

127. Ibid.; and Haiman, "Tale of Two Countries," 30.

128. Lawson and Ysmal, "France," 117; and Jacques Gerstlé, Keith R. Sanders, and Lynda Lee Kaid, "Commonalities, Differences, and Lessons Learned from Comparative Communication Research," in Kaid, Gerstlé, and Sanders, *Mediated Politics in Two Cultures*, 278.

129. Haiman, "Tale of Two Countries," 30.

130. See ibid., 26, 28; Suzanne Daley, "A Rough Week on Chirac Campaign Trail," *New York Times*, March 8, 2002, http://proquest.com; and Lawson and Ysmal, "France," 103–104, on election campaign rules and practices, relating to various media, at the turn of the twenty-first century in France.

131. See Price, *Concise History of France*, 2nd ed., 438, 440.

132. See ibid., 438.

133. Craig R. Whitney, "Killing of Immigrant Likely to Hurt Far Right at French Polls," *New York Times*, February 28, 1995, http://proquest.com.

134. It has been noted that the Nazi Party used a similar slogan on one of its posters in 1931. The Nazi poster showed a hugely grotesque Jew towering over a group of workers, with the slogan "Five hundred thousand unemployed, four hundred thousand Jews, the solution is simple." Philip Gourevitch, "The Unthinkable," *New Yorker*, April 28, 1997, http://www.newyorker.com/archive.

135. See Whitney, "Killing of Immigrant"; and Wolfreys, "Neither Right Nor Left?" 270, on the 1995 French presidential election campaign, including the controversy surrounding the attack and murder committed by FN party members, and for the election results.

136. See Price, *Concise History of France*, 2nd ed., 450.

137. See Roger Cohen, "France Starts Divided Rule with Jospin as Premier," *New York Times*, June 3, 1997, http://proquest.com.

138. Victor Mallet and Raphael Minder, "'Don't Be Afraid to Dream,' Le Pen Tells Jubilant Far-Right Supporters of NATIONAL FRONT PARTY," *Financial Times of London*, April 22, 2002, http://proquest.com.

139. See Ministry of Foreign Affairs of France, "Elections and Referenda," http://ambafrance-au.org.

140. See Price, *Concise History of France*, 2nd ed., 449–450, for the results of 2002 presidential runoff and legislative elections.

141. Ministry of Foreign Affairs of France, "Elections and Referenda."

142. Charlot and Charlot, "France," 149–150.

143. Ibid., 150–151.

144. See Jane Kramer, "Round One: The Battle for France," *New Yorker*, April 23, 2007, 31, 35, on the positions of the candidates in the French 2007 presidential elections.

145. See Ministry of the Interior of France, "Resultats de l'Election Presidentielle," http://French.about.com; and Elaine Sciolino, "Sarkozy Wins in France and Vows Break with Past," *New York Times*, May 7, 2007, http://www.nytimes.com, for the results in 2007.

146.   See Peter Schwarz, "French Presidential Election: Extreme Right Candidate Le Pen Profits from the Bankruptcy of the 'Left,'" *Asian Tribune*, April 20, 2007, http://www.asiantribune .com; and Doug Sanders, "Style and Image Take Centre Stage as Voters Choose a New President," *Globe and Mail* (Toronto), April 21, 2007, http://www.theglobeandmail.com/ servlet/storyLAC.2007042FRANCE.21/Tpstory/TPInternational1/Europe, on the 2007 campaign.

Chapter Five

1.   David Butler and Dennis Kavanagh, *The British General Election of 1997* (London: St. Martin's Press, 1997), 57.
2.   See Nanci Lamb Roider, "Simon de Montfort and the Baronial Crisis of 1258–65," http:// www.triviumpublishing.com/articles/simondemontfort.html#19. Earlier parliaments, with elected representatives, probably met during the reign of Edward the Confessor in the early eleventh century, and definitely under William the Conqueror later in that century, according to Members of the House of Commons, *The Old & New Representation of the United Kingdom Contrasted; and an Account of the Various Alterations Made at the Late General Election* (Westminster, UK: Vacher & Son, 1833), vii–viii.
3.   Roider, "Simon de Montfort."
4.   Members of the House of Commons, "The Palace of Westminster," viii–ix, http://www.parlia ment.uk/works/palace.cfm.
5.   The election statutes in the fifteenth century were frequently ignored, however, allowing for the illegal exclusion of commoners. K. N. Houghton, "Theory and Practice in Borough Elections to Parliament during the Later Fifteenth Century," *Bulletin of the Institute of Historical Research* 39 (1966): 130, 133–134; and Clive Behagg, "The Government and the People: The Movement for Parliamentary Reform, 1815–32," in *Years of Expansion British History, 1815–1914*, 2nd ed., ed. Michael Scott-Baumann (London: Hodder & Stoughton, 2002), 33.
6.   Behagg, "Government and the People," 33.
7.   See David Boothroyd, *The History of British Political Parties* (London: Politico's Publishing, 2001), 42, 47, 151–152, 157, on the beginnings of the Liberal and Conservative parties.
8.   See Frank O'Gorman, *The Long Eighteenth Century: British Political and Social History 1688– 1832* (London: Arnold, 1997), 50.
9.   Michael C. McGee, "The Rhetorical Process in Eighteenth Century England," *Fragments*, http://www.mcgees.net/fragments/essays/archives/rhetorical_process_England.htm.
10.   See H. T. Dickinson, *The Politics of the People in Eighteenth-Century Britain* (New York: St. Martin's Press, 1995), 32; and Behagg, "Government and the People," 53.
11.   See Karen M. Ford, "Britain (Eighteenth Century)," in Cull, Culbert, and Welch, *Propaganda and Mass Persuasion*, 52; William B. Gwyn, *Democracy and the Cost of Politics in Britain* (London: Athlone Press, 1962), 8–9; and Dickinson, *Politics of the People*, 41, 49–55, on electioneering for House of Commons seats and suffrage in the sixteenth, seventeenth, and eighteenth centuries.
12.   Dickinson, *Politics of the People*, 45.
13.   See ibid., 32, 36–37, 41–42, 47–49; McGee, "Rhetorical Process"; Frank O'Gorman, *Voters, Patrons, and Parties: The Unreformed Electoral System of Hanoverian England 1734– 1832* (Oxford, UK: Clarendon Press, 1989), 68–78, 90–105, 129, 139–140; Linda Colley, *Britons: Forging the Nation 1707–1837* (New Haven, Conn.: Yale University Press, 2005), 342; Behagg, "Government and the People," 39, 41–42, 48–50; Gwyn, *Democracy and the Cost of Politics*, 17–18, 37; and *The Times* (of London), "Irish Electioneering," November 21, 1835, on political campaigns and meetings in England and Ireland in the eighteenth and early

nineteenth centuries.

14. See Colley, *Britons*, 345–347, 349; and Malcolm Pearce and Geoffrey Stewart, *British Political History 1867–2001*, 3rd ed. (London: Routledge, 2002), 18, on the rise of the Whigs, the Reform Act of 1832, and the Chartist movement.

15. Adam McNaughton, "The Ephemera of John Smith," http://special.lib.gla.ac.uk/exhibns/ephemera/political.html.

16. *British Parliamentary Election Results 1832–1885*, ed. F. W. S. Craig (London: Macmillan, 1977), 539.

17. Later (in 1840), as attorney general, Campbell prosecuted a Chartist leader, who had been charged with responsibility for an attack on the town of Newport, reputedly by about ten thousand armed men. The result was a verdict of guilty of high treason. John Campbell, *Life of John, Lord Campbell: Lord High Chancellor of Great Britain; Consisting of a Selection from His Autobiography, Diary, and Letters*, vol. 2, ed. Mary Hardcastle (London: John Murray, 1881), 29–30, 126, 132–135.

18. National Portrait Gallery, London, "James Aytoun," http://www.npg.org.uk; George Eastman House, "Hill & Adamson," http://www.geh.org/fm/hill/htmlsrc/m198123960004_ful.html; and National Library of Scotland, "Broadside Ballad Entitled 'Aytoun, The Friend of the People!!'," http://www.nls.uk/broadsides/broadside.cfm/id/16508/criteria/aytoun.

19. See *British Parliamentary Election Results 1832–1885*, 539.

20. Campbell, *Life of John, Lord Campbell*, 43–44.

21. See Behagg, "Government and the People," 121.

22. See H. J. Hanham, *The Reformed Electoral System in Great Britain, 1832–1914* (London: Historical Association, 1968), 22, 32, 35; David Cooper and Edward Townley, "Whigs, Liberals and Conservatives, 1846–68," in Scott-Baumann, *Years of Expansion*, 205; and Brendan Bruce, *Images of Power: How the Image Makers Shape Our Leaders* (London: Kogan Page, 1992), 14–15, on the effects of the Reform Act of 1867, particularly the growth of political parties and their promotional efforts.

23. See Nicholas J. Cull, "Elections (Britain)," in Cull, Culbert, and Welch, *Propaganda and Mass Persuasion*, 110–111; Hanham, *Reformed Electoral System*, 25–26; H. J. Hanham, *Elections and Party Management: Politics in the Time of Disraeli and Gladstone* (1959; repr., Sussex, UK: Harvest Press, 1978), 191, 197; Cooper and Townley, "Whigs, Liberals and Conservatives," 190; *New York Times*, "What the Victory Means," April 24, 1880, http://proquest.com; David Cooper and Edward Townley, "Gladstone and Disraeli, 1868–86," in Scott-Baumann, *Years of Expansion*, 236; and Wood, *Story of Advertising*, 13, on electioneering and reforms in Great Britain between 1861 and 1886, Gladstone's campaigning practices and advertising, and British elections during this period.

24. Hanham, *Elections and Party Management*, 201–202.

25. Ibid., 202.

26. *Preston Guardian*, "The Queen or the Pope?" November 28, 1868, quoted in ibid., 308;

27. See Trevor Lloyd, *The General Election of 1880* (London: Oxford University Press, 1968), 106, 158–159; Hanham, *Elections and Party Management*, 229, 232; and Pearce and Stewart, *British Political History*, 44.

28. See Hanham, *Elections and Party Management*, 249, 252, 305; Peter Hischberg, "Of Polls and Prejudice," *Haartetz.com*, April 3, 2005, http://www.haaretz.com; Trevor Lloyd, *General Election of 1880*, 105–107; and Pearce and Stewart, *British Political History*, 44, on broadsides, posters, and campaign issues in British elections in the second half of the nineteenth century.

29. See Cooper and Townley, "Gladstone and Disraeli," 247–248; Pearce and Stewart, *British Political History*, 50, 116–119; and *British Electoral Facts 1885–1975*, ed. F. W. S. Craig (London: Macmillan, 1976), 1, on the 1885 election.

30. See Pearce and Stewart, *British Political History*, 49.

31. See Cooper and Townley, "Gladstone and Disraeli," 248; Mike Byrne, "Britain in a New

Century: Labour, Liberals and Unionists," in Scott-Baumann, *Years of Expansion*, 402; and *British Electoral Facts 1885–1975*, 2, on the expansion of the electorate by 1886, its political consequences, and issues and results in the British election that year.

32. Pearce and Stewart, *British Political History*, 49.

33. See ibid., 47–49; and Cooper and Townley, "Gladstone and Disraeli," 247–249, on the weakening of the Liberal Party after 1886.

34. See *British Electoral Facts 1885–1975*, 6, for the results of the 1906 election.

35. See Boothroyd, *History of British Political Parties*, 115, 139, 141; and Clive Behagg and Michael Lynch, "Trade Unions and the Rise of Labour, 1867–1906," in Scott-Baumann, *Years of Expansion*, 355, 373, on the trade-union movement and the formation of the British Labour Party at the end of the nineteenth century.

36. See Edward Townley, "From Conservative Domination to Liberal Revival: 1886–1906," in Scott-Baumann, *Years of Expansion*, 312; Mike Byrne and Michael Lynch, "Foreign and Imperial Policy, 1830–1914," in Scott-Baumann, *Years of Expansion*, 339; Byrne, "Britain in a New Century," 404–405; Pearce and Stewart, *British Political History*, 100–104; William D. Rubenstein, *Twentieth-Century Britain: A Political History* (New York: Palgrave Macmillan, 2003), 18; and Crowley, "Propaganda Poster," 119, on the events and policies that led to the Liberals regaining power in 1906.

37. The London School of Economics and Political Science (LSE), *Catalogue of Collection 519: Political and Tariff Reform Posters* (London: LSE, n.d.), 11.

38. Rubenstein, *Twentieth-Century Britain,* 24.

39. *The Times* (of London), "Some Election Posters," November 30, 1910.

40. *The Times* (of London), "Campaign Publications," November 30, 1910.

41. See ibid., Richard Cockett, "The Party, Publicity, and the Media," in Anthony Seldon and Stewart Ball, eds., *Conservative Century: The Conservative Party since 1900* (New York: Oxford University Press, 1994), 547; and Wring, *Politics of Marketing,* 26.

42. See *The Times* (of London), "Campaign Publications"; *The Times* (of London), "Some Election Posters," November 30, 1910; *The Times* (of London), "Election Posters," January 15, 1910; Gwyn, *Democracy and the Cost of Politics,* 196; and Cockett, "Party, Publicity," 547, on the popularity, cost, and use of posters and other print and nonprint political material in the early twentieth century in Great Britain.

43. The Parliament Bill, which reformed the House of Lords, was introduced in 1910 and passed in 1911. It prevented the upper body from dealing with financial legislation and blocking other legislation indefinitely. Byrne, "Britain in a New Century," 418.

44. See *British Electoral Facts 1885–1975*, 7; Rubenstein, *Twentieth-Century Britain,* 48; *New York Times*, "British Parties Practically Tied," January 24, 1910, http://proquest.com; LSE, *Catalogue of Collection 519*, 6; and *The Times* (of London), "Some Election Posters," on issues and posters in the British elections of 1910.

45. Rubenstein, *Twentieth-Century Britain,* 32–35.

46. See *British Electoral Facts 1885–1975*, 8.

47. See Rubenstein, *Twentieth-Century Britain,* 37, 39, 43, 57, on George's political strategy.

48. *The Times* (of London), "Election Posters," December 1, 1910.

49. Crowley, "Propaganda Poster," 104.

50. *British Electoral Facts 1885–1975*, 7–8.

51. Pearce and Stewart, *British Political History*, 205–206.

52. Rubenstein, *Twentieth-Century Britain,* 56–57.

53. Actually, the *first* women's political group in Great Britain was established in Sheffield in 1857, and, ten years earlier, the first known suffrage handbill was printed. P. W. Wilson, "Under the Franchise Bill Soon to be Passed They Will Outnumber the Men Voters by 2,000,000—New-Won Rights Bring Large Responsibilities," *New York Times*, April 24, 1927, http://proquest.com; and ibid., 59–60.

54. WSPU demonstrations boasted as many as an estimated two hundred fifty thousand participants. Rubenstein, *Twentieth-Century Britain*, 61; and Gallo, *Poster in History*, 159.

55. Rubenstein, *Twentieth-Century Britain*, 61.

56. *The Times* (of London), "Mr. Lloyd George and Militant Methods," October 24, 1913.

57. Most Conservative MPs also did not favor enfranchisement. Rubenstein, *Twentieth-Century Britain*, 59, 61.

58. See ibid., 75, 78–79, 83–84, 99; and Pearce and Stewart, *British Political History*, 129–130, on World War I and politics in Great Britain during the conflict.

59. See Rubenstein, *Twentieth-Century Britain*, 100.

60. See ibid., 87, 100; and P. W. Wilson, "Under the Franchise Bill," on George's coalition, suffrage reform, and redistricting.

61. See Rubenstein, *Twentieth-Century Britain*, 43, 93, 101–102, 105, for the 1918 election results, on the growth of the Labour Party, and political events and developments in Great Britain in 1917 and 1918.

62. See ibid., 132.

63. See ibid., 124–128, 132–133; The National Museum of Labour History, "NMLH.1995.39.38," *Catalogue of the People's History Museum*, http://82.71.77.169; and Pearce and Stewart, *British Political History*, 258, on the dissolution of George's coalition and the 1922 election.

64. See John Ramsden, "Conservative Party," in the *Oxford Companion to Twentieth-Century British Politics*, ed. John Ramsden (Oxford, UK: Oxford University Press, 2002), 158; Rubenstein, *Twentieth-Century Britain*, 132, 139, 148; and Pearce and Stewart, *British Political History*, 226, 260, 394, on campaign themes, communication media, and Stanley Baldwin in the 1920s, and the 1923 election.

65. See *British Electoral Facts 1885–1975*, 13–14; and Rubenstein, *Twentieth-Century Britain*, 148, for the 1924 election results.

66. See *New York Times*, "Britain Is Flooded with Party Posters," October 21, 1924, http://proquest.com; Bob Franklin, *Packaging Politics: Political Communications in Britain's Media Democracy*, 2nd ed. (London: Arnold, 2004), 119; and *New York Times*, "Voting in Great Britain," October 29, 1924, http://proquest.com, on the 1924 election, campaigning, printed material, and expenditures.

67. See *New York Times*, "Britain Is Flooded," on the election posters during the 1924 campaign; see *The Times* (of London), "Posters in City Streets," March 15, 1922, on a citizen's reaction to them in this period.

68. Rubenstein, *Twentieth-Century Britain*, 166; and David Butler and Gareth Butler, *Twentieth-Century British Political Facts 1900–2000*, 8th ed. (London: Macmillan, 2000), 287.

69. Rubenstein, *Twentieth-Century Britain*, 158, 162.

70. Ibid., 163–164; and Ernest Marshall, "The News of Europe in Week-End Cables," *New York Times*, May 5, 1929, http://proquest.com.

71. Ralph D. Casey, "The National Publicity Bureau and British Party Propaganda," *Public Opinion Quarterly* 3 (1939): 630.

72. See Rubenstein, *Twentieth-Century Britain*, 148, 167.

73. See ibid., 166; Pearce and Stewart, *British Political History*, 266; and Wring, *Politics of Marketing*, 27.

74. See Rubenstein, *Twentieth-Century Britain*, 167.

75. See Wring, *Politics of Marketing*, 15.

76. *New York Times*, "Topics of the Times: Political Advertising Refused," May 14, 1929, http://proquest.com.

77. Cockett, "Party, Publicity," 557.

78. Ibid.

79. See Franklin, *Packaging Politics*, 4.

80. J. C. C. Davidson, cited in Cockett, "Party, Publicity," 548.

81.   Cockett, "Party, Publicity," 553, 557.

82.   See Rubenstein, *Twentieth-Century Britain*, 167, 169–171, 175, 177, 179, 182–183; and Ferdinand Kuhn, Jr., "Patriotism Is Issue in British Campaign," *New York Times*, October 23, 1931, http://proquest.com, on the events in Great Britain that led up to the 1931 election, the campaign, its posters, and the results.

83.   Casey, "National Publicity Bureau," 631–632.

84.   See ibid.," 632–634, on the broadsides, posters, and billboards of the 1935 British election campaign.

85.   See Rubenstein, *Twentieth-Century Britain*, 183, 196.

86.   See ibid., 186–193, 200; Wring, *Politics of Marketing*, 33; and Keith Laybourn, "(James) Ramsey MacDonald," in Ramsden, *Oxford Companion*, 410, on the 1935 election and its posters and aftermath in Great Britain.

87.   *New York Times*, "Balwin Addresses Millions by Radio," October 17, 1924, http://proquest. com.

88.   See Cockett, "Party, Publicity," 557–559, 560–561.

89.   See Rubenstein, *Twentieth-Century Britain*, 159; Butler and Butler, *Twentieth-Century British Political Facts*, 235; and Wring, *Politics of Marketing*, 23, on the role of radio and posters in British elections in the 1920s and 1930s.

90.   See Paddy Scannell, "Public Service Broadcasting and Modern Public Life," *Media Culture & Society* 11 (1989): 137.

91.   Marshall, "News of Europe."

92.   Ibid.

93.   See Rubenstein, *Twentieth-Century Britain*, 164; and Cockett, "Party, Publicity," 559–560, on "image management" in British politics in posters and newsreels.

94.   See Rubenstein, *Twentieth-Century Britain*, 200, 207–208, 214–217; and Nicholas J. Cull, "Churchill, Winston (1874–1965)," in Cull, Culbert, and Welch, *Propaganda and Mass Persuasion*, 78, 80, on Chamberlain's leadership record before World War II, and on Churchill's political career and media abilities through the war.

95.   See R. B. McCallum and Alison Readman, *The British General Election of 1945* (London: Oxford University Press, 1947), 154.

96.   See Rubenstein, *Twentieth-Century Britain*, 226, 228, 229–231; McCallum and Readman, *British General Election of 1945*, 13, 44, 139–140; and *British Electoral Facts 1885–1975*, 21, on political developments in Great Britain after World War II, campaign radio addresses, the use of photographs of Churchill in posters, and the results of the 1945 election; see British Library of Political and Economic Science, "Beveridge, William Henry, 1879–1963, 1st Baron Beveridge of Tuggal, Economist: Munitions Labour Papers," http://www.aim25.ac.uk/cgi-bin/search2?coll_id=5771&inst_id=1, on Beveridge.

97.   McCallum and Readman, *British General Election of 1945*, 237–239, 241–242, 248; and Appendix 1 in Butler and Kavanagh, *British General Election of 1997*, 255.

98.   See Wring, *Politics of Marketing*, 34.

99.   D. E. Butler and Richard Rose, *The British General Election of 1959* (London: Frank Cass, 1960), 18–19.

100.   Coleman, Prentis & Varley (memorandum, 1950), cited in Cockett, "Party, Publicity," 567.

101.   See H. G. Nicholas, *The British General Election of 1950* (London: Macmillan, 1951), 241; Rubenstein, *Twentieth-Century Britain*, 232–250; and Pearce and Stewart, *British Political History*, 446, on the 1950 election and its issues, legislation that affected the number of posters, and the antinationalization advertising campaign in Great Britain.

102.   Ian McAllister, "Campaign Activities and Electoral Outcomes in Britain 1979 and 1983," *Public Opinion Quarterly* 49 (1985): 491.

103.   See Rubenstein, *Twentieth-Century Britain*, 259.

104.   D. E. Butler, *The British General Election of 1955* (London: Macmillan, 1955), 49–51.

105.   See Rubenstein, *Twentieth-Century Britain*, 250–252, 254–255; and Brian Girvin, "The Party
          in Comparative and International Context," in Seldon and Ball, *Conservative Century*, 715, on
          the issues of the 1951 and 1955 British elections, and the events during this period.
106.   See Butler and Rose, *British General Election of 1959*, 75, 84, 93, on television and radio
          ownership and party broadcasts in Great Britain in the 1950s.
107.   See Cull, "Elections (Britain)," 111; and Weir and Beetham, *Political Power and Democratic
          Control*, 86, 88, on British legislation in the 1950s and beyond.
108.   Hugh Gaitskell, quoted in Butler and Rose, *British General Election of 1959*, 20.
109.   Cockett, "Party, Publicity," 22.
110.   Ibid.
111.   Butler and Rose, *British General Election of 1959*, 17.
112.   See ibid., 21.
113.   See ibid., 17, 24, 26, 41, 255, on the 1959 British election campaign, and the role of
          consultants.
114.   See ibid., 19–23, 139.
115.   See Appendix 1 in Butler and Kavanagh, *British General Election of 1997*, 255.
116.   David Butler and Michael Pinto-Duschinsky, *The British General Election of 1970* (London:
          Macmillan, 1971), 263.
117.   See Rubenstein, *Twentieth-Century Britain*, 279, 286
118.   See Butler and Pinto-Duschinsky, *British General Election of 1970*, 133–134.
119.   See Butler and Butler, *Twentieth-Century British Political Facts*, 272, 294.
120.   Butler and Pinto-Duschinsky, *British General Election of 1970*, 133.
121.   See David Butler and Dennis Kavanagh, *The British General Election of 1979* (London:
          Macmillan, 1980), 132; and Wring, *Politics of Marketing*, 73, on the reactions to the "Yesterday's
          Men" poster and the advertising firm that designed the campaign.
122.   See Butler and Pinto-Duschinsky, *British General Election of 1970*, ix, 108–109, 135; Appendix
          1 in Butler and Kavanagh, *British General Election of 1997*, 255; and Brian McNair, *An
          Introduction to Political Communication*, 2nd ed. (London: Routledge, 1999), 109.
123.   See Butler and Butler, *Twentieth-Century British Political Facts*, 272.
124.   See Butler and Pinto-Duschinsky, *British General Election of 1970*, 109; Cockett, "Party,
          Publicity," 571; Rubenstein, *Twentieth-Century Britain*, 286, 294; and Pearce and Stewart,
          British Political History, 492, on the Conservatives' political-advertising strategies and the 1970
          election results.
125.   Butler and Pinto-Duschinsky, *British General Election of 1970*, 311.
126.   See ibid., 289–290.
127.   See ibid., 289–290, 310, 312–313, on printed campaign material, particularly posters, in the
          1970 British election, and regulations for posters.
128.   See Goldman, *Conflicting Accounts*, 46–48, on the campaign for the Conservatives in 1978–
          1979.
129.   See Butler and Kavanagh, *British General Election of 1979*, 12, on the issues in 1979; and
          Appendix 1 in Butler and Kavanagh, *British General Election of 1997*, 255, for voting results.
130.   Butler and Kavanagh, *British General Election of 1979*, 139.
131.   Maurice Saatchi, quoted in Goldman, *Conflicting Accounts*, 332.
132.   Butler and Kavanagh, *British General Election of 1979*, 133, 139, 225–227.
133.   Margaret Scammell and Holli A. Semetko, "Political Advertising on Television: The British
          Experience," in Kaid and Holtz-Bacha, *Political Advertising in Western Democracies*, 31; and
          Sabato, *Rise of Political Consultants*, 129.
134.   Sabato, *Rise of Political Consultants*, 129.
135.   See ibid., 130–131, for the script.
136.   See Butler and Kavanagh, *British General Election of 1979*, 71–72, 132–134, 139, 141, 225–
          227, 295; and Pearce and Stewart, *British Political History*, 518–520, on the 1979 Conservative

and Labour campaigns.

137.   See, for example, Patrick Barrett, "Tories Swap Vitriol for Humour in Bid to Unseat Blair," *Guardian Unlimited*, March 23, 2004, http://www.guardian.co.uk/uk_news/story.

138.   Goldman, *Conflicting Accounts*, 13.

139.   Butler and Kavanagh, *British General Election of 1979*, 45; and Crowley, "Propaganda Poster," 104.

140.   See Butler and Kavanagh, *British General Election of 1979*, 45.

141.   Ibid., 36.

142.   Sabato, *Rise of Political Consultants*, 327.

143.   See Butler and Kavanagh, *British General Election of 1997*, 255.

144.   Karen S. Johnson and Camille Elebash, "The Contagion from the Right: The Americanization of British Political Advertising," in Kaid, Nimmo, and Sanders, *New Perspectives on Political Advertising*, 306–307, 311.

145.   David Butler and Dennis Kavanagh, *The British General Election of 1987* (New York: St. Martin's Press, 1988), 109.

146.   Ibid., 217.

147.   See ibid., 215.

148.   See ibid., 249.

149.   Ibid.; and Wring, *Politics of Marketing*, 4.

150.   Wring, *Politics of Marketing*, 96–97.

151.   See Sackman, "Learning Curve Towards New Labour," 147–158.

152.   Scammell and Semetko, "Political Advertising on Television," 19.

153.   Anonymous German citizen, quoted in Ian Traynor, "Hoots of Laughter from Streets of Bonn," *Guardian Unlimited,* April 19, 1997, http://politics.guardian.co.uk/politicspast/story/0,9061,449872,00.html.

154.   1992 survey results reported in David Butler and Dennis Kavanagh, *The British General Election of 1992* (London: St. Martin's Press, 1992), 242.

155.   See ibid., 116, 240, on exposure to billboards, posters, leaflets, and political television broadcasts during the 1992 election campaign in Great Britain; see Weir and Beetham, *Political Power and Democratic Control*, 90, on Conservative expenditures for posters then.

156.   The Labour Party chose to spend its money more on leaders' tours and meetings, and grants to constituencies. Reported in Weir and Beetham, *Political Power and Democratic Control*, 89.

157.   The value of the free television time in the last month of the 1997 election campaign, for example, was estimated at five million pounds for each major political party. Ibid., 86, 88.

158.   Jennifer Lees-Marshment, *Political Marketing and British Political Parties: The Party's Just Begun* (Manchester, UK: Manchester University Press, 2001), 168.

159.   See Craig R. Whitney, "British Chief Set for a Close Vote," *New York Times*, January 30, 1992, http://proquest.com: Butler and Butler, *Twentieth-Century British Political Facts*, 239; and Butler and Kavanagh, *British General Election of 1992*, 267–268, on the 1992 Labour billboard campaign and for the voting results.

160.   See Butler and Kavanagh, *British General Election of 1997*, 219, 243, on the number of posters displayed and expenditures on them.

161.   In 1996, 4.1 million pounds were spent on posters by the Conservative Party (£2.5m) and the Labour Party (£1.6m); 1.645 million pounds were spent on press ads (£0.981m and £0.664m, respectively). Ibid., 44–45.

162.   See ibid., 242.

163.   Weir and Beetham, *Political Power and Democratic Control*, 89.

164.   See Butler and Kavanagh, *British General Election of 1997*, 219.

165.   See ibid.

166.   See ibid., 219, 251, on the political marketing video disseminated by the Referendum Party during the 1997 British election campaign, and the party's share of the vote.

167. Ibid., 60.
168. See ibid., 34, 98–99; Wring, *Politics of Marketing*, 145–146; McNair, *Introduction to Political Communication*, 120; and United Kingdom Parliament, "General Election Results, 1 May 1997," Research Paper 01/38, March 29, 2001, http://www.parliament.uk/commons/lib/research/rp2001/rp01-38.pdf, on Labour's political marketing strategies during the 1997 election campaign, and for voting data.
169. See United Kingdom Parliament, "General Election Results, 7 June 2001," Research Paper 01/54, June 18, 2001, http://www.parliament.uk/commons/lib/research/rp2001/rp01-54.pdf.
170. See Butler and Kavanagh, *British General Election of 2005*, 200, 204.
171. Patrick Hennessy, "Blair Plans Snap Election in February," *Telegraph.co.uk*, October 31, 2004, http://www.telegraph.co.uk/news/main.jhtml?xml=/news/2004/10/31/ixnewstop.html.
172. Survey data on media influence during the 2001 British election campaign reported in Butler and Kavanagh, *British General Election of 2001*, 215; see Giles Wilson, "Voters-Wanted Posters: Britain's Political Parties Take to the Streets to Get Their Message Out," *Slate*, June 6, 2001, http://www.slate.com/id/109543, on posters and billboards from that campaign.
173. Philip Webster and Peter Riddell, "Tories Taunt 'Liar' Blair as Battle Gets Personal," *The Times* (of London), April 27, 2005, http://proquest.com; and Peter Riddell, Sam Coates, and Tom Baldwin, "'Liar Blair' Tactic Backfires on Howard as Tories Slip in the Polls," *The Times* (of London), April 30, 2005, http://proquest.com.
174. Scammell and Semetko, "Political Advertising on Television," 32.
175. See ibid., 21–22, 37–39; Butler and Kavanagh, *British General Election of 1997*, 239; and Cockett, "Party, Publicity," 575, on the "Americanization" of British election campaigns, and for election results in 1992.
176. Scammell and Semetko, "Political Advertising on Television," 35.
177. Franklin, *Packaging Politics*, 129.
178. Ibid.
179. *The Economist*, "Britain: Hot Air; Political Paraphernalia," April 30, 2005, http://proquest.com.
180. See Stephen Armstrong, "Media: Poster Power: Who Will Really Fight—and Win—the Next Election?" *Guardian* (Manchester, UK), November 27, 2000, http://proquest.com.
181. Patrick Wintour and Lucy Ward, "Election Delay: Spending: Parties Rush to Cancel Costly Posters for Hold-up," *Guardian* (Manchester, UK), April 3, 2001, http://proquest.com.
182. Ibid.
183. Butler and Kavanagh, *British General Election of 2005*, 42, 90–91.
184. Adrian McMenamin, quoted in Eric Pfanner, "On Advertising: Marketing to Voters in Britain," *International Herald Tribune*, April 18, 2005, http://proquest.com.
185. Ibid.
186. See Franklin, *Packaging Politics*, 121–125, 127.
187. Ibid., 124.
188. Ibid., 125.

Chapter Six

1. See Plasser, *Global Political Campaigning*, 295.
2. Ibid., 298.
3. See Colin A. Hughes, "Australia and New Zealand," in Butler and Ranney, *Electioneering*, 93–94.
4. Holtz-Bacha and Kaid, "Comparative Perspective on Political Advertising," 10; and James Manor, "India," in Butler and Ranney, *Electioneering*, 116.

5.   Hughes, "Australia and New Zealand," 103.

6.   Ralph Negrine, *The Communication of Politics* (London: Sage Publications, 1996), 152.

7.   Lynda Lee Kaid and Christina Holtz-Bacha, "Political Advertising Across Cultures: Comparing Content, Styles, and Effects," in Kaid and Holtz-Bacha, *Political Advertising in Western Democracies*, 223.

8.   Plasser, *Global Political Campaigning*, 21.

9.   See ibid., 42, for the results of the survey of foreign campaign professionals.

10.   See ibid., 2–3, 27, 63, 72, 246–247, on the activity of American and U.S.-connected political consultants.

11.   See J. Müller-Brockmann and S. Müller-Brockmann, *History of the Poster*, 157–158; and A. Livingston and I. Livingston, *Thames & Hudson Dictionary*, 59.

12.   See Gallo, *Poster in History*, 216.

13.   Steven Heller and Seymour Chwast, *Graphic Style: From Victorian to Digital*, rev. ed. (New York: Harry N. Abrams, 2000), 200. Originally published 1988.

14.   Cheles, "Picture Battles in the Piazza," 142.

15.   Ibid.

16.   Philip van Praag, Jr., "The Netherlands: The 1989 Campaign," in Bowler and Farrell, *Electoral Strategies and Political Marketing*, 150, 152.

17.   *L'Espresso*, June 7, 2001, cited in Plasser, *Global Political Campaigning*, 298.

18.   See N. C. Bipindra, "Parties Give a Go-By to Posters in City," *Times of India*, April 13, 2004, http://timesofindia.indiatimes.com/articleshow/613012.cms; Satbir Silas and K. N. Kumar, "Elections in India: A Monumental Exercise," *India Perspectives*, July 2004, 7, http://meaindia.nic.in/; and Philip Oldenburg, "Introductory Essay: A Portrait of Elections in India," http://www.columbia.edu/cu/sipa/REGIONAL/SAI/digital/Introductory%20essay.html, on posters and other paraphernalia in election campaigns in India.

19.   Veejay Archary, quoted in Gill Moodie, "Posters Get Thumbs Down," *Sunday Times* (Johannesburg, South Africa), February 29, 2004, http://www.suntimes.co.za/2004/02/29/news03.asp.

20.   See Hans Anker, "The 2003 Parliamentary Elections in the Netherlands: Restoration or Change?" in European Association of Political Consultants, *Election Time: The European Yearbook of Political Campaigning 2003* (Leibnitz, Austria: Hartinger Consulting, 2004), 207.

21.   *Blog@Stefangeens.com*, "The First Quinquennial Swedish EU Parliamentary Election Poster Slogan Review," May 29, 2004, http://www.stefangeens.com/000392.html.

22.   World Audit, "About Us," http://www.worldaudit.org/publisher.htm; World Audit, "Democracy Table November 2006," http://www.worldaudit.org/democracy.htm; and World Audit, "Democracy Table May 2007," http://www.worldaudit.org/democracy.htm.

23.   World Audit, "About Us"; and World Audit, "Democracy Table May 2007."

24.   Paul de Bendern, "Algeria Told to Stop Clashes Before President Vote," *Reuters*, April 2, 2004, http://dehai.org/archives/AW_news_archive/0612.html.

25.   Philip Van Niekerk, "Street Talk: Virtual Utopia of Boers 'n' Whores Apartheid Diehards Download Dreams of Running the World," *Guardian* (Manchester, UK), September 24, 1995, http://proquest.com; and Costas Panagopoulos and Christopher Cullen, "South Africa Votes 2004," *Campaigns & Elections*, April 2004, 41.

26.   See Plasser, *Global Political Campaigning*, 295.

27.   See Bernard Magubane, "South Africa," in *The Oxford Companion to Politics of the World*, 2nd ed., ed. Joel Krieger (New York: Oxford University Press, 2001), 784; Richard P. Hunt, "Strijdom Victor in South Africa," *New York Times*, April 17, 1958, http://proquest.com; and Nelson Mandela, "Address by Nelson Mandela on Behalf of the ANC Delegation to the Conference of the Pan-African Freedom Movement of East and Central Africa" (speech, Addis Ababa, Ethiopia, January 1962), http://www.anc.org.za/ancdocs/speeches/1960s, on the anticolonial and antiracist movements in South Africa to 1960.

28. Roger Thurow, "South African Whites Shift to the Right, Delaying Movement to Soften Apartheid," *New York Times*, February 25, 1988, http://proquest.com.

29. See Nicholas J. Cull, "Africa," in Cull, Culbert, and Welch, *Propaganda and Mass Persuasion*, 10; Leonard Thompson, *A History of South Africa*, 3rd ed. (New Haven, Conn.: Yale University Press, 2001), 190–204; and Magubane, "South Africa," 784, on apartheid and the resistance to it.

30. See Cull, "Africa," 10; Bill Keller, "White South African Party Seeks Black Maids' Votes," *New York Times*, February 28, 1993, http://proquest.com; Meshack M. Khosa and Yvonne G. Muthien, "Election Management in South Africa: An Evaluation of the 1999 Election," *International Institute for Democracy and Electoral Assistance*, http://archive.idea.int; and Bill Keller, "Nation Is Elated," *New York Times*, April 20, 1994, http://proquest.com, on the use of political media by the ANC, and on the 1994 election campaign and results in South Africa.

31. Jon Sawyer, "Clinton's Pollster Aided Nelson Mandela's Election Campaign," *St. Louis Post-Dispatch*, June 16, 1994, http://proquest.com.

32. Plasser, "American Campaign Techniques Worldwide," 47.

33. Bill Keller, "South African Election Is Campaign of Paradoxes," *New York Times*, January 3, 1994, http://proquest.com; and Bill Keller, "Mandela and de Klerk Open Fire in Battle for Votes," *New York Times*, February 3, 1994, http://proquest.com.

34. Keller, "South African Election."

35. See Plasser, "American Campaign Techniques Worldwide," 47; Panagopoulos and Cullen, "South Africa Votes 2004," 41; Andy David, "Smoke, Mirrors, Posters, Buses and Taxis," *Mail & Guardian*, September 24, 2004, http://www.themedia.co.za; Khosa and Muthien, "Election Management in South Africa"; and Daniel Silke and Robert Schrire, "The Mass Media and the South African Election," in *Election '94 South Africa: The Campaigns, Results and Future Prospects*, ed. Andrew Reynolds (New York: St. Martin's Press, 1994), 135, on the 1999 South African election campaign, and the use of media, particularly posters, in it.

36. See World Audit, "Democracy Table November 2006"; and World Audit, "Democracy Table May 2007," for "democracy" ratings for Asia; see Newnations, "Taiwan: Update No: 038," April 30, 2007, http://www.newnations.com/headlines/tw.php, for a report on Taiwan as it approached its 2007 elections; see Francis Fukuyama, "Asia's Democratic Values: How Ronald Reagan Helped Transform the Region for the Better," *Wall Street Journal*, May 25, 2005, http://proquest.com, on election campaign trends in Asia.

37. See Jonathan Lewis and Brian J. Masshardt, "Election Posters in Japan," *Japan Forum* 14 (2002): 392–393, 396, 399–400, for results of this study of Japanese election posters.

38. Subsequently, these posters were ordered taken down by the party, even though this tactic had been used previously in Thai campaigns without any complaints and was not prohibited by the election laws. There were reports that foreign officials had objected. Thanyaporn Kunakornpaiboonsiri, "Controversial Posters Upset Diplomats," *The Nation* (Thailand), January 20, 2005, http://lexis-nexis.com.

39. See K. Nesan, "Gujarat Election Opens Door for More Communal Violence in India," *World Socialist Web Site*, December 28, 2002, http://www.wsws.org; and Tekwani, "Visual Culture in Indian Politics," 12, on issue-oriented posters in Indian election campaigns; see Plasser, *Global Political Campaigning*, 250, 295, on recent election campaign trends in India and survey results on Indian campaign managers' evaluations of media.

40. See Lewis and Masshardt, "Election Posters in Japan," 373–404, on the popularity and use of posters in Japanese elections; see Tekwani, "Visual Culture in Indian Politics," 3, on election posters and billboards in India.

41. See Toshihide Umeda, "Posters from the 1930s: The Social Context," *Ohara Institute for Social Research*, http://oohara.mt.tama.hosei.ac.jp/english/explanation.html.

42. See Elise K. Tipton, *Modern Japan: A Social and Political History* (London: Routledge, 2002), 55–58; and Ian Neary, *The State and Politics in Japan* (Cambridge, UK: Polity Press, 2002), 24

on Japanese political history in the late nineteenth century, particularly the Constitution of 1889.

43. See Umeda, "Posters from the 1930s"; and Neary, *State and Politics in Japan*, 24, on the 1925 law and the extension of suffrage.

44. See Umeda, "Posters from the 1930s."

45. See *New York Times*, "Japanese Predict a Drawn Election," February 19, 1928, http://proquest. com; Ohara Institute for Social Research, "Images of Japanese Labor and Social Movement in Pre-1945 Japan," http://oohara.mt.tama.hosei.ac.jp/senkyo01/index.html; and Tipton, *Modern Japan*, 116, on election campaigns and political events in Japan from 1928 to 1932.

46. See National Diet Library, "Reconstruction of Japan," http://www.ndl.go.jp/modern/e/cha5/index.html.

47. See National Diet Library, "Reconstruction of Japan: Rebuilding Political Parties and General Election," http://www.ndl.go.jp/modern/e/cha5/description05.html; Neary, *State and Politics in Japan*, 51, 61–62; and *Japanese Politics Central*, "Elections: Lower House Election Results, 1946–2000," http://jpcentral.virginia.edu/Elections.htm, on politics in post-World War II Japan, and the elections of 1946 and 1958.

48. See Tipton, *Modern Japan*, 169–170.

49. See Robert Trumbull, "On Election Posters All the Japanese Are Happy," *New York Times*, January 22, 1967, http://proquest.com, on posters in the 1960s in Japanese election campaigns and on laws regulating them; see Sterngold, "Advertising"; and Lewis and Masshardt, "Election Posters in Japan," 382–383, on such legislation afterward; see Sheryl WuDunn, "Japan Tries Aggressive Campaigning, Politely," *New York Times*, October 17, 1996, http://proquest.com, on poster utilization during the 1996 Japanese election campaign period.

50. See Lewis and Masshardt, "Election Posters in Japan," 399.

51. See ibid., 382–383, 390; James Brooke, "Inuyama Journal: A Campaign as Japanese as Baseball and Apple Pie," *New York Times*, April 24, 2003, http://proquest.com; WuDunn, "Japan Tries Aggressive Campaigning, Politely"; Trumbull, "On Election Posters"; Sterngold, "Advertising"; and Gerald L. Curtis, "Japan," in Butler and Ranney, *Electioneering*, 225–226, on legal restrictions on election campaign media in Japan in the last decade of the twentieth century and first decade of the twenty-first.

52. See Neary, *State and Politics in Japan*, 70–71, 74, 90; *Japanese Politics Central*, "Elections: Lower House Election Results, 1946–2000"; and Tipton, *Modern Japan*, 191, on Japanese election results from 1963 to 1990, and on political developments in Japan in the 1980s.

53. See Neary, *State and Politics in Japan*, 76; and *Japanese Politics Central*, "Elections: Lower House Election Results, 1946–2000."

54. See Neary, *State and Politics in Japan*, 74–75; Tipton, *Modern Japan*, 204; and Sterngold, "Advertising," on loss of support for the LDP and election poster campaigns in Japan in 1989.

55. Neary, *State and Politics in Japan*, 91.

56. See ibid., 91–92; and *Japanese Politics Central*, "Elections: Lower House Election Results, 1946–2000," for the results of the lower-house elections of 1993 in Japan and political developments around them.

57. See Neary, *State and Politics in Japan*, 93.

58. See ibid., 94, 96, 102; and the *Web KANZAKI*, "Political Parties in Japan: 1874–1998," http://www.kanzaki.com/jinfo/PoliticalParties.html, on political events in Japan from 1994 to 2000.

59. See Lewis and Masshardt, "Election Posters in Japan," 398.

60. Philbert Ono, "PhotoHistory 2001 (Heisei 13)," *PhotoGuide Japan: A Guide to Photography in Japan*, http://photojpn.org/notes/node.

61. See Neary, *State and Politics in Japan*, xxi, 102–103, 112; Justin McCurry, "We Shall Miss Him," *Japan Times*, September 16, 2006, http://search.japantimes.co.jp; Anthony Faiola,

"Japan's Koizumi Breaks the Mold," *Washington Post*, September 10, 2005, http://proquest. com; Lewis and Masshardt, "Election Posters in Japan," 394–395; *Japanese Politics Central*, "Elections: Koizumi Wins Landslide Victory in Lower House Election," September 11, 2005, http://jpcentral.virginia.edu/LH-seats-1958-1990.htm; and Bruce Wallace, "Japan's Koizumi Wins in a Landslide," *Los Angeles Times*, September 12, 2005, http://proquest.com, on Koizumi's rise to power, his image management, the 2001 election campaign and its posters, and the 2005 election results and its aftermath.

62. See Jim Frederick, "The Mythmaker," *Japan Times*, September 16, 2006, http://search. japantimes.co.jp; David McNeill, "Good Riddance," *Japan Times*, September 16, 2006, http://search.japantimes.co.jp; Masami Ito, "Diet Closes for Summer, Puts Lid on Koizumi Legacy," *Japan Times*, June 17, 2006, http://search.japan times.co.jp; Richard Lloyd Parry, "A Professional Disaster," *Japan Times*, September 16, 2006, http://search.japantimes.co .jp; McCurry, "We Shall Miss Him"; Faiola, "Japan's Koizumi Breaks the Mold"; Sebastian Moffett and Ginny Parker Woods, "Urban Renewal: As Japan Votes, Aid to Countryside Hangs in Balance," *Wall Street Journal*, September 7, 2005, http://proquest.com; Simon Tisdall, "World Briefing: Latter-day Samurai Could Transform Politics," *Guardian* (Manchester, UK), September 12, 2005, http://proquest.com; and Kim Moogwi, "Communication Failure," *Japan Times*, September 16, 2006, http://search.japantimes.co .jp, on Koizumi's image and accomplishments.

63. Bruce Wallace, "For Politicians in Japan, Net Is No-Go Zone," *Los Angeles Times*, September 9, 2005, http://proquest.com.

64. See ibid.; and Curtis, "Japan," 227, on the Internet and Japanese political campaigns, the role of advertising and political consulting firms, and election posters in Japan recently.

65. Jonathan Manthorpe, *Forbidden Nation: A History of Taiwan* (New York: Palgrave Macmillan, 2005), xi; and Dennis Roy, *Taiwan: A Political History* (Ithaca, N.Y.: Cornell University Press, 2003), 93.

66. See Harvey J. Feldman, "Taiwan Moves Toward a Two-Party System," *New York Times*, December 27, 1986, http://proquest.com.

67. See Manthorpe, *Forbidden Nation*, xii; Roy, *Taiwan*, 10, 172–173; John F. Cooper, "The Role of Minor Political Parties in Taiwan," *World Affairs* 155 (1993), http://www.questia .com; and *Economist.com*, "Taiwan: Political Forces," October 20, 2005, http://www.economist. com/countries/Taiwan, on political events in Taiwan from 1949 to 1989.

68. See *Economist.com*, "Taiwan."

69. See ibid.; Roy, *Taiwan*, 175, 192, 230–231, 235; Nicholas D. Kristof, "As Free Election Comes to Taiwan, Will the End of Claims to China Follow?" *New York Times*, December 21, 1991, http://proquest.com; David W. Tsai, "Taiwan Voted for Status Quo, not One China; A Stinging Defeat," *New York Times*, January 6, 1992, http://proquest.com; Charles A. Radin, "Taiwan Ruling Party Holds On; Foes Show Strength in Local Polls," *Boston Globe*, November 28, 1993, http://proquest.com; Mark Landler, "An Embarrassment of Riches Hurts Taiwan's Ruling Party," *New York Times*, January 23, 2000, http://proquest.com; *Taipei Times*, "Democratic Electoral System," http://ecommerce.taipeitimes.com/yearbook 2004; and Erik Eckholm, "Taiwan's Opposition Party Tones Down Call for Independence," *New York Times*, May 6, 1999, http://proquest.com, on the KMT and its control of the mass media until 1997, and the results of the 2000 elections in Taiwan.

70. See Liz Sly, "Taiwan's Ruling Party Facing Strong Challenge; Rival Party Surges as 3-Way Election Heads to the Wire," *Times-Picayune* (New Orleans), March 16, 2000, http:// proquest.com; Roy, *Taiwan*, 230; Gary D. Rawnsley, "As Edifying as a Bout of Mud Wrestling, The 2000 Presidential Election in Taiwan," in *Political Communications in China: The Construction and Reflection of Identity*, ed. Gary D. Rawnsley and Ming-Yeh T. Rawnsley (London: RouledgeCurzon, 2003), 117–118; Gary D. Rawnsley, "An Institutional Approach to Election Campaigning in Taiwan," *Journal of Contemporary China* 12 (2003): 768; Eric

Sautedé, "Electioneering Taiwan-style," *China Perspectives* 29 (2000): 55; Institute of Asia-Pacific Studies, University of Nottingham, "2000 Election—DPP—Campaign Products," http://www.nottingham.ac.uk/iaps/taiwan; Institute of Asia-Pacific Studies, University of Nottingham, "2000 Election—DPP—Candidate Websites," http://www.Nottingham.ac.uk/iaps/taiwan; and Myra Lu, "Presidential Election Drawing Near, Voters Go Wild for Campaign Merchandise," *Taipei Journal*, February 3, 2000, http://th.gio.gov.tw/p2000/p10.htm, on KMT and DPP strategies, slogans, and campaign paraphernalia during the 2000 Taiwanese elections.

71. See Rawnsley, "Institutional Approach to Election Campaigning," 105, 114–115; and Gary D. Rawnsley, "The Day after the Night Before: Thoughts on the 2004 Presidential Election in Taiwan," *Taiwan Perspective*, April 12, 2004, http://www.tp.org.tw, on Web sites and poster propaganda during the 2000 elections in Taiwan.

72. See Roy, *Taiwan*, 234.

73. See Christian Schafferer, "The 2001 National and Local Elections in Taiwan" Institute of Asia-Pacific Studies, University of Nottingham e-paper (2002), 2–4, 7–10, 17, http://www.nottingham.ac.uk; and Michael Turton, "Election Time in Taiwan," http://users2.ev1.net//~turton/election/election.html, on political events, the campaign, and the aftermath of the 2001 election in Taiwan.

74. See Manthorpe, *Forbidden Nation*, 238; Richard Gunde, "The Election in Taiwan: A Forum," *AsiaMedia*, http://www.asiamedia.ucla.edu/article.asp?parentid=9435; and *Taipei Times*, "Taiwan Yearbook 2004: Democratic Electoral System," http://ecommerce.taipeitimes.com/yearbook2004/P073.htm, on the 2004 election campaign in Taiwan.

75. Martin Williams and Joy Su, "Taiwan: Pan-Blue Poster Likens Chen to bin Laden, Saddam," *Taipei Times*, March 23, 2004, http://www.asiamedia.ucla.edu/taiwan.

76. Anonymous person, quoted in Gunde, "Election in Taiwan."

77. Anonymous persons, quoted in Joy Su and Martin Williams, "Taiwan: Hu Sued Over 'Repulsive' bin Laden Advertisement," *Taipei Times*, March 25, 2004, http://www.asiamedia.ucla.edu/taiwan/print.asp?parentid=9469.

78. Anonymous person, quoted in ibid.

79. Su and Williams, "Taiwan: Hu Sued."

80. See *AsiaMedia*, "Taiwan Election/Referendum, March 20, 2004," http://www.asia/media.ucla.edu/taiwan.

81. Rawnsley, "Day after the Night Before."

82. Ibid.

83. *Taipei Times*, "Taiwan Yearbook 2004."

84. Ibid.

85. Brian D. Gooch and John W. Rooney, Jr., "Belgium in 1848," http://www.ohiou.edu/~chastain/ac/belgium.htm; and *The Times* (of London), "Electioneering in Belgium," November 5, 1845.

86. See Craig R. Whitney, "In the East, the Selling of Democracy Takes on a New Fervor," *New York Times*, January 21, 1990, http://proquest.com; and Fred Martin, "Politics at The Club Tomaj," *New York Times*, May 20, 1990, http://proquest.com, on the work of external consultants in post-Communist Eastern Europe; see World Audit, "Democracy Table May 2007"; and World Audit, "About Us," for "democracy" ratings for Europe.

87. Commission of the European Communities, Eurobarometer 31A: European Elections, 1989: Post-Election Survey, June–July 1989, cited in Pippa Norris, *A Virtuous Circle: Political Communications in Post-Industrial Societies* (Cambridge, UK: Cambridge University Press, 2000), 157.

88. Timo Kivi, "From Election Winner to Iraq Victim," in European Association of Political Consultants, *Election Time: The European Yearbook of Political Campaigning 2003*, 49, 51.

89. See Peter Finn, "A Turn from Tolerance; Anti-Immigrant Movement in Europe Reflects Post-

Sept. 11 Views on Muslims," *Washington Post*, March 29, 2002, http://proquest.com.

90. See Mads Qvortrup, "The Emperor's New Clothes: The Danish General Election of 20 November, 2001," *West European Politics* 25 (2002): 209.
91. See ibid., 206–207.
92. See Helena Bachmann, "With Friends Like These … : Switzerland," *Time Europe*, February 14, 2000, http://www.time.com/time/magazine/europe/magazine; J. Sean Curtin, "Anti-immigrant Party Makes Big Gains in Swiss Election," *Japanese Institute of Global Communications*, Report #61, October 29, 2003, http://www.glocom.org; and Deutsche Welle, "Racism Overshadows Swiss Election," November 10, 2003, http://www.dw-world.de/dw/article/0,,993364,00. html.
93. Jonas Attenhofer, "Did Someone Say Racism?" *Haartetz.com*, November 16, 2007, http://www.haaretz.com; and *Jane's*, "Swiss Election Highlights Social Divides," October 26, 2007, http://www.janes.com.
94. *New York Times*, "Italian Posters on Way," May 26, 1953, http://proquest.com.
95. Cheles, "Picture Battles in the Piazza," 125.
96. See Gundle, "Italy," 184.
97. See ibid., 173.
98. See Christoph Hofinger, Answer Lang, and Eva Zeglovits, "Austrian Presidential Elections: Authenticity as the Key to Success," in European Association of Political Consultants, *Election Time: The European Yearbook of Political Campaigning 2004* (Leibnitz, Austria: Hartinger Consulting, 2005), 38.
99. See ibid., 40–41, 45.
100. See ibid., 42–43.
101. Ibid., 43.
102. See Martin Kitchen, *A History of Modern Germany 1800–2000* (Malden, Mass.: Blackwell, 2006), 73–75, 78–79, 86–88, 91.
103. See ibid., 103–105, 121, 145; Jonathan Sperber, *The Kaiser's Voters: Electors and Elections in Imperial Germany* (Cambridge, UK: Cambridge University Press, 1997), 1; U.S. Library of Congress, "Germany: Bismarck and Unification," http://lcweb2.loc.gov; *The Times* (of London), "Germany," October 1, 1886; U.S. Library of Congress, "Germany: Political Parties," http://lcweb2.loc.gov; and Stephen Padgett and Tony Burkett, *Political Parties and Elections in West Germany: The Search for a New Stability* (New York: St. Martin's Press, 1986), 31–33, on Prussian and German election campaigns and political events from 1861 to 1912, and on the rise to power and rule of Bismarck.
104. Brett Fairbairn, "Interpreting Wilhelmine Elections: National Issues, Fairness Issues, and Electoral Mobilization," in *Elections, Mass Politics, and Social Change in Modern Germany: New Perspectives*, ed. Larry Eugene Jones and James Retallack (Cambridge, UK: Cambridge University Press, 1992), 27.
105. See ibid., 28; U.S. Library of Congress, "Germany: Political Parties"; George Renwick, "Parties Are Recast for German Voting," *New York Times*, January 8, 1919, http://proquest.com; Kitchen, *History of Modern Germany*, 179; and *New York Times*, "Germany's Many Parties," June 11, 1893, http://proquest.com, on German political parties from the 1870s to 1919.
106. See *New York Times*, "Hot Campaigns for Convention Stir Germany," January 4, 1919, http://proquest.com.
107. See Renwick, "Parties Are Recast."
108. See Leslie Cabarga, *Progressive German Graphics: 1900–1937* (San Francisco, Calif.: Chronicle Books, 1994), 8, 14–18, on posters and German advertising during this period.
109. See Padgett and Burkett, *Political Parties and Elections*, 38.
110. See ibid., 38–41; E. J. Feuchtwanger, *From Weimar to Hitler: Germany, 1918–33*, 2nd ed. (New York: St. Martin's Press, 1995), 37; and Mary Fulbrook, *A Concise History of Germany*, 2nd ed. (Cambridge, UK: Cambridge University Press, 2004), 217, on the SPD and the political

events in post-World War I Germany.

111.   See Padgett and Burkett, *Political Parties and Elections*, 90.

112.   See Feuchtwanger, *From Weimar to Hitler*, 81–82.

113.   See ibid., ix, 81, 83, 107, 326; and Padgett and Burkett, *Political Parties and Elections*, 89–90, on the political parties of the center and right in post-World War I Germany.

114.   See Feuchtwanger, *From Weimar to Hitler*, 82, 326; and Erich Matthias, "German Social Democracy in the Weimar Republic," in *German Democracy and the Triumph of Hitler: Essays in Recent German History*, ed. Anthony Nichols and Erich Matthias (New York: St. Martin's Press, 1971), 48.

115.   See Feuchtwanger, *From Weimar to Hitler*, 326, 328.

116.   See ibid., 326.

117.   See ibid.

118.   Walter Rinderle and Bernard Norling, *The Nazi Impact on a German Village* (Lexington, Ky.: University Press of Kentucky, 1993), 89.

119.   Ibid., 90–91, 244.

120.   Corey Ross, "Mass Politics and the Techniques of Leadership: The Promise and Perils of Propaganda in the Weimar Republic," *German History* 24 (2006), 202.

121.   See ibid., 207; and Richard J. Evans, "German Social Democracy and Women's Suffrage 1891–1918," *Journal of Contemporary History* 15 (1980): 545, 550, 552, on the propaganda approaches of the SPD, KPD, and the Nazi Party and on German political parties and women's suffrage.

122.   David Pike, *Lukács and Brecht* (Chapel Hill, N.C.: University of North Carolina Press, 1985), 165.

123.   Adolf Hitler, *Mein Kampf*, trans. Ralph Manheim (Boston: Houghton Mifflin, 1943), 182.

124.   Bruce, *Images of Power*, 24.

125.   Gustave Le Bon, *The Crowd: A Study of the Popular Mind* (New York: Macmillan, 1896), 118.

126.   Ibid., 125–131.

127.   Ibid., 126.

128.   Bruce, *Images of Power*, 24–25.

129.   Servando González, "The Swastika and the Nazis: A Study on the Origins of the Adoption of the Swastika by Adolf Hitler as a Symbol of the Nazi Movement," http://www.intelinet.org/swastika/swastika_intro.htm.

130.   See Edward L. Bernays, *Propaganda* (New York: Horace Liveright, 1928), 23, 25.

131.   Ibid., 23, 48, 52.

132.   Blumenthal, *Permanent Campaign*, 19.

133.   Bernays, *Propaganda*, 11.

134.   National Socialist German Workers Party, Propaganda Abteilung, *Propaganda*, http://www.calvin.edu/academic/cas/gpa/prop27.htm#anchor254328.

135.   Ibid.

136.   Ralf Georg Reuth, *Goebbels*, trans. Krishna Winston (New York: Harcourt Brace, 1993), 143.

137.   Hitler, *Mein Kampf*, 176.

138.   Joseph Darracott, introduction to *The First World War in Posters,* ed. Joseph Darracott (New York: Dover Publications, 1974), ix.

139.   M. L. Sanders and Philip M. Taylor, *British Propaganda During the First World War, 1914–1918* (London: Macmillan, 1982), 142–148.

140.   Hitler, *Mein Kampf*, 178–180.

141.   Ibid., 180–181.

142.   Ibid., 177–180.

143.   Rinderle and Norling, *Nazi Impact on a German Village*, 88.

144.   Thomas Childers, *The Nazi Voter: The Social Foundations of Fascism in Germany, 1919–1933*

(Chapel Hill, N.C.: University of North Carolina Press, 1983), 266.

145. Rinderle and Norling, *Nazi Impact on a German Village*, 88.

146. Ibid., 75, 89–91, 99, 102.

147. Joseph Goebbels, "Knowledge and Propaganda," (speech, Nazi Party meeting, Berlin, Germany, January 9, 1928), http://www.calvin.edu/academic/cas/gpa/goeb54.htm.

148. Rinderle and Norling, *Nazi Impact on a German Village*, 91–92.

149. Ibid., 91.

150. Ibid., 92–93, 103.

151. For election results, see Feuchtwanger, *From Weimar to Hitler Germany*, 326.

152. Rinderle and Norling, *Nazi Impact on a German Village*, 99.

153. See Feuchtwanger, *From Weimar to Hitler*, 328.

154. Ibid., 326, 328.

155. Childers, *Nazi Voter*, 194–195.

156. See ibid., 196–197; Feuchtwanger, *From Weimar to Hitler*, 264–266, 268; and *New York Times*, "Bruening Uses Ruse to Campaign on Air," March 1, 1932, http://proquest.com.

157. See Childers, *Nazi Voter*, 194; Rinderle and Norling, *Nazi Impact on a German Village*, 103–104; *New York Times*, "Election in Reich Finds Foe Aiding Foe," March 8, 1932, http://proquest.com; *New York Times*, "Bruening Uses Ruse"; and *New York Times*, "Campaign in Full Blast," April 8, 1932, http://proquest.com, on the Nazi Party's propaganda campaigns in 1932.

158. See Feuchtwanger, *From Weimar to Hitler*, 326.

159. Ibid.

160. Ibid.

161. See *New York Times*, October 5, 1932, http://proquest.com; Childers, *Nazi Voter*, 199; Rinderle and Norling, *Nazi Impact on a German Village*, 106, 108–109, 114; and Frederick T. Birchall, "Nazi Campaign Starts," *New York Times*, October 16, 1933, http://proquest.com, on the Nazis use of billboards, film, and radio from summer 1932 to fall 1933.

162. Ernst Growald, quoted in Ross, "Mass Politics," 204.

163. Michelle Bowen-Charoensawadsiri, "Bernhard and His Creations," http://www.angelfire.com/art2/frainis; and A. Livingston and I. Livingston, *Thames & Hudson Dictionary*, 31.

164. See Kitchen, *History of Modern Germany*, 318–319, 324; Padgett and Burkett, *Political Parties and Elections*, 204; and Clifton Daniel, "Germans Vote on Europeanism vs. Neutralism," *New York Times*, September 6, 1953, http://proquest.com, on post–World War II political developments in Germany, and on the elections of 1949.

165. See Padgett and Burkett, *Political Parties and Elections*, 200, 206; and Fulbrook, *Concise History of Germany*, 214.

166. Konrad Adenauer, quoted in Daniel, "Germans Vote."

167. See ibid.; Padgett and Burkett, *Political Parties and Elections*, 200, 209; Fulbrook, *Concise History of Germany*, 214; Kitchen, *History of Modern Germany*, 333; Clifton Daniel, "Electoral Drive in Bonn Is Sedate," *New York Times*, August 24, 1953, http://proquest.com; and *New York Times*, "Specialists Assail Dulles," September 4, 1953, http://proquest.com, on the West German elections of 1957, and the campaigns and posters in the 1950s.

168. Kitchen, *History of Modern Germany*, 337.

169. See Padgett and Burkett, *Political Parties and Elections*, 200, 209.

170. See Max Kaase, "Germany," in Butler and Ranney, *Electioneering*, 161.

171. See ibid., 200, 209, 214–215,

172. See Kitchen, *History of Modern Germany*, 342; and Padgett and Burkett, *Political Parties and Elections*, 200.

173. See Kitchen, *History of Modern Germany*, 337, 354, 358–360; and Padgett and Burkett, *Political Parties and Elections*, 200, 222, on the rise of Willy Brandt and on the West German elections from 1961 to 1972.

174. See Padgett and Burkett, *Political Parties and Elections*, 200, 224–229, on political and economic developments in West Germany from 1972 to 1976, and on the election campaign and its advertisements in 1976.

175. See Kaase, "Germany," 161.

176. See Padgett and Burkett, *Political Parties and Elections*, 233, 235; Elim Papadakis, "Social Movements, Self-Limiting Radicalism and the Green Party in West Germany," *Sociology* 22 (1988): 451; and Kitchen, *History of Modern Germany*, 372, on the 1980 West German election campaign and its aftermath.

177. See Padgett and Burkett, *Political Parties and Elections*, 200, 243, on the election results of 1983 in West Germany.

178. See Hermann Schmitt, "Are Party Leaders Becoming More Important in German Elections? Leader Effects on the Vote in Germany, 1961–1998" (paper presented at the annual meeting of the American Political Science Association, Washington, D.C., August 31–September 3, 2000), 6–8, http://www.dieterohr.de/download/schmidt_ohr_aug28.pdf, on the effects of television on German political campaigns; see *New York Times*, "Regulating Campaigns"; and Negrine, *Communication of Politics*, 156–157, on government regulation of political broadcasts in Germany.

179. See R. E. M. Irving and W. E. Paterson, "The West German General Election of 1987," *Parliamentary Affairs* 40 (1987): 352–353.

180. See ibid., 335–337, 345; James M. Markham, "Germany Expected to Carry on with Kohl," *New York Times*, January 18, 1987, http://proquest.com; Federal Statistical Office of Germany, "March 6, 1983 Bundestag Election Results—Federal Republic of Germany Totals," http://www.electionresources.org; and Federal Statistical Office of Germany, "January 25, 1987 Bundestag Election Results—Federal Republic of Germany Totals," http://www.electionresources.org, on the campaign and election results in West Germany in 1987.

181. See Kitchen, *History of Modern Germany*, 381–388, on the collapse of Communist rule in East Germany and the move toward reunification.

182. See ibid., 388, 390.

183. See ibid., 394–396; Henry Kamm, "As the East Germans Vote Today, They Choose for Europe as Well," *New York Times*, March 18, 1990, http://proquest.com; John Tagliabue, "Former East Germans Vote, And Kohl Is the Big Winner," *New York Times*, October 15, 1990, http://proquest.com; Stephen Kinzer, "Kohl Is Savoring 'This Happy Hour,'" *New York Times*, November 25, 1990, http://proquest.com; and Serge Schmemann, "Kohl's Campaign Foe: Standard-Bearer Who Leaves Party and People Cold, *New York Times*, November 28, 1990, http://proquest.com, on the 1990 elections and the campaigns in both Germanys.

184. Christina Holtz-Bacha and Lynda Lee Kaid, "Television Spots in German National Elections," in Kaid and Holtz-Bacha, *Political Advertising in Western Democracies*, 75.

185. Klaus Schoenbach, "The 'Americanization' of German Election Campaigns: Any Impact on the Voters?" in *Politics, Media, and Modern Democracy*, ed. David L. Swanson and Paolo Mancini (Westport, Conn.: Praeger, 1996), 97.

186. See Kaase, "Germany," 158–159; and Bernhard Boll and Thomas Poguntke, "Germany: The 1990 All-German Election Campaign," in Bowler and Farrell, *Electoral Strategies and Political Marketing*, 128–129, 132–133, on the use of various media in the December 1990 German elections, and on the CDU and SPD organizations.

187. See Schmemann, "Kohl's Campaign Foe."

188. See Federal Statistical Office of Germany, "January 25, 1987 Bundestag Election Results"; and Kitchen, *History of Modern Germany*, 396.

189. See Federal Statistical Office of Germany, "January 25, 1987 Bundestag Election Results"; and Kitchen, *History of Modern Germany*, 296.

190. See Steven E. Finkel and Peter R. Schrott, "Campaign Effects on Voter Choice in the German Election of 1990," *British Journal of Political Science* 25 (1995): 369

191. Schoenbach, "'Americanization' of German Election Campaigns," 98–102.
192. It was estimated that more than fifty thousand persons voted in the first election. Adam Zamoyski, *The Polish Way: A Thousand-Year History of the Poles and Their Culture* (New York: Franklin Watts, 1988), 95–96, 126–127.
193. In the 1922 parliamentary elections, four different Jewish parties ran lists. *New York Times*, "The Polish Elections," November 5, 1922, http://proquest.com.
194. See Zamoyski, *Polish Way*, 35, 100–101, 273–274, 276–277, 340–343; Hieronim Kubiak, "Parties, Party Systems, and Cleavages in Poland: 1918–1989," in *Cleavages, Parties, and Voters: Studies from Bulgaria, the Czech Republic, Hungary, Poland, and Romania*, ed. Kay Lawson, Andrea Römmele, and Georgi Karasimeonov (Westport, Conn.: Praeger, 1999), 78; Jerzy Szapiro, "Poles Cold to New Vote Plan," *New York Times*, August 18, 1935, http://proquest. com; Anita J. Prazmowska, *History of Poland* (New York: Palgrave Macmillan, 2004), 191–192; and *New York Times*, "New Parliament Elected in Poland," October 27, 1952, http://proquest. com, on the political history of Poland from the late 1200s to 1989.
195. Danuta A. Boczar, "The Polish Poster," *Art Journal* 44 (1984): 25.
196. See Prazmowska, *History of Poland*, 206–208; and Michael T. Kaufman, "Underground Urges Boycotts and Protests in Poland," *New York Times*, June 17, 1984, http://proquest.com, on Solidarity in the 1980s and its propaganda.
197. See John Tagliabue, "Solidarity Says Warsaw Is Playing Campaign Tricks," *New York Times*, May 25, 1989, http://proquest.com.
198. See Prazmowska, *History of Poland*, 210; John Tagliabue, "Slogans Ready, Solidarity Takes Stab at the Hustings," *New York Times*, May 10, 1989, http://proquest.com; and John Tagliabue, "For Solidarity, a Dab of Election Glitz," *New York Times*, May 13, 1989, http://proquest.com, on the resurrection of Solidarity, and the 1989 Polish election.
199. No overt party designations were stated. Stephen Engelberg, "In Polish Race, No Parties Need Apply," *New York Times*, November 23, 1990, http://proquest.com.
200. See Susan Rose-Ackerman, *From Elections to Democracy: Building Accountable Government in Hungary and Poland* (New York: Cambridge University Press, 2005), 57, on the provisions of the new Polish constitution; see Joshua A. Tucker, *Regional Economic Voting: Russia, Poland, Hungary, Slovakia, and the Czech Republic, 1990–1999* (New York: Cambridge University Press, 2006), 312, for the results of this election.
201. See Joshua A. Tucker, *Regional Economic Voting*, 313; and U.S. Library of Congress, "Solidarity," http://www.countrysides.us/poland/81.htm, for the results of the 1991 Polish parliamentary elections.
202. See Stephen Engleberg, "Low Turnout Seen for Polish Vote," *New York Times*, October 16, 1991, http://proquest.com; Stephen Engleberg, "Poles Vote Today in Anxious Mood," *New York Times*, October 27, 1991, http://proquest.com; and U.S. Library of Congress, "Democratic Union," http://countrystudies.us/poland/83.htm, on the events surrounding the 1991 parliamentary elections in Poland.
203. See U.S. Library of Congress, "Democratic Union"; U.S. Library of Congress, "The Olszewski Government," http://countrystudies.us/poland/68.htm; Prazmowska, *History of Poland*, 212; Thomas Lundberg, "Political Transition in Hungary and Poland: Positive Signs for Lasting Democracy," in The Center for Voting and Democracy, *Voting and Democracy Report: 1995*, http://fairvote.org/reports/1995/chp7/lundberg2.html; and Jerzy Lukowski and Hubert Zawadzki, *A Concise History of Poland*, 2nd ed. (New York: Cambridge University Press, 2006), 322–325, on political events in Poland after the 1991 elections.
204. See László Kontler, *A History of Hungary* (New York: Palgrave Macmillan, 2002), 467–470; and Celestine Bohlen, "Hungarian Prime Minister Reports That Moscow Has Agreed to Withdraw Its Troops," *New York Times*, January 24, 1990, http://proquest.com, on the political events in Hungary in 1989 and 1990.
205. See Kontler, *History of Hungary*, 249.

206.   See ibid., 251, 253–259; Miklós Mólnar, *A Concise History of Hungary*, trans. Anna Magyar (Cambridge, UK: Cambridge University Press, 2001), 186, 188; and Laszlo Deme, "The Society for Equality in the Hungarian Revolution of 1848," *Slavic Review* 31 (1972): 71, 75, on the 1848 Hungarian Revolution and the events the next year.

207.   See Kontler, *History of Hungary*, 281.

208.   See ibid., 281, 284, 286; *The Times* (of London), "Hungary," January 7, 1869; and *New York Times*, "Bloodshed in Hungary," January 26, 1905, http://proquest.com, on Hungarian politics in the 1860s and 1870s.

209.   See Kontler, *History of Hungary*, 296, 299–300; and Mólnar, *Concise History of Hungary*, 234, 250–253, on political events during the first two decades of the twentieth century in Hungary.

210.   See *New York Times*, "Hungary's Rulers," September 7, 1947, http://proquest.com.

211.   See Mólnar, *Concise History of Hungary*, 290–291, 299–301; Kontler, *History of Hungary*, 338–340, 349–350, 353, 391, 394–396; and Malcolm W. Browne, " 'Dry' Election Day Quiet in Hungary," *New York Times*, June 17, 1975, http://proquest.com, on dictatorships in Hungary after both world wars, and on the election of 1945.

212.   See University of Essex, International Foundation for Election Systems, and Association of Central and Eastern European Electoral Offices, "Hungary: 1990 Parliamentary Elections," http://www2.essex.ac.uk/elect/electer/hu_er_nl.htm#90; Central Intelligence Agency, "Hungary," http://www.cia.gov/cia/publications/factbook/geos/hu.html; Kontler, *History of Hungary*, 470, 476; György G. Márkus, "Hungarian Cleavages and Parties prior to 1989," in Lawson, Römmele, and Karasimeonov, *Cleavages, Parties, and Voters*, 74; and Mólnar, *Concise History of Hungary*, 338, on the 1990 Hungarian elections.

213.   György G. Márkus, "Cleavages and Parties in Hungary after 1989," in Lawson, Römmele, and Karasimeonov, *Cleavages, Parties, and Voters*, 143.

214.   Cornell University, *Hungarian Poster Collection #4481* (Ithaca, N.Y.: Cornell University, Rare and Manuscript Collections, Carl A. Kroch Library, n.d.), 7–8.

215.   See Celestine Bohlen, "Divisions Bedevil Hungary Parties," *New York Times*, April 7, 1990, http://proquest.com; Kontler, *History of Hungary*, 476; and Cornell University, *Hungarian Poster Collection #4481*, 7–9, 12–13, on Hungarian election posters in 1990, and the use of imagery from them in the Baltic countries the next year.

216.   See Celestine Bohlen, "A Democratically Evolving Hungary Heads Into Unknown at Polls Today," *New York Times*, March 25, 1990, http://proquest.com; and F. Martin, "Politics at The Club Tomaj," on the use of posters, banners, and TV spot ads in the 1990 Hungarian election campaign.

217.   See Kontler, *History of Hungary*, 476; and University of Essex et al., "Hungary: 1990 Parliamentary Elections," on the seats held and coalition-building in the legislature.

218.   See Kontler, *History of Hungary*, 477–478; University of Essex et al., "Hungary: 1990 Parliamentary Elections"; János Simon, "Cleavages and Spaces of Competition in Hungary," in Lawson, Römmele, and Karasimeonov, *Cleavages, Parties, and Voters*, 219–222, 231; Mólnar, *Concise History of Hungary*, 340–341, 349–351; Szonja Szelényi, Ivan Szelényi, and Winifred R. Poster, "Interests and Symbols in Post-Communist Political Culture: The Case of Hungary," *American Sociological Review* 61 (1996): 466–477; and Marina Popescu and Gábor Tóka, "Campaign Effects and Media Monopoly: The 1994 and 1998 Parliamentary Elections in Hungary," in *Do Political Campaigns Matter? Campaign Effects in Elections and Referendums*, ed. David M. Farrell and Rüdiger Schmitt-Beck (London: Routledge, 2002), 58, on political propaganda campaigns and events in Hungary from 1990 to 1994, and on the election results in 1990 and 1994.

219.   See Popescu and Tóka, "Campaign Effects and Media Monopoly," 60.

220.   See ibid.; Bohlen, "Democratically Evolving Hungary"; Crowley, "Propaganda Poster," 133; and András Szekfü, "Hungary Joins the EU: A Communications Analysis of the Referendum,"

in European Association of Political Consultants, *Election Time: The European Yearbook of Political Campaigning 2003*, 91–92, 97–98, on the use of media in Hungarian election campaigns in the 1990s.

221.   See Lyman G. Chaffee, "Poster and Political Propaganda in Argentina," *Studies in Latin American Culture* 5 (1986): 80, 82, on the use of posters for political purposes in Latin America.

222.   See Lyman G. Chaffee, *Political Protest and Street Art: Popular Tools for Democratization in Hispanic Countries* (Westport, Conn.: Greenwood Press, 1993), 103.

223.   See ibid., 102–103, 105, on posters in election campaigns in Argentina from the 1890s through the 1950s.

224.   See ibid., 117, 121, on campaign posters in the 1983 and 1989 elections in Argentina; see World Audit, "Democracy Table May 2007," for "democracy" rankings for Latin American countries.

225.   See Alan Angell, Maria D'Alva Kinzo, and Diego Urbaneja, "Latin America," in Butler and Ranney, *Electioneering*, 52, on media in Brazil, particularly in its election campaigns.

226.   See *Brainy Encyclopedia*, "Evo Morales," http://brainyencyclopedia.com/encyclopedia/e/ev/evo_morales.html, on the 2002 Bolivian elections and the Morales poster.

227.   *Café Chile*, "The Mega Circus Blitz of Election Frenzy, … " December 6, 2005, http://café chile.blogspot.com.

228.   See Plasser, *Global Political Campaigning*, 286, 295, for survey results on campaign advertising media in Latin America.

229.   Central Intelligence Agency, *Memorandum for the Record; Subject: Genesis of Project FUBELT*, September 16, 1970, http://www.gwu.edu/~nsarchiv/NSAEBB/NSAEBB8/ch03-01.htm.

230.   See Lois Hecht Oppenheim, *Politics in Chile: Democracy, Authoritarianism, and the Search for Development*, 2nd ed. (New Haven, Conn.: Westview Press, 1999), 3, 27, 281; Arturo Valenzuela, "The Scope of the Chilean Party System," in *Parties, Elections, and Political Participation in Latin America*, ed. Jorge I. Domínguez (New York: Garland Publishing, 1994), 109; and Associated Press, "Allende Backers Warned by Junta not to Bear Arms," *New York Times*, September 13, 1973, http://proquest.com, on the 1970 election campaign in Chile, and on Allende and the UP; see Edy Kaufman, *Crisis in Allende's Chile: New Perspectives* (New York: Praeger, 1988), 6; and Senate Select Committee to Study Governmental Operations with Respect to Intelligence Activities, *Covert Action in Chile 1963–1973* (Washington, D.C.: U.S. Government Printing Office, 1975), http://foia.state.gov/Reports/ChurchReport.asp, on U.S. antileftist efforts in Chile in the 1960s and 1970s, including monies expended.

231.   Valenzuela, "Scope of the Chilean Party System," 103.

232.   See ibid., 103, 107; Oppenheim, *Politics in Chile*, 10; and U.S. Library of Congress, "Chile: Military Interventions, 1925–32," http://countrystudies.us/chile/20.htm, on Chilean political and constitutional history; see Jack Ray Thomas, "The Socialist Republic of Chile," *Journal of Inter-American Studies* 6 (1964): 203–220; and Jack Ray Thomas, "The Evolution of a Chilean Socialist: Marmaduke Grove," *Hispanic Journal of American Historical Review* 47 (1967): 22–37, on Grove.

233.   See Kaufman, *Crisis in Allende's Chile*, 183.

234.   Ibid.

235.   Salvador Allende, quoted in Norman Gall, "The Chileans Have Elected a Revolution," *New York Times*, November 1, 1970, http://proquest.com.

236.   See Kaufman, *Crisis in Allende's Chile*, 183.

237.   Jose Yglesias, "Report from Chile: The Left Prepares for an Election," *New York Times*, January 11, 1970, http://proquest.com.

238.   Senate Select Committee to Study Governmental Operations with Respect to Intelligence Activities, *Covert Action in Chile*.

239.   David Kunzle, "Art of the New Chile: Mural, Poster, and Comic Book in a 'Revolutionary

Process,'" in *Art and Architecture in the Service of Politics*, ed. Henry A. Millon and Linda Nochlin (Cambridge, Mass.: MIT Press, 1978), 366–367.

240. Ibid., 367.

241. See Valenzuela, "Scope of the Chilean Party System," 108; Malcolm W. Browne, "Smog Is Now a Problem Even High in the Andes," *New York Times*, August 1, 1970, http://pro quest.com; and Gall, "Chileans Have Elected a Revolution," 27, 106, on the role of television in the 1970 Chilean election campaign, the lowering of the voting age, the election result, and the selection of Allende by the Congress.

242. See Jan Lahmeyer, "Honduras: Historical Demographical Data of the Whole Country," http://www.populstat/Americas/hondurasc.htm; and Jan Lahmeyer, "Mexico: Historical Demographical Data of the Whole Country," http://www.populstat/Americas/mexicoc.htm.

243. See Central American Business Consultants, "International Free Trade Zone," http://www. ca-bc.com/zipinternacional/about_honduras.html; and U.S. Library of Congress, "The Suazo Córdova Administration," http://countrystudies.us/honduras/26.htm, on political, economic, and military developments in Honduras in the 1970s and 1980s.

244. See Darío A. Euraque, *Reinterpreting the Region and State in Banana Republic Honduras, 1870–1972* (Chapel Hill, N.C.: University of North Carolina Press, 1996), 45, on suffrage in Honduras.

245. See ibid., 7, 45–62, 66–67, 77; Central American Business Consultants; U.S. Library of Congress, "Political Parties," http://countrystudies.us/honduras/90htm; "Honduras— History," *Mongabay.com*, http://www.mongabay.com/reference/countrystudies/Honduras/ HISTORY.html; Ralph Lee Woodward, Jr., *Central America: A Nation Divided*, 3rd ed. (New York: Oxford University Press, 1999), 179, 271–272; and U.S. Library of Congress, "The Suazo Córdova Administration," on the political and economic history of Honduras from the 1880s to 1980s.

246. See U.S. Library of Congress, "The Struggle of Electoral Democracy: The Elections of 1985," http://countrystudies.us/honduras/28.htm; and U.S. Library of Congress, "Political Parties," on the constitutional crisis of 1985 in Honduras.

247. Mark Rosenberg, quoted in U.S. Library of Congress, "Political Parties."

248. See ibid.; James LeMoyne, "Hondurans to Elect Chief; The Question Is 'How?'" *New York Times*, November 13, 1985, http://proquest.com; U.S. Department of State, "Background Note: Honduras," http://www.state.gov/r/pa/ei/bgn/1922.htm; H. Joachim Maitre, "Fear and Loathing in the Honduran Campaign," *New York Times*, November 22, 1985, http://proquest. com; *New York Times*, "Hondurans Vote for a President Today," November 24, 1985, http:// proquest.com; and U.S. Library of Congress, "Struggle of Electoral Democracy," on the 1985 Honduran election campaign.

249. See U.S. Library of Congress, "Struggle of Electoral Democracy," for the results of the 1985 election in Honduras.

250. See Central American Business Consultants, "International Free Trade Zone"; Woodward, Jr., *Central America*, 273–274; *Honduras This Week*, "Election Results: Madero Wins!" November 26, 2001, http://ww.marrder.com/htw/2001nov; Central Intelligence Agency, "Honduras," http://www.cia.gov/cia/publications/factbook/geos/ho.html; and U.S. Library of Congress, "Political Parties," on the aftermath of the 1985 Honduran election, and on political developments since then.

251. See *Biography Resource Center* (Farmington Hills, Mich.: Thomson Gale. 2007), s.v. "Benito Juárez," Document Number: K1616000524, http://galenet.galegroup.com/servlet/BioRC, from *Historic World Leaders* (Detroit: Gale Research, 1994); Glen W. Taplin, *Middle American Governors* (Metuchen, N.J.: Scarecrow Press, 1972), 56; Instituto de Investigaciones Jurídicas, "Constitución Política de la República Mexicana de 1857," http://www.juridicas.unam.mx/ infjur/leg/conshist/pdf/1857.pdf; and U.S. Library of Congress, "The Constitution," http:// countrystudies.us/mexico/81.htm, on Juárez and the history of Mexico from 1821 to 1857;

see Gustavo Ernesto Emmerich, "Las Elecciones en México, 1808–1911: ¿Sufragio Efectivo?, ¿No Reeleccion?" in *Las Elecciones en México: Evolución y Perspectivas*, 3rd ed., ed. Pablo González Casanova (Mexico City: Siglo Veintiuno Editores, 1993), 52; and Brian R. Hamnett, "Liberalism Divided: Regional Politics and the National Project during the Mexico Restored Republic, 1867–1876," *Hispanic American Historical Review* 76 (1996): 662, on voting results from 1853 to 1877; see Laurens Ballard Perry, *Juárez and Díaz: Machine Politics in Mexico* (DeKalb, Ill.: Northern Illinois University Press, 1978), 4, 18–21, on suffrage and turnout after 1857; see Richard A. Warren, *Vagrants and Citizens: Politics and the Masses in Mexico City from Colony to Republic* (Wilmington, Del.: Scholarly Resources, 2001), 67, 80–81, 102–104, 164–165, on voter eligibility and turnout in Mexico City for earlier congressional elections in the 1820s and 1830s, with turnout possibly over 70 percent of the adult male population in 1826 and 1828, but declining afterward.

252. Under the Mexican Constitution at this time, the chief justice became president when the office was vacant. Biography Resource Center, s.v. "Benito Juárez."

253. See Emmerich, "Elecciones en México," 53.

254. See ibid.

255. See the *New York Times,* "Mexican Affairs," July 25, 1866, http://proquest.com; *New York Times,* "Mexico," October 24, 1867, http://proquest.com; Perry, *Juárez and Díaz,* 88; Jim Tuck, "Mexico's Lincoln: The Ecstasy and Agony of Benito Juarez (1806–1872)," *Mexico Connect,* http://www.mexconnect.com/mex_/history/jtuck/jtbenitojuarez.html; Walter V. Scholes, "El Mensajero and the Election of 1871 in Mexico," *Americas* 5 (1948): 61–67; and Biography Resource Center, s.v. "Benito Juárez," on the events in Mexico from 1858 to 1872; see Hamnett, "Liberalism Divided," on the divisions of the Liberal Party for much of the nineteenth century, as well as the election of 1871; see Frank Averill Knapp, Jr., *The Life of Sebastián Lerdo de Tejada, 1823–1889: A Study of Influence and Obscurity* (New York: Greenwood Press, 1968), 164, 249–256, 262, on Lerdo de Tejada.

256. See Alan Knight, *The Mexican Revolution*, vol. 1 (Lincoln, Nebr.: University of Nebraska Press, 1986), 20, 41, 98; and Nicholas J. Cull, "Mexico," in Cull, Culbert, and Welch, *Propaganda and Mass Persuasion*, 247, on Mexico under Díaz.

257. Matthew White, "Death Tolls for the Major Wars and Atrocities of the Twentieth Century," http://users.erols.com/mwhite28/warstat2.htm; and Héctor Aguilar Camín and Lorenzo Meyer, *In the Shadow of the Mexican Revolution: Contemporary Mexican History, 1910–1989,* trans. Luis Alberto Fierro (Austin: University of Texas Press, 1993), 71.

258. Linda Hall, "Mexico," in Krieger, *Oxford Companion to Politics*, 542.

259. See "1917 Constitution of Mexico," http://www.ilstu.edu/class/hist263/docs/1917const.html. Translated from *Constitución Política de los Estados Unidos Mexicanos*, Trigésima Quinta Edición (México, D.F.: Editorial Porrua, S.A., 1967). Originally published by the Pan American Union, General Secretariat (Washington, D.C., Organization of American States, 1968); and Daniel C. Levy and Gabriel Székeley, *Mexico: Paradoxes of Stability and Change,* 2nd ed. (Boulder, Colo.: Westview Press, 1987), 65, on the Constitution of 1917 and on the expansion of suffrage; see Ann L. Craig and Wayne A. Cornelius, "Houses Divided: Parties and Political Reform in Mexico," in *Building Democratic Institutions: Party Systems in Latin America*, ed. Scott Mainwaring and Timothy R. Scully (Stanford, Calif.: Stanford University Press, 1995), 255, on the formation of the PRI and its solidification of power.

260. See Frank Ralph Brandenburg, "Mexico an Experiment in One-Party Democracy" (PhD diss., University of Pennsylvania, 1956), 31; Camín and Meyer, *In the Shadow,* 179, 240, 258; Philip B. Taylor, Jr., "The Mexican Elections of 1958: Affirmation or Authoritarianism?" *Western Political Quarterly* 13 (1960): 722; and Craig and Cornelius, "Houses Divided," 258, for these Mexican election results.

261. See Craig and Cornelius, "Houses Divided," 276; and Frank Brandenburg, *The Making of Modern Mexico* (Englewood Cliffs, N.J.: Prentice-Hall, 1964), 1, on Diaz Ordaz, his term in

office, and the PRI.

262. See U.S. Library of Congress, "Institutional Revolutionary Party (PRI)," http://countrystu dies.us/mexico/84.htm.

263. See Camín and Meyer, *In the Shadow*, 176–177, on socioeconomic status in Mexico; see James W. Wilkie, *The Mexican Revolution: Federal Expenditure and Social Change since 1910*, 2nd ed. (Berkeley, Calif.: University of California Press, 1970), 282; and Hall, "Mexico," 542, on nationalization and reforms in Mexico, and the political organization of the lower class; see Camín and Meyer, *In the Shadow*, 179; U.S. Library of Congress, "National Action Party," http://countrystudies.us/mexico/85.htm; U.S. Library of Congress, "Institutional Revolutionary Party (PRI)"; and Carlos Gil, ed., *Hope and Frustration: Interviews with Leaders of Mexico's Political Opposition* (Wilmington, Del.: Scholarly Resources, 1992), 149, 151, on opposition to PRI rule, the PAN, and on changes in PRI orientation since the mid-1980s.

264. See William Branigin, "Strengthened Opposition Charges Fraud in Mexico," *Washington Post*, July 15, 1988, http://proquest.com.

265. See U.S. Library of Congress, "Carlos Salinas de Gortari," http://countrystudies.us/mexico/45 .htm; Camín and Meyer, *In the Shadow*, 241–242; and Craig and Cornelius, "Houses Divided," 268, on the 1988 Mexican presidential election campaign; see Elaine Pofeldt, "Posters Clarify Mexican Politics," *Los Angeles Times*, October 1, 1988, http://proquest.com, on the campaign posters in 1988.

266. Fidel Velasquez, quoted in David Asman, "The Americas: Mexican Opposition Is Given a Few Feet and Takes a Mile," *Wall Street Journal*, September 16, 1988, http://proquest.com.

267. See Camín and Meyer, *In the Shadow*, 242–243; Angell, D'Alva Kinzo, and Urbaneja, "Latin America," 45, 47; U.S. Library of Congress, "President Salinas," http://countrystudies.us/ mexico/46.htm; Branigin, "Strengthened Opposition Charges Fraud"; Storer H. Rowley, "Monopoly Ends as Mexico's Top Political Game," *Chicago Tribune*, July 17, 1988, http://proquest.com; Instituto Federal Electoral de México, "México: 1988 Legislative Elections," *Edmund A. Walsh School of Foreign Service, Center for Latin American Studies, Georgetown University, Political Database of the Americas*, http://pdba.georgetown.edu/Elec data/Mexico/dipde1988.html; and Instituto Federal Electoral de México, "México: 1979 Legislative Elections," *Edmund A. Walsh School of Foreign Service, Center for Latin American Studies, Georgetown University, Political Database of the Americas*, http://pdba.georgetown.edu/ Elecdata/Mexico/dipde1979.html, on the disputed results of the 1988 Mexican elections.

268. See Jorge I. Dominguez and James A. McCann, "Whither the PRI? Explaining Voter Defection in the 1988 Mexican Presidential Elections," *Electoral Studies* 11 (1992): 214–219, on factors affecting voters to switch from the PRI to other parties in the 1988 presidential election in Mexico.

269. Taylor, Jr., "Mexican Elections of 1958," 742.

270. See Craig and Cornelius, "Houses Divided," 258, on votes for the PAN from 1958 to 1988.

271. See Instituto Federal Electoral, "Resultados Electorales," http://graficos.eluniversal.com.mx/ tablas_presidente/presidentes.htm.

272. See U.S. Library of Congress, "National Action Party"; and Jorge I. Dominquez and James A. McCann, "Shaping Mexico's Electoral Arena: The Construction of Partisan Cleavages in the 1988 and 1991 National Elections," *American Political Science Review* 89 (1995): 34, 40; U.S. Library of Congress, "Democratic Revolutionary Party," http://countrystudies.us/mexico/86. htm; U.S. Library of Congress, "Institutional Revolutionary Party (PRI)"; U.S. Library of Congress, "President Salinas"; Jeanine Braithwaite, Kalanidhi Subbarao, Soniya Carvalho, Aniruddha Bonnerjee, and Kene Ezemenari, *Safety Net Programs and Poverty Reduction: Lessons from Cross-Country Experience* (Washington, D.C.: World Bank, 1997), 143; and Hall, "Mexico," 543, on the PAN and its increased electoral success and on the 1994 Mexican presidential election, campaign, and on the causes of the PRI victory.

273. Homero Aridjis, quoted in Sam Dillon, "Whoever Wins, Vote in Mexico Will Be Fateful,"

New York Times, July 2, 2000, http://proquest.com.

274. Craig and Cornelius, "Houses Divided," 270.

275. Vicente Fox Quesada, quoted in CBC News Online, "The Coca-Cola Kid: Mexico's Vicente Fox," June 29, 2006, http://www.cbc.ca/news/background/mexico/fox-vicente.html.

276. Vicente Fox Quesada, quoted in Sam Dillon, "Mexico's Election, the Race is Real," New York Times, March 12, 2000, http://proquest.com.

277. See ibid.,"; Craig and Cornelius, 207–271; Julia Preston, "Joy in Street of Capital as Reign of 71 Years Ends for the PRI," New York Times, July 3, 2000, http://proquest.com; and CBC News Online, "Coca-Cola Kid," on support for the PAN from businessmen, beginning in the 1980s, changing PAN strategy (and its impact), and Fox and his political strategy.

278. See Sam Dillon, "TV Proves Most Potent Campaign Tool in Mexico," New York Times, September 9, 1999, http://proquest.com.

279. Ron Mader, "Election 2000: Rate the Partys' [sic] Webmaster Skills before the 2000 Elections," Mexico Connect Business, http://www.mexconnect.com/mex_/travel/rmader/rmpoliticalweb.html.

280. See ibid.; Dillon, "TV Proves Most Potent"; Dillon, "Mexico's Election"; Susan Ferriss, "Ruling Party Faces Test in Today's Vote," Atlanta Journal-Constitution, July 2, 2000, http://proquest.com; Plasser, Global Political Campaigning, 234; Nathan Tabor and Jim Kouri, "Mexicans Hire Bush Advisor to Stop U.S. Border, Illegal Immigrations Reforms," Renew America, December 30, 2005, http://www.renewamerica.us/tabor/051230; and Michael Barone, "Insight," Jewish World Review, October 28, 1999, http://www.jewishworldreview.com/michael/barone102899.asp, on the use of mass media in Mexican election campaigns from 1994 to 2000.

281. See Tim McGirk, "Newsmakers of 2000: Vicente Fox Quesada," Time Europe, December 25, 2000, http://www.time.com/time/europe/magazine.

282. See Dillon, "Mexico's Election"; Edward Hegstrom, "Lifting Barriers at Border Urged," Houston Chronicle, June 16, 2000, http://proquest.com; Ferriss, "Ruling Party Faces Test"; Dillon, "Whoever Wins"; Barone, "Insight"; and CBC News Online, "Coca-Cola Kid," on issues and campaign strategy in the 2000 Mexican presidential election.

283. See Barone, "Insight"; Dudley Althaus, "The Task: Pour a Foundation," Houston Chronicle, http://www.chron.com; and Mary Beth Sheridan, "May Test Faith in Mexico's Political System," Los Angeles Times, July 2, 2000, http://proquest.com, on the 2000 Mexican election campaign and its posters.

284. See Dillon, "Whoever Wins"; and Dillon, "Mexico's Election," for these poll results.

285. See Instituto Federal Electoral de México, "México: 2000 Federal Elections," Edmund A. Walsh School of Foreign Service, Center for Latin American Studies, Georgetown University, Political Database of the Americas, http://pdba.georgetown.edu/Elecdata/Mexico/fed2000.html.

286. See Juanita Darling, "Landmark Vote," Los Angeles Times, July 4, 2000, http://proquest.com.

287. See Instituto Federal Electoral de México, "México: 2000 Federal Elections."

288. Carlos Elizondo Mayer-Serra and Agustin Basave, quoted, respectively, in Atlanta Journal-Constitution, "Jolted PRI Leaders Say Party Isn't Dead Yet," July 5, 2000, http://proquest.com.

289. See Instituto Federal Electoral de México, "República de México: Elecciones Presidenciales 2006," Edmund A. Walsh School of Foreign Service, Center for Latin American Studies, Georgetown University, Political Database of the Americas, http://pdba.georgetown.edu/Elecdata/Mexico/pres06.html and Instituto Federal Electoral de México, "República de México: Elecciones Legislativas 2006," Edmund A. Walsh School of Foreign Service, Center for Latin American Studies, Georgetown University, Political Database of the Americas, http://pdba.georgetown.edu/Elecdata/Mexico/leg06.html, for the 2006 election results; see BBC News, "EU Says Disputed Mexico Vote Fair," July 8, 2006, http://news.bbc.co.uk/1/hi/world/americas/5160188.stm, on the conclusion of fairness by observers.

290. See John Lyons, "Politics & Economics: Attack Ads Stir Up Mexican Campaign," Wall Street

Journal, April 11, 2006, http://proquest.com; and Danna Harman and Sara Miller Llana, "The Dirt Is Being Flung before Mexico Vote Sunday," *USA Today,* June 30, 2006, http://proquest. com, on campaign strategies for the 2006 Mexican election; see *CBC News Online,* "Coca-Cola Kid," on Fox's record.

291.　See Michaela Cosgrove, e-mail communication to Margaret Fay, September 28, 2005; and Robert Mayer, "On the Other Side," *Publius Pundit,* June 1, 2006, www.publiuspundit.com/wp/index.php/?m=200606, on election posters and bumper stickers in twenty-first century Mexico.

Chapter Seven

1.　See Doll, *Poster War,* 31.

2.　See George I. Vogt, "When Posters Went to War: How America's Best Commercial Artists Helped Win World War I," *Wisconsin Magazine of History* 84, no. 2 (2000–2001): 44.

3.　MRUK survey results reported in Andrew Denholm, "Parties' Billboard Sideswipes are Negative Campaigning Writ Large," *Scotsman,* May 2, 2003, http://election.scotsman.com/index.cfm?id=498912003.

4.　William L. Miller, Harold D. Clarke, Martin Harrop, Lawrence Leduc, and Paul F. Whiteley, *How Voters Change: The 1987 British Election Campaign in Perspective* (New York: Oxford University Press, 1990), 9–10.

5.　Ibid., 234.

6.　Devlin, "Political Commercials," in Kaid and Holtz-Bacha, *Political Advertising in Western Democracies,* 187.

7.　Darrell M. West, *Air Wars: Television Advertising in Election Campaigns, 1952–2004,* 4th ed. (Washington, D.C.: CQ Press, 2005), 173.

8.　Finkel and Schrott, "Campaign Effects on Voter Choice," 370–374.

9.　Thomas E. Patterson and Robert D. McClure, *The Unseeing Eye: The Myth of Television Power in National Politics* (New York: G.P. Putnam's Sons, 1976), 135.

10.　Stephen Armstrong, "Media: Poster Postures Ad Agencies Are in the Front Line of the Battle to Win Next Year's Election," *Guardian* (Manchester, UK), September 16, 1996, http://proquest.com.

11.　All "significant" results referred to in this chapter are *statistically* significant.

12.　R. J. Johnston, "Campaign Expenditure and the Efficacy of Advertising at the 1974 General Election in England," *Political Studies* 27 (1979): 114–119, for the multiple-regression study; see R. J. Johnston and C. J. Pattie, "Campaigning and Advertising: An Evaluation of the Components of Constituency Activism at Recent British General Elections," *British Journal of Political Science* 28 (1998): 678, on posters and leaflets in election campaign advertising in Great Britain.

13.　Johnston and Pattie, "Campaigning and Advertising," 678–680.

14.　Ibid., 682–685.

15.　Ibid., 685.

16.　Finke, *Fresh Ideas in Invitations,* 100.

17.　John Gruber and J. J. Sedelmaier, "Sic Transit," *Print 52,* no. 4 (1998): 65.

18.　Ibid.

19.　Jennifer Porter Gore, "First American Tells Customers It's All About Them," *Bank Marketing* 30, no. 11 (1998): 12.

20.　Joan Lund, "How We Made 850,000 Beer Drinkers Shout," *World Advertising Research Center,* http://www.warc.com/Search/CaseStudies.

21.　Phillip Coffey, "An Evaluation of Wildlife Preservation Trusts' Production of Threatened Species Posters as an Aid to *In Situ* Conservation," *Dodo: Journal of Wildlife Preservation Trusts*

28 (1992): 144, 149.

22. Leonid S. Shkolnik, "Experimental Study of the Efficiency of Posters for Children," *Voprosy Psychologii* 3 (1985): 140–144. PsycINFO Abstract.

23. Eunice Belbin, "The Effects of Propaganda on Recall, Recognition and Behavior: II. The Conditions Which Determine the Response to Propaganda," *British Journal of Psychology* 47 (1956): 259–262.

24. Edmund Bruce Piccolino, "Depicted Threat, Realism, and Specificity: Variables Governing Safety Poster Effectiveness" (PhD diss., Illinois Institute of Technology, 1966), 105, 121–122.

25. S. Laner and R. G. Sell, "An Experiment on the Effect of Specially Designed Safety Posters," *Occupational Psychology* 34 (1960): 156–158, 161–165.

26. Reagan Outdoor Advertising, "Case Studies: Calvin Coolidge," http://www.reaganoutdoor.com/index.php?id=42.

27. Elizabeth M. Tucker, "The Power of Posters: Examining the Effectiveness of 30–Sheet Posters," *Outdoor Advertising Association of America*, September 11, 1999, 4–6, 8–10, http://www.oaaa.org/images/upload/research/200324847172083611150.pdf.

28. Ibid., 1.

29. Richard Hunt, "Vote Valley: Changing the Agenda in a Local Government Debate," *World Advertising Research Center*, http://www.warc.com/Search/CaseStudies; and *BBC.co.uk*, "Charlton Athletic FC," http://www.bbc.co.uk/london/content/articles/2005/05/18/charlton_athletic_team.shtml.

30. Bruce Pinkleton, "The Effects of Negative Comparative Political Advertising on Candidate Evaluations and Advertising Evaluations: An Exploration," *Journal of Advertising* 26, no. 1 (1997): 19, 23–25.

31. Sharyne Merritt, "Negative Political Advertising: Some Empirical Findings," *Journal of Advertising* 13, no. 3 (1984): 14, 27, 30–36.

32. Ronald Paul Hill, "An Exploration of Voter Responses to Political Advertisements," *Journal of Advertising* 18, no. 4 (1989): 14, 17–20.

33. Mike R. Rubinoff and Diane T. Marsh, "Candidates and Colors: An Investigation," *Perceptual and Motor Skills* 50 (1980): 869–870.

34. Wendy Winter, "The Perception of Safety Posters by Bantu Industrial Workers," *Psychologia Africana* 10 (1963): 127, 132. 134.

35. See Molly S. Joss, *Looking Good in Presentations*, 3rd ed. (New York: Coriolis, 1999), 102–103; John deLemos, *Planning and Producing Posters* (Worcester, Mass.: Davis Publications, 1947), 18; and Horn, *Contemporary Posters*, 42–43;

36. ArtLex, "Blue," http://www.artlex.com; and Pantone, "Every Heart Beats True," http://pantone.com/aboutus.

37. Amitava Chattopadhyay, Gerald Gorn, and Peter R. Drake, "East, West, Blue Is Best," *HKUST Business School Newsletter*, http://www.bm.ust.hk/newsletter/autumn2000/autumn00-10.htm; and Pantone, *Colorteam—Consumer Color Preference Study*, http://pantone.com/products.

38. See A. B. Blankenship, George Edward Breen, and Alan Dutka, *State of the Art Marketing Research*, 2nd ed. (Chicago: NTC Business Books, 1998), 390; Harold F. Clark, Jr., "Brand Ideas and Their Importance: "When Do You Tell the Agency What the Brand Means?" in *How to Use Advertising to Build Strong Brands,* ed. John Philip Jones (Thousand Oaks, Calif.: Sage, 1999), 28; Al Lieberman, *The Entertainment Marketing Revolution: Bringing the Moguls, the Media, and the Magic to the World* (Upper Saddle River, N.J.: Financial Times Prentice Hall, 2002), 238; and Jan S. Slater, "The Case for Collectible Brands," in Jones, *How to Use Advertising*, 255, 258, on effective use of slogans in advertising.

39. James Curran, "The Boomerang Effect: The Press and the Battle for London 1981–6," in *Impacts and Influences: Essays on Media Power in the Twentieth Century,* ed. James Curran,

        Anthony Smith, and Pauline Wingate (London: Methuen, 1987), 129–133, for an example of successful use of political slogans.

40.   Charles J. Stewart, Craig Allen Smith, and Robert E. Denton, Jr., "The Persuasive Functions of Slogans," in Jackall, *Propaganda*, 402–403, 407, 413–414, 420.

41.   Van den Bulck, "Estimating the Success," 484.

42.   Shawn W. Rosenberg, Lisa Bohan, Patrick McCafferty, and Kevin Harris, "The Image and the Vote: The Effect of Candidate Presentation on Voter Preference," *American Journal of Political Science* 30 (1986): 108, 117–122.

43.   Shawn W. Rosenberg, "The Image and the Vote: Manipulating Voters' Preferences," *Public Opinion Quarterly* 51 (1987): 34–38, 41–44.

44.   Shawn W. Rosenberg, Shulamit Kahn, Thuy Tran, and Minh-Thu Le, "Creating a Political Image: Shaping Appearance and Manipulating the Vote," *Political Behavior* 12 (1991): 349–359.

45.   See Lynda Lee Kaid, Chris M. Leland, and Susan Whitney, "The Impact of Televised Political Ads: Evoking Viewer Responses in the 1988 Presidential Campaign," *Southern Communication Journal* 57 (1992): 289–290; and Montague Kern, *30-Second Politics: Political Advertising in the Eighties* (New York: Praeger, 1989), 50, 80–81, 95–97.

46.   Kern, *30-Second Politics*, 76–77, 99–100.

47.   Van den Bulck, "Estimating the Success," 481.

48.   Ibid., 471, 482, 486.

49.   Donald L. Shaw and Thomas A. Bowers, "Learning from Commercials: The Influence of TV Advertising on the Voter Political 'Agenda,'" (paper presented at the annual conference of the Association for Education in Journalism, Fort Collins, Colo., August 1973), 6–8. ERIC Document Microfiche ED079 765.

50.   Robert D. McClure and Thomas E. Patterson, "Television News and Political Advertising: The Impact of Exposure on Voter Beliefs," *Communication Research* 1 (1974): 16–19.

51.   Shaun Bowler, David Broughton, Todd Donovan, and Joseph Sniff, "The Informed Electorate? Voter Responsiveness to Campaigns in Britain and Germany," in Bowler and Farrell, *Electoral Strategies and Political Marketing*, 208–214.

52.   MORI May 24–30, 2001 survey, reported in Butler and Kavanagh, *British General Election of 2001*, 214.

53.   Butler and Kavanagh, *British General Election of 2001*, 214.

54.   MORI May 24–30, 2001 survey, reported in Butler and Kavanagh, *British General Election of 2001*, 214.

55.   *Die Bundestagswahl* report, October 1976, vol. 3, 3.02A, reported in Klaus Schoenbach, "The Role of Mass Media in West German Election Campaigns," *Legislative Studies Quarterly* 12 (1987): 387.

56.   Tokyo Electoral Commission surveys, reported in Lewis and Masshardt, "Election Posters in Japan," 376.

57.   Paul E. Schaffner, Abraham Wandersman, and David Stang, "Candidate Name Exposure and Voting: Two Field Studies," *Basic and Applied Social Psychology* 2 (1981): 200–202.

58.   Paul F. Lazarsfeld, Bernard Berelson, and Hazel Gaudeet, *The People's Choice: How the Voter Makes Up His Mind in a Presidential Campaign*, 3rd ed. (New York: Columbia University Press, 1968), 75–96, 98.

59.   Wojciech Cwalina, Andrzej Falkowski, and Lynda Lee Kaid, "Role of Advertising in Forming the Image of Politicians: Comparative Analysis of Poland, France, and Germany," *Media Psychology* 2 (2000): 124–140.

60.   Rosenberg, Kahn, Tran, and Le, "Creating a Political Image," 349–359.

61.   Eurobarometer 31A, "European Elections," No. 11,819, EU–12, June-July 1989, reported in Norris, *Virtuous Circle*, 157–158.

62.   See McAllister, "Campaign Activities and Electoral Outcomes," 496–498.

63. MORI/Electoral Commission, June 9–18, 2001 survey, reported in Butler and Kavanagh, *British General Election of 2001*, 215.

64. Tokyo Electoral Commission surveys, reported in Lewis and Masshardt, "Election Posters in Japan," 378.

65. Filip Boen, Norbert Vanbeselaere, Mario Pandelaere, Siegfried Dewitte, Bart Duriez, Boris Snauwaert, Jos Feys, Vicky Dierckx, and Eddy Van Avermaet, "Politics and Basking-in-Reflected-Glory: A Field Study in Flanders," *Basic and Applied Social Psychology* 24 (2002): 205, 207, 209.

Chapter Eight

1. Theodore White, quoted in R. W. Apple, Jr., "Old Pros Appraise the '88 Campaign," *New York Times*, November 6, 1988, http://proquest.com.

2. John Powers, "Can We Talk?" *Boston Globe*, October 27, 1996, http://proquest.com.

3. See Avraham Shama, "The Marketing of Political Candidates," *Journal of the Academy of Marketing Sciences* 4 (1976): 764–777.

4. Nicholas Lemann, "Remember the Alamo: How George W. Bush Reinvented Himself," *New Yorker*, October 18, 2004, 153.

5. Kaid and Holtz-Bacha, "Political Advertising Across Cultures," 221–222.

6. McNair, *Introduction to Political Communication*, 144; and Sterngold, "Adverting."

7. Risatti, "Contemporary Political Poster," 11–12, 15.

8. See Sabato, *Rise of Political Consultants*, 192.

9. Eleanor Randolph, "Two Campaigns Escalate the Rhetoric in Ad War," *Los Angeles Times*, September 28, 1996, http://proquest.com.

10. Ibid.

11. Jamieson, *Packaging the Presidency*, 520.

12. Bruce, *Images of Power*, 44.

13. See Kenneth L. Hacker, "Conclusion: Present and Future Directions for Presidential Candidate Image Research," in *Presidential Candidate Images*, ed. Kenneth L. Hacker (Lanham, Md.: Rowman & Littlefield, 2004), 241.

14. Robert Justin Goldstein, "Flag-Burning: Overview," http://www.fac.org/Speech/flagburning/overview.aspx.

15. Adrian Beard, *The Language of Politics* (New York: Routledge, 2000), 63.

16. Sabato, *Rise of Political Consultants*, 192.

17. Fritz Plasser, Christian Scheucher, and Christian Senft, "Is There a European Style of Political Marketing?" in *Handbook of Political Marketing*, ed. Bruce I. Newman (Thousand Oaks, Calif.: Sage, 1999), 99.

18. Ibid.

19. Bryant, "Paid Media Advertising," 90.

20. Labour shadow minister, quoted in Butler and Kavanagh, *British General Election of 1992*, 256.

21. Julia Bigham, "Commercial Advertising and the Poster from the 1880's to the Present," in Timmers, *Power of the Poster*, 215.

22. Charles Flowers, "Image and Idea in a Wired Decade: The 1990s," in Gallo, *Poster in History*, 319.

23. Ibid., 320.

24. Jeffrey H. Birnbaum, "Consultants Deliver Politics to Voters' Inboxes, at a Price," *Washington Post*, August 29, 2004, http://proquest.com.

25. Ibid.

26. James Spencer, personal communication to Margaret Fay, November 7, 2005.

27.   Todd Olsen, personal communication to Margaret Fay, December 12, 2005.

28.   David Moceri, "Email Microtargeting," *VIBEdirect*, http://www.goarticles.com/cgi-bin/showa .cgi?C=13209.

29.   Kate Folmar and Lisa Vorderbrueggen, "Campaign Workers Scramble to Rally Voters for State Election," *Mercury News* (Sacramento, Calif.), October 30, 2005, http://www.mercury news.com.

30.   Outdoor Advertising Association of America, "Political Advertising: A 'How To' Guide" (2005), 2, http://www.oaaa.org/pdf/A_How_to_Guide2005.pdf.

31.   See press releases, Outdoor Advertising Association of America, http://www.oaaa.org/press center/news.asp.

32.   See Ogden, "Volume VI"; and Michel Marriott, "Movie Posters That Talk Back," *New York Times*, December 12, 2002, http://proquest.com.

33.   Murdo Macleod, "Britons' Love of TV Goes Down the Tube," *Scotsman.com*, December 18, 2005, http://news.scotsman.com/entertainment.cfm?id=2426052005.

H

I

S

T

V

W

Y

Z